Windows® Server For Dummie.

MW00998225

Windows Server 2003 Administrative Tools

You can access any of these programs by using the Start⇔Administrative Tools menu or by typing the name of the launch file in the Run dialog box (Start⇔Run).

Name	Launch File	Description
Active Directory Domains and Trusts	domain.msc	Manages trusts between domains
Active Directory Sites and Services	dssite.msc	Manages sites involved in Active Directory replication
Active Directory Users and Computers	dsa.msc	Manages users, groups, computers, and other objects
Component Services	comexp.msc	Manages COM+ applications
Computer Management	compmgmt.msc /s	Starts and stops services, manages disks, and provides access to other computer management tools for local and remote administration
Data Sources (ODBC)	odbcad32.exe	Manages ODBC drivers and data sources
DHCP	dhcpmgmt.msc /s	Manages DHCP, which assigns TCP/IP settings to clients
Disk Defragmenter	dfrg.msc	Starts the Disk Defragmenter utility
Distributed File System	dfscmd	Manages DFS, which creates a single shared hierarchy of resources from multiple hosts
DNS	dnsmgmt.msc /s	Manages DNS, which resolves host names into IP addresses
Event Viewer	eventvwr.msc /s	Accesses various log files under Windows Server
Internet Services Manager	mmc.exe H:\W2KSVR\System32\inetsrv\iis.msc	Manages Web and FTP Internet services
Licensing	llsmgr.exe	Manages licenses and client use
Performance	perfmon.msc /s	Monitors the performance of a system or network
Routing and Remote Access	rrasmgmt.msc /s	Manages remote connections and routing activities
Terminal Services Licensing	licmgr.exe	Manages client access to terminal services

Windows® Server 2003 For Dummies®

Cheat Sheet

Important TCP/IP Command-Line Utilities

Each of these utilities performs some useful function. The *Help String* column shows how to get online help for syntax details on each command.

Name	Help String	Description
ARP	arp /h	Displays and modifies the address translation table maintained by the TCP/IP Address Resolution Protocol
IPCONFIG	ipconfig /?	Displays all current TCP/IP network configuration data
NETSTART	netstart /?	Displays protocol statistics and current TCP/IP network connections
N3LOOKUP	nslookup	Displays information about known DNS servers
PING	ping	Verifies connections to local or remote computers (Ping stands for Packet InterNet Groper, an excellent IP troubleshooting tool)
ROUTE	route	Displays and manipulates network routing tables
TRACERT	tracert	Displays the route from your machine to a specified destination

Important Net Commands

Each of these command-line utilities performs some useful NetBIOS networking functions. Use Net Help to get general help or Net Help <*command*> to get help on a specific Net command.

Name	Description
Net accounts	Provides a command-line tool to manage user accounts
Net computer	Adds or deletes computers in a domain database
Net help	Provides access to all Net command help files
Net helpmsg	Explains Windows Net error messages
Net print	Allows you to view or control print jobs
Net send	Sends messages to other computers or users on a network
Net share	Allows you to display, create, or delete network shares
Net use	Allows you to connect or disconnect a computer from a share by name

For Dummies: Bestselling Book Series for Beginners

Windows® Server 2003

FOR

DUMMIES®

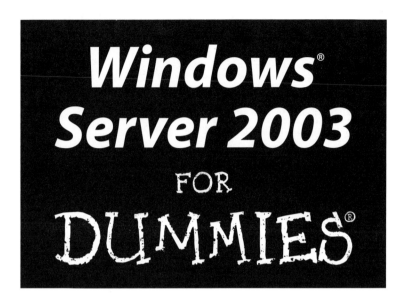

by Ed Tittel with James Michael Stewart

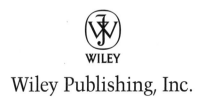

Wiley Publishing, Inc.

Windows® Server 2003 For Dummies®

Published by
Wiley Publishing, Inc.
909 Third Avenue
New York, NY 10022

www.wiley.com

About the Authors

Ed Tittel is a grizzled veteran of the publishing game, with several hundred magazine articles and more than 100 books to his credit. Ed has worked on numerous *For Dummies* books, including *HTML 4 For Dummies,* 3rd Edition (with Natanya Pitts and Chelsea Valentine) and *XML For Dummies*, 3rd Edition, (with Frank Boumphrey), as well as books on many other topics. Ed presides over a small, Austin, Texas-based company called LANWrights that specializes in network-oriented training, writing, and consulting. When Ed's not busy writing, he likes to shoot pool, cook, and hang out with his Labrador retriever, Blackie. You can reach Ed by email at `etittel@lanw.com` or through his Web page at `www.lanw.com/staff/etbio.htm`.

James Michael Stewart has been working with computers and technology for more than eighteen years. Michael is an independent consultant working as a writer and trainer. His work focuses on security, Windows NT, 2000, XP, and 2003, intranets, and the Internet. Michael has coauthored numerous books on Microsoft certification and administration and has written articles for print and online publications. He has developed certification courseware and training materials as well as presented these materials in the classroom. He is also a regular speaker at Networld+Interop. He has been an MCSE since 1997 and holds the following certifications: CISSP, TICSA, CIW Security Analyst, CTT+, CCNA, MCSE NT & W2K, and iNet+. Michael graduated in 1992 from the University of Texas at Austin with a bachelor's degree in Philosophy. His computer knowledge is self-acquired, based on more than 18 years of hands-on experience. He spends his spare time reading, Texas two-stepping, cycling, woodworking, and managing his tenants as a slumlord. You can reach Michael by e-mail at `michael@impactonline.com`.

Author's Acknowledgments

As always, thanks to the LANWrights folks who worked on this book: Mary Burmeister and Kim Lindros. On the Wiley side, special thanks to Susan Pink, Bob Woerner, and Amanda Foxworth. I'd also like to thank Jason Zandri for his much-appreciated and very welcome assistance with the final revision of the book, and Michael Stewart for his earlier and equally welcome revisions for RC1. Well-known Windows author and expert John Savill, creator of a widely used Windows resource Web site (www.ntfaq.com), wrote Chapters 11 and 12 of this book. We'd like to acknowledge his contribution and thank him for his sterling efforts. Personally, I want to thank my Mom and Dad for making my career both possible and attainable. Finally, I want to thank my new bride, Dina Kutueva, for coming into my life rather later than sooner. Welcome to America! Also, my thanks to Blackie, my ever-faithful Labrador sidekick who urges me constantly into the wider world beyond my keyboard.

— ET

Thanks to my coauthor, Ed Tittel, for including me in this book. To my editor Mary Burmeister for putting up with me on yet another book project. To my parents, Dave and Sue, thanks for your love and consistent support. To Mark, thanks for always being there. To HERbert and Quin, stop tracking the cat litter all over the house! And finally, as always, to Elvis: If I'm ever feeling down, I just remember your sparkling leather jumpsuit with the big collar — and fall on the floor laughing.

— JMS

Publisher's Acknowledgments

We're proud of this book; please send us your comments through our online registration form located at www.dummies.com/register/.

Some of the people who helped bring this book to market include the following:

Acquisitions, Editorial, and Media Development

Project Editor: Susan Pink

Acquisitions Editor: Bob Woerner

Technical Editor: Allen Wyatt, Discovery Computing, Inc.

Editorial Manager: Carol Sheehan

Media Development Supervisor: Richard Graves

Editorial Assistant: Amanda Foxworth

Cartoons: Rich Tennant (www.the5thwave.com)

Production

Project Coordinator: Regina Scott

Layout and Graphics: Amanda Carter, Seth Conley, Tiffany Muth, Julie Trippetti, Jeremey Unger, Mary Virgin

Proofreaders: Laura Albert, Andy Hollandbeck, Carl Pierce, Angel Perez, TECHBOOKS Production Services

Indexer: TECHBOOKS Production Services

Special Help
Ethel M. Winslow

Publishing and Editorial for Technology Dummies

Richard Swadley, Vice President and Executive Group Publisher

Andy Cummings, Vice President and Publisher

Mary C. Corder, Editorial Director

Publishing for Consumer Dummies

Diane Graves Steele, Vice President and Publisher

Joyce Pepple, Acquisitions Director

Composition Services

Gerry Fahey, Vice President of Production Services

Debbie Stailey, Director of Composition Services

Contents at a Glance

Table of Contents

Introduction

● ●

*W*elcome to *Windows Server 2003 For Dummies,* the book that helps anyone who's unfamiliar with Windows Server 2003 (or networks in general) find his or her way around a Windows Server 2003-based network. In a wired world, networks provide the links that tie all users together. Even if you're not using a network already, you probably will use one someday! This book tells you what's going on, in basic, straightforward terms.

Although a few fortunate individuals may be acquainted with Windows Server 2003 and networks already, a lot more of us are not only unfamiliar with networking but also downright scared of it. To those who may be worried about the prospect of facing new and difficult technologies, we say, "Don't worry. Be happy." Using a network is not beyond anyone's wits or abilities — it's mostly a matter of using a language that ordinary people can understand.

Ordinary folks are why this book talks about using Windows Server 2003 and networks in simple — and deliberately irreverent — terms. Nothing is too highfalutin to be mocked, nor too arcane to state in plain English. And when we do have to get technical, we'll warn you and make sure to define our terms to boot.

This books aims to help you meet your needs. You'll find everything you need to know about Windows Server 2003 and networking in here, so you'll be able to find your way around — without having to learn lots of jargon or obtain an advanced degree in computer science along the way. We want you to *enjoy* yourself. If networking really is a big deal, it's important that you be able to get the most out of it. We really want to help!

About This Book

This book is designed so you can pick it up and start reading at any point — like you might read a reference book. In Parts I and II, networking basics are covered: concepts and terminology in Part I, and the design and deployment of network hardware in Part II. In Parts III through V, you'll find ample coverage of Windows Server 2003 and related networking topics. Part III covers installation and configuration of Windows Server 2003, whereas Part IV covers its maintenance and management. Part V completes this picture with chapters on a variety of troubleshooting topics.

Each chapter is divided into freestanding sections in which each one relates to the chapter's major theme. For example, the chapter on installing network interface cards, or NICs, contains the following collection of information:

- A description of a NIC and how it works
- The various PC buses for which NICs are available
- How to begin the installation process by documenting your current configuration
- How to insert a NIC into a PC
- How to configure a NIC after it's installed in your PC
- What to do when Plug and Play fails to live up to its promises
- Troubleshooting techniques to try when NIC installation doesn't work on the first (or second) try

You don't have to memorize the contents of this book. Each section supplies just the facts you need to make networking with Windows Server 2003 easy to use. On some occasions, however, you may want to work directly from the book to make sure you keep things straight.

How to Use This Book

This book works like a reference, so start with a topic that interests you. You can use the table of contents to identify general areas of interest or broad topics. The index, however, is your best tool for identifying detailed concepts, related topics, or particular Windows 2003 capabilities, tools, or controls.

After you find what you need, you can close the book and tackle whatever task you've set for yourself — without having to grapple with unrelated details.

If you've never worked on a network before, it's a good idea to read Parts I and II in their entirety. Likewise, if you're new to Windows Server 2003, you might want to read all of Parts III and IV. Otherwise, dig in wherever your fancy moves you!

When you need to type something at the keyboard, you'll see text that looks like this: **TYPE THIS**. You're expected to enter this text at the keyboard, and then press the Enter key. Because typing stuff can sometimes be confusing, we always try to describe what it is you're typing and why you need to type it.

This book occasionally suggests that you consult the Windows Server 2003 online help, printed manuals, and Resource Kit and even Microsoft's TechNet

CD for additional information. In most cases, though, you find everything you need to know about a particular topic right here — except for some of the bizarre details that abound in Windows Server 2003.

If there's a topic we don't cover in this book that you need to know more about, we suggest you look for a book on that subject in the *For Dummies* series, published by Wiley Publishing, Inc. In addition, a whole world of Web information about Windows Server 2003 is available on the Internet, and the Microsoft Web site at `www.microsoft.com/windowsserver2003/ default.mspx` is not a bad place to start looking for such information.

Foolish Assumptions

We're going to climb out on a limb and make some potentially foolish assumptions about you, our gentle reader. You have or are thinking about getting a computer, a network, and at least one copy of Windows Server 2003. You know what you want to do with these things. You might even be able to handle all these things yourself, if somebody could only show you how. Our goal with this book is to decrease your need for such a somebody, but we don't recommend telling him or her that out loud — at least, not until you've finished this book!

How This Book Is Organized

The book is divided into six major parts, each of which consists of two to seven chapters. Each chapter covers a major topic and is divided into sections, which discuss some particular issue or concern related to that topic. That's how things in this book are organized, but how you read it is up to you. Choose a topic, a section, a chapter, or a part — whatever strikes your fancy or suits your needs — and start reading.

Part I: Laying the Network Foundation

Part I covers networking concepts and terminology, including the basics of networked communications and what makes networks work — usually, some magical combination of hardware and software. Look here for discussions about networking terms and concepts, such as client, server, protocol, and topology. If you're not familiar with networks, this part should come in handy. If you're already a seasoned networker, you can skip this part (and Part II).

Part II: Hooking Up the Hardware

Part II covers everything you need to know to build or extend a network or simply to understand what's really happening on an existing network. It starts with coverage of network design and layout principles, and continues with a discussion of how to install and configure NICs in a PC. After that, it examines the wiring that links network devices and talks about how multiple networks can interconnect. Part II concludes with a review of all the software components you're likely to encounter on a Windows 2003-based network and why you need them.

Part III: Servers, Start Your Engines!

Part III tackles Windows Server 2003 head on, starting with its installation and configuration. It covers the issues involved in installing and configuring network hardware specifically for Windows Server 2003. It also covers how to install and manage print servers and services on a Windows 2003-based network, how to handle Transmission Control Protocol/Internet Protocol (TCP/IP) addresses, and how to set up and manage directory services, domains, and trust relationships in a Windows 2003-based environment. Part III is where you figure out how to put the basic pieces of a network together using Windows Server 2003.

Part IV: Running Your Network

Part IV picks up where Part III leaves off — that is, it talks about living with and managing a Windows 2003-based network after the initial installation and configuration phase is complete. It begins with a discussion of how to manage users and groups on a Windows 2003-based network, including details on profiles, policies, and local and global groups. Next, it covers how Windows 2003 controls access to NTFS files and directories, and how to manage network-accessible file system resources called shares.

After a network's users, groups, and data assets are in place, rebuilding such a setup from scratch can be a real pain. That's where a backup comes in handy, so Part IV covers the ins and outs of backing up and restoring a Windows Server 2003 machine, plus other aspects of fault tolerance. After that, a review of network security principles and practices should help to prepare you to protect your data from accidental loss and from would-be hackers and crackers.

Part V: Troubleshooting

Part V takes a long, hard look at the common causes of trouble on Windows 2003-based networks and explores those areas that are most likely to fall prey to trouble. It begins with a look at some key Windows 2003 tools for troubleshooting systems, and then continues on to explore tips, tricks, and techniques for troubleshooting a Windows 2003-based network. Part V concludes by exploring the handling of problems with Active Directory.

Part VI: The Part of Tens

Part VI follows the grand tradition of *For Dummies* books, all of which include "The Part of Tens." Here, you'll find lists of information, tips, tricks, and suggestions, all organized into short and convenient chapters. This supplemental information is designed to be both helpful and informative and is supplied at no extra charge.

Icons Used in This Book

The icons used in this book point you to important (and not so important) topics in the text.

This icon lets you know that you're about to encounter information that's important to understand if you really want to *get* what's going on with networking or with Windows Server 2003. It may be painful at times, but you have to slog through it.

Oh gee, we're getting so old that we can't recall what this one means. Maybe you should check one out and see whether it's worth watching for!

This icon lets you know that you're about to be swamped in technical details. We include this information because we love it, not because we think you have to master it to use Windows Server 2003 or networks. If you aspire to nerdhood, you probably want to read it; if you're already a nerd, you'll want to write us about stuff we left out or other information we should put in!

This icon signals that helpful advice is at hand. We also use it when we offer insights that we hope make networking or using Windows Server 2003 more interesting or easier. For example, whenever we include a shortcut that improves your productivity, it's usually marked with the Tip icon.

This icon means what it says — you'd better be careful with the information it conveys. Nine times out of ten, it's warning you not to do something that can have nasty or painful consequences, as in accidentally wiping out the contents of an entire hard drive. Whoops!

Where to Go from Here

With this book at your side, you should be ready to wrestle with Windows Server 2003 and the networks it connects to. Find a subject, turn to its page, and you'll be ready to jam. Feel free to mark up this book, fill in the blanks, dog-ear the pages, and do anything else that might make a librarian queasy. The important things are to make good use of it and to enjoy yourself while you're at it.

Please check out the Web page at `www.dummies.com`. Be sure to take the opportunity to register your purchase online or to send the authors e-mail with feedback about your reading experience.

Part I
Laying the Network Foundation

The 5th Wave   By Rich Tennant

"You the guy having trouble staying connected to the network?"

In this part . . .

In this introductory part of the book, you get background material about local area networks, or LANs. We present the barest essentials: how computers communicate with each other, why communication isn't a bad thing, and what makes networks work. We also cover vital concepts, including *protocols,* which are the rules of communication that computers use to exchange information, and *topologies,* which are the ways in which network wiring can be arranged.

Along the way, you discover all kinds of basic network terminology and concepts that you may never have heard of but that everyone, including Microsoft, assumes that you know when you work with Windows Server 2003.

Each chapter presents its information in small, easy-to-read sections. If information is really technical (mostly worth skipping, unless you're a glutton for punishment), it's clearly marked as such. Even so, we hope you find this information useful — and maybe even worth a giggle or two.

Chapter 1

Making Networks Make Sense

*I*f you've ever used a cell phone or watched a TV show, you've used a network, perhaps without even realizing it. Much of the world's modern communications infrastructure, including wired and wireless telephones, cable and broadcast TV, and the Internet, depends on networks.

Windows Server 2003 needs a network, too. Because servers exist to provide file, print, directory, Web, security, and other services to clients across a network, using Windows Server 2003 without a network is like using a telephone that's not plugged into the wall. Although that phone may have some value as abstract art, its real value comes from its capability to connect you with other people or services. The same is true for Windows Server 2003.

In this chapter, we introduce you to the various components that make up a Windows Server 2003-based network and briefly discuss how each one works.

What's This about a Network?

A *network* requires at least two computers linked in a way that enables them to talk to each other. Most networks use electrical wires of some type to convey signals and data between computers. However, numerous types of networking media, including wireless technologies and fiber-optic cables, also support networked connections. In other words, you can get from here to there in many ways on modern networks!

A network's key ingredients always include some type of physical connection that allows computers to talk (and listen) to some kind of communications medium. Even if that network medium is wireless, something must physically connect computers to an antenna or to a similar device that allows those computers to broadcast and receive signals.

But there's more to networking than hardware. Although cables and connections are essential, they are purely decorative and can serve no useful purpose without software. In the following sections, you find out a bit more about the hardware and software that make networks work.

No hardware means no connections!

First and foremost, networking requires working connections to enable computers to communicate with each other. *Networking hardware* creates connections between computers and a network and defines the medium (or media) that allows information to flow from sender to receiver.

Networking hardware covers a broad range of devices, many of which you may find on your networks. In the first part of this book, we help you understand the roles and functions these devices play on a network.

From the most basic perspective, computers need the following hardware to talk to each other on a typical network:

- **A network interface card (NIC)** plugs into a computer and attaches to a network cable (or other medium, if something else is used). It turns computer bits into signals on the wire for outgoing stuff and turns incoming signals into bits for incoming stuff.

- **Connectors** make it possible to attach a network interface to the network medium. For wireless media, connectors attach antennas or other broadcast devices to interfaces. Connectors bring all the separate pieces of networking hardware together, so to speak.

- **Cables** convey signals from sender to receiver, using either electrical signals for wire cables or light pulses for fiber-optic cable. In the case of wireless media, the medium consists of the broadcast frequencies used to transmit information between senders and receivers.

- **Additional network devices** tie bigger, more complex networks together. These devices range from relatively simple hubs used to interconnect interfaces on star-wired networks (see Chapters 4 and 7) to repeaters used to link individual cable segments, as well as bridges, routers, and gateways (see Chapter 7). Hardware plays an important role in networking. Not only does it attach computers to a network, but it also interconnects multiple networks to manage how and when data flows from one network to another.

A simple view of networking

Networking boils down to these three critical requirements:

- **Connections** include the necessary hardware to connect a computer to a network, plus cables (called the *network medium*) that ferry messages between computers. The hardware that hooks a computer to a network is called a *network interface*. In most cases, attaching a PC to a network requires inserting an adapter board called a *network interface card (NIC)*. Without a physical connection, a computer can't use the network.

- **Communications** define rules that computers must follow to exchange and interpret information. Because each computer may run different software, interconnected computers need a shared language to enable them to exchange messages and data. Without shared communications, computers can't exchange data, even though they may share a common network medium.

- **Services** are what computers talk about. In other words, services represent what computers do for each other, including sending or receiving files, messages, print jobs, and so on. Unless computers can perform services for each other across a network, a computer can't respond to requests from other computers, nor can it request things from other computers.

Without software, networks don't work

Software lets computers access and use hardware, whether that hardware is used for networking-related functions or for other purposes.

By now, you should understand that hardware provides the necessary connections that make networking possible, and software supports the communications and services needed to access the hardware and the network to which the hardware is attached.

Many different types of software play a supporting role when networking modern computers. This software includes special-purpose programs called *device drivers,* which allow a computer to address a network interface and exchange data with that interface. The software collection also includes full-blown applications that can access data on a local computer or on a server across the network with equal aplomb. The software also includes a bunch of other stuff that sits between device drivers and applications.

Throughout this book, we show you how to recognize the various pieces of software involved in networking and how to best configure that software to work with Windows Server 2003 on a network.

Investigating Your Network's Facilities

If you tour an average network, you can't help but discover that many different types of equipment and a variety of related software are in use. If you inventory all the components in a network, you can use that data to figure out what's attached to your network and what functions various devices perform on your network.

The infrastructure that makes networking possible is made up of the equipment that hooks computers into a network, the cables or other networking media that ferry information between computers, and the hardware and software used to create and control a network. You may also call the collection of connections, cables, interfaces, and other equipment *glue* because these elements bind computers into a working network.

The three phases of networking

Network software falls into one of three categories: host/terminal, client/server, and peer-to-peer. Each category reflects a certain type of networked communication.

✔ **Host/terminal networks** are based on an old-fashioned model for networking, even if they don't use old-fashioned stuff. In this network's original version, users access information using a device called a *terminal,* which consists of nothing more than a screen, a keyboard, and a network connection. All the software runs on a powerful computer called a *host,* which resides elsewhere on the network. The lowly terminal doesn't do anything more than provide a way for users to access remote data and applications (which is why such devices are also known as *dumb terminals*). In more modern versions, PCs can act like terminals by using *terminal emulation software,* which the PC uses to access a host. The PC still provides some local smarts and access to local word-processing software, spreadsheets, and so on. In fact, Windows Server 2003 supports host/terminal capabilities through a facility called Terminal Server.

✔ A **client/server network** consists of a collection of smart machines. One or more of these machines acts as a server and has lots of storage space, a powerful processor, and networking software so it can handle requests for services from other machines. The other machines that interact with the server are called clients. Sometimes, client/server networks are also called *server-based networks* to emphasize the server's key role. Windows Server 2003 provides a foundation for the client/server network, which is the subject of this book. However, Novell NetWare and UNIX servers also play similar roles on modern networks.

✔ On a **peer-to-peer network**, any machine that can be a client can also act as a server. Unlike client/server networks, no special-purpose machine acts as a server. On a peer-to-peer network, all machines are more or less alike in capability and in the services they offer. If you use the built-in networking included in Windows XP Professional, Windows 2000 Professional, Windows NT Workstation, or Windows 95, 98, SE, or Me, you're using this type of networking software.

Workstations for everyone!

One of networking's primary advantages is that a network takes what you do at your desk — and we bet you usually call it "work" — and lets you do what you do more efficiently by allowing you to interact with remote resources and data. This means you can access a file on a server as if it's part of your own disk drive, send a job to a printer elsewhere on the network as if it were hooked directly to your machine, and so on. Sharing resources remains the most highly touted benefit of networking because it connects your desktop computer to file stores, printers, applications, and information resources that would otherwise be inaccessible or too expensive to add to every desktop computer.

The terms *network client, desktop computer,* and *workstation* are all used more or less synonymously in the networking world. No matter what you call them, these machines are where users do the bulk of their work (and perhaps some play at odd moments).

A *desktop* is also the area of a computer that displays the program icons and the wallpaper.

One of the key goals that drives networking is to interconnect all the desktops in an organization, whether they run a DOS, Windows, UNIX, Linux, or Macintosh operating system, so that they can communicate and share resources. Some of the resources shared by workstations include large disk arrays, expensive color or laser printers, CD-ROM jukeboxes, and high-speed Internet connections (all of which would be too expensive to connect to every desktop machine).

On most networks, the ratio of desktop machines to users is pretty close to one-to-one. In other words, each user has access to a workstation attached to the network, even if that user is not the only person who works on that machine. Because workstations are where requests for services originate, such machines are known as network clients, or more simply, as *clients.*

When you call such a machine a *workstation,* you emphasize its capability to support an individual user more or less independently. When you call such a machine a *client,* you focus on its connection to the network. Whatever you call it, it's a machine that sits on your desk and is connected to a network.

A server is always at your service

Networking is about obtaining access to shared services. Because networks are useless unless you can do something with them, access to services is what networking is all about.

On modern networks, servers provide the capabilities necessary to obtain access to resources or to do things. For example, when you send a print job to a networked printer, you can assume that, somewhere in the background, a print server is handling the job. Likewise, when you request a file from a network drive, a file server is probably involved. When you poke around in the network directory — you guessed it! — a directory server is pulling the strings. For every service, some type of server handles and responds to requests. Sometimes, a single server provides many services; at other times, a server provides only a single service.

Computers that provide services to clients are generically called *servers*. A server's job is to listen for requests from clients for whatever service or services it offers, and to satisfy any valid requests for its services. In fact, validating service requests is an important part of what servers do — you wouldn't want just anyone to be able to print the salaries for everyone in your company just because a user asks a print server to do so. You want that server to verify that Bob is *allowed* to access that file before you let him print it! Throughout this book, you find out more about such validations and other key aspects of what it takes for a server to provide services.

The common path of networking

A common pathway must exist between any computer that requests services and any computer whose job it is to satisfy such requests. Just as you need a highway to drive from one city to another, you need a pathway over which your computer can send and receive data. On a network, that's the job of the media that tie all the various pieces together.

Look around and observe the types of cables and connections used on your network. Get a sense of the structure of your network so you can tell which highways the users use — from the side roads that only the folks in the accounting or shipping department use to the main road that all users use.

When you observe how all the pieces fit together — workstations, servers, and media — you get a reasonably complete view of your network. Figure 1-1 depicts a simple network diagram that shows these purely physical elements of a network. Notice that clients (desktop machines) outnumber servers, and that media tie all the pieces together. Networking follows the law of supply and demand, so the more clients you have, the more (or bigger) servers you'll need — and the more work will get accomplished!

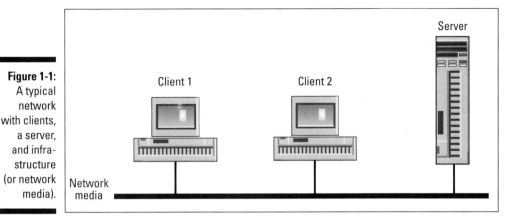

Figure 1-1:
A typical
network
with clients,
a server,
and infra-
structure
(or network
media).

What Is the Sound of a Working Network?

Figuring out whether a network is functioning is both easy and hard, and most observers, including novices and experts alike, agree that telling when a network's *not* working is easier than telling when it is! A client must know how to ask for services from the network and must state precisely what it's requesting. Likewise, a server must know how to recognize and evaluate incoming requests for its services and how to respond appropriately. Only then can a network work correctly.

Understanding how this constant stream of requests and replies works means looking a little deeper into how clients state their requests and how servers satisfy them. In the following sections, we examine the mechanics of this give-and-take.

Knowing how to ask is where the game begins

Knowing how to ask for network services requires some ability to distinguish between what's available locally on a client machine and what's available remotely from the network. Determining what's local and what's remote is the key to handling network access correctly. This determination depends on specialized software to handle the job in the background, so users don't necessarily have to know the difference.

A computer's main control program is called its *operating system (OS)* because it defines the software environment that lets a computer operate and run the applications and system services that get things accomplished on a machine. Most modern operating systems include built-in networking capabilities to augment their control over local resources and devices.

Certain modern operating systems can be called *network operating systems (NOSs)* when they create network server environments. Their built-in networking capabilities include a range of network services as part and parcel of the underlying operating system. Windows Server 2003 certainly fits this bill because it offers a broad range of powerful, flexible networking capabilities.

Right out of the box, Windows Server 2003 understands the differences between local and remote resources. The same is true for most modern desktop operating systems, including Windows XP Professional, Windows 2000 Server and Professional, Windows NT Server and Workstation, Windows 9*x,* the Macintosh OS, as well as that old (but still modern) warhorse, UNIX.

In Windows Server 2003, Windows XP Professional, Windows 2000, Windows NT, Windows 9*x,* Macintosh, and UNIX operating systems, and through add-ons to DOS and Windows 3.*x,* a special piece of software known as a *redirector* keeps track of what's local and what's remote when users or applications request resources. The redirector takes generic requests for services and sends any that can't be satisfied locally to the appropriate service provider elsewhere on the network (in other words, to the appropriate server). Therefore, if you ask for a file that resides on a server elsewhere on the network, the redirector hands your request off to that machine and makes sure that the results of that request are delivered properly.

What's on today's menu?

For a computer to use network services, the computer must know how to ask for them. That's what a *requester* does. But knowing what to ask for is as important as knowing how to ask. In most cases, applications supply the necessary information about network services that they want to access, either through information supplied from a requester or through knowledge built directly into an application itself.

E-mail clients and Web browsers represent good examples of applications with sophisticated, built-in networking capabilities. On the other hand, file system access tools, such as Windows Explorer, My Computer, and My Documents, rely on the redirector to furnish them with views of (and access to) shared files and printers elsewhere on the network.

Please note that applications with built-in networking knowledge offer *transparent* access to network services because the applications know how to ask for services and, often, what to ask for on the user's behalf. Programmers design such computer applications to be transparent to keep the applications out of sight and out of mind; therefore, the user remains blissfully unaware of cumbersome networking details and trivia. File managers, printer controls, and other tools with access to both local and remote resources, however, require users to be able to tell the difference between what's local and what's remote. In fact, such tools usually force users to request access to remote resources explicitly and directly.

Increasingly, finding out which services a network can provide is becoming more and more implicit. This is why all editions of Windows Server 2003 support a set of directory services to catalog and describe the services that the network can deliver to its users. Likewise, Windows Server 2003 supports the Distributed File System that allows directories on multiple machines all around a network to appear as a single network drive to users. Therefore, users don't have to know where individual files or folders reside.

Such sophisticated mechanisms make it easier than ever before for users to request and access resources implicitly without having to know how to request those resources or having to determine exactly where they reside. Nevertheless, some explicit knowledge about such things is necessary if you want to make the most of Windows Server 2003's networking capabilities.

It's All about Sharing Resources

The mechanics of requesting resources depend on having access to the right software tools to determine when network requests are necessary. The software delivers the request to a server whose job is to listen for such requests and to satisfy all legitimate ones. Ultimately, a server's job is to make resources available to all authorized users. This feature makes sharing possible and helps explain the most powerful benefit of networking — namely, to provide a single, consistent way for multiple users to obtain secure and managed access to files, printers, scanners, data, applications, and more.

The secret to sharing is to find a way to make sure that everyone can obtain access to a shared resource. For example, for access to print services, a temporary storage space must hold incoming print jobs until each one's turn to be printed comes up. Therefore, sharing a printer means not only providing access to the device itself, but also keeping track of who's in line, providing a place where pending jobs can reside, and sometimes notifying users when a print job has been successfully completed. All these mechanisms make sharing work easier and explain why servers are so important to any network.

Because servers bring services and data together in a single machine, servers provide a natural point of control and maintenance for the important devices, services, and data on a network, which are, of course, the things that everybody wants to share.

Windows Networking Trends

Microsoft is leaping into a new era in which local networking and Internet access is integrated unlike ever before. Windows Server 2003 is Microsoft's next step toward a goal of end-to-end communication structures that enable companies and individuals to electronically communicate easily, efficiently, and securely. Windows Server 2003 is built on technology from Windows 2000, which in turn was built on technology from Windows NT. The Windows Server 2003 family embraces several types of servers, including the following:

- **Windows Server 2003, Web Edition:** A server system optimized for Web serving and hosting. This edition supports up to four processors and 2GB of RAM per computer.

- **Windows Server 2003, Standard Edition:** A server designed to replace Windows 2000 Server. It can be used as a member server or as a domain controller on small to medium-sized networks. The Standard Edition supports up to four processors and 4GB of RAM per computer. It is also the subject of this book.

- **Windows Server 2003, Enterprise Edition:** You can think of the version as Windows Server 2003, Standard Edition with lots of bells and whistles. This souped-up version allows you to use up to eight CPUs (processors) and up to 32GB of RAM on a single server (which helps improve performance). Windows Server 2003, Enterprise Edition supports up to eight-node clustering (combining two or more computers in such a way that they all share the workload to support a single, large application or network service).

- **Windows Server 2003, Datacenter Edition:** This is a high-end Windows operating system that supports even more CPUs and RAM than Windows Server 2003, Enterprise Edition (up to 64 CPUs and 64GB of RAM). It has the same features as the Enterprise Edition, plus more. Windows Server 2003, Datacenter Edition can support more than 10,000 simultaneous users in certain situations and up to eight-node clustering.

There are also versions of Windows Server 2003, Enterprise Edition and Windows Server, Datacenter Edition designed for the Intel 64-bit Itanium CPU.

Although these versions vary, they're more alike than different. Therefore, this book can help you master the basics for any of these types of Windows Server 2003 products.

Based on the capabilities of Windows Server 2003, we see the following trends emerging for Windows networking in this millennium:

- ✔ **Use of Active Directory:** Active Directory is Microsoft's name for the directory services supported by Windows Server 2003. Active Directory makes it easier for users to identify and access network resources and for applications to use such resources directly and automatically. Currently, you can't see much evidence of this capability, but it will change the way we use Windows — and networks — in the future.

- ✔ **Access to dynamic disk storage:** Windows Server 2003 supports a variety of sophisticated directory-sharing technologies. Dynamic disk storage enables network administrators to define collections of files and directories gathered from multiple servers around a network and present them to users as if the files and directories reside on a single network drive. This makes creating, identifying, and accessing collections of shared files easier.

- ✔ **Consistent naming services:** Part of locating resources on a network is knowing their names (or how to find them). Windows Server 2003 uses a single enhanced method to translate human-intelligible names for network resources into computer-intelligible network addresses, which makes managing and interacting with network resources far simpler.

- ✔ **Web-based management console:** In Windows Server 2003, a single Microsoft Management Console (MMC) plays host to management tools (called *MMC snap-ins*) for all system services, resources, and facilities. This console makes the Windows Server 2003 interface simpler and its many capabilities more visually consistent and therefore easier to learn and manage. In fact, this capability works on any computer with a suitable Web browser (and an administrative password).

- ✔ **Simplified Web content creation and delivery:** One of the primary goals of the Windows Server 2003 family is to bring high-end, high-profit Web services and applications to end users (that is, customers) in an efficient manner. Through the use of optimized Web tools, new programming language structures, and content development architectures, Windows Server 2003 is poised to revolutionize how enterprise Web sites are created, deployed, and maintained.

As all these capabilities are used, the trends in Windows networking should be clear:

- ✔ Easier, more straightforward access to network resources

- ✔ Simplified administration and management of such resources

- ✔ More sophisticated tools and technologies to describe, deliver, and control network resources

Get used to it!

Chapter 2

Networking the Client/Server Way

● ●

In This Chapter

▶ Requesting services

▶ Delivering services

▶ Listening in on a client/server conversation

▶ Networking natively means networking nicely

▶ Adding on enhances network capabilities

▶ Understanding the Microsoft network (and its alternatives)

▶ Managing network access

▶ Using the Windows Server 2003 network services

● ●

*F*or most applications, using Windows Server 2003 in a networked environment means buying into the client/server model. To help you understand this networking model, which best explains why it's necessary for Windows Server 2003 to exist, we explore the client/server model in detail in this chapter. Along the way, you discover more about the types of capabilities and services that make client/server networks work and the various ways that clients and servers interact on such networks.

Clients Request Services

In Chapter 1, we explain that clients ask for services and that both hardware and software are necessary to make networking work on any computer. In this chapter, we take a closer look at the various pieces and parts involved in a client/server relationship to help you understand what happens when a client requests a service from a server.

At the most basic level, a client must have a network connection available to transmit a request for services. Likewise, the client must have the correct software installed to formulate an intelligible request and pass it to the network, which is where a server can notice and respond to such a request.

Making the connection

To request network services, a client must have the following hardware:

- **Network interface card (NIC):** A NIC (also called a network adapter or a network board) allows a computer to interact with the network. Before a NIC can transmit signals onto the network medium and receive signals from that network medium, you must configure it.

- **Physical connection:** The link between the computer and its network must work properly. This means that clients can transmit outgoing signals and receive incoming signals through their network connections. Likewise, the network cabling itself — also known as the network medium — must be properly configured and interconnected for signals to travel from sender to receiver.

This takes care of the connections part in a three-part simple model for networking, which requires that connections, communications, and services all be available and working.

Software uses the connection

The software on the client computer handles the communications and services necessary for the network to operate. Here's a list of software that you normally find on a networked client computer, starting from the hardware level (or as close as software can get to hardware) and working up to the applications that request network services:

- **Network driver:** A special-purpose piece of software that enables a computer to send data from the computer's *central processing unit* (CPU) to the NIC when an outgoing message is ready to be sent. The network driver also forwards a request for immediate attention (called an *interrupt*) to the CPU when an incoming message arrives. You might say that the driver allows the PC to communicate with the NIC, which in turn communicates with the network.

- **Protocol stack:** A collection of communications software that provides the type of "shared language" necessary for successful networking. The protocol stack governs which formats network messages can assume, and it defines a set of rules for how to interpret their contents. Two computers must use the same protocol stack to communicate. We cover protocol stacks thoroughly in Chapter 3.

- **Redirector:** A redirector, or equivalent software, issues requests for remote resources or services to the protocol stack and receives the incoming replies from the protocol stack. With a redirector running in the background, applications don't need to be explicitly network aware, because the redirector handles network connections.

✔ **Network-aware application:** Network-aware applications understand when service requests can be satisfied locally or must be satisfied remotely. In the latter case, a redirector may be present, but it may not necessarily handle certain types of network services (such as e-mail or Web-page access). However, the redirector can handle other types of network services, such as providing access to a file stored elsewhere on the network that's applied as an attachment to an e-mail message. In such a case, the redirector grabs a copy of that file across the network and attaches it to the outgoing e-mail message.

When a client makes a request for a resource or service that requires access to the network, either the application (if it's network aware) or a redirector (if the application isn't network aware) formulates a formal request for a remote service. Satisfying the request may involve the transfer of a small amount of data (as when requesting a listing of a directory on a machine elsewhere on the network). However, it may also involve transferring a large amount of data (as when sending a large file off to be printed or when copying a large file from the client machine to a server).

The request is ferried through the protocol stack that the client and server have in common. For short requests, a handful of short messages travel from the client and are reassembled and handled by the server. For large information transfers, the client breaks up the file into hundreds or thousands of small information packages, each of which is shipped across the network separately and then reassembled on the receiving end.

The protocol stack tells the network driver to send little packages of data (called *frames* or *packets*) from the computer, through the NIC, and across the network to the intended recipient (the server). On the receiving end, the same thing happens in reverse, with a few additional considerations that you find out about in the following section.

Servers Deliver Services

In the preceding section, you found out that clients ask for services and that servers provide them. What handling requests on the server side really means is that a special bit of software, called a *listener process,* runs continuously on the server and listens for requests for a particular service. When a request arrives, the listener process handles it as quickly as possible.

Servers thread through a maze of requests

What usually happens on most server operating systems — including Windows Server 2003 — is that the listener process simply recognizes that a request has arrived. The listener process checks the identity and the associated permissions of the client, and if the client is who it says it is and has the correct permissions for the service, the listener process grants the request for service. It does so by starting a temporary process (called an *execution thread* in Windows-speak; think of this as a very small program) that exists just long enough to handle whatever service the client requests — after which, the temporary process disappears. For example, a request for a particular file on a server would result in the creation of a temporary process that exists just long enough to copy the requested file across the network. As soon as the copy completes, the temporary process goes poof!

Using a listener process to create short-lived execution threads allows a server to handle large numbers of requests, because the listener process never stays busy for long handling individual requests. As soon as the listener process creates a thread to handle one request, it checks for other pending requests and handles them if necessary; otherwise, the listener process goes back to listening for new incoming requests. Typically, a server has one or more listener processes for each service that the server supports.

Servers are demand-driven. That is, their job is to respond to requests for services from clients. A server rarely initiates activity. This reactive mode of server operation helps explain why the client/server model is also known as a *request/response* or a *request/reply* architecture, in which clients make requests and servers respond or reply to them.

Other than the necessary listener processes and a set of service applications that actually perform services, servers need the same hardware components that clients do. Servers need one or more NICs with a working connection to the network to allow data to enter and leave the server.

Software is similar on the server side

On the software side, servers also need the following elements so that their services can be available across the network:

- ✓ **Network drivers** enable the server to communicate with its NIC. This software lurks in the background and exists only to tie the computer to the NIC.

- ✓ **Protocol stacks** send and receive messages across the network. This software also lurks in the background and provides a common language shared with clients used to ferry information across the network.

- ✓ **Service applications** respond to requests for service and formulate replies to those requests. This software runs in the foreground and does the useful work. The service application includes the listener process, the temporary execution threads, and some type of configuration or management console so that it can be installed, configured, and altered as needed. Typical service applications include directory services (Active Directory), database engines (SQL Server or Oracle), and e-mail servers (Exchange).

Most, if not all, software that resides on a server is network aware because delivering information across a network is a server's primary function.

Decoding a Client/Server Conversation

You may be wondering what the steps are in a conversation between a client and server. Examining the exact contents of such a message exchange wouldn't do you much good. However, the following sequence presents a typical request to print a file on a network printer (and, by necessity, through a print server) from a spreadsheet program:

1. A user requests print services in the spreadsheet program by clicking the printer icon or by choosing File⇨Print. Assume that a network printer is set as the default printer for the designated print job.

2. The spreadsheet program formats the spreadsheet and then builds an appropriate print file. A print file includes the text and graphics that make up a file's content. It also includes instructions on how (bold, italic, and so forth) and where (top, bottom, left, right) to place the elements to be printed.

3. The spreadsheet program sends the print file to the printer.

4. The local networking software (assuming it's a Windows XP redirector) recognizes that the printer is on the network and sends a print request to print that file to the print server. The redirector accesses name and network address information through a Windows networking service (called the Browse Service, which talks to a browser server on the network) to figure out where to send the print file.

5. On the server side, the listener process recognizes and checks out the user's print request. We'll assume it's legal, so the listener process creates a temporary execution thread to handle delivery of the incoming print file packets from the client. This temporary thread tells the client to start sending the print file.

6. Having now obtained permission to start shipping the file, the protocol stack on the client chops the file up into small chunks (called *packets*) that are delivered to the temporary thread on the server.

7. The temporary thread on the server oversees delivery of the file and places it into a temporary holding area (called a *spool file*) where the print server stores all pending print jobs. The print server places the job in the *print queue,* which stores the print jobs in the order in which they are received.

8. When the print job reaches the head of the queue, the server creates another temporary thread to ship the job to the printer. In many cases, a different protocol carries data from the server to the printer than the one the client uses to ship data to the server in the first place.

9. In a final (and optional) step, the print server creates another temporary thread to send a message to the client computer stating that the print job is complete. Here, the same protocol used to transport the file from the client to the server is often used to send this message back to the client.

What's worth noting here is that a kind of conversation occurs between client and server. The client initiates this conversation when it asks for permission to print, and then it sends the print job to the print server. The server takes over from there, storing the incoming print file in its spool file, managing the queue, and then printing the file when its turn comes. The conversation ends when the server sends notification of job completion to the client.

Requests for other services, such as access to a database server, an e-mail server, or even a file server, are similar to the previous interchange. In such cases, the conversation usually ends when the server sends a data table, message, or file in reply to the client's initiating requests. This request/reply sequence is really what makes modern networks work.

Clients and Network Access Software

Speaking historically, some of the ugliest problems with PCs have been networking related. Before the release of Windows for Workgroups in 1993, Microsoft PC operating systems — primarily, Windows 1.x, 2.x, and 3.x, and all versions of DOS up through Version 6.0 — included no built-in networking facilities.

Therefore, to put PCs on a network, users had to not only deal with installing and configuring NICs and the driver software that makes them work, but also purchase or otherwise obtain networking protocol software and networking services software from other vendors. Because neither those users nor Microsoft provided any of these products themselves, these products were called *third-party components*.

Suffice it to say, networking PCs before the days of built-in networking typically meant adding two or more third-party networking products to the mix of hardware and software components on each machine. Typically, one product was required to supply the protocol stack necessary for networked communications, and one or more other products were needed to access whatever services may use that protocol stack to do things across the network. For example, you would buy a protocol stack such as TCP/IP (Transmission Control Protocol/Internet Protocol) for your PC from Chameleon Software, then buy e-mail software from QUALCOMM, and then tie it all together by guess and by gosh.

Starting with Windows for Workgroups, and then picking up in a major way with Windows 95 and Windows NT, Microsoft made networking a lot easier for ordinary mortals. It did so by providing built-in networking components as a part of the operating system. Although this made life hard for third-party vendors who had been making good livings from their protocol stacks and add-on service products, it definitely made using networks vastly simpler. It was especially appealing to users who wanted networking to be something you could "set and forget" rather than "set and regret" or "fret and reset!"

Today, Windows 98, SE, Me, NT, 2000, XP, and 2003 include all the elements necessary for networking — from multiple types of protocol stacks to many different types of client and server capabilities. If you base your network entirely on Microsoft technologies or if the majority of your clients and servers use Microsoft technologies, handling networking is just like handling other parts of the Windows operating systems. That is, you still have to know something about what you're doing (which is why you're reading this book, right?), but you don't have to be a rocket scientist to install, configure, and maintain the necessary protocol and service components.

In some compelling cases, however, you may have to mess with third-party networking components, as in days of yore. For example, your network may use a non-Microsoft server, such as NetWare or UNIX, to provide network services. Or perhaps the collection of built-in services delivered with Windows XP or Windows 2003 doesn't include something that you need, and you must add it to the mix yourself.

An example of a useful component that you may decide to add for yourself is the *Network File System* (NFS). On UNIX-dominated networks, NFS plays the same role for sharing files that built-in file sharing plays on Microsoft networks. If you want to use this capability on Windows XP or Windows 2003, you can purchase and install an add-on pack called Microsoft Windows Services for UNIX. Third-party vendors, such as Sun Microsystems (the inventor of NFS) and Intergraph (the purveyor of the fastest NFS implementation for Windows 2003), also offer NFS.

Since 1993, software vendors have come a long way in making their interfaces more Windows-like, making the process of installation and configuration more intuitive for administrators. Today, you can usually find help files and wizards to assist you when installing and configuring third-party components. Also, many third-party networks function using the Windows native networking facilities with little or no alteration.

The critical issue in choosing between built-in Microsoft networking components and third-party alternatives (which we cover in detail in Chapters 3 and 8) is the type of functionality your clients need. Certain client capabilities offered by third-party vendors may not work in the native Microsoft framework. If those third-party components don't work with the Microsoft components, you may have to weigh the requirements for this third-party functionality against the complexity of installing and configuring third-party networking software.

If requirements for third-party software are absolute or if their functionality is essential, you have no choice but to bite the bullet and face a possible configuration nightmare. For example, access to certain driver features in NetWare client software that aren't supported in the Microsoft counterpart may force you to use Novell software — like it or not. Otherwise, you're better off sticking with native Microsoft client software.

Built-in Functions versus Network Add-ons

You may want to enable clients to access networking services that aren't built into the Microsoft Windows client software. Giving users access to this type of functionality always requires additional software, such as the software necessary to access NFS. Although Windows 95, 98, SE, Me, NT, 2000, XP, and 2003 can all support NFS, that support is not built into those operating systems. Therefore, providing users with access to NFS requires obtaining, installing, and configuring additional software on their computers.

Adding new software to network clients, such as installing an application on a Windows operating system, is far less traumatic (and more common) than the situation in the preceding section, in which you had to change out the Microsoft client software for Novell client software. The application must be compatible with that operating system, and you must install and configure it correctly. However, software that uses only existing protocols and drivers on a Windows machine augments the Windows built-in capabilities, rather than replacing (or displacing) them. Therefore, adding compatible products, such as QUALCOMM's Eudora e-mail package, Ipswitch's WS_FTP Pro file transfer program, or the Netscape Navigator Web browser, to Windows XP and Windows 2003 is quite easy.

Nevertheless, many network administrators try to avoid adding unnecessary protocols and services to Windows. They do so because each additional protocol and service consumes system resources, such as memory and disk space. Granted, additional protocols and services may not use much memory if they're never or rarely used, but disk space is something services always consume!

One of the most profound ways to improve the performance of a Windows 2003 machine is to eliminate unnecessary protocols and services, as well as the *bindings* that tie protocols and services together. By default, Windows 2003 binds all protocols and services, even when those bindings may not be necessary (or wanted). Therefore, a bit of post-installation cleanup can improve performance as well as remove unwanted software connections. This is true of every version of Windows since Windows for Workgroups 3.11. (Managing bindings is covered further in Chapter 18.)

Adding third-party client applications or services to Windows machines is okay. This is especially true because most such software uses Windows built-in networking capabilities under the hood.

Managing Network Components

Modern Windows operating systems — by which we mean Windows 95, Windows 98, SE, Me, NT 4.0, 2000, XP, and 2003 — include support for two collections of client software for networking:

✔ Client for Microsoft Networks

✔ Client for NetWare Networks (or Client Service for NetWare)

These two client-software collections appear in Figure 2-1, which shows the General tab of a Local Area Connection object in Windows Server 2003. These two different sets of client software provide access to two different sets of network resources.

Figure 2-1: The General tab of a Local Area Connection object from a Windows Server 2003 system.

Client for Microsoft Networks, as the name suggests, includes the necessary components for a machine to act as a client on a Microsoft network. Likewise, Client for NetWare Networks includes similar components needed to act as a NetWare network client. Additional software components come into play on Windows Server 2003 and on client machines (such as Windows 95, 98, SE, Me, 2000, and XP), all of which we cover in Chapter 8.

You can use the Windows 2003 utility called My Network Places (if it's not on the desktop, look in Windows Explorer) to view information about resources available on your network. By default, this icon displays a list of all the network shares you've created and the computers they reside on. However, you can instruct it to show all kinds of displays. In Figure 2-2, for example, you see a complete list of all the computers in the same domain as the listing machine.

Figure 2-2:
My Network
Places
shows the
computers
in your
nearby
network
neighbor-
hood.

Unmasking the Microsoft network

In addition to the basic network client components used by Windows Server 2003 to communicate with a Microsoft or NetWare-based network, numerous other networking components are essential to the functional operation of a network:

- **MultiProtocol Router (MPR):** Distributes requests for network services to a specific *network provider,* which represents some type of network client environment. (It routes requests for Microsoft services to the Microsoft network provider and requests for Novell services to the NetWare network provider.) MPR allows a Windows system to support multiple simultaneous client connections. MPR also defines a single common interface so that applications can access features common to all networks through a single set of interface calls.

✔ **Microsoft Network Provider:** Defines an open interface that allows third-party vendors to integrate support for their networks. Microsoft Network Provider also grants access to (and management of) network resources and components through common utilities, such as My Network Places and the Network Connections utilities. Microsoft Network Provider offers a single set of well-defined functions to browse servers, to connect to or disconnect from servers, and to interact with other network resources.

✔ **Installable File System Manager (IFSMGR):** This file-system access facility integrates multiple file systems through a single interface. IFSMGR also allows remote file-system access requests to look exactly the same as local file-system access requests in their structure and functions. (They differ only in how requested objects are addressed.)

✔ **Client for Microsoft Networks Redirector:** This software component checks all application requests for resources. It hands off any requests for remote resources to the network interface but passes requests for local resources to the local operating system.

✔ **NetBIOS interface:** This protocol interface defines a high-level request/response protocol that carries requests for remote resources (and their replies). In particular, the NetBIOS interface uses a special messaging protocol, called *Server Message Block* (SMB), to carry requests from clients to servers and responses to those requests from servers back to their originating clients.

✔ **Network protocols designed to support Microsoft's Network Driver Interface Specification (NDIS) Version 3.1 or higher:** This refers to the built-in networking protocols for Windows operating systems that we discuss further in Chapter 3.

✔ **A generic NDIS interface:** This programming convention defines a standard code interface to network adapters in Windows operating systems. It allows driver developers to interact with NICs using a well-known, well-documented set of program calls to move data from the computer to the NIC for outgoing messages, and from the NIC back to the computer for incoming messages.

✔ **A specific NDIS adapter driver:** This device driver translates generic network interface formats into formats specific to whatever NIC or NICs are installed in a Windows computer. (Note that Windows NT, 2000, XP, and 2003 support multiple NICs in a single machine but neither Windows 95 nor Windows 98 offers this capability.)

Figure 2-3 shows this collection of Microsoft Network components and how the various components interact with an application that makes requests and the network that carries those requests to a server and delivers the corresponding replies to those requests. Please note that although all Windows operating systems are all similarly constructed and use similar components, details among these individual operating systems vary.

Figure 2-3:
The
component
structure
for the
Client for
Microsoft
Networks.

Understanding the Novell network

Even though the component structure for Client for NetWare Networks is similar to that for Client for Microsoft Networks (which we cover in the preceding section), their differences lie in specific NetWare-focused components that replace Microsoft counterparts. At many steps along the way from the application to the NDIS driver, different components specific to NetWare are used instead. The resulting collection of components is as follows:

- ✓ **MultiProtocol Router (MPR):** This software component is common to all network clients for Windows operating systems. As is the case with Microsoft Network/Microsoft Windows Network, MPR hands off network service requests to the appropriate network provider.

- ✓ **A NetWare-compatible Network Provider:** This software component provides access to and management of NetWare-accessible network resources and components through common utilities, such as the My Network Places and the Network Connections utilities. Like its Microsoft counterpart, the NetWare-compatible Network Provider offers a single set of well-defined functions to browse servers, to connect to or disconnect from servers, and to interact with network resources.

- ✓ **Installable File System Manager (IFSMGR):** This file system access facility integrates multiple file systems through a single interface for

consistent local and remote access to NetWare-based file and print
resources when Client for NetWare Networks is at work.

✔ **Client for NetWare Networks Redirector:** This software component
hands off requests for remote resources to the NetWare network interface
and passes requests for local resources to the local operating system.

✔ **One of several Network protocols:** Client for NetWare Networks can
use either Internet Package Exchange/Sequenced Package Exchange
(IPX/SPX) or TCP/IP to access the network.

✔ **Generic NDIS interface:** This device driver defines a standard interface
to network adapters in Windows operating systems. The same interface
works for Microsoft and NetWare clients.

✔ **A specific NDIS adapter driver:** This device driver translates generic
network interface formats into formats specific to whatever NIC or NICs
are installed in a Windows computer. (Note that Windows NT, 2000, XP,
and 2003 support multiple NICs in a single machine but neither Windows
95 nor Windows 98 offers this capability.)

Note the absence of a separate NetBIOS interface in this collection. This
omission means that NetWare doesn't use NetBIOS-based names to navigate
its networks. Client for NetWare Networks loses none of its NetBIOS capabilities even though there's no separate NetBIOS interface; applications still need
and get NetBIOS support. Notice also that MPR, the installable file system,
the protocols (except for the range of choices), and the NDIS components
remain more or less the same for both Microsoft and NetWare clients.

Observing this component-based software structure, you may feel compelled
to ask whether you can mix and match software components from Novell and
Microsoft. Unfortunately, you must go all one way (Microsoft) or the other
(Novell) when installing network client software components on a Windows
machine. No good comes of trying to meld the two!

You can run both Microsoft and NetWare clients side by side without difficulty,
but you can't mix Novell components and Microsoft components willy-nilly on
any Windows machine. Therefore, you can use Microsoft software to access
both Windows Server 2003 and NetWare servers or Novell software to access
both Windows Server 2003 and NetWare servers. But you can't use Microsoft
software to access Windows Server 2003 and NetWare software to access
NetWare servers on the same machine.

Managing Access to Resources

Part of each request that a client makes for a network resource includes the
client's own identification. Another part names the resources that the client
is requesting from the network. Clients normally use a password to access

resources on a peer-to-peer network, which Microsoft calls *share-level access control* (because each password applies to a single shared resource).

In a Microsoft client/server network, the user's level of permissions governs that user's ability to access resources. In Microsoft-speak, *user-level access* means that when a user identifies himself or herself in a request for service, the user's account name determines which requests the server can honor and which ones it must deny.

The server checks which resources the user has permission to access, and it checks also whether the operation that the user requests is allowed. For example, Bob may be allowed to read a certain file, but he may not be able to write to or delete that file. If he requests a read operation, the request is permitted, but if he requests a write or delete operation, that request is denied.

Handling requests on a client/server network involves more work than may be immediately apparent, because a *security check* controls access and restrictions. Setting up permissions requires an understanding of which names to attach to resources, to the domains in which they reside, and to the users who state such requests. Much of what you find out in Chapters 8, 11–14, and especially in Chapters 15, 16, and 18 touch on these terms and concepts and explain them to your heart's content.

A Windows Network Services Sampler

In the previous sections, we covered the request/response mechanism that handles all requests for network services and the ways in which responses occur. In this section, we explain what you can do within this structure. The following is an alphabetical list of common services that you're likely to find on a Windows Server 2003-based network:

- ✔ **Alerter:** Provides the capability to send alarms and alerts to specific recipients when events occur in Event Viewer or thresholds are exceeded in System Monitor.

- ✔ **Computer Browser:** Manages the list of computer and resource names on a specific network, so users can browse a list of what's out there (and available) in Network Neighborhood and other utilities.

- ✔ **Messenger:** Provides a way for Windows Server 2003 to deliver on-screen messages to designated recipients in response to explicit commands or to alarms and alerts.

✓ **Net Logon:** Handles user attempts to log on to the network and ferries information among all *domain controllers* in a single Windows Server 2003 domain.

✓ **Network DDE:** Allows dynamic updates to occur across a network. DDE *(Dynamic Data Exchange)* refers to a dynamic update technology used to propagate updates from one file or document to another when embedded objects in one document must reflect changes to that object in another document.

✓ **NTLM Security Support Provider:** Provides a Windows Server 2003 security model that's compatible with LAN Manager (LM). This service handles encryption and delivery of logon requests that can't use more modern Windows security models.

✓ **Plug and Play:** Makes a Windows 2003 machine Plug-and-Play compatible.

✓ **Print Spooler:** Handles the storage of files for pending print jobs. This is the service that manages the scheduling and retention of pending print jobs until their turn to print comes up.

✓ **Routing and Remote Access Service (RRAS):** Covers a whole range of RRAS services. RRAS provides dial-in and dial-out communications services for up to 256 simultaneous connections on a single Windows Server 2003 and offers a range of routing services as well.

✓ **Server:** Acts as the basic listener process for requests for service on a Windows Server 2003. (In fact, stopping the Server service is a good way to temporarily disable network access to a server.) Although its name may suggest otherwise, this service is necessary on Windows client machines and Windows Server 2003 machines alike.

✓ **Telephony Service:** Makes it possible for Windows 2003 to use the built-in Windows Telephony Application Programming Interface (TAPI) to access modems, telephones, Integrated Services Digital Network (ISDN), and general Digital Subscriber Line (xDSL) devices through a standard dialer and telephone book interface. Therefore, it is also a key component of RRAS service.

✓ **Workstation:** Allows a Windows 2003 machine to issue requests for service. This is what supports client-side activity.

To view a comprehensive list of the services available in Windows 2003, check out the Services utility that appears in the Administrative Tools section of the Start menu or Control Panel.

Although this laundry list doesn't include every service in Windows Server 2003, it does represent the most common services that you're likely to see running on most computers. Throughout this book, we give you a much better idea of what these and other services can do, as well as how you install, configure, and maintain them.

Chapter 3

Matters of Protocol

. . . .

. . . .

*I*n this chapter, you examine the communications and messages that move around on networks. We tell you more about what senders send and receivers receive while you investigate the sets of rules — called *protocols* — that govern how computers exchange information across a network.

In essence, networked communications rely on a shared set of rules for exchanging information and for defining how data looks at the most basic level, such as how to present data digitally (or "What's a one, and what's a zero?"). These rules also dictate the formats for and meanings behind the addresses that indicate where "here" and "there" are on a network, that identify message types and content, and that offer lots of other critical information to boot.

When Computers Communicate

Many of the ways that computers communicate and that humans communicate share common elements. Take a phone call, for example:

✔ Phone calls use highly formulaic introductions to connect the right speakers on each end of the connection. ("Is this the Phlogiston residence? May I speak to Phil, please?") Computers take a similar tack for network communications in that a sender often begins by asking the receiver if a conversation can begin, and only after permission is granted does any actual exchange of data occur.

✔ Taking turns talking on the phone requires careful listening skills and sensitivity to open spaces in the other party's talk, so each party can speak when the opportunity arises. Computers have no intuition, so they exchange explicit signals when one party wants to switch from listening to talking. In fact, some communications techniques allow both parties to talk — and listen — at the same time!

✔ Ending a phone conversation can be a matter of mutual agreement or it can involve well-known signals that one party wants to end the conversation. ("I have to let you go now" is a famous human example.) Computers also exchange signals to indicate that a network conversation is ready to end and then conclude by breaking their connection to each other.

✔ Humans possess coping skills to help them recognize unplanned endings to conversations, such as a failed cordless phone battery, driving beyond a cell boundary, or an outright connection failure. They also have the smarts to try again or give up, depending on whether they've satisfied their communication goals. Computers are more simple-minded; they wait until communications resume or a fixed interval of time (called a *timeout period*) elapses before recognizing that a connection is dead and that the conversation is over. Then it's up to the application that initiated the link to decide whether to try again or give up.

Understanding the differences between human communications and computer communications can help you understand networking better. The biggest difference, it seems, is that humans can navigate by the seat of their pants far better than computers can.

The secret's in the interpretation . . .

When humans communicate on the phone, what we say (or hear) is always interpreted and often misunderstood. What you think you said isn't always what another person thinks he or she heard you say. Human communication relies on shared rules and meanings as well as a common frame of reference. Computers rely on these same elements to communicate; but because computers can't make judgment calls or use their intuition, these elements must be spelled out completely. Computers can do only what they're programmed to do.

For computers to exchange data, every element must be explicitly supplied. Computers can't pick up implications and hidden meanings. To communicate, computers have to begin with complete agreement about the following issues (as stated from a computer's point of view):

- What's my address? How do I learn my address? How do I learn other computers' addresses?

- How do I signal another computer to indicate that I'm ready to send (or receive) a message, that I'm busy, or that I can wait if it's busy?

If you think about the phone system, these issues are the same for humans dialing a telephone and computers dialing a modem. In fact, these questions can be restated as follows:

- What's my phone number? How do I learn my phone number? How do I learn the phone numbers for other parties that I want to reach?

- How do I place a call? How do I recognize a busy signal? How do I get the phone to keep dialing if the number I want to reach is busy? (Note also that the phone system handles busy and ring signals, so both computers and humans can tell when a call is going through and when the party they're trying to reach is busy.)

Agreeing on a set of rules

Building a complete and consistent set of rules for computer communications is a time-consuming, nitpicky business that's entirely capable of driving most ordinary people bonkers. In the early days of the computer industry, individual companies or groups would put hordes of programmers to work building computer communications programs to solve specific, isolated problems.

But as time went on, programmers realized that this approach produced lots of unique ways for computers to communicate that worked only in the confines of small, isolated technical communities. After the need to communicate spreads farther, serious incompatibilities prevented such communities from exchanging data unless one community willingly gave up its way of communicating and adopted another's way of communicating.

The U.S. government played a key role in bringing order to this network chaos. When the government tried to get computers from Company A to work with computers from Company Z, it soon realized that it had a monster compatibility problem. A consensus soon emerged that a common set of rules for networking would make communication easier. Likewise, early network pioneers quickly learned that networking was difficult, if not downright impossible, when all players didn't follow the same set of rules.

If this tale had a storybook ending, it would be "Today, there's only one set of networking rules that everyone uses wisely and well." Alas, that's not the case. The degree of networking chaos has decreased significantly, but many sets of mutually incompatible networking protocols are still in use because hardware and software vendors try to stay on the "bleeding edge" by inventing new rules as they boldly go where no network has gone before.

These fundamental questions must be answered, and they represent just the beginning of a large and complex collection of details that have to be nailed down, codified, and implemented for computers to be able to communicate across a network. The answers to this entire collection of questions are the basis for a set of rules for computer communications; in fact, these rules represent the rules of the road — or protocols — for networking.

Following Protocol

The sets of networking rules that we talk about in the previous section are usually called *networking protocols* — but sometimes they're also called *networking standards*, *standard networking protocols*, and so on. You get the idea — these rules are shared by some group that seeks to communicate amongst themselves and define a common method for computers to communicate with one another. Any particular protocol defines a language, a structure, and a set of rules to support such communications.

Lots of work goes into defining a set of networking protocols, and even more work goes into building software to implement it. This is a huge project, and the amount of work necessary to pull it off explains why users, software developers, and hardware manufacturers all find it convenient to stick to the protocols that best fit their needs.

In diplomacy, protocol establishes a rigid set of procedures and etiquette that representatives from sovereign governments follow to prevent all-out war. For example, protocol helps explain why diplomats refer to screaming matches as "frank and earnest discussions" and to knotty disagreements as "constructive dialogs." Political doubletalk aside, the word *protocol* captures the flavor of rules for network communications quite nicely.

Whales come in pods, protocols in suites

Although this book deals primarily with Windows Server 2003 and the Microsoft protocols, the protocols included in Windows 2003 represent only part of a large body of well-known and well-defined networking protocols. Microsoft does a good job of allowing multiple protocols to run at the same time in Windows 2003, including the Internet standard Transmission Control Protocol/Internet Protocol (TCP/IP) and Novell's Internet Package Exchange/Sequenced Package Exchange (IPX/SPX).

Upon examination of any networking implementation, you're likely to observe that protocols rarely, if ever, appear in the singular. Most networking protocols consist of a collection of specific message formats and rules for interaction, each with its own name and functions, rather than a single, monolithic collection of formats and rules. For that reason, protocols may also be called *protocol suites,* not because they like to lounge around on comfortable furniture, but because they travel in packs, like wild dogs.

Making standards happen

One interesting fact about networking rules is that both vendors and standards groups call their protocols *standards.* Some vendors wax eloquently about differences between de facto and de jure standards. *De facto* means "It's not official, but a lot of people use it, so we can call it a standard if we want to." *De jure* means "It's a standard because the ABC (a standards-setting body) has declared it so and published this four-foot-high stack of books to prove it!"

Behind the often-heated discussions about what is and isn't a standard lurks a control issue. Purists — including academics, researchers, and techno-weenies — flatly assert that only a standards-setting group can be objective and fair. Therefore, only such a group can select the very best that technology has to offer by putting it in its standard — making it the best possible standard.

The other heat source comes from the vendors' desperate race to keep up with the marketplace (and customer demands for better, faster, cheaper technology) by struggling to get products finished and out the door. "Of course, we must control our technology," they say. "How else can we keep up?"

The objectivity, fairness, and leading-edge characteristics of most protocol standards may not be open to dispute, but establishing standards involves assembling groups of individuals who must agree on their contents. This takes time. Meanwhile, technology races ahead. (Nothing goes stale faster than leading-edge technology.)

It doesn't matter whether networking protocols are standards or not, whether de facto or de jure. The markets are where the action is. Vendors must involve themselves in all sides of any debate because they must bet on all the technology horses in any race. Some astute vendors, including Microsoft, publish their standards and give customers and industry experts enough documentation to both create workable networks and keep up with the rapid pace of development as well.

Some standards bodies have been wise enough to realize that a standard is viable only when widely used. These groups have allowed hardware and software vendors to deal with the real-world issues involved in getting products to market. The winners in both camps are the most popular protocols. Microsoft's protocol selections for Windows Server 2003 (and other Windows versions) include the leading standard protocol, TCP/IP, and the widely used vendor protocol NWLink IPX/SPX/NetBIOS (IPX/SPX originated with Novell NetWare).

Protocols permeate all aspects of networking

If one key concept explains why protocols are necessary, it's that protocols handle the movement of information between the hardware on the network interface and the applications that access the network. The reason why one computer can't talk to another computer without both sharing a common set of protocols is that both the sender and the receiver must be able to understand the other's operations, data formats, and delivery mechanisms. Without this common frame of reference, networking can't work.

Protocols fill the gap between a network's hardware and its software; they're used by programs that let your computer access the network. These protocols ferry data from applications all the way down to hardware, where a protocol says "send this message," to talk to the network. Going the other way, the protocol tells the hardware "give me the message," when the hardware indicates an incoming message has arrived.

Most protocols don't care what type of network they're talking through. In most cases, protocols are unaware of the network technology used, which might be Ethernet, token ring, or tutti-frutti. This indifference is possible because the part of the software that provides hardware access resides in a *device driver* for the network interface. The protocols themselves originate from other sources. (In Windows 2003, they reside in software components installed as part of the operating system, unless third-party components have been installed to displace built-in ones.) Therefore, when a protocol talks to the network interface, it's really communicating through a device driver to send data to (or to receive data from) the network. Specific device drivers tell a protocol exactly how to talk to the network interface (or interfaces) in your machine.

As we explain in Chapter 2, some applications include built-in networking capabilities that use a special software interface. Such network-aware applications are becoming increasingly common as networks become ubiquitous. Most Microsoft applications include some type of network intelligence, but the amount of such brainpower varies according to each application's focus and capabilities. Other applications may use standard application programming interfaces (APIs) and obtain network access anyway, totally unaware that a network is involved. This is where redirectors and other key system elements play a part. Whether applications are network-ready or use external networking facilities, as soon as they access the network, they use protocol software (and device drivers) to accept incoming or send outgoing messages.

The key to network access from applications or the operating system depends on access to a protocol suite. As we explain in Chapter 2, Windows 2003 includes all the components necessary to support network-aware and network-oblivious applications, which makes Windows Server 2003 itself quite network-aware indeed. Even though applications (and the operating system) may make requests for network service, the protocols do the dirty work, packaging messages to be sent across the network and then unpacking incoming messages into a readable form.

On other operating systems, such as Windows 95, 98, SE, Me, NT, 2000, and XP, UNIX, OS/2, and the Macintosh OS, built-in networking software also handles the network interface and those protocols and services that use it. DOS and older Windows 3.*x* versions, however, use client networking software that Microsoft supplies with Windows Server 2003 (or some other alternative from a third party).

Protocols as Postal Centers

Most of the action that occurs between applications and hardware consists of taking messages, breaking them down, and stuffing them into envelopes as those messages move farther from the application and closer to the hardware. From the other direction — from hardware to application — protocols unpack envelopes and reassemble individual pieces to build complete messages. We hope that the resulting message is meaningful, but remember GIGO, that immutable law of computing — garbage in, garbage out.

Exploring a post office analogy here may be useful. The post office handles anything that has an address on it and has sufficient postage to pay its way, as long as it conforms to the legal dimensions for a letter or a package. How is a letter delivered? It works something like this:

1. You address a letter, stick on a stamp, and drop it in a mailbox.

2. The mail carrier picks up the letter.

3. The mail carrier delivers the letter to the local post office.

4. Mail sorters check the zip code and route the letter.

5. The letter goes to the post office that serves the destination zip code.

6. Mail sorters check the street address and route the letter to the appropriate mail carrier.

7. The mail carrier delivers the letter to the address of its recipient.

At least, that's the way it's *supposed* to work. The basic requirements for successful mail delivery are timely pickup, short transit time, and correct delivery. Factors that affect transit time and delivery are correct identification of and routing to the destination address, plus potential transportation delays between sender and receiver.

The similarity between networking protocols and the postal service lies in the capability to recognize addresses, route messages from senders to receivers, and provide delivery. The major difference is that the postal service, unlike networking protocols, doesn't care what's in the envelopes we send as long as they meet size, weight, and materials restrictions. Networking protocols are very unpostman-like in that they care a great deal about what's in the envelopes we send. One of the main jobs of a networking protocol is to divide the contents of our envelopes and put them into smaller envelopes for delivery.

For example, suppose that you want to copy a 10MB file from your computer to another machine on your network. The file consists of a spreadsheet with some charts and graphics that include a sales forecast for the next quarter, so you want it to arrive quickly and correctly.

To use the post office (or what net-heads call snail mail), you would copy the file to a floppy disk and mail it to its recipient. However, that's not fast enough for most computer users. Over the network, it gets there in about 30 seconds (compared to the days it would take via snail mail). As the file moves from your workstation to the other machine, it's chopped into lots of small packages and then reassembled into its original 10MB form upon receipt.

Size restriction — that is, the biggest chunk of data that can move across the network in a single message — is only one reason that network messages are broken up and put into multiple envelopes. Handling addresses is another reason. In the post office example, the post office cares about the destination zip code, whereas the delivering mail carrier cares only about the street address. Likewise, one protocol may care about only the name of the computer to which the file is to be shipped. However, at a lower level, the protocol needs to know where to direct the chunks of data moving from sender to receiver so that the file can be correctly reassembled upon delivery.

For senders, the protocol software spends most of its time taking things apart to send them accurately and completely. On the receiving end, the protocol software spends its time stripping off packaging information and putting things back together again. The sender and receiver also exchange information during this process to monitor the accuracy and effectiveness of their communications and to determine if and when delivery is complete. Protocols also keep track of the quality and usability of network links.

In short, a lot more communication and activity is involved in sending and receiving messages across a network than is required to route mail from the sending post office to the receiving one. But the mail analogy remains a pretty good explanation for how things work in general (ignoring the routine rooting around inside messages performed by protocols but not by the post office).

The Dance of the Seven Layers

Network protocols are grouped according to their functions, such as sending and receiving messages from the network interface, talking to the hardware, making it possible for applications to do their things in a network environment, and talking to the software.

This group organization involves stacking multiple layers of functionality, where software is associated with each layer. When the software that supports a particular network protocol loads on a computer, it's called a *protocol stack.* All computers on the network load all or part of the stack. They use the same parts of the stack, called *peer protocols,* when they communicate with each other as — you guessed it — peers.

The best-known collection of networking layers was developed as part of an open networking systems effort in the 1980s called the *Open Systems Interconnection* (OSI) initiative. This model is known as the *OSI reference model* (also simply called the OSI model) because it defines a common frame of reference for understanding how networks work. Even though the OSI initiative never really achieved widespread adoption, the OSI model remains a standard tool to explain how network communications are structured and how they behave. The OSI model is shown in Figure 3-1.

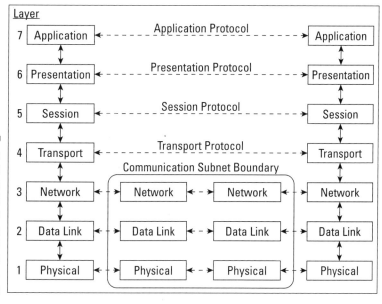

Figure 3-1: The OSI reference model breaks networking protocols into seven layers.

The OSI model consists of seven layers, as follows (working from the bottom up):

- ✔ **Physical layer:** This is the layer where the network hardware operates. Rules for this layer govern the types of connectors used, what types of signaling techniques carry data across the network, and the types of cable or other networking media that the physical, tangible part of the network uses. In some sense, this is the only part of the OSI model that you can see and touch.

- ✔ **Data Link layer:** This layer handles communication with the network hardware. For outbound messages, the Data Link layer enables the conversion of the bits that computers use to represent data into equivalent signals needed to move data across the network. For inbound messages, it reverses the process by enabling the conversion of signals into their equivalent bits. The Data Link layer is also where low-level hardware addresses for individual network interface cards (NICs) and other devices are handled.

- ✔ **Network layer:** This layer routes messages between senders and receivers, which means that it also handles translation between human-readable network addresses and computer-readable network addresses (which are not the same as the hardware addresses that the Data Link layer handles). Each message that passes through this layer includes the sender's and the receiver's addresses to identify the parties involved. The Network layer moves data from sender to receiver when they aren't both attached to the same cable segment.

- ✔ **Transport layer:** This layer chops up large messages into so-called *Protocol Data Units* (PDUs), or packets, and sends them across a network. It also puts PDUs back together to reconstitute messages upon receipt. The Transport layer can also include data integrity checks by adding a bit pattern to each message based on a mathematical calculation before sending. This same calculation is repeated by the sender, and the result is compared to the value calculated beforehand. If both values agree, the Transport layer assumes that the transmission was accurate and correct; if they don't agree, the Transport layer requests that the PDU be resent. This integrity function is optional; therefore, some Transport layer protocols include an integrity check and others don't.

- ✔ **Session layer:** This layer sets up ongoing network conversations (called *sessions*) between sender and receiver. This kind of ongoing connection makes it easier for computers to exchange large amounts of data, or to maintain a connection when data moves regularly between both parties to a session. Therefore, the Session layer handles *session setup* (which is like dialing a phone), *session maintenance* (which is like having a phone conversation), and *session termination,* or *teardown* (which is like ending a phone conversation and then hanging up the phone).

✔ **Presentation layer:** This layer converts data for network delivery. The assumption that drives this activity is that the sender and the receiver may not share a common set of data types, formats, or representations. Therefore, the Presentation layer converts data from formats created by the sender into a generic format for network transit, and then converts that generic form into a format specific to the receiver upon delivery. This conversion process allows programmers on both sides of the network connection to assume generic formats for network data, and to handle the details necessary to deliver that data to a specific client more easily.

✔ **Application layer:** This layer's name is something of a misnomer. It doesn't refer to the application or service that seeks to send or receive data across a network. Rather, it refers to an interface between the protocol stack and applications or system services. The Application layer defines the methods by which applications or system services can request network access and by which they can obtain access to incoming data from the network.

Each layer functions more or less independently of the others. But the job of any given layer is to provide services for the layer above it and to deliver data to the layer below. (The lowest level of the OSI model, the Physical layer, simply sends data on to a receiver or to the Data Link layer, depending on whether the communication is coming or going.)

The encoding that a layer does on the sending side is decoded by the same layer on the receiving side. Therefore, the layered OSI model helps emphasize that protocols on the sending end accept data from applications, convert that data into a generic form, manage conversations, prepare data to be sent across the network, address and route data, and then convert that data into signals for transmission across the network.

On the receiving end, that process is reversed: The protocols convert signals into data, figure out where that data is to be delivered, reconstitute incoming messages into their original containers, manage conversations, prepare the data for the client computer, and deliver that data to an application.

Some wags like to claim that there's an eighth layer to the protocol stack, and that it's the most important layer of all. It's called the Politics and Religion layer, and it jokingly refers to the organizational beliefs and requirements that drive network use. Even though there's no such layer in the OSI model, you'd be well-advised to keep this layer in mind any time you have to sell networking technology to upper management in your organization!

Windows 2003 Protocols (and More)

Just as diplomatic protocols grease the wheels of international relations, network protocols keep the network wheels turning. By getting to know these players, you gain more insight into how your network operates. As a bonus, you'll also be better equipped to troubleshoot protocol-related problems.

Windows Server 2003 includes support for two primary protocol suites:

- ✔ **TCP/IP (Transmission Control Protocol/Internet Protocol):** A set of standard protocols and services developed for the U.S. government in the 1970s and 1980s. TCP/IP is now the most widely used networking protocol suite in the world.
- ✔ **IPX/SPX (Internet Package Exchange/Sequenced Package Exchange):** The NetWare core protocols, developed by Novell in the early 1980s.

Windows 2003 Server also includes built-in support for a few specialty protocols. These include *AppleTalk,* the networking protocol native to the Macintosh operating system, and Reliable Multicast Protocol, a networking protocol used to improve the delivery of transmissions to multiple recipients simultaneously.

You can use just one or several protocols on your network, which accounts for both the blessings and curses of Windows 2003 networking. In the following sections, we tell you about each of these protocols and give you some guidance about when and why you may want to use one or more of them. Don't worry if the acronyms are unfamiliar or the terminology seems strange; concentrate on finding out how the protocols work to connect programs and services to your network (and your network's users). After you understand these concepts, you'll know all the really important stuff.

TCP/IP: The Internet suite

Transmission Control Protocol/Internet Protocol (TCP/IP) grew out of research funded by the Department of Defense (DoD) that began in the 1970s when the feds realized that they needed a technology to help them link all their dissimilar computer systems into a single network. These protocols in the TCP/IP suite are sometimes called the *DoD protocols* because the DoD requires that all computers it purchases be able to use them. Likewise, TCP/IP is known as the *Internet protocol* because it's the foundation upon which the Internet runs.

TCP/IP is actually an acronym for two members of the protocol suite: the Transmission Control Protocol (TCP) and the Internet Protocol (IP). According to Dr. Vinton Cerf, one of the Internet's founding technologists, more than one million networks are part of the Internet itself, but an equal number (or more) of private networks also use TCP/IP.

Here there be acronyms!

To set up and troubleshoot a Windows 2003-based network, you need to understand what the various protocols do to make educated guesses about the types of problems that each protocol may develop. When working with these protocols, you have to toss around awkward collections of letters (and sometimes numbers) with aplomb.

You should know which acronyms belong together and how the pieces of the various protocol stacks fit together. When things get weird — and we're sorry to report that they sometimes do — you have to know about the Windows 2003 rogue's gallery of protocols so you can run down the possible perpetrators.

Most protocol families are rife with abbreviations and acronyms. Take heart from this fact: Although familiarity may breed contempt, it can also enable you to navigate this complex bowl of alphabet soup!

With a global community of nearly 100 million users, TCP/IP is the most widely used of all the networking protocols. TCP/IP is also deeply rooted in the UNIX community because of its inclusion in early-1980s public releases of the free *Berkeley Software Distribution* (BSD) of UNIX and its subsequent inclusion in the official AT&T/Bell Labs offering of UNIX shortly afterward.

Because TCP/IP was designed to allow dissimilar types of computers to interconnect and communicate, TCP/IP works on more types of hardware than any other networking protocol. Therefore, you shouldn't be surprised that most commercially available operating systems — including Windows, Macintosh, and UNIX — include built-in TCP/IP implementations.

Two versions of TCP/IP are in use today. Version 4 is based on a 32-bit addressing scheme. This is the version of TCP/IP used by default on Windows 2003 as well as all previous network-capable Microsoft Windows operating systems. TCP/IP version 6 is based on a 128-bit addressing scheme. TCP/IP version 4 is so widely used that nearly all of the possible addresses have already been assigned to systems. Several technologies have been developed to help manage this issue (such as private IP address, which cannot be routed, or using NAT proxies to hide the internal addresses of a network from the Internet), but things are getting crowded. TCP/IP version 6 has so many addresses that every person on the planet could have 4.86×10^{28} IP addresses (that's a lot of a lot).

Windows Server 2003 can use TCP/IP version 6 if you install it (as did Windows 2000 and Windows XP). However, the only place where you can use it is either within a private network or when connected to I2 (the new exclusive, high-speed, trendy version of the Internet that only government, military, and educational organizations can access).

Because TCP/IP is the foundation for the Internet and the most widely used networking protocol, we consider it to be the default choice for most networks. Although learning and using TCP/IP can be a chore, it provides more functions and capabilities than any other protocol. In fact, Microsoft recommends TCP/IP as the best protocol to use with Windows Server 2003.

IPX/SPX: The original NetWare protocols

Internet Package Exchange (IPX), *Sequenced Package Exchange* (SPX), and *NetWare Core Protocol* (NCP) are the original Novell NetWare protocols. IPX, SPX, and NCP, with more than 48 million users, are among the most widely used networking protocols worldwide. You can use IPX with NetWare for a variety of operating systems, including DOS, Windows 3.*x*, Windows 9*x*, Windows 2000, Windows XP, Windows Server 2003, Macintosh, OS/2, and some varieties of UNIX.

You normally need these protocols only if you use NetWare 4.*x* or older versions on your network. With the release of NetWare version 5.0, Novell provides native NetWare support for TCP/IP, so we expect IPX/SPX usage to diminish over time. Please note that because Microsoft didn't want to pay Novell to use the IPX/SPX trade name, Microsoft calls IPX/SPX NWLink. (In Windows 9*x*, it's called the IPX/SPX-compatible protocol.)

IPX/SPX is a pretty well-behaved protocol with advanced routing capabilities. Therefore, it works on networks of all sizes. But using IPX/SPX typically means a NetWare 4.*x* server (or some older version) is somewhere on your network. You can wean yourself from this protocol over time or do without it altogether as your organization follows the inexorable trend toward TCP/IP, the protocol of the Internet (with which IPX/SPX is incompatible).

Other faces, other protocols

On networks where you work, other, less common protocols may crop up, such as the following:

- **DLC (Data Link Control):** A legacy protocol used to connect to a network-attached printer and some IBM mainframes. This protocol has been dropped from Microsoft's operating systems. It appeared with limited acclaim under Windows 2000, but it's gone gone gone from Windows XP and Windows 2003. If you need network-attached printer access, you'll probably use TCP/IP or some vendor proprietary protocol. Likewise, if you need to communicate with mainframes or other extreme legacy systems, you'll use TCP/IP, a gateway, or a vendor proprietary protocol. DLC can still be used on a Windows Server 2003 system, but you'll need to find a third-party vendor to provide an installation disk because Microsoft left it out of the goodie bag (that is, the distribution CD).

- **NetBIOS (Networked Basic Input-Output System):** NetBIOS is an API developed by IBM and refined by Microsoft. NetBIOS, along with NetBEUI, formed the original networking components for LAN Manager and Windows NT. NetBIOS also works with IPX/SPX and TCP/IP, so don't assume that NetBIOS requires NetBEUI. (It doesn't.) If you're working on a network with only Windows 2000, Windows XP, and Windows 2003 systems, you can opt to not use NetBIOS at all!

- **NetBEUI (NetBIOS Enhanced User Interface):** NetBEUI is a fast, efficient, but nonroutable local-area protocol developed by IBM and refined by Microsoft. NetBEUI and NetBIOS were the original networking components for LAN Manager and Windows NT. NetBEUI has gone the way of the dodo, at least according to Windows XP and Windows 2003. Out of sight, out of mind. NetBEUI can still be used on a Windows Server 2003 system, but you'll need to find a third-party vendor to provide an installation disk.

- **AppleTalk:** The name of a set of protocols created by Apple Computer, whose Macintosh computer was one of the first mass-market computers to include built-in networking hardware and software. In most cases, where you have a Macintosh, you have some need for AppleTalk. To offer file and print access to Macintosh clients, Microsoft includes a networking component called Services for Macintosh. This add-in module (which isn't installed during Windows Server 2003's initial setup) allows Mac users to access files, printers, and services on a Windows Server 2003.

- **ISO/OSI:** A nifty palindrome that stands for the *International Organization for Standardization Open Systems Interconnection* protocol suite. OSI has never lived up to its original goal to succeed TCP/IP. Some OSI protocols are in broad use in Europe, where they have established a foothold. OSI is out there in industry, government, academia, and business because many governments, including the U.S. government, require systems to be OSI-compliant.

  Like TCP/IP, OSI is available for a broad range of systems, from PCs to supercomputers. Most protocol stacks resemble the OSI reference model for networking, and this model remains the most enduring legacy of the effort that went into OSI networking in the 1980s. Numerous third-party ISO/OSI implementations are available for Windows 2003, mostly from European companies, but Microsoft itself doesn't include these protocols with the operating system.

- **SNA:** This refers to IBM's *Systems Network Architecture,* its basic protocol suite for large-scale networking and mainframe access. Because SNA was a pioneering protocol, companies that invested heavily in mainframe technology also usually invested in SNA. Many SNA networks are still in use, but the number is dropping because SNA is old, cumbersome, and expensive, and because TCP/IP is eating SNA's lunch — even on mainframes.

Connection types classify protocols

IP, IPX, and NetBEUI are *connectionless* protocols, and SPX and TCP are *connection-oriented*. What does this mean? Must you care?

All these protocols operate at lower levels. Earlier in this chapter, we told you that a lower-level protocol's most important jobs are to break up arbitrarily long messages into digestible chunks when sending data across a network and then put them back together upon receipt. These chunks (called *packets*) form the basic message units for data moving across a network. These packets are further divided and stuffed into their envelopes by the access method in use. Such envelopes are called *frames*. Look at it this way: Packets move up and down the protocol stack; frames dance across the wires.

Connectionless protocols work the same way as mailing letters through the postal service. You drop the letter into a mailbox and expect the post office to deliver it. You may never know whether or not the letter actually gets there — unless it's a bill! IP, IPX, and NetBEUI provide no guarantee of delivery, and frames can arrive in any order.

Connection-oriented protocols, on the other hand, use a handshake to start communications, where the would-be sender asks the receiver whether it can accept input before it starts sending. After transmission is underway, connection-oriented protocols treat each message like a registered letter, where you get a return card to verify its receipt. SPX and TCP packets are sequenced so that when they arrive, they can be reassembled in their original order, which makes them more reliable. Connection-oriented protocols can also request redelivery or send error notices when packets are damaged or lost en route from sender to receiver.

IP and other connectionless protocols are typically fast and impose little overhead but are considered lightweight and unreliable. TCP and other connection-oriented protocols run more slowly than their connectionless counterparts because they keep track of what has been sent and received and because they monitor the status of the connection between sender and receiver. More record-keeping and data-check information is built into each packet, which raises overhead requirements but also increases reliability.

The networking world includes hundreds of other protocol suites, each with its own collection of acronyms and special capabilities, but you don't need to know most of them. If you haven't seen a protocol that runs on your network in this chapter, you probably know more about it than we do anyway!

Mixing Protocols

Sometimes, you may need more than one networking protocol on a computer. This may occasionally require you to go through some interesting contortions, but Windows Server 2003 is accommodating about supporting multiple protocols. In fact, you can run both TCP/IP and IPX/SPX (NWLink) (plus any other native or third-party, vendor-provided protocol) on a single Windows

Server 2003 machine on multiple network interface cards without too much hassle. The same is true of Windows 98, SE, Me, XP, and 2000.

Likewise, Macintoshes can run AppleTalk and TCP/IP together easily, and UNIX can run as many protocol stacks together as you may need to obtain the range of network services necessary. A UNIX machine's protocol collection can include TCP/IP, NetBEUI, OSI, IPX, and more.

Chances are that your biggest problems in using multiple protocol stacks will occur on older PCs running DOS or Windows 3.*x*, where the lack of built-in networking automatically makes installing and using multiple protocols more difficult. Likewise, limited memory management capabilities and the lack of support for modern device drivers make hybrid networking a challenge.

Seeing What's Up on Your Server

With Windows Server 2003, inspecting your system to see which protocols are installed is pretty simple. Just launch the Network Connections utility (choose Start⇨Control Panel, right-click Network Connections, and then choose Open). Next, click the Advanced menu, and then choose Advanced Settings. You see the results of these actions in Figure 3-2.

The figure shows that we practice what we preached in this chapter by running only TCP/IP on our network. (Figure 3-2 shows that TCP/IP is bound to all the services that show up for our local area connection.) The only protocols that you have to worry about on your network are the ones that show up in this window (or the protocols that you know are supposed to show up but don't, as the case may sometimes be).

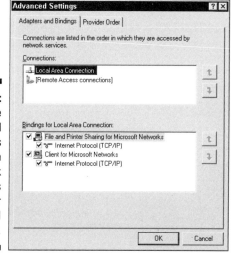

Figure 3-2:
Use the Advanced Settings dialog box in Network Connections to check for installed protocols.

Chapter 4

My Kingdom for a Topology!

*W*hen mathematicians get together, they enjoy nothing more than making up new terminology to bedevil the rest of us. (Maybe they don't want computer scientists to corner the market on obtuse terminology.) Mathematics is where the networking term *topology* originates; a topology describes the way computers are wired together on a network. Beyond bedevilment, topologies provide a concise and accurate way to describe how a network's various pieces and parts come together. In this chapter, we tell you about various topologies that you can mix and match to create networks.

However, topologies don't tell the whole story about network design. You must also consider the specific hardware you use and how that hardware interacts with other hardware — the *hardware implementation,* if you will.

Perhaps jealous of the mathematicians and their coining of cool terms, a group of computer scientists coined the term *networking technologies,* to identify the specific hardware and signaling methods used in a network. Perhaps jealous of that group of computer scientists, another group decided that it was more useful to think about the same hardware and signaling methods in terms of *access methods,* a way of thinking that concentrates more on how the hardware gets permission to transmit signals across the network medium.

This chapter also gives you the skinny on specific hardware implementations, network technologies, and access methods that take a topology and make it into a real, working network.

What Is a Topology, Really?

Mathematically speaking, a topology is an arrangement of lines between points in a graph. In a network, the word *topology* refers to the way wires (lines) stretch between computers (points in a graph). Therefore, when you hear the word *topology* at a networking conference, what's being talked about is the arrangement of computers in a network.

You can lay out network wiring in many ways. Figure 4-1 shows the two most common layouts — the star topology and the bus topology. Another common layout, called a *ring topology,* uses a wiring pattern laid out in a circle, where the last computer in the ring links back to the first computer.

Figure 4-1:
Star and bus wiring layouts often appear together.

Bus   Star

Topologies can be combined in many interesting ways. If you use a bus to link a number of separate stars together, you end up with a *distributed-star network,* also known as a *hybrid network.* Most networks are hybrids of some type, but in general, networks work better if you keep things simple.

The star of the network world

A *star topology* consists of separate wires that run from a central point — usually attached to a single device called a *hub* (hubs are explained later in this section) — to individual devices attached to the other end of each wire. A *bus topology* is a single cable to which all devices on a network (or on some part of a network, as is more often the case) are attached.

If you break a wire in a star topology, only one link is affected, and everything else keeps working. If you break a wire on a bus topology, however, everything connected to that bus loses the capability to access the network.

In a star topology, the hub at the center of the star acts as a relay for computers attached to its arms, like this:

1. The sending computer sends a chunk of data across the wire aimed at some destination computer.

2. The hub sitting between the sender and the receiver passes the message to the destination computer — if it's attached to the same hub — or to some other hub or network device, if it's not hooked to the same hub.

3. The hub to which the destination computer is attached sends the message to that computer (assuming that both the sender and receiver reside in a star topology — however, nothing prevents networking across different topologies, as long as the right types of links exist between them).

On a large network, the middle step might be repeated several times, as data jumps from the sender to the hub to the receiver, or from hub to bus to hub (and so on), until the data eventually reaches its destination computer.

Get on the bus!

In a bus topology, every computer on the same wire sees every message that travels across that wire. If the sender and the receiver are on the same wire, called a *segment,* messages travel very quickly. If the sender and the receiver are not on the same wire, a special message-forwarding computer, called a bridge or a router, passes the message from the sender's wire on toward the receiver's wire by copying the message and retransmitting that message.

Bridges and routers are discussed in detail later in this chapter. For now, think of a *bridge* as a device that forwards information from one network to another based on *Media Access Control* (MAC)-level addresses. A router, on the other hand, routes information from one network to another based on network addresses.

Just as you can forward a message through multiple hubs in a star topology, you can forward a message through multiple bridges or routers on a bus topology.

Run rings around your network

The other remaining major topology is called a ring. Real rings are seldom built because they can fail completely if a cable breaks. That's why networking technologies, such as the *Fiber Distributed Data Interface* (FDDI) use true ring topologies that include dual cables and a fault tolerance scheme to allow the network to recover from the break of any single cable.

In fact, most so-called ring topologies are really star- or bus-wired networks that impose a logical ring structure on the physical wiring, whatever its actual topology may be. Therefore, you'll find that network technologies, such as ARCnet (short for *Attached Resource Computer Network*), support logical rings atop star- or bus-wired networks, and other technologies such as token ring, support logical rings atop star-wired networks (or distributed star-wired networks). This arrangement appears in Figure 4-2.

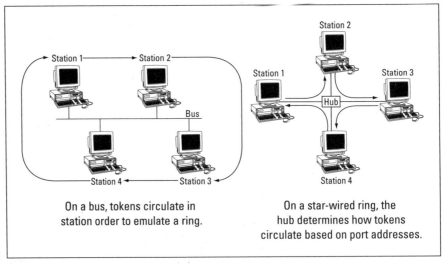

Figure 4-2:
Physical stars or buses can support logical rings.

On a bus, tokens circulate in station order to emulate a ring.

On a star-wired ring, the hub determines how tokens circulate based on port addresses.

Physical versus logical

Network topologies can be physical or logical. The physical topology of a token ring network is normally a star, but the way data moves from one computer to another is a ring. ARCnet can be a physical bus or star (or some combination of the two), but logically it's a ring. Not even Ethernet is exempt from this confusion. When Ethernet is wired as a bus, it acts like a bus; but when Ethernet is wired as a star, it still acts like a bus.

More than just a simple token

Networks use sets of rules, called *protocols,* to communicate with one another. Some network technologies use *tokens* to control these communications. Other network technologies opt for a free-for-all, in which any computer can send data whenever the network's not busy. Networks that send tokens are called *token-passing networks*. They use a token-passing protocol to control network access — that is, they must wait for a usable token to arrive when they want to send data.

On the free-for-all side, things are a bit more complicated: Computers must listen to the media to determine whether it's in use (indicated by active signals on the media). If a computer wants to transmit, it stops and listens, like the well-mannered little computer it is, to see whether someone else is talking. If the computer doesn't hear any signals, it can go ahead

and transmit right away. When another computer does the same thing at more or less the same time, data from one computer collides with data from another, and both computers must back off and try again.

You want to have something in place to deal with these kinds of collisions. Ethernet implements *Carrier Sense Multiple Access with Collision Detection* (CSMA/CD), whereas ARCnet and token ring implement token-passing protocols. The names that describe how these technologies access network media are called *access methods.* People often confuse topologies with access methods or network technologies, but now that we've got this source of confusion straightened out, the details of the various network technologies described in this chapter should make more sense.

Rings are attractive because they keep track of who gets to send a message by circulating an electronic permission form, also known as a *token,* around and around the network. Only the computer with possession of the token can transmit a message on the network, which eliminates any possibility that two computers might try to send a message at the same time. On average, every computer waits about the same amount of time for the token to come around; therefore, each computer has an equal shot at network access over time. This approach allows a network's available bandwidth to be used more fully before the network starts to slow down.

When thinking about networks, don't confuse a network's topology and the network technology in use. The topology identifies the network's wiring scheme, plain and simple. The topology describes how communications move among the computers and other devices on a network. The network technology, sometimes called an access method, identifies how the network behaves and what types of interfaces and equipment it requires. Therefore, the network technology also describes the network's physical characteristics in great detail, including

✔ The network's electrical characteristics

✔ The type of signaling that the network uses

✔ The type of connectors that the network uses

✔ The types of interfaces and how they work together

✔ The maximum message size

✔ Everything else necessary to build a working environment

The topology deals with network layout; the network technology (or access method) deals with how a network operates. Put another way, a topology names the wiring scheme in use, and the network technology defines what physical components you must buy to make those wires work.

A Network Technology Primer

You can break down all the various network technologies available in today's marketplace according to five categories. Therefore, by answering all five of the following questions, you can distinguish any one type of network technology from another:

✔ What access method, protocol, and topology does the network use?

✔ How does the network work?

✔ What are the network's technical pros and cons?

✔ What types of network media does the network support?

✔ How business-friendly (cost, availability, and so on) is this network?

In the following sections, we examine the pros and cons of various network technologies — just as you must do when you have to apply a certain technology to a particular topology with the goal of best serving the needs of your users.

And the technology contestants are . . .

When you talk about network technologies, you're talking about a specific type of hardware and associated driver software that, when added to a PC, can produce a working network connection. The working part, however, is contingent on the right infrastructure — cables, connections, and ancillary equipment (such as bridges or routers) — also being available.

For the purposes of this book, there are two primary network technologies (but that's a tremendous oversimplification, as you'll find out later):

> ✔ Ethernet
>
> ✔ Token ring
>
> ✔ Other

Okay, you caught us sneaking in a third, catch-all entry (we almost called it *miscellaneous*) to give us the opportunity to say something about several of the multitude of other available (but less common) network technologies that we choose not to cover in detail in this book. In fact, recent industry analyses indicate that it's about 75 percent likely that your network uses (or will use) one or both of the first two network technologies mentioned in the preceding list. Thus, even though we cover only a small number of technologies in depth, we cover most networks to some degree.

Meet Ethernet, the most popular network technology

Ethernet is the best known, most widely used, versatile, and readily available network technology around. As such things go, Ethernet has been around longer than most, since the mid-to-late 1970s. Ethernet was the brainchild of Xerox's Palo Alto Research Center (PARC) and later adopted by Digital, Intel, and Xerox (which is why older 15-pin connectors for ThickWire Ethernet are sometimes called DIX connectors). Ethernet has long been a networking commodity, which means that plenty of vendors play in this market and that lots of options and choices are available for this technology.

Ethernet uses the CSMA/CD access method. The sidebar titled "Ethernet: Network bumper cars," shown later in this chapter, explains what this stuff means in everyday English, insofar as the subject allows — which isn't so very far, alas.

The easiest way to describe CSMA/CD is like this: "Listen before sending. Listen while sending. If garbage happens, quit sending and try again later."

Ethernet's strengths and weaknesses

Ethernet's strengths are as follows: It's robust and reliable, and it comes in a broad, affordable range of flavors. Ethernet's weaknesses include the inevitability of collisions and the more difficult troubleshooting techniques that a bus network requires. Ethernet's base speed of 10 Mbps (short for *megabits per second*) is on the slow end for modern networks, but plenty of higher-speed Ethernet versions are now available. (We give you the goods on these in Chapter 7.)

Ethernet does not perform well for high-traffic applications or when real-time delivery is needed (for video and multimedia), nor does it degrade gracefully when high traffic volumes occur. In fact, with Ethernet's CSMA/CD access method, the effective ceiling on its bandwidth is between 56 and 60 percent of total bandwidth (or between 5.6 and 6.0 Mbps on a 10-Mbps Ethernet). That's the level of use beyond which the increasing probability of collisions often results in network slowdowns or failures.

Ethernet: Network bumper cars

The acronym that describes Ethernet's media access method is CSMA/CD, for *Carrier Sense Multiple Access with Collision Detection*. (The auditory equivalent of a collision is an echo.) When a collision occurs, you must repeat the transmission. The following list provides a definition for each term in this access method acronym:

✓ **Carrier Sense:** Everyone attached to the network is always listening to the wire, and no one can send while someone else is sending. When a message moves across the wire, an electrical signal called a *carrier* is used. By listening to the wire, a device knows when it's busy, because it senses the presence of the carrier.

✓ **Multiple Access:** Any device attached to the network can send a message whenever it wants, as long as no carrier is sensed at the time. This means that multiple senders can (and sometimes do) begin sending at roughly the same time — when they think things are quiet — and that's why it's called *multiple access.*

✓ **Collision Detection:** If two or more senders begin transmitting at roughly the same time, sooner or later their messages run into each other, causing a *collision*. Collisions are easy to recognize because they produce a garbage signal that is completely unlike a valid transmission. Ethernet hardware includes *collision-detection* circuitry that immediately halts transmission when a collision is observed. When a collision occurs, each sender waits a random time interval before listening to the wire to retry its transmission.

When planning bandwidth consumption for an Ethernet network, use 55 percent of the total bandwidth (5.5 Mbps on a 10-Mbps network, 55 Mbps on a 100-Mbps network, and so on) as the ceiling for usable bandwidth on any network segment. If you plan to consume Ethernet's entire bandwidth when designing a network, you'll be designing a network that's headed for trouble!

There's no shortage of bandwidth available to Ethernet customers today. Most newer Ethernet network interface cards (NICs) are 10/100 designs, which means they can sense whether they're used on a 10-Mbps or 100-Mbps Ethernet network and set their speeds accordingly. Today, Gigabit Ethernet, with an amazing 1,000 Mbps of total theoretical bandwidth, lifts the ceiling on network capacity to new heights but retains compatibility with other Ethernet versions.

All the flavors of Ethernet

Ethernet comes in all the basic flavors. That is, Ethernet runs on any of the major media types — twisted-pair, coaxial cable (multiple versions, in fact), and fiber optic — and works with both bus and star topologies. One unusual variant — 100BaseVG-AnyLAN — uses a different access method called *demand priority* that gives this implementation interesting capabilities. (100BaseVG-AnyLAN is covered in detail in Chapter 7.)

Also, you can easily find Ethernet devices that allow you to mix and match media; so you can use Ethernet to build networks of just about any size and for even the most hostile environments (such as factory floors or engine rooms, where lots of heavy-duty equipment can create major interference).

In addition, Ethernet technologies support some innovative uses of bandwidth, so you'll occasionally hear about varieties such as switched Ethernet and full-duplex Ethernet. The former variety depends on a special kind of device (called a switch, naturally) that allows any two nodes to establish a private end-to-end connection. Therefore, switched Ethernet allows pairs of machines to use the entire bandwidth of the network medium. (This is a great way to squeeze extra life out of 10-Mbps Ethernet systems.) Full-duplex Ethernet is limited to 100BaseVG-AnyLAN and uses two pairs of wires so that machines can send and receive data at the same time, thereby doubling overall bandwidth.

The business end of Ethernet

Despite its age, Ethernet remains the most widespread and popular network technology. Of the major media types available, twisted-pair leads the pack for new Ethernet installations, but a lot of coaxial cable is still in use. Fiber-based Ethernet is usually limited to networks in campus environments, where long distances and electrical interference issues are greatest. However, it's also used in hostile environments or for high-bandwidth applications, including both 100-Mbps and gigabit implementations.

The primary reasons for Ethernet's unshaken popularity are as follows:

- **Affordability:** Cabling is cheap and interfaces range from $20 for bottom-end NICs to less than $200 for powerful server NICs. Ethernet is not the cheapest of all the network technologies, but it's darn close!

- **Freedom of choice:** Ethernet supports all types of media, numerous bandwidths, and lots of gear to build hybrid networks. Vendors galore offer Ethernet hardware. For specialized network hardware or media needs, chances are good that some Ethernet variety meets them. If some option isn't available, it's probably on someone's drawing board.

- **Experience:** Ethernet's longevity means that Ethernet-savvy individuals are easy to find. Also, lots of technical and training material on Ethernet makes expertise relatively easy to build.

- **Continuing innovation:** At 10 Mbps, basic Ethernet is no speed demon. However, vendors make high-speed network switches for Ethernet that can deliver the entire 10 Mbps to individual connections, and higher-speed Ethernet varieties are readily available and widely used. As bandwidth needs grow, engineers have found ways to increase Ethernet's capabilities to match those needs, as the formalization of Gigabit Ethernet as an IEEE standard (802.3z, in fact) attests.

If you're asked to build a new network and no compelling reasons exist to choose another network technology, choose Ethernet because of all the reasons previously mentioned!

Taking on token ring

Token ring has gained a substantial foothold in the marketplace, although it hasn't been around in commercial form as long as Ethernet. Token ring is based on technology refined and originally marketed by IBM, so it's most commonly found in environments where IBM is entrenched. When PCs started taking desktop space away from dumb terminals hooked to IBM mainframes, IBM took action. They developed token ring to tie all those new PCs into their mainframe computers.

Token ring uses a token-passing access method in a collection of individual point-to-point links between pairs of devices arranged in a circular pattern. *Point-to-point* means that one device is hooked directly to another. For token ring, point-to-point describes the connection between a computer and a hub, which may, in turn, be attached to other hubs or computers. Although the devices used with token-ring networks act like hubs, they are more properly known as *multistation access units* (MAUs or MSAUs) or *controlled attachment units* (CAUs). The reason they're not really hubs (and that they're more expensive than most hubs) derives from these devices' capabilities to reconfigure themselves on the fly as nodes enter and leave the network. This is more difficult than simply sensing whether a connection is working and requires more expensive hardware to handle the job.

Token ring is mathematically fair to everyone who participates, and it guarantees that the network isn't overwhelmed by traffic. Token ring is said to be *fair* because it constantly passes the right to transmit around the network. This is accomplished in the form of a special message called a *token*. To send a message, a computer must wait until it obtains possession of the token. The token is not released until the message has been delivered (or until it's obvious that it can't be delivered). Everyone gets the same opportunity at using the token.

The easiest way to think about how token ring works is as follows: To send a message, your system waits for the token. When the token comes by, if it's not already carrying a message, your system tacks your message to the token, and then sends the token (and the message) on to its intended recipient. The recipient, upon getting a token addressed to it, copies the attached message and passes the token on around the ring. When the token comes back to your system, it strips off your message and sends the token (now empty of cargo) to the next computer downstream on the ring.

Token ring's strengths and weaknesses

Token ring's strengths include equal access for all devices and guaranteed delivery. Token ring works reliably and predictably, even when loaded to capacity. Token ring is available in two speeds: 4 Mbps and 16 Mbps. The older, slower version runs at 4 Mbps. This is 40 percent of the theoretical bandwidth for 10-Mbps Ethernet, but only slightly slower than basic Ethernet's effective speed.

A newer, higher-speed version of token ring runs at 16 Mbps, or 160 percent of basic Ethernet's theoretical bandwidth. It can handle three to four times as much data because it allows simultaneous use of multiple tokens while using 100 percent of total bandwidth. Waiting in the wings is a full-duplex implementation of token ring that works much like switched Ethernet. For higher speeds, a 100-Mbps version of token ring is under construction.

We hear you thinking "If token ring is so great, why buy Ethernet?" Token ring has weaknesses that have less to do with technical considerations and more to do with inflexibility and expense. Token ring's major downside is that it requires the expensive MAUs we discussed in the preceding section. Also, token ring requires that two strands of cable be run from each computer to each hub port. (One for the outbound trip, the other for the return trip.) These requirements add to token ring's expense and reduce the maximum legal distance between computers and hubs. Token ring is also more complicated and requires fancier connectors than Ethernet.

Token ring's many flavors

Token-ring implementations for twisted-pair and fiber-optic media are available, but twisted-pair is by far the most common implementation and is the most likely medium when tying desktops to hubs. Fiber-optic is the cable of choice for spanning longer distances and daisy-chaining MAUs. Only limited amounts of *shielded twisted-pair* (STP) cabling are used on token-ring networks. Because of individual cable length limitations and maximum ring-size limitations, cabling a token-ring network takes more planning and number crunching than cabling an Ethernet network.

The business end of token ring

From a cost-benefit perspective, there's not enough benefit in token ring's reliability, fairness, and guaranteed performance to offset its higher costs. Today, token ring costs from 75 to 150 percent more than Ethernet without necessarily providing significant performance or reliability advantages.

Although there are two schools of thought on this issue — "Forget token ring. Ethernet rules." and "We're token-passing fools. What's Ethernet?" — we're not about to climb out on either limb. If someone offers you token ring at a price that's too good to pass up or if that's what circumstances dictate you must use, go ahead and use it. Token ring works just fine. However, we don't recommend it as a technology of choice for starter networks because of its expense and complexity.

What other network technologies are there?

If you're thinking, "What else is there?" you may be wondering why this book omits your network technology of choice. We hate to be the bearer of sad tidings, but if you're not using either Ethernet or token ring, you may be networking too hard (or at least networking the hard way). Sorry!

In fact, hundreds of other types of network technologies are in use today. At least one such technology exists for every letter in the alphabet from *A* for ARCnet to *X* for xDSL. If you think that such acronym overkill may end up making your head spin, you're not alone. The proliferation of exotic network technologies can be a problem for Windows Server 2003, too. A word to the wise: If you're using an exotic network technology, make sure that Windows Server 203 works with it before you spend any money on the software.

The good news is that Windows 2003 runs over a reasonable subset of network technologies. The bad news is that you'll have to do some research to find out whether what you're using is one of the technologies that Windows 2003 supports. Worse yet, you'll have to work harder to do basic stuff that less exotic network technologies take for granted, and you may have to pass on some sophisticated capabilities as well, such as network-attached printers and other peripheral devices.

Doing without Ethernet or token ring does not necessarily bring with it such harrowing consequences, however. In the following two sections, we do your homework for you and cover a couple of potentially useful network technologies that occur on a reasonably large subset of enterprise networks and are supported by Windows 2003.

Find your way to FDDI

One workhorse network technology found on many networks, especially in campus environments, is called the *Fiber Distributed Data Interface* (FDDI). FDDI uses a token-passing access method. FDDI cable uses a real ring topology, but consists of two rings. One ring transmits messages clockwise; the other transmits messages counterclockwise. If either ring fails, the other automatically takes over as a backup. Better still, if both rings get cut in the same place — watch out for guys with backhoes on your campus — the two rings automatically splice together to form a ring that's twice the length of the original ring and still able to function.

FDDI's biggest advantage is reach, now that its 100-Mbps speed is no longer such a big deal. FDDI supports rings as big as 100 kilometers in circumference (that's about 62 miles for non-metric types). FDDI can support as many as 500 active devices on a single ring, which is more than the other network technologies we discuss in detail in this chapter.

On the downside, FDDI requires fiber-optic cables for runs of any length. There's a CDDI (where *C* stands for copper), but it doesn't support cable runs longer than 75 feet, so it's impractical except for workstation connections.

Cost is another negative for FDDI. Fiber-optic cables are more expensive to buy and install than other types of cable, and FDDI NICs cost between $700 and $1800 each. FDDI looks good primarily for the central line of a campus network (the *backbone,* to use the technical term), if Gigabit Ethernet is not an option (or a requirement).

Accelerating to ATM

A rising star in the area of high-speed networking is ATM, an acronym for *asynchronous transfer mode.* In the last few years, several companies have introduced ATM-based *local area network* (LAN) equipment. Long-distance telephone companies already use ATM versions that run at 155 and 622 Mbps, and current ATM specifications support speeds of 1.2 and 2.4 *gigabits per second* (Gbps) as well.

ATM is a fast-switching technology that requires a hub-like switching device and network interfaces for each computer. You can expect to spend at least $2000 per workstation (including allocated switch and fiber-optic cable costs) to bring ATM to your computers. That probably explains why ATM is far more popular as a backbone technology than for networking computers.

Figure 4-3 gives you the skinny on the comparative speeds of the different network technologies (which will help you a little), but the best way to find out what's what is to go online and seek out the collective wisdom that's so readily available. You can check in on any of Microsoft's Usenet Windows 2003-focused newsgroups through `news://msnews.microsoft.com`; use Microsoft's own online service, Microsoft Network (MSN), at `www.msn.com`; or drop in on any of the numerous Windows 2003-focused mailing lists and ask, "Does my (fill in the name of your network technology here) work with Windows Server 2003?" If you don't have access to online information resources, ask around. With so many users worldwide, you shouldn't have to look far to find someone who can help you.

About Ancillary Equipment

Numerous network devices, besides computers, are sometimes required to help you build networks — especially when networks grow beyond the confines of a simple workgroup. Without dwelling too much on features and more sophisticated functions, here's a list of devices available for most major network technologies (or that incorporate interfaces based on such technologies) that you can use to extend or interconnect existing networks:

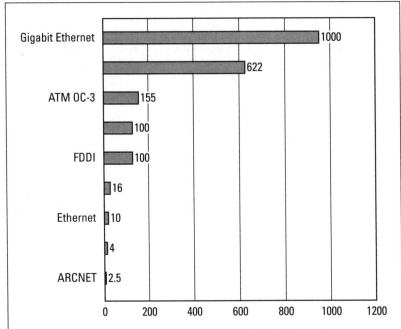

✔ **Repeater:** A *repeater* is a simple networking device that copies incoming signals from one connection and then sends them to one or more other connections (called *ports*). The notion behind the name is that this device "repeats" exactly what — and everything that — it "hears." Repeaters can link only media segments that use the same network technology, but those segments can be different media types. Repeaters operate at the Physical layer of the Open Systems Interconnection (OSI) model. (See Chapter 3 for an explanation of the OSI model.)

Use repeaters when you reach the legal limits for cable lengths that a network technology can support. Repeaters allow you to extend your networks farther than they could otherwise go. Note that network technologies also have rules about the maximum number of repeaters that occur between any sender and any receiver on a network.

✔ **Bridge:** A *bridge* is a network device that examines the addresses of incoming network traffic and copies incoming messages to other network segments only if their destinations can be reached through (or on) those segments. The notion behind the name is that these devices act as semi-intelligent links between networks and check low-level hardware addresses to decide what can pass from one network segment to another. Bridges operate at the Data Link layer (at the MAC sublayer, in fact) of the OSI model. We explain the OSI model in Chapter 3.

Not only can bridges link media segments for the same network technologies, but so-called translation bridges can interconnect network segments that use different network technologies. (Linking FDDI and Ethernet is a common example.) The protocols on both sides of the device must remain the same, however.

Use bridges when your network includes nonroutable protocols, such as NetBEUI or Data Link Control (DLC), and such traffic must be forwarded from one network segment to another. Note that some routers (next item) include bridging functions, and that hybrid devices called brouters (item after next) can perform both bridging and routing functions.

✔ **Router:** A *router* is a sophisticated network device that reads and resolves network addresses from incoming traffic. Routers perform all kinds of interesting functions on such data, including filtering incoming data by address, managing multiple protocols, either blocking or allowing certain types of protocols as well as certain ranges of addresses associated with certain protocols, and more. Routers operate at the Network layer of the OSI model. (See Chapter 3 for details.)

Routers can interconnect dissimilar network technologies and can even reformat data for transmission on an outgoing port whose technology differs from that of the incoming port. The most common example here is when 16-Mbps token ring and Ethernet are linked. Because token ring supports much larger message units than Ethernet, a router may have to break up a single token-ring message into as many as 44 equivalent Ethernet messages.

Routers are what make it possible for two separate networks to function independently yet still exchange information when they must. Routers make phenomena such as the Internet possible and have played a critical role in its growth. Use routers when you seek to operate and control your own network(s) and connectivity to other networks is also required.

✔ **Brouter:** A *brouter* combines the functions of a bridge and a router. That is, it acts like a bridge for nonroutable protocols and like a router for routable protocols. Brouters are most commonly used on networks that have both kinds of protocols in use. They are also used when a local network requires bridging of nonroutable protocols, but access to the Internet or some other public network requires routing of routable protocols. Brouters operate at both the Data Link and Network layers of the OSI model. (We explain this model in Chapter 3.)

✔ **Gateway:** A *gateway* is a device that translates application information from one type of environment for some other type of environment. A typical example is an e-mail gateway that translates between Microsoft Exchange formats and the native Internet e-mail format known as the *Simple Mail Transfer Protocol* (SMTP), and vice versa.

Other gateways can translate between dissimilar protocol suites, such as Systems Network Architecture (SNA) and Transmission Control Protocol/Internet Protocol (TCP/IP). Still other gateways support moving data between other dissimilar applications of the same type, such as database management systems or transaction processing systems. Gateways operate primarily at the upper layers of the OSI model (which we explain in Chapter 3) and are concentrated at the Session, Application, and Presentation layers.

As you climb this set of ancillary network devices (beginning with the lowly repeaters and moving up to gateways), their sophistication and capabilities increase but their speed and overall handling capacity decline. That's because each step up this ladder involves increased processing and data-handling capabilities, which take time and programming smarts and therefore lowers their overall throughput.

You often find items at the lower end of this ladder — such as repeaters and bridges — sold as simple black boxes that are more or less ready to plug in and use. Routers and brouters, on the other hand, are usually special-purpose, high-powered, high-speed computers that accept two or more interface cards (one for each connection that you make to this device).

Windows 2003 includes powerful built-in routing capabilities, such as its *Routing and Remote Access Server,* or RRAS. Also, additional software, such as Internet Security and Administration Server (ISA Server), can be added to Windows Server 2003 to enhance its capabilities. Gateways, on the other hand, usually occupy a general-purpose computer, but they are also normally dedicated to performing only that job.

Mixing and Matching Network Technologies

Networks can easily mix and match topologies within the confines of a single network technology, but interconnecting network technologies requires more sophisticated equipment. Here's a brief rundown of the issues:

✔ **Interconnecting different media in a particular network technology:** Most vendors offer simple devices (that is, repeaters and bridges) to interconnect network segments that use different types of media, such as twisted-pair (10BaseT) and coaxial (10Base2) cable for Ethernet. Windows Server 2003 can handle multiple network interfaces, each with a different media type as well.

- ✔ **Interconnecting different network technologies in a network:** As long as the protocols stay the same, routers or brouters can handle the job, such as interconnecting token-ring and Ethernet segments. Likewise, the built-in routing capabilities of Windows Server 2003 allow it to function as a router to interconnect different network technologies with ease. It just can't do those things as quickly as special-purpose, high-end routers, such as those from Cisco Systems and Nortel Networks.

- ✔ **Interconnecting fundamentally different protocols or applications:** Gateways shine when fundamentally different protocols or applications must exchange data. This exchange involves considerably more effort and intelligence than the lower-level services that bridges and routers provide. However, gateways must also be sensitive to many more nuances and levels of functionality than other devices. This probably explains why they're more prone to problems than other choices.

In its TCP/IP settings, Windows 2003 asks for the address of a gateway. In this particular instance, Windows 2003 is using the term *gateway* in a different sense than what we've been discussing here. When configuring its TCP/IP settings, Windows 2003 considers the term *gateway* to be synonymous with the term *router* and, in fact, points to a device that can forward packets not directed to the local cable segment for delivery to the outside world. Be sure to keep this in mind when you configure TCP/IP for Windows 2003!

Part II
Hooking Up the Hardware

The 5th Wave   By Rich Tennant

"I guess you could say this is the hub of our network."

In this part . . .

*H*aving covered basic networking terminology and concepts in Part I, we try to cover something more tangible in Part II — namely, the bits and pieces of equipment and cabling that are necessary to the proper operation of any network.

You explore the basic principles of network layout and design as you seek to translate networking concepts into a working network. After that, you tackle the ins and outs of network interface cards, or NICs, as they're more commonly known in the networking trade. With cards in place in your computers, the cables that connect them come next.

Along the way, you can figure out how to build a new network or extend an old one and how to take stock of an existing network. You also discover how to bring the parts of the network together to create a harmonious whole rather than a hodgepodge of bits and pieces. Your goal is to understand who the players are and how to make them function well as a gung-ho team.

Chapter 5

Network Design Basics

*W*hether you're constructing a complete network or simply renovating an existing network, the basic approach is the same. You begin by planning what you want to implement, and then you gather the ingredients necessary to realize your plans. Next, you have to execute those plans according to the blueprint that you devised. The execution of any successful plan involves bringing all the pieces together, applying solid organizational principles to your network, and documenting what you add (and what's already in place) to your network.

Begin at the Beginning: Requirements

Whenever you set forth on a network project, begin by analyzing your requirements. If you're building a network from scratch, this phase can take weeks or even months of effort; if you're simply extending or repairing an existing network, planning may take a day of your time or less.

Whatever your project's scope, your plan should contain the following:

> ✔ **A brief statement of your overall objectives, plus a more lengthy statement of requirements that addresses the following: what applications and services users need to access; estimates of user-to-server bandwidth requirements; and estimates of server-to-server bandwidth requirements (where applicable).**

For example: The new XYZ Inc. network will provide 60 users with access to Windows Server 2003 file and print services, plus access to a SQL Server sales and inventory database. Each user will require no more than 1-Mbps bandwidth, and there are no server-to-server bandwidth requirements during business hours because all backups are scheduled for after-hours and weekends.

✓ **A complete list of all the elements that you must purchase or otherwise acquire to meet those objectives.**

For example: Three different department servers (Accounting, Manufacturing, and Sales) will act as routers to link two network segments of 10 users each, for a total of 6 user segments based on 10-Mbps Ethernet. The three servers will be connected with a 100-Mpbs Ethernet backbone using 100BaseT. We will purchase six 16-port 10/100 Ethernet hubs (one per user segment) to leave room for growth, and three two-CPU 500-MHz Intel Zeon Pentium II server machines, each with 512MB RAM and 24GB of disk space. The Accounting server will have an 80GB DLT tape drive attached so that we can back up all three servers across the backbone.

✓ **A description of the role each element will play on the network, the location of each element on the network, the configuration of each element, and the time during the installation process in which you plan to add each element to the network.**

You should use a map or a set of plans to help you place cables, computers, and other components, and a timeline to indicate the order in which you have to install everything.

For example: The Accounting server will handle users from the Accounting and Purchasing departments; the Manufacturing server will handle users from the Manufacturing and Engineering departments; the Sales server will handle users from Administration as well as from the Sales and Marketing departments. All servers, the backbone, and all hubs will be installed when the company is closed between Christmas and New Year. The network should be operational when normal business operations resume. A map of this network appears in Figure 5-1.

✓ **A test plan that describes how you plan to test individual elements, individual cable segments, and the entire network to make sure everything functions properly after you finish the installation.**

For example: The three servers will be installed first and tested individually the weekend before the Christmas break. On December 23 and 24, the 100-Mbps backbone will be installed. On December 28, the backbone will be tested. On December 28 and 29, the hubs will be installed and tested. On December 30, workstations on all existing 10-Mbps cable segments will be connected to the new 10/100 hubs and tested individually. From December 31 to January 2, automated testing software will exercise the entire network. On January 3, a network technician will visit our site with Bob, the site administrator, and any last-minute changes, repairs, and adjustments will be performed. We believe the network will be ready for use on January 4.

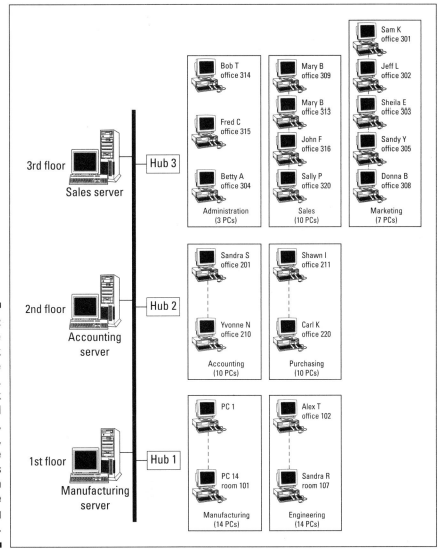

Figure 5-1:
A simple network map of the XYZ Inc. network shows all hubs, servers, and cable segments overlaid on a simple building floor plan.

This plan helps you to decide where you must place key network elements — such as servers, hubs, and other network devices. More importantly, the plan also helps you determine what type of network technology and bandwidth you need to deploy to meet your objectives. Because most businesses work on a budget, building a plan also helps you make sure that you won't try to spend more than you're allowed to spend or incorporate more exotic technologies than you can afford.

Your network implementation plan should also help you evaluate your current network backbone or plan a new one to be able to carry all the traffic that normally comes together on such critical network segments. (We discuss backbones in more detail in Chapter 7.)

Network Design's Barest Basics

The possible implementations from which you can choose when designing a network are innumerable. To help you distinguish between what's improbable, possible, feasible, and recommended when designing your network, here's a set of guidelines that should be helpful:

✔ **Select a network technology:** When adding to or expanding an existing network, this decision is easy — it simply requires choosing something identical to or compatible with whatever you're using. For new networks, you need to analyze what kinds of applications and services users require. For ordinary office work (e-mail, word processing, spreadsheets, basic database access, and so on) 10-Mbps Ethernet works well. For high-traffic or real-time applications — such as Computer Aided Design (CAD), imaging, video conferencing, and voice over network — 100 Mbps to the desktop makes more sense.

✔ **Stay close to the resources:** When designing a network, the smartest thing you can do is minimize the distance between users and the resources they use most. This applies to printers (so users enjoy easy access to output), servers (so cable runs needn't be too long), and other services (such as fax machines, scanners, and copiers) that users need to access to do their jobs.

✔ **Build an online work environment:** When designing a network, you also have to take into account current working patterns and arrangements in your offices. (For example, if the Accounting and Purchasing departments work together all the time, perhaps they should share a server.) This also applies to the type of network you build. For small companies, centralized control and tight security may hamper your workers; in large companies, centralized control and tight security are the norm. You must serve the communities that currently exist in your organization and use the network to help users communicate and be as productive as possible.

✔ **Arrange servers, hubs, and other key resources:** The places where wiring congregates — namely at punchdown blocks, wiring centers, and equipment rooms (or closets) — sometimes dictate where certain equipment must be placed. Be sure to check the distance between those locations and the areas where workers reside. In most cases, offices are designed to support cabling from a centrally located wiring center or equipment room for groups of offices. If that's not the case in your workspace, you may have to add new equipment rooms and wiring centers or move workers to bring them closer to existing facilities. Either of these solutions takes time and costs serious money, so be sure to get your management involved in deciding which options make the most sense and how your organization will handle these changes.

✔ **Build better backbones:** Depending on your network technology choice, you'll probably want to arrange your network to include a special highway for data to travel across when multiple network cables come together. This can happen between servers, as with the XYZ Inc. example that appears at the beginning of this chapter. Such portions of the network are called *backbones.*

A backbone can be something as simple as a so-called *collapsed backbone,* in which a high-speed switch links multiple cable segments and provides a single, high-speed connection between *all* cable segments. A backbone can also be as complex as a *staged backbone,* in which intermediate segments jump from normal 10 Mbps-Ethernet to switched Ethernet or 100-Mbps Ethernet at the server (as in the XYZ Inc. example mentioned at the beginning of this chapter). More complex backbones might even include a segment of Gigabit Ethernet on the innermost segment, where traffic is heaviest.

✔ **Plan for growth:** When planning a network, include at least 30 percent spare, unused capacity in your design. This spare capacity should include network ports (unused ports on hubs), unused network cables in offices and cableways, and bandwidth on individual network segments. That way, you can grow within your current environment for a while without having to redesign your network on a regular basis. If your annual growth rate exceeds 30 percent, design at least one year's planned growth into your network — better yet, one year's planned growth *plus* 30 percent.

✔ **Work within the system:** As you discover when you start deploying a network in any organization, networks have a political as well as a technical side. When you plan a network, you should work within your system in at least two ways: First, make sure that management knows about and approves of what you plan. Second, make sure that you handle the work, contracts, purchases, and so on within the rules and regulations of your organization. If you neglect either of these guidelines, the only thing you'll learn how to network is trouble!

✔ **Check your design:** After you put a network design down on paper, review that design against what you know about the network technologies it uses. Be especially careful to check maximum cable lengths, maximum number of devices per segment, and maximum number of cable segments and devices between any two ends of the network against the rules that apply to the technologies you plan to use. You don't want to build a network that tries to break these rules. If you do, your network may not work, or worse, it may work for a while and then quit working when you add users or devices. If you check your work before you build, you won't try to build something that can't work or that's inherently prone to trouble.

✔ **Ask for a sanity check:** After you've put a network design down on paper and checked your work, you should also solicit input from one or more networking experts. Redesigning a network is always easier while it's still on paper; you don't want to fix a flawed design after you've built a network. The more qualified advice you get before you start building, the better off you'll be in the long run. In fact, this advice is worth paying for because it can save you a world of hurt (or your job, for that matter).

Although this list of network design principles is not exhaustive, it should lead you toward designing a network that works best for your organization. Because these guidelines consider work patterns, politics, and organizational rules as well as technology, the resulting network should serve your organization well for more than just technical reasons.

Deciding Where Networking Devices Must Go

After your plan is in place, you must purchase the necessary equipment, cables, connectors, and so on and start deploying the components that make a network work. When you start situating key network equipment — including servers, hubs, and routers — you need to make some important decisions about where to put them.

For small organizations of 25 people or less, using separate locked facilities to store hubs and servers may not make sense. Small organizations tend to be more informal and are less likely to have the kind of budget that supports a full-time information systems (IS) staff. In these circumstances, you usually want to situate your networking gear along with all your other gear — out in the open with other equipment for easy access to one and all. If you do put the networking gear out in the open, make sure that only users with valid passwords can log onto such equipment. Otherwise, locking it up is highly recommended.

Larger organizations tend to be more concerned about security and control, and, therefore, they usually situate key networking components in locked equipment rooms and in locked wiring closets or wiring centers at various locations around their offices. Because the equipment has to be close to the wiring, it's not uncommon for servers to reside in wiring closets along with punchdown blocks, hubs, and other networking equipment.

Only authorized personnel should be allowed to access these facilities. Likewise, only authorized personnel should be allowed to add users or equipment to the network, usually within a system of regularly scheduled updates or maintenance. In office buildings, for example, this usually means one or two wiring closets or equipment rooms per floor, where only authorized personnel have keys or access codes to get into these rooms.

Choose an approach to situating your servers that makes sense for your organization, and stick with it. If you're going to follow rules for placing equipment, share those rules with employees so that they know what's going on. In fact, formulating a security policy for most networks is a smart move, and you should regularly explain that policy to your employees in detail. (For more information on this subject, see Chapter 18.)

Most small- to medium-sized companies — such as the fictitious XYZ Inc. mentioned at this chapter's outset — put their servers into small, locked rooms at each end of the floors they occupy in an office building. This keeps the distances between users' desktops and the wiring centers acceptably low, and puts their servers alongside the punchdown blocks and hubs they use, which helps manage wiring. This approach also provides controlled access to the equipment and software that makes their networks work in a small number of closely managed locations. Finally, it addresses the need for adequate ventilation and power control that hubs and servers require for proper operation, which many wiring closets do not offer.

Always Check Your Work!

Normally, you install cable and equipment at the same time you build a network. You may run your own cables for your network and perform all equipment installation and configuration yourself, you may contract both the cable and equipment installation out to third parties, or you may choose some point between these two extremes. Whichever way you go, somewhere along the way you'll be ready to put the finished pieces of your network together.

When it comes to installing cabling, we highly recommend that you employ experienced cable installers with good references. The company that owns or operates your office building may even require a licensed cable installer to perform any such work. Here's why this is a good idea:

✔ Adherence to building and fire codes is mandatory, but it can also be tricky; using an experienced professional is a good way to avoid trouble.

✔ Cable placement and routing are sensitive; trained professionals know how to avoid potential trouble spots and always test their work to make sure that the network will behave properly.

✔ High-speed networks are much more finicky and prone to installation difficulties than lower-speed networks. The faster you want your network to go, the better off you'll be if you leave the cabling to an expert.

We strongly advise that you bring up your network in small, manageable pieces. When installing multiple cable segments, bring up individual segments one at a time and test them to make sure each one works before connecting all of them. Likewise, if you're installing a backbone or a server cluster, test individual components separately before trying them out en masse.

When you install equipment, apply the same principles. After you install and configure a machine, check it by itself to make sure it works before attaching it to the network. This is as appropriate for hubs and routers as it is for server and desktop computers.

Our suggestions on piecewise checking and gradually increasing the complexity of your network come from experience. We found out the hard way that throwing everything together at once can cause problems that are too hard to troubleshoot because you have to deal with too many unknowns.

Don't Take Your Eyes off the Ball

After you build a network, you may be tempted to rest for a while to enjoy your success. After all, you've earned it, right? Well, although you should certainly pat yourself on the back, you should also realize that the real work begins as soon as users start using the network (or a new portion of an existing one). If you're responsible for a network, you must not only keep things running for the moment, but also keep them running — and running well — over time.

Whereas the network you build or extend may meet your users' initial needs, any network's capability to meet users' continuing needs diminishes over time. Growth, change in technologies, and new applications and services guarantee that nothing stays the same for long in the workplace — this includes your network as well as the systems and services that the network delivers to your users.

Therefore, you need to conduct regular reviews of how well your network meets users' needs. In small or slow-growing organizations, you may have to review the network only once a year. In large or fast-growing organizations, you should review the network on a quarterly basis.

Your network review should include at least these three elements:

- **Traffic analysis and usage review:** You can conduct this yourself by using the built-in Windows Server 2003 tools and facilities such as System Monitor and third-party software tools. The idea is to take a snapshot of your network during ordinary-load, light-load, and peak-load conditions. If any of these loads encroach on the boundaries of what the current design can reasonably support, start planning to extend and expand your network. See Chapter 19 for more information on using System Monitor.

- **User interviews:** You can interview selected users on a one-on-one basis in your organization or hold meetings with individual workgroups and departments. The idea is to give employees a chance to share their observations, gripes, and wishes regarding the network. This can give you a great opportunity to not only gauge user satisfaction and networking knowledge, but also determine whether you should give employees additional training on how to use the network more effectively.

- **Management review:** You should also meet with members of management regularly to find out what they're planning and what future information processing needs they're considering. You can also gauge management's impressions of and beliefs about the network as you report your findings from the previous two items to them.

If you perform these reviews and keep in touch with upcoming changes and requirements, you can keep your network and your organization better synchronized. Planning for change and growth is essential to modern networks because they've become critical business tools that organizations depend on to do their work. If you take an active approach and plan, you can stay ahead of the curve!

Every Network Map Tells a Story

Earlier in this chapter, we introduce you to most of the basic principles involved in designing and building a network. By now, you have a pretty good idea about how networks work. As you spend more time around networks, however, you may realize that what they *do* isn't nearly as important as what you *know* about what they do.

Whether you wrestle with networks only occasionally or full-time, you may discover that there's nothing like a network map to help you find and keep track of things on your network.

It's not a map; it's the whole enchilada!

Calling the collection of data that describes your network a *map* doesn't do this concept justice. A network map is certainly more than a mere drawing that shows where network components live on your network — but creating such a drawing is a great way to start building a network map. If you look at the following list of things that a network map should contain, you'll see why such a map is more than a mere depiction:

- A list of all computers on your network, with supporting documentation
- A list of all network equipment — such as servers and hubs, plus any repeaters, routers, and so on — with supporting documentation
- A list of all printers and other similar equipment on the network — such as scanners and fax machines — with supporting documentation
- Lines to indicate where cables run and where junctions, taps, and other media-related elements are located

Capturing data for your network map

Because a network map is so important and such a powerful tool, pause right here and start one immediately. Be prepared to spend some time and energy on this project, because most of the data that makes up a network map is scattered all over the place.

Building a detailed network map is a worthwhile investment. It will pay for itself many times over as you come to depend on it. At worst, you discover more about your network than you ever wanted to know (but not more than you'll ever *need* to know). At best, you get to know your network so well that it will seldom throw you a curve ball — and you may even find some things to tweak and tune while building that map.

Start at the foundation

Obtaining a set of your building's architectural drawings or engineering plans can help a great deal. If you can find any drawings or plans, take them to an architect's supply store and make copies that you can mark up and use as a base map. (Most plans are created using an old-fashioned, ammonia-based copying system called *blueline*. You can copy even large-sized plans for less than $25 per plan.)

If a professional cabling outfit installed your network, you should be able to get a copy of the cabling plans, which work even better than architectural drawings or engineering plans because they probably already show where the cable is laid and how much of it you have. This is another good reason why do-it-yourself may not be the best way to cable your network.

If no such plans are available, you can sketch a room-by-room layout on rectangular grid paper (such as an engineering pad) to make it easy to draw to scale. Be sure to mark the location of machines, approximate locations for cable runs, and so on.

Anything on your network should be on the map

Anything that merits attention or costs money is worth recording on your map. You don't need to go into great detail about each and every connector or note the exact length of every cable. (Approximate lengths within a meter or so are useful, however.) Indicate every major cable run, every computer, and every piece of gear attached to the network.

You probably won't have enough room to write all this information on the map itself. Therefore, you should key information to a machine or cable name and record the actual details in a file on your computer. Or, if you prefer to do things your own way, that's fine — just make sure you know how to find what you've recorded. Whatever scheme you adopt, use it religiously. Also, make brief notes about how your scheme works, so that someone else can use your map if you're not available to explain it.

Take stock of your network

The information you gather while producing a network map creates a detailed inventory of what's on your network and where everything is located. Unfortunately, you quickly find out that this is a *lot* of information.

To make keeping an inventory easy for yourself (and for anyone who follows in your footsteps), build a template or form that you can fill out for each item on the network. This approach forces you to collect consistent information — and makes delegating information gathering to others easier. Include all of the following information for each computer on the network:

✔ **The hardware configuration for each machine:** This should include a list of all interfaces and their settings, information about installed RAM and drives, and the make and model of the keyboard, display, and so on. If you can find out who sold you the equipment, write that down, too.

Keeping track of equipment is typically the accounting department's responsibility. Check with them for a copy of your company's capital assets or a depreciable items inventory (if available). This type of documentation normally includes serial numbers and other identification for hardware on the network. If no one in your company has gathered such information, collect it yourself. It's valuable.

✔ **The software configuration for each machine:** This should include listings of configuration files, operating system data (including version number, most recent Service Pack applied, and so on), as well as a list of programs and versions installed on the machine.

✔ **The network configuration for each machine:** This should include the make and model of each network interface card (NIC), plus a list of driver files with names, version numbers, dates, and sizes. You can capture such data to a file easily on Windows systems by choosing Start⇨Programs⇨Accessories⇨System Tools⇨System Information⇨Hardware Resources; use this as the basis for this inventory. (On Windows XP and Windows Server 2003 systems, the menu selection begins with Start⇨All Programs.)

In addition to information on each computer, your inventory should also include the following data:

✔ **A list of other equipment, such as hubs, routers, and printers:** Include the manufacturer, model, make, and serial number for each piece of equipment. If the equipment includes memory modules, disk drives, or plug-in interface cards, get information about them, too. If the equipment uses software or firmware, record the name, version, release date, and any other information you can garner about such items.

✔ **A list of all the cable segments on the network:** Give each segment a unique name or number, and associate your records with whatever type of identifier you use for those segments. Record the type and make of cable, its length, the locations of its ends, and any significant connections or intermediate locations that you may have to visit in the future.

✔ **A list of all the vendors who've worked on your network or its machines:** Include names and phone numbers of contacts at each operation. This can be a valuable resource for technical support and troubleshooting. Over time, add the names and phone numbers of tech support or other individuals at these organizations who prove to be knowledgeable and helpful.

Essentially, the information gathered while creating and maintaining a network map forms a database of everything anyone needs to know about your network. To improve access to and usability of this data, consider storing the text for your network map in an honest-to-gosh database engine. If this is too labor-intensive, a file- or paper-based approach works but takes more effort to maintain over time. Whichever method of recording data for your map you use, be sure to keep your inventory complete and up-to-date.

Applications such as Visio and HP OpenView can help you create network maps. Search your favorite Web browser's computer or networking section using the keywords *network map* to find other applications and companies that can help you with this process.

When the network changes, so does the map!

One thing that you can always be sure of when it comes to networks: They're always changing. Your map is only as good as the information it contains. And the map only remains useful if that information is an accurate reflection of the real network in your organization.

Whenever anything changes on your network, make updating the map and its associated database a priority. Sitting down and checking your map is much less work than walking around and looking at the real objects that the map shows. If the map is current, you can keep on top of things from the comfort of your office. If it's out of date, you'd better start walking!

Chapter 6

Installing Network Interface Cards

*B*uckle up, because it's time to hook the network up to your prospective Windows Server 2003 in preparation for putting that sucker to work!

For most PCs, whether they run Windows Server 2003 or some other operating system, the *network interface* (or interfaces, if a machine has more than one network connection) comes in the form of *network interface cards,* known affectionately as NICs.

For the uninitiated, NIC is pronounced "nick" just like what sometimes happens when you shave. NICs provide the essential link between the network medium and a computer that needs to access the network.

In this chapter, you find out about the basic types, functions, and capabilities of NICs, and how to choose the right type to use in your server. Along the way, you have a chance to pick up lots of tips and tricks about setting up these all-important components correctly the first time and every time.

What Makes a NIC Tick?

A typical NIC is an add-in card that's configured to work inside your PC. Its role is to work both sides of the network connection, like this:

- ✔ The NIC plugs into your computer's bus (or a special adapter slot) so that it can talk to the CPU (or CPUs) and the CPU can talk to it. This essentially defines a NIC's most important role — namely, it permits a computer to access the network medium and vice versa.

- ✔ A NIC's accommodation for a network connection (where the medium plugs in) requires an external connector to connect the network medium to the NIC in some form or fashion. Some NICs include more than one connector, so if you change your network (or your mind), you don't have to throw out the old NIC and put in a new one.

- ✔ Your network technology determines the details of how a NIC accesses the network medium. There are NICs for Ethernet, token ring, Fiber Distributed Data Interface (FDDI), and so on. NICs don't normally support more than one network technology.

Figure 6-1 shows all the important connections on a NIC, including the bus connector (which makes the NIC and the CPU accessible to one another) and the media interface (which makes the NIC and the networking medium accessible to each other). Media connectors vary with the networking technology and physical media in use. By learning to recognize what you have, you can select the NIC or NICs that are right for your network.

Figure 6-1:
The NIC creates a bridge between your computer and the network.

RJ-45 connector

BNC connector

DB-15 AUI connector

Media interfaces

Bus connector

Figure 6-1 shows a so-called *three-way combo card* for Ethernet, with an RJ-45 connector for *twisted pair* (10BaseT), a BNC connector for *ThinWire* (10Base2), and an AUI connector for *ThickWire* (10Base5). If this sounds like sheer gibberish, don't worry — you can explore exactly what all this gobbledygook means in Chapter 7.

Not all NICs take the form of adapter cards that plug into a bus inside your computer. Some laptops, portables, and other machines can't accommodate standard internal interfaces like conventional desktop PCs can. Especially on laptops, you must often install PC card adapters (formerly known as PCMCIA, or Personal Computer Memory Card International Association, adapters) according to your networking whims.

PC cards look a lot like fat credit cards and are about the same size. You slide them into and out of your computer's PC card slot. Laptops sometimes require a NIC PC card for a network connection in the office and a modem for remote access to network resources when the laptop owner is away from the office.

Find the Newest Bus — and Use It Well!

If your computer is a desktop or server PC, you must match its NIC (or NICs) to an internal bus (or buses) with an open slot (or slots). In this section, we introduce information about a variety of buses that you may find in your PCs, and we offer tips about which ones are better than others.

Because Windows Server 2003's primary job is handling network service requests, install the fastest, most capable NIC(s) that works on your PC. Then you can expect the best possible performance for your network clients!

The business end of a NIC plugs into a PC bus and is called an *edge connector*. You can recognize the types of interfaces that your computer includes by looking at a computer's bus slots. Likewise, looking at your NIC can tell you for which type of bus it's made. Figure 6-2 shows the three types of buses covered in this section — ISA, EISA, and PCI — with their respective edge connectors.

NICs come in a variety of flavors that generally correspond to PC bus architectures that have found their way in and out of vogue since the 1980s. Here's a brief list of these architectures:

- **Industry Standard Architecture (ISA):** ISA is pronounced "ice-ah" and describes the bus that most PCs have used since IBM introduced the PC/AT in 1985. ISA is still a common PC bus, but you should use a faster bus type, such as PCI, for better Windows Server 2003 performance.

ISA

EISA

PCI

✔ **Extended ISA (EISA):** EISA is pronounced "eesa." This type of bus is
fairly difficult to find today. It represented an attempt to extend the
capabilities of the ISA bus. EISA is *backward compatible* with ISA, which
means that you can plug an ISA card into an EISA slot and it will work
even though EISA and ISA cards use slightly different edge connectors
(refer to Figure 6-2). Although EISA cards provide better performance
than ISA cards and were designed specifically for servers, EISA never
really caught on.

✔ **Micro Channel Architecture (MCA):** MCA is a 32-bit bus developed by
IBM, with most of the same advantages as EISA: higher speed and a
broader, 32-bit data path. If you have a Micro Channel PC, you must buy

Micro Channel NICs to go with it because MCA is a replacement bus, not necessarily an expansion bus. MCA's main advantage is that you can usually plug in a NIC and it handles its own configuration. This convenience does not come cheap, however — MCA NICs cost more than other NICs. MCA buses are rare today except in high-end IBM machines such as Reduced Instruction Set Computer (RISC) workstations or AS/400s.

✔ **VESA Local Bus (VLB):** VESA stands for *Video Electronics Standards Association.* VLB is a 32-bit bus technology that runs at speeds up to 66 MHz. A VLB slot uses one 32-bit MCA slot plus another standard ISA, EISA, or MCA slot. This lets manufacturers design NICs that use the local bus or the standard bus at the same time. VLB supports a bus management technique known as *bus mastering,* which enables the board to take control of the bus and frees the CPU to handle other tasks, thereby speeding up overall system performance. Because VLB depends on MCA, VLB is pretty much passé. You'll be hard pressed to find a new system with VLB.

✔ **Peripheral Component Interconnect (PCI):** The PCI, developed by Intel, provides a high-speed data path between the CPU and up to ten peripherals while coexisting with ISA or EISA (like other expansion buses). Like VLB, PCI supports bus mastering to free up the CPU. With PCI, you plug ISA or EISA boards into their usual slots, and plug high-speed PCI controllers into PCI slots. PCI supports 32- and 64-bit implementations, with clock speeds up to 100 MHz and data transfer rates up to 132 Mbps. It's no wonder that PCI has more or less won the bus wars and that it has become the high-speed local PC bus of choice. PCI offers the best performance for peripheral adapter cards, and when it comes to server NICs, that's the name of the game!

High-speed buses such as EISA and PCI are great, and emerging standards such as *FireWire* (which is Apple's implementation of IEEE 1394) and *Fibre Channel* are even better because high-speed buses meet a server's need for speed in spades. On the other hand, you may not always have the money or open slots to use a high-speed connection, so do the best you can.

For more information on the Institute of Electrical and Electronic Engineers (IEEE) 1394 standard, search your favorite Web browser using the keywords *IEEE 1394* or search the IEEE Web site at www.ieee.org.

Because Windows 2003 supports FireWire and Fibre Channel, high-speed options for networking are broader than for any other Windows server versions. However, we still feel that PCI is the best game in town when it comes to providing high performance and advanced features because it's widely available and supported in Windows 2003. In addition, many vendors offer PCI-based NICs with advanced features suitable for use on Windows Server 2003.

FireWire and Fibre Channel may become better options in the future, but for now, the competition out there in the marketplace is not yet fierce enough to bring prices down from their stratospheric levels. That's why we recommend obtaining the fastest available PCI NIC for your network technology of choice: You can use PCI to make your Windows Server 2003 as fast at networking as it can be, which is highly desirable on a network server of any kind.

Selecting Speedy Server NICs

Certain built-in NIC features affect network performance significantly. Poor NIC performance hurts doubly on a server because it limits access to its services for everyone. In fact, on networks where all users share a common medium, such as Ethernet, a slow NIC on any computer on a single-cable segment decreases available bandwidth for all network users as long as that slow NIC stays busy.

When selecting a NIC for a Windows Server 2003 computer, start by identifying the network media and the connector that the card must fit. This means recognizing the type of network technology in use and deciding what type of connector the NIC must provide. After covering these basics, you have to consider numerous other NIC options to boost a card's speed and data-handling capabilities. Because server performance is critical, you improve your overall network performance by exploiting speedy NIC options.

Here's a select set of NIC options to look for in any card you want to use in a Windows Server 2003 machine (you may not be able to find a NIC that supports all of these, but try for as many as you can find — and afford):

- **Bus mastering:** Enables a NIC to control a computer's bus so that it can initiate and manage data transfers to and from the computer's RAM. Bus mastering allows the CPU to focus on other tasks. It offers the biggest performance boost of any of the items mentioned here and can increase network performance from 20 to 70 percent. Although bus mastering cards cost more than NICs that don't master the bus, they're essential for server use.

- **Direct Memory Access (DMA):** Enables NICs to transfer data directly from on-board RAM buffers into a computer's main RAM without requiring the CPU's involvement in the data transfer. DMA can boost NIC performance by as much as 20 to 25 percent.

- **On-board coprocessors:** Coprocessors are CPUs built into a NIC itself. They enable NICs to handle data without involving the CPU. Most modern NICs include coprocessors to boost network performance, so it's hard to estimate their overall contribution to performance improvements.

✔ **RAM buffering:** Incorporates additional RAM on a NIC to provide storage space for incoming and outgoing data. Extra buffering boosts network performance because it enables a NIC to process data as fast as possible, without having to pause to empty and refill its buffers.

✔ **Plug-and-Play compatibility:** One of the best features in Windows Server 2003, compared to earlier versions of Windows NT, is its improved support for Microsoft's Plug-and-Play architecture. In English, PnP (as it's usually abbreviated) means that you can insert a device into a PC and it will happily — and correctly — configure itself. Although this confers no performance advantages, we mention it here as an essential feature because it improves *your* performance by speeding installation incredibly. Earlier Windows servers often required contortions to get hardware devices installed and running. A PnP-compatible NIC or other device is a snap to install on Windows 2003!

✔ **Shared adapter memory:** Causes a NIC's buffers to map directly into computer RAM addresses. This fools the computer into thinking that it's writing to its own memory when it's really accessing a NIC's buffers. In other words, the computer treats a NIC's RAM as if it were its own.

✔ **Shared system memory:** Reverses the preceding item, and enables an on-board NIC processor to write to an area in the computer's RAM as if it were NIC buffer space. This enables a NIC to treat computer RAM as its own and may be preferable to shared adapter memory because it allows a NIC to manage memory and frees the CPU for other tasks.

As network traffic loads go up, the value of these options follows apace. When selecting a NIC for your server, purchase the fastest PnP-compatible NIC you can afford. Invest in a 32-bit, bus-mastering, PnP-compatible NIC that uses either shared adapter or shared system memory and includes added buffer space, and you won't be disappointed.

Preparing to Stick in the NIC

Before you start mucking around inside your PC, be prepared. Messing with your system is one of the few things that can flat-out kill a computer — or you! If you take some preventive steps at the outset, you can ward off all kinds of trouble, and probably get back to work more quickly.

NIC installation maneuvers can turn out one of two ways. With luck, your brand-new NIC will be safely ensconced in your PC, doing exactly what it's supposed to do. Otherwise, it will be back in its original packaging, ready to be exchanged for whatever it is that you now know you *really* need!

Here are some tips that should improve your installation experience:

- **Unplug any PC before you open it:** Electricity is your friend, but there's no reason to get personal with it. *Never, never, never* open a PC that's plugged into a wall socket. This mistake can get you or your machine (or both) fried. This is, technically speaking, not a good thing.

- **If you can't go forward, make sure you can go back:** Sometimes, after you install a NIC, you turn on the computer and get a big, fat, resounding nothing! The worst case of all may require sending the computer to a professional for repair. In the not-so-bad (and more common) case, if you take out the new stuff and reverse any software changes you've made, you're back where you started.

  Reverse software changes, you ask? This brings us to a crucial preemptive step that you must always take before fiddling with hardware. *Before* you start messing around, back up any system that will be affected. Backing up confers two vital benefits. First, assuming the worst happens and a DOA computer results, you can install your backup on another similarly configured machine and keep working until the original computer gets back from the shop. Second, if the new installation doesn't work, you can use the backup to restore the machine to the pristine state it presumably enjoyed before you mucked it up.

  Before you go the backup route on a machine you've rendered comatose by adding new hardware, try rebooting using the Last Known Good Configuration (LKGC) option. This rolls back recent Windows 2003 Registry changes and may enable you to keep working. However, like our other worst-case scenario, the key to using the LKGC is to have a good Registry configuration available. Make sure that you reboot your machine when your machine appears to be working properly again; that way, the saved version of the Registry should maintain your computer in its working condition.

- **Figure out what you're dealing with:** A PC can act like a minefield when you add another interface to an already jam-packed machine. If you don't have an inventory of what's installed as well as related configuration data, prepare that list now. This makes quick work of installation and may head off configuration anxiety. Time may be money, but remember: It always takes longer to do it over than it does to do it right the first time.

  One of the many benefits of the built-in PnP support in Windows 2003 is that it goes through what's called an *enumeration phase* each time the system boots. This phase occurs also when a new hardware device is added to the system or an existing device is removed from the system.

In plain English, this means Windows 2003 keeps track of what's what, hardware-wise, on a system and can even keep up with changes that occur while the system is running. This is more meaningful on laptops, where PC cards may come and go while the system is running, than on server machines, where you'd typically have to shut down a system to add or remove an interface card.

In any event, with the help of Windows 2003, you can now look in the Hardware Resources folder of the Computer Management utility to obtain a current list of devices and related settings on any Windows Server 2003 machine. (Use the following menu sequence: Start — All Programs⇨Accessories⇨System Tools⇨System Information⇨Hardware Resources.)

✔ **Give yourself room to maneuver:** Clear some work space for yourself. Find some small paper cups or other small containers to hold screws and connectors. If you're really going to take things apart, label what goes where to help eliminate guesswork during reassembly. Also, make sure that you have the right tools for the job. Go to a computer store and get one of those $30 to $100 general-purpose computer toolkits that comes in a nifty zip-up case.

You build up static as you walk on carpet or move around in dry conditions. Therefore, always carry NICs in antistatic wrappers. Ground yourself before you reach inside a machine or handle computer hardware. To dissipate static buildup, use antistatic wristbands or heel-caps. Also, keep non-conductive materials (such as polyester clothing and Styrofoam cups) away from electronic components. These materials can generate static charges quickly.

✔ **Learn the lay of your LAN:** You will eventually connect any installed NIC to a network. Part of the configuration drill is knowing the names and addresses of other servers, users, and networks around you. Before you start, read the installation requirements provided by the NIC's manufacturer and go over any of the details that you may need to supply during installation. This heads off any need to stop partway through the process to dig up missing information. Invest the ounce of prevention that helps avoid expensive, time-consuming cures!

Beware the Golden Fingers!

Reading motherboard or adapter manuals from offshore manufacturers gives you a unique opportunity to decipher the bizarre forms that written English can sometimes take in the hands of non-native speakers. For example, one Taiwanese company describes an edge connector (the part of the NIC that plugs into a PC's bus slot) as "golden fingers."

Even if those fingers are brass rather than gold, make sure they're firmly seated and fully connected when you plug a NIC into an empty bus slot. That is, make sure that the edge connector is hidden from view and that the network interface on the side of the card is well positioned in the cutout on the back of your PC case. Don't jam the edge connector into the computer's bus socket; rock it carefully if you must. Too much force can peel the golden fingers away; if that happens, you need a replacement card.

You should also screw the NIC's metal tab into place, using the screw that attached the placeholder before it was removed. Figure 6-3 shows a placeholder.

Figure 6-3:
Place-
holders
close off
empty slots
and keep
dust and
dirt out of
your PC.

Screw notch

Two things are worth noting about PC placeholders:

✔ Be careful with the little screw that holds the placeholder in position. If you drop a screw, you can usually get it to show itself more readily by picking up the PC case and rocking it back and forth gently. *Never* use a magnetized screwdriver to pick up a screw you've dropped; otherwise, you computer's data may become screwy.

✔ Be sure to put the placeholder in a toolbox or spare-parts drawer so you can find it again later. If you ever have to remove the NIC (or any other card) from your PC, you'll need the placeholder to close the case again. Some cases use odd-sized placeholders, so life will be simpler if you can find the right placeholder when you need it.

Old-Fashioned NIC Configuration

If you're lucky enough that your Windows Server 2003 PC includes only PnP-compatible adapter cards, you can probably skip this section with a certain amount of glee. Your NIC will probably configure itself without any help from you, but if you encounter hardware configuration problems when you try to add your NIC (or some other device) to a Windows 2003 system, you may want to read this material over anyway.

Configuring a non-PnP NIC for Windows 2003 requires making all the right hardware selections and choosing the appropriate software settings. In short, you have to deal with numerous settings and make sure that the right configuration information is furnished to the NIC's software drivers. Read on for the gory details!

NICcus interruptus

Activity on a network can occur at any time. To receive incoming data and to handle outgoing traffic, a NIC must be able to signal the CPU or the bus (for incoming traffic) and vice versa (for outgoing traffic).

The most common way to handle such activity is to reserve an *interrupt request* (IRQ) for a NIC's use. PCs typically support from 15 to 23 IRQs, numbered 0 through 15 or 23, depending on the number of interrupt controllers installed. Interfaces use IRQs to signal activity. Each NIC must have its own unique IRQ value in a range that the card itself can handle.

These variables help explain why mapping a PC's configuration is a good idea. Your mission, whether you like it or not, is to find an IRQ that no other adapter is using and that your new NIC can accept. If such an IRQ is not available, you must alter another card to free up a usable IRQ. For PCI NICs, this exercise is not so difficult because PCI handles IRQs itself.

Setting IRQs usually means making software settings, setting DIP switches (DIP stands for *dual in-line package*), or moving jumpers. The software stuff is self-documenting, but we explain how to use DIP switches and jumpers next.

Flick all DIP switches the right way

Most *DIP switches,* which are really banks of individual switches, indicate which way is on or off. If you can't tell and the manual doesn't help, call the vendor's tech support department right away (or see whether it has a Web site). The vendor will know the answer, and this will save you unnecessary and potentially dangerous guesses or experiments. Figure 6-4 shows a typical DIP switch. DIP switches are found on ISA NICs; you won't find them on PCI NICs.

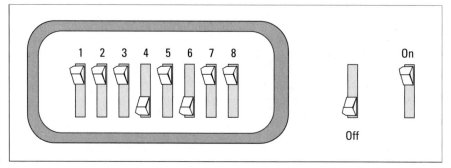

Figure 6-4:
DIP
switches
often
control a
NICs
various
settings.

Jumping blocks for fun and networking!

Jumper blocks consist of two rows of adjacent pins, interconnected with teeny-tiny widgets called *jumpers* (see Figure 6-5). Pins are numbered with designations that start with *J* followed by a number (for example, J6).

Sliding a jumper over both pins turns a jumper on. To turn a numbered pin set off, remove the jumper from both pins and slide it over one of the two pins so that it sticks out from the pin block (as in the middle position in Figure 6-5). Often, when you set IRQs with jumpers, you insert one jumper for an entire block of pins. The pin set you jump selects one IRQ. In that case, make sure that the jumper is firmly seated on both pins.

Figure 6-5:
A typical
jumper
block has
multiple
pins, with
individual
jumpers.

Beware de defaults

Before you worry too much about DIP switches or jumpers, check the NIC manual to find out where the factory set the IRQ by default. If the default setting is available, you can stick with that default and do nothing else. Consider it a blessing when this happens!

Sail into the right I/O port

Each card in a system has a unique input/output (I/O) port address, with certain addresses reserved for particular interfaces, especially video cards. NICs are choosy and normally get an I/O port address assigned from a range of addresses reserved for their use. This address is generally set by software or by a DIP switch on most NICs because of the broad range of settings possible.

I/O ports let a computer read from or write to memory that belongs to an interface. When an interrupt is signaled, it tells the computer to read from or write to an I/O port. The information written to or read from the I/O port's address is copied across the bus between the NIC and the CPU.

Can we be direct? Setting DMA

Some NICs use a technique called *direct memory access* (DMA) to move information between the NIC and the CPU. This speeds copying information from computer memory to the NIC and vice versa. This technique has become less necessary (and less common) as computers and equipment have become faster. You probably won't have to mess with this on a newer NIC, but it's a common setting for older ones.

DMA matches two areas of memory: one on the computer and another on the NIC. Writing to the memory area on the computer automatically copies data to the NIC and vice versa. Setting a DMA address means finding an unoccupied DMA memory block to assign to your NIC. Again, your earlier research on what settings are already occupied helps you avoid conflicts. Choose an unoccupied address block and make the right NIC settings to match it. If you encounter a conflict, you have to figure out some way to resolve it. Remember to check your defaults here, too.

MemBase is not a new boy band

NICs contain their own RAM, called *buffer space,* to provide working room to store information coming on and off the network. This buffer space must be assigned an equivalent region in the PC's memory called the *memory base address,* or MemBase for short.

Just as with IRQs and DMA, this setting must be unique. Watch out for potential address conflicts and steer around them. If software doesn't do the job automatically, you usually use jumpers to set the MemBase on your NIC. Common settings for NICs include C000h, D000h, and D800h.

If a NIC is on the Microsoft Hardware Compatibility List (HCL), a possible configuration is probably listed there (www.microsoft.com/hwdq/hc1/) too, so you won't have to figure everything out without help. Also, be sure to check your NIC's installation software before you install Windows 2003, in case you need to find a driver for the card (as we explain further in the following section).

In the Driver's Seat

After you install NIC hardware, you must deal with device driver software. If your NIC is of recent vintage, the drivers on the disk included with the card may actually be worth using.

In that case — which we rank right up there with your chances of winning the lottery — you can load the disk, run an installation program, supply a few values here and there, and be ready to rock and roll. If you're not that lucky, you'll have to chase down drivers on your own.

Our advice: Always determine the latest and greatest drivers for your NICs before you start installing them. Ask for help in the following order:

1. From the company that sold you the NIC.

2. From the vendor that built the card.

3. On the Internet. Use a search engine to search for the NIC by vendor and model. This usually produces usable information, if not usable software.

Bringing the NIC to the Cable

Okay, the software is installed and the hardware is plugged in. All that's left is hooking the NIC up to the network. For modular technologies, such as twisted-pair Ethernet or token ring, this means inserting the LAN cable's modular connector into a receptacle on the NIC. For other technologies, it means hooking up a T-connector or a transceiver cable from the LAN to your NIC. Whichever option applies, make sure that the connection is tight and that the NIC is seated solidly in its slot. Then you're ready to fire it up!

When Trouble Shoots at You, Be Ready to Shoot Back!

You've navigated the maze of potential address conflicts and have set your NIC to the correct settings. The software is installed, so everything should work, right? Well, it usually does (loud cheers and high fives) but sometimes it doesn't (serious grinding and gnashing of teeth). You learn that things aren't working in one of four ways:

✔ **Your PC doesn't boot:** This one is obvious. When you can't boot, it's time to undo what you just did. First, restore the system to its state before you started messing around (that is, remove any newly installed hardware or connection cables). If that works, you know that the new hardware (the NIC) is the problem. If your system doesn't work when you return to square one, you have bigger problems. Time to visit the repair shop!

✔ **Your PC boots but doesn't load the drivers:** The most common reasons that drivers fail to load are as follows:

  • **Loose connections:** Make sure that the wire is tight and properly seated on the NIC and that it's plugged into something on the other end.

  • **Installation problems:** Make sure that the drivers are in the right directory, and that this directory is referenced in your bootup file or defined in your PATH statement. Because Windows 2003 actively searches your hard drive for drivers (as long as your NIC is on the HCL), this normally isn't a problem for Windows 2003 machines.

  • **Conflict:** You may have missed something and introduced a conflict. Try all your other stuff; it's a dead giveaway if something else has quit working, too. Time to return to square one and recheck all system settings. Something somewhere is squirrelly, so be extra careful!

The good news is that such a problem is most likely to result from a loose connection or a configuration boo-boo. If it's not one of those, it may be time for a visit to the repair shop!

✔ **Your PC boots partway but hangs on a blue screen:** Sometimes, Windows 2003 starts booting but hangs up on a solid-blue screen filled with white text that starts with an error code. This condition is known as the blue screen of death (also known as BSOD) to Windows aficionados.

If a BSOD appears during installation, it's usually related to some type of hardware driver problem. If it happens right after you install a NIC but Windows 2003 has booted before, guess what? The NIC driver you just installed isn't working properly and will have to be replaced with one that works. Make sure you have the latest and greatest driver. If in doubt, send the vendor an e-mail or call tech support. If this problem occurs during an initial installation of Windows 2003, it may not be clear what's causing the problem. If that's the case, consult Chapter 22, which covers installation and configuration tips.

✔ **You try to use the network and it fails to respond:** This is a subtle variant on NIC driver problems and usually results from one or more of the same causes. You're treated to an extra layer of mystery here because a conflict may result from an application rather than a driver. Or the network may be stymied by an incorrect NIC setting, an incorrect network configuration, or an invalid login sequence (that is, the software works okay but you're telling it to do the wrong stuff). You must work your way through a careful process of elimination to find an answer. Good luck, and take lots of breaks. Remember that it's okay to ask for help!

After you've made it over any humps and can communicate with the network, you're ready to get to work. Or, if you're a fledgling network administrator, you'll have the pleasure of helping someone else get to work for the first time. Either way, you'll have pushed the networking wave another machine ahead!

Chapter 7

Hooking Up Your Network

*B*uying computers does not make a network! You have to interconnect computers to enable them to communicate. You can set up communications among computers in several ways; the one you choose depends on your budget and bandwidth needs. Okay, most of it depends on your budget!

Transmission media is a fancy, generic term for cabling and atmospheric transmission. The media provide the means by which computers talk to each other across a network. In fact, computers can communicate through the air-waves using broadcast transmissions, through the wiring in a building, or through fiber-optic cabling across a campus. Linking long-haul or Internet connections to local networks means that there's almost no limit to what your network can access!

In this chapter, you examine different methods to interconnect networks using cables and other media. You find out which media are appropriate for desktop access and which work best for server-to-server activity. You also discover more about network anatomy as we tackle two ticklish subjects — namely, backbones and wide area network (WAN) links.

Make a Network Medium Happy!

A happy network medium has nothing whatsoever to do with a TV psychic. Rather, finding the right network medium means implementing network cabling that won't cause bottlenecks. Depending on whether you're building a network from the ground up or starting from scratch, you may need to take a different approach to evaluating cabling options for your network:

✔ If you step into a job where a local area network (LAN) is already in place, cabling is probably in place, too. Evaluating the type, capabilities, and usability of an inherited network is almost always a good idea. That way, you can decide whether you can live with what you have, or whether some change will do the network good. You may learn, for example, that old cabling causes so many difficulties that you're better off replacing or upgrading it. (We've popped out ceiling tiles and found badly spliced cables hidden from view.)

✔ If you're planning a brand-new network, one of your concerns is to determine your cabling needs. Decide which network cabling you're going to use *before* ordering equipment for your network because you can often order computers and peripherals with the appropriate network interface cards (NICs) preinstalled and preconfigured. (Of course, NICs are preinstalled and preconfigured on an existing network, which means your choices have already been made for you.) The more work you save yourself, the better!

✔ If a contractor handles your cabling maintenance, don't assume that every old cable gets replaced if it's not completely up to snuff. A contractor may choose to reuse substandard cables to save on material costs. Without proper wiring, your network may be in constant trouble (or it may not work at all).

If you work with a cable contractor, require that contractor to test each network cable and insist that the contractor provide you with those test results. In fact, many companies hire one contractor to install cables and another to test them. By doing so, they ensure that the common tendency to overlook errors or potential sources of problems on a network can be avoided — plus, it never hurts to get a second opinion.

The most common cabling technology for LANs is *baseband cable,* which is cable set up for baseband transmission. For this reason, we concentrate on baseband cable in this book. Check out the sidebar titled "Use the right pipes in your network's plumbing" for a description of baseband transmission and how it differs from broadband transmission.

If you know what to look for, the name of a particular type of cable can tell you all about its transmission properties. Ethernet cable notation (set down by the Institute of Electrical and Electronic Engineers, or IEEE) breaks down as follows:

✔ The speed of the Ethernet in Mbps

✔ The cable's technology — broadband or baseband

✔ The cable's rated distance in hundreds of meters or the type of cable — twisted-pair or fiber-optic cable

Use the right pipes in your network's plumbing

Wiring in a network is like plumbing in a house. Just as pipes form the pathways through which water flows to and from your plumbing fixtures, a network's wiring provides the pathways through which computers transmit data using electric signals. The amount of data that computers can move through a wiring system at any one time depends on the characteristics of the wires, or pipes, installed. The larger the pipes, the more data that computers can send simultaneously.

You can think of a network's *bandwidth* as the size of a network's pipes. Bandwidth represents a range of usable frequencies and is measured in hertz (Hz). A higher hertz rating for a network medium means higher available bandwidth. Higher bandwidth translates into bigger pipes to carry data. Just because you have big pipes, however, doesn't mean you always get to fill them completely. Therefore, it makes sense to try to measure the actual amount of data (called *throughput*) flowing through the pipes.

Different types of cabling are rated for different amounts of data flow at different distances. Remember, however, that even if a pipe is big enough to handle all the water you send through it, that pipe can still get clogged. As a result, although a given amount of data can

theoretically flow through a cable, in the real world you may see less data flow than the maximum bandwidth indicates. Plumbers will tell you that mineral deposits and other obstructions can often restrict the water flow in pipes. In keeping with our metaphor, we can say that noise, cross-talk, electromagnetic interference (EMI), and other network maladies can often degrade the actual performance of your cable. *Throughput*, commonly measured in bits per second (bps), describes the actual amount of data that's flowing through a cable at any one time.

If you take one pipe and divide it into little pipes, you've just reinvented the concept of *broadband transmission* (in which multiple transmissions at different frequencies use the same networking medium simultaneously). If the pipe is kept whole instead of subdivided, you end up with the concept of *baseband transmission* (in which the entire bandwidth is used to carry only one set of frequencies and one transmission at a time).

Whew! Got all that? Maybe it's time to call Roto-Rooter!

For example, 10Base5 is an Ethernet designation that stands for [10 Mbps] [baseband] [5 x 100 meters = 500 meters]. From the name alone, you can tell that the baseband cable is rated to handle up to 10 Mbps on a segment up to 500 meters (1,640 feet) long.

Any time you see a *T* or an *F* in such a name, replace that letter with either *twisted-pair* or *fiber-optic,* respectively. For example, *10BaseT* means that this particular baseband Ethernet cable is rated at up to 10 Mbps using twisted-pair cables. Likewise, *10BaseF* means the same thing, except that it uses fiber-optic media instead of twisted-pair.

Cabling is easy, but comes in many varieties

Wiring and cables come in all sizes and shapes. Each type of cable has associated distance limitations. Each type also has different price tags, transmission characteristics, and so forth. The more common types of cable you find on modern networks are twisted-pair, coaxial, and fiber-optic.

Twisted-pair cable: Call it "teepee" for short!

Twisted-pair wiring comes in two flavors: unshielded twisted-pair (UTP) and shielded twisted-pair (STP). To explain shielded versus unshielded wiring in the simplest terms possible, STP incorporates a foil or wire braid around its wires, which are twisted together in pairs; UTP doesn't.

UTP

You've probably been exposed to UTP cable if you have any type of phone system in your organization. You may have even seen such cabling inside the walls of your home (if you watched the contractors build it).

A UTP cable consists of pairs of copper wires where a color-coded plastic jacket encases each wire. Individual pairs are twisted together, and the entire cable is wrapped in an outer jacket. Figure 7-1 depicts a cross section of a typical UTP cable. The number of twists in a cable is important because the twists improve transmission characteristics for the wires involved and improve resistance to interference. This puts a whole new twist on twisted-pair!

Figure 7-1: Let's twist again, like we did last summer.

Outer casing

Twisted-pair

Notice that the *U* in UTP means *unshielded.* That notation is included because another type of twisted-pair cable is *shielded* — STP (shielded twisted-pair). The difference is that STP includes an extra layer of shielding around the twisted wires. Both types of cable are used in modern networks, but UTP is more common because STP is more expensive. You find out more about STP later in this section.

Voice-grade UTP (CAT 1 and 2 — the next paragraph has the skinny on CAT ratings) is the kind of cable installed in most homes and in older phone systems. *Voice-grade UTP cable* is made to carry voice signals and is quite cheap. Some organizations discover that they have extra phone wires already pulled and terminated in offices, so they try this cable for networking. The problem is that voice-grade UTP is not made to carry data. If you have a small LAN with little traffic, this cable may work. If you're building a big network with huge database applications, however, voice-grade UTP is unacceptable. You need to install UTP cable with a higher CAT rating.

What's a CAT rating? *CAT* stands for *category*. The Electronic Industries Association (EIA) places ratings on UTP cable based on how fast such a cable can transmit data. Here's the current roster of CAT ratings that you can find in use in the workplace:

- ✔ **CAT 1 and 2:** Use only for voice and low-speed data

- ✔ **CAT 3:** Use for data speeds up to 16 Mbps

- ✔ **CAT 4:** Use for data speeds up to 20 Mbps

- ✔ **CAT 5:** Use for data speeds up to 100 Mbps

- ✔ **CAT 5 Enhanced:** Use for data speeds up to 200 Mbps

- ✔ **CAT 6:** Use for data speeds up to 600 Mbps

CAT 6 cable is different from its CAT 1 – 5 counterparts. Each pair is individually wrapped in foil shielding, and then all pairs are enclosed in another layer of foil shielding. This extra shielding helps protect the cable from noise and other disturbances. The only question we have left is, "Why is CAT 6 called UTP when the cable is shielded?" Alas, some burning questions must go unanswered!

If you're already using UTP cable on your network and you're not sure how it's rated, call in a cable contractor to test your cables to see what you have.

If you plan to install CAT 5 cable for your network, make sure that the connectors used from one end of the network to the other are also rated CAT 5. If you follow whatever connection your computer makes on the network through the wall and so on, you find numerous components along the way, including wall plates, punchdown blocks, and patch panels. All these need to be rated CAT 5 for the network to function properly at the rated data speeds.

UTP cable is cheaper and more widespread than STP, but it has a few minor foibles that you may not like. Because it's unshielded, UTP is prone to interference from external sources, such as fluorescent lighting. It's not unusual to pop ceiling tiles and find UTP cables strung over light fixtures or near elevators. This placement can lead to network interference; therefore, you should be careful how and where you place your cables.

KEY CONCEPT

10BaseT

10BaseT is a pretty popular version of Ethernet in broad use on today's networks. It's a star topology that uses hubs connected with twisted-pair cable. And as its IEEE name indicates, it's an Ethernet standard rated for a transmission speeds of 10 Mbps. 10BaseT requires at least CAT 3 UTP. You can install CAT 5 for 10BaseT networks to anticipate moving to higher bandwidths such as 100BaseT. The following list tells you what you would need to construct a 10BaseT network starting from the device to the computer room:

- **NICs:** Ethernet NICs with RJ-45 connections

- **Cable:** CAT 3-5 UTP from NIC to transceiver (if it's an external transceiver)

- **Transceiver:** Can be external or on board the NIC

- **Cable:** CAT 3-5 UTP from transceiver (or NIC) to wall

- **Wall plate:** RJ-45 sockets

- **Cabling in wall:** CAT 3-5 UTP

- **Punchdown block:** Incoming UTP wires are brought here and are pressed down into a block of wires using a special tool

- **Cable:** CAT 3-5 UTP from punchdown block to patch panel

- **Cable:** CAT 3-5 UTP patch cable from patch panel to hub

The following are some limitations to note when implementing 10BaseT:

- **Distance:** From network device to hub, cable runs can't exceed 100 meters (328 feet).

- **Nodes:** Can't use more than 1024 nodes on a network without subdividing that network and adding a routing device between the subdivisions.

- **Hubs:** You may not plug more than 12 additional hubs into a main hub to increase the total number of network devices accessible.

Another cost factor for twisted-pair cable is that it requires you to connect workstations through a hub. Although you can buy simple eight-port hubs for under $50, the added cost may still become a consideration if you're planning a large network. On the plus side, so-called *smart hubs* can be advantageous on a network because they can help you manage your cabling — but those smarts show up on the price tags for such equipment. At the very least, less expensive hubs always have blinking lights that can tell you which ports are active and whether data is transmitting.

In most cases, you'll be using UTP for your network cabling — that is, unless you need the extra shielding of STP or fiber-optic cabling. Most off-the-shelf NICs support UTP/STP only (it's getting harder and harder to find the combo cards that support both UTP/STP and coax). Plus, most network connection devices, such as hubs, repeaters, bridges, and routers have only UTP/STP ports.

STP: The shielding improves performance

STP, shielded twisted-pair, adds an extra layer of shielding around its twisted pairs. This shielding is a wire mesh or foil layer that sits between individual pairs and the outer jacket. STP can transmit data at speeds of up to 155 Mbps across spans of up to 100 meters (328 feet), but such implementations are atypical (and quite expensive). Normally, you find token-ring network implementations of 4 – 16 Mbps based on STP (but sometimes on UTP as well).

The most predictable places to find STP implementations are on older token-ring and LocalTalk networks or in older IBM mainframe environments. IBM is token ring's original designer, and it still makes and sells token-ring parts. That's why most "Big Blue" shops use token-ring networks.

STP cable may require electrical grounding, and it's not much fun to install. STP cable is thick and less flexible, which makes it harder to route and handle than UTP. STP's connectors are bothersome and don't always plug in easily either. STP cable is expensive, so unless you require the higher bandwidth that STP can deliver, you may do better to stick with UTP to simplify your network's installation and to keep costs down.

Coaxial (coax) cable

Coaxial cable, also called *coax,* was once the most popular transmission medium for networks. However, with the cost of UTP dropping significantly in the last few years, it's getting hard to find coax cabling, NICs, and other network connection devices. Older networks used coaxial cable exclusively before UTP arrived in the mid-1980s. Initially, only thick coaxial cable (which we like to call "frozen yellow garden hose") was available. Thick coax is quite cumbersome to handle and a real pain in the neck to install. Imagine pulling a frozen garden hose through the ceiling and then having to connect *transceivers* (an abbreviation for transmitter/receiver) to that cable! Maybe a frozen garden hose is easier, after all. . . .

Coaxial cable incorporates two layers of insulation. Beginning in the middle of the cable and spanning outward, the cable has a copper wire surrounded by a foam insulator, which is surrounded by a wire mesh conductor that is then surrounded by an outer jacket of insulation. This jacket, in turn, is surrounded by a plastic casing, called *cladding.* Figure 7-2 shows a cross section of a well-dressed piece of coaxial cable.

The way you determine the cost of the different types of coaxial cable is simple. The larger a cable's diameter, the more it costs. In this case, bigger is not necessarily better, but it is more expensive. Table 7-1 shows some coax cable ratings based on the U.S. military's Radio Grade (RG) cable specifications.

Outer casing

Wire mesh conductor

Inner insulation

Copper wire

Figure 7-2:
An inside
view of coax
cable.

Table 7-1		Coax Cable Classifications	
Classification	*Name*	*Ohms*	*Use*
RG-8 and RG-11	ThickNet	50	Thick Ethernet
RG-58	ThinNet	50	Thin Ethernet
RG-59	Broadband	75	Cable television
RG-62	ARCnet	93	ARCnet

When selecting any version of RG-58 for a network, make sure you select one of the varieties that has a braided-wire core, either RG-58A/U or RG-58C/U (the military equivalent). Although a solid-core variety called RG-58/U is available, it's not covered in the IEEE specification for 10Base2, and may occasionally cause problems if used on a 10Base2 network.

You probably noticed that we slipped in some new terms in Table 7-1, such as ThickNet and ThinNet. These are just different classifications for coaxial Ethernet cable. We describe them in more detail in the following sections because they're frequently implemented in smaller organizations.

Know your network trunks!

A *trunk,* or network segment, consists of an entire cable segment on a network that spans from one repeating device to another, to which individual computers may (or may not) be attached. For 10Base2, a trunk may span only 185 meters (607 feet) and may have no more than 30 devices attached to it. Each device on a 10Base2 trunk must be spaced at least 50 cm (20 inches) from the next device.

You may not use a single unbroken cable segment that's more than 91.5 meters (300 feet) long. That means you must have at least three devices on a segment that spans 185 meters (607 feet). If you ignore these restrictions, your network is likely to experience difficulties. You

can, however, add repeating devices to network trunks and, therefore, extend the length of your network.

Repeating devices take an incoming signal from the network, strip out the noise, amplify the signal, and pass the data onto the next segment of the network. In 10Base2, however, even if you use repeaters, the network's maximum span has physical limitations. The total network span cannot exceed more than 925 meters (3035 feet), and you cannot (theoretically) place more than 1024 devices on a single 10Base2 internetwork across all cable segments (practically, experiments indicate that the real limit is more like 900 devices).

Coax cable cost is directly proportional to its diameter. The thicker the diameter, the more the cable costs; not coincidentally, related equipment costs more, too.

10Base2 (ThinNet)

ThinNet goes by some aliases, such as RG-58, CheaperNet, ThinWire, and 10Base2. Remember that 10Base2 means that this cable is rated at 10 Mbps and can span a distance of 185 meters (okay, so they didn't want to put the notation of 10Base1.85) without any repeating devices. (That's the equivalent of approximately 607 feet for you non-metric types.) It's a thinner type of coax cable (hence the names ThinWire and ThinNet) and is quite popular because it's cheap (hence the name CheaperNet).

ThinNet is flexible and easy to work with because it's quite thin. You find ThinNet coax in smaller organizations that have only one floor or suite of offices because it's cheaper than CAT 5 UTP and STP and doesn't require dedicated connecting devices such as hubs.

Because 10Base2 cable is thicker than UTP, it requires funny-shaped connectors that you've probably seen in Radio Shack but didn't recognize. These connectors are called *British Naval Connectors* (BNCs) or *T-connectors.* The latter name describes this connector's shape. The top part of the T interconnects cable segments, and the bottom of the T attaches the cable to a computer's NIC. In addition, 10Base2 requires terminating resistors at each end of each cable segment, one end of which is often grounded.

So, how do you connect computers and devices to a network using 10Base2? First, picture a straight line with devices attached to it. 10Base2 is a *bus topology* (see Chapter 4), so it extends in a straight line where each device on the network attaches between two cable segments. Devices attach to the network through the bottom of a T-connector that plugs into the NIC on the back of each computer.

Install terminating resistors on the unused sides of the T-connectors at each end of a 10Base2 network.

When installing a 10Base2 network, track the number of devices that an individual cable segment supports and how long any such segment of cable becomes. Table 7-2 lays out key information that you need to review before installing a 10Base2 network or when checking out an existing installation.

Table 7-2	10Base2 Limitations	
	Trunk Segment	**Entire Network**
Max length	185 meters (607 feet)	925 meters (3035 feet)
Max nodes	30	1024
Min node distance	50 cm (20 inches)	50 cm (20 inches)
Max # repeaters	n/a	4
Max # segments	n/a	5

10Base5 (ThickNet)

10Base5, or ThickNet, is a thicker coaxial cable and is, therefore, more expensive than 10Base2. It's also less pliable and subject to more stringent bend radius restrictions. (In English, this means that if you bend it sharply, the cable doesn't work properly.) If you can visualize trying to poke a little hole into a frozen garden hose, you quickly realize that you need some type of special clamping or tapping device to get through the thick outer layers.

To connect network devices to 10Base5 coax, you must have special mechanical devices called *vampire taps* — instead of the T-connectors that 10Base2 uses. The tap clamps onto the coax cable and penetrates through the coax to its inner conductor. You need to use transceivers to convert a digital signal from the computer into an electrical signal on the wire, and vice versa.

10Base5 uses external transceivers and can support transceiver cables up to 15 meters (50 feet) long, which allows the 10Base5 cable to act as a type of backbone and the transceiver cables to extend to desktop machines. This makes routing the frozen yellow garden hose quite a bit easier because it doesn't have to snake its way from computer to computer as do 10Base2 cables.

A typical 10Base5 cable layout is shown in Figure 7-3. This arrangement also explains why 10Base5 cable is used primarily for network backbones or on older networks that haven't changed since their original installations (usually in the 1970s or early 1980s, when this cable represented the only available Ethernet technology).

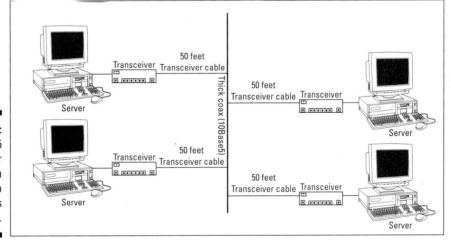

Figure 7-3:
10Base5 transceiver cables can span up to 15 meters (50 feet).

Table 7-3 lists the distance and nodal limitations on 10Base5 networking.

Table 7-3	10Base5 Limitations	
	Trunk Segment	**Entire Network**
Max length	500 meters (1640 feet)	2500 meters (8200 feet)
Max nodes	100	1024
Min node distance	2.5 meters (8 feet)	2.5 meters (8 feet)
Max # repeaters	n/a	4
Max # segments	n/a	5

Although 10Base5 allows five cable segments to be tied together, it's interesting to note that only three of those cables can contain network devices. This limitation is known as the 5-4-3 rule in Ethernet: On any path from one terminator to another on a network, up to five cable segments may be joined by up to four repeating devices, but only three of those cable segments may be populated with more than two devices.

If you have a small network and a restricted budget, coax can be a good choice, but because of expense factors and ease of installation, ThinWire is invariably a better choice for such installations than ThickWire. You may, however, decide to mix these two cable types if the distance limitations of ThinWire don't allow your cables to span sufficient distance.

You can buy pre-fab cables of different lengths to speed up network installation. Otherwise, you have to purchase special crimping tools and build such cables yourself. If you decide to build your own, spend the extra $200 or so to buy a low-cost cable tester to make sure your cables are put together properly. You can find tools such as cable scanners, Time Domain Reflectometers (TDRs), and crimping tools, along with white papers and cabling specs at www.microtest.com — Microtest is the most popular vendor of cabling equipment today.

Fiber-optic cable

Fiber-optic cable is different than twisted-pair and coax cable because it transmits data using light signals instead of electrical impulses. When you look at the layout of the cable, it appears similar to coax, but it has a glass or plastic fiber as its inner conductor instead of a copper wire. Figure 7-4 shows you what the inside of a fiber-optic cable looks like.

Figure 7-4:
An inside view of fiber-optic cable.

Outer jacket

Buffer coating

Cladding

Core

In Figure 7-4, notice that the inner glass core is sometimes called buffer coating, and the entire cable has another strong jacket around it. The outer jacket is designed to be thick enough to protect the inner fiber from being broken when the cable is handled (with care, that is).

Although it has a higher price tag than electrical cables, fiber-optic cable can also handle greater bandwidth, which means that it can transfer more data over longer distances. Fiber-optic cable is largely immune to electromagnetic interference (EMI) and other sources of noise that affect electrically conductive cables. One factor that adds to the expense of fiber-optic cable is the care required during installation. A knowledgeable technician must carefully polish each glass fiber with specialized tools and then add special connectors to the cable.

You often find fiber-optic cable installed between buildings in campus environments or between floors in a building. You rarely see fiber pulled to the desktop because of the expense involved — you must use fiber-optic NICs, and two cables must be attached to each workstation because one cable transmits outbound signals and the other receives inbound signals. Although the appetite for bandwidth is always increasing, don't expect your desktop to have a high-fiber diet anytime soon!

In some locations, such as hospitals, it's necessary to run fiber-optic cable to some desktops because X-ray and MRI equipment can interfere with electrical cables. Also, the bandwidth requirements for medical imaging equipment can be so extreme that conventional electrical cables can't handle the traffic involved.

For light signals to pass through a fiber-optic cable, a transmitter has to be attached to one end of the cable and a receiver attached to the other end. This is why two cables are needed to permit any one device to send and receive signals. On the transmitting end, an injection laser diode (ILD) or a light-emitting diode (LED) sends light pulses down the cable. These light pulses reflect within the glass core and bounce against the mirror-like cladding through the length of the cable until they reach a photo diode receiver at the cable's other end. Notice that data flows in only one direction. The receiver converts incoming light pulses into electrical signals and passes the data to the NIC.

Because of the way that light pulses travel through fiber-optic cable, splicing two such cables requires great care so that the cable's signal-carrying capabilities are not reduced. Otherwise, a light pulse may arrive at the splice but may not make it through to the other end of the cable. We call this situation a *bad splice,* but your users will call it much worse names!

Fiber-optic cable is the most expensive type, but it offers the highest bandwidth and the most room for future bandwidth growth.

A final note about cabling

If you're going to install cable yourself instead of hiring a cable contractor, here are a few final notes we'd like to share with you:

✔ **Obtain a copy of the blueprints for your building or floor and make sure that all the electrical devices and outlets are clearly marked.**

This map assists you in placing cable away from electrical devices or motors that can interfere with your network. You don't want to install cable near elevator motors, transformers, or other heavy-duty electrical devices (unless you're using fiber-optic cable, and even then, you need to protect it from potential sources of damage or wear and tear).

✔ **Obtain all relevant local, state, and federal building code regulations and make sure that your plans conform to such ordinances.**

You need to evaluate these requirements before purchasing any cable because some codes require you to purchase plenum-rated, fire-retardant cable. Other codes require you to use plenum-rated cable only when you run cable through locations that are likely to catch fire rapidly. In any case, it behooves you to know the rules before you purchase and install a network.

Plenums are the air-handling spaces between the ceiling of one floor and the bottom of the floor above where cable is often strung. Fires spread more rapidly in these areas because air carries fire rapidly; therefore, plenum-rated cable is mandated for use in such spaces to keep fire and smoke from spreading through a building.

✔ **Determine which parts of the network you can build and maintain on your own and which parts you need to subcontract.**

For example, if you have the time and inclination to build cables and also have the time to troubleshoot the network when those cables don't work, so be it. We recommend that you buy as much prefabricated cable as possible and make cables only when you absolutely must. Why? Because companies that make cables do it all the time, and they're good at it. If you make cables for your network only occasionally, you may introduce problems.

✔ **Try to hire a contractor to install cable for your LAN.**

The wiring is your network's infrastructure. If the wiring is not installed properly, it can cause endless network snafus. Wiring contractors should provide you with bids, install the cabling, label all cables, test and certify all cables, and provide you with final documentation. You're responsible to keep them on track. Don't assume that a contractor will follow local ordinances unless you make him or her do it. Put all expectations in writing and keep tabs on the work.

Raising the Bandwidth Ceiling

As organizations have come to depend on LANs and WANs, they've put more applications and information on their networks. Speedy retrieval of such information becomes critical to such organizations. This retrieval is where the need for additional bandwidth most often manifests itself.

Conventional text-only documents don't normally put much strain on a network. But today, data often takes the form of audio, video, graphics, and other types of multimedia. Such files or data streams are much larger than plain-text files and often impose delivery deadlines on networks. If this is hard to picture, think how frustrating it is when the audio track and the video track get out of synch on your TV, and then multiply this frustration by several orders of magnitude. Then, think about what delivering time sensitive audio, video, or multimedia data across a network really requires.

Such complex forms of data can easily consume the full bandwidth of an ordinary 10-Mbps network while handling only one or two users' needs. That's why an increasing appetite for higher-bandwidth networks is emerging in the workplace. Such added bandwidth is increasingly necessary to handle the more complex types of data traversing the network and to prepare the infrastructure to deal with emerging applications, such as network teleconferencing, network telephony, collaborative development, and all kinds of other gee-whiz technologies now under construction.

This is why we feel compelled to tell you about some of the cabling alternatives available for today's networks that might be able to handle tomorrow's bandwidth needs. Please read the sidebars in this chapter for the full picture if you really want to understand what's out there!

100-Mbps Ethernet

Two flavors of 100-Mbps Ethernet are available today, each with its own particular access method: CSMA/CD (this means Carrier Sense Multiple Access with Collision Detection; we discuss it in detail in Chapter 4) and demand priority (as described later in this chapter). When proposals for 100 Mbps were solicited, two factions emerged: one that used the same CSMA/CD access method used in conventional Ethernet (now known as Fast Ethernet or 100BaseT), and another that used a demand priority access method (now known as 100BaseVG-AnyLAN).

Both factions put proposals forward to implement their approaches. Curiously, both proposals were ultimately accepted as standards, but each one fell under different IEEE committees. Today, the Fast Ethernet standard falls under the 802.3 standards family, and the 100BaseVG-AnyLAN standard falls under the IEEE 802.12 standards family.

100BaseT is similar to 10BaseT except that it runs 10 times faster. When implementing 100BaseT, you need to use equipment designed for 100BaseT throughout your network, but otherwise, designing and building the network is pretty much the same as for 10BaseT. It's even possible to mix and match 10BaseT and 100BaseT technologies on a single network, but you need to include hubs that have 10-Mbps and 100-Mbps capabilities to bring these two worlds together.

100BaseVG-AnyLAN offers the same bandwidth as 100BaseT but uses four pairs of wires instead of two pairs in each cable. Doubling the number of pairs enables a different access method, called *demand priority,* to control access to the network medium. In addition, 100BaseVG-AnyLAN permits devices on the network to receive and transmit at the same time (that's one reason why the number of pairs in the cable is doubled).

100BaseVG-AnyLAN hubs help manage the demand priority scheme and provide arbitration services when multiple requests for network access occur at more or less the same time. When using the CSMA/CD access method, workstations listen before sending, and they transmit as soon as they recognize that the medium is not in use. This arrangement leads to collisions when two or more stations begin to broadcast at more or less the same time, especially as network utilization increases. When a demand priority device wants to transmit data across the network, it signals the hub, and the hub determines when that device may access the network. This setup eliminates collisions and allows networks to function at higher utilization rates than CSMA/CD can support.

On the downside, networking equipment and cabling for 100BaseVG-AnyLAN is more expensive than that for 100BaseT, even though 100BaseVG-AnyLAN offers better performance. Perhaps that's why 100BaseT has proven more popular in the marketplace than 100BaseVG-AnyLAN has.

Gigabit Ethernet

You're probably wondering what you can implement on your network when you start running out of bandwidth even with 100-Mbps technology. From there, the next step up is to Gigabit Ethernet. Although Gigabit Ethernet technologies are currently available, they're not yet in broad use. However, because the need for speed will never decrease, we want to give you a taste of this technology so you can salivate over it — even if it's unlikely to show up in your office any time soon.

To begin with, Gigabit Ethernet is not typically used as a networking solution for the desktop. (In fact, no conventional PC or other desktop machine can come close to saturating a Gigabit Ethernet network.) Rather, Gigabit Ethernet is used primarily as a backbone technology, especially in large networks where certain pathways need to carry huge amounts of traffic. Ideally, Gigabit Ethernet helps boost server-to-server communications and permits ultra-fast data transfers between switches on a network backbone.

Gigabit Ethernet uses the CSMA/CD access method and the same frame size and formats as conventional Ethernet. Therefore, you can integrate this technology into existing Ethernet networks easily, and you don't need to buy new protocol analyzers, network management software, and so forth.

To jump on the Gigabit Ethernet bandwagon, the devices you need to add to your network include

✔ Suitable NICs and connectors for your servers

✔ Proper cables (fiber-optic, in most cases, though twisted-pair options are under development)

✔ Upgrades to the routers and switches that handle Gigabit Ethernet traffic

In some cases, this emerging standard may require you to replace certain pieces of equipment; but modern routers and switches need only new EPROM chips and upgrades for certain interface cards. Eventually, as the price of the technology drops, you may even consider adding Gigabit Ethernet interfaces into your high-end workstations. This probably won't be necessary for a few more years, however.

The Gigabit Ethernet Alliance offers a terrific white paper on this technology. You can download it at `www.10gea.org/` (look in their Technology section for the 10GEA white paper). It gives a great overview of Gigabit Ethernet and describes what types of applications demand this kind of network speed.

The Backbone's Connected to . . . Everything Else!

As mentioned in this chapter, 10Base5 and Gigabit Ethernet are both well suited for network backbones. If networks have backbones, do they also have hip bones and tailbones? How about it?

In networking, the *backbone* is a particular cable segment that connects other cable segments or that provides a high-speed link to accommodate high-volume network traffic on cable segments where large quantities of traffic aggregate. If you think about this situation for a minute and take a quick look at Figure 7-5, you should begin to understand that saying "a cable segment that connects other cable segments" and "a cable segment where large quantities of traffic aggregate" are two ways of saying the same thing.

Backbone

Manufacturing
(Network C)

Accounting
(Network A)

Shipping and Receiving
(Network D)

Sales
(Network B)

Figure 7-5:
A backbone
ties together
all the
pieces of a
network.

Administration
(Network E)

Simply put, a backbone provides a link to tie together many other cables. As the demand for network bandwidth goes up for individual users, the amount of traffic that backbones must carry increases accordingly. Backbones also often provide links to outside resources, such as the Internet, or access to massive centralized data collections, such as mainframe databases and their ilk.

More Than One Network Is an Internetwork

Another subtlety of networking has to do with the relationship between individual cable segments and the network that encompasses all of them. For historical reasons too tedious to relate, the term *network* is often used to describe only those devices that attach to a single cable segment.

The many flavors of WAN links

WAN links run the gamut of functionality, bandwidth, and associated costs, and include a broad range of technologies. These days, Windows Server 2003 does a good job of supporting all types of WAN links because of its multiprotocol and router support, including:

 Integrated Services Digital Network (ISDN): This relatively low-speed digital link connects through the telephone system, giving it nearly global reach. Windows Server 2003 includes built-in drivers for a variety of ISDN interfaces and supports a broad range of ISDN-based bandwidths. Normal ISDN connections occur through a so-called basic rate interface (BRI) and support one or two 64 Kbps data channels for a maximum bandwidth of 128 Kbps. Monthly costs for a typical ISDN connection vary from a low of $100 a month to as high as $500 a month in some markets. Some ISDN rates accumulate on a per minute basis, so be sure to check with your local telecom company.

 General Digital Subscriber Line (xDSL): This term describes a higher-bandwidth technology that also uses conventional phone lines to handle digital data. (There are many types of DSL lines; therefore, the *x* stands for general.) Windows Server 2003 includes drivers for a range of xDSL devices. Most conventional xDSL devices offer bandwidths that range from 256 Kbps to as high as 1.544 Mbps. xDSL costs are still unclear in many markets, but it looks like xDSL will ultimately replace ISDN.

 Cable modems: Cable modems use CATV coaxial cables to send and receive network data. Although cable modems are not available in all markets, most metropolitan areas serviced by national cable TV companies, such as Time Warner or Cox Communications, now offer cable modem connections. Cable modems usually offer high bandwidth downstream (up to 1.544 Mbps for incoming data) but less bandwidth upstream (up to 512 Kbps for outgoing data). Cable modems are way cheap and can cost as little as $40 a month (but the medium is shared, unlike all the other alternatives mentioned here, so more users means less individual bandwidth).

 Satellite links: Several of the satellite television providers have begun to offer high-speed satellite access to the Internet. In most cases, the download speed is only 2 to 10 times faster than the upload speed, but if you can't get an ISP or telecom connection to your network, it's a way to go. Most satellite uplinks range from about $50 a month to nearly $500.

 T1/E1 or T3/E3: These terms name the most common high-end digital services for medium-sized companies and larger. T1/T3 describes two classes of digital service available in North America; E1/E3 describes two similar classes of service available in Europe and elsewhere. Bandwidth for T1 is 1.544 Mbps; for T3 it's 45 Mbps; for E1 it's 2.048 Mbps; and for E3 it's 34.368 Mbps. All these services cost at least $500 a month and use expensive equipment. T3/E3 costs $20,000 a month or more in most markets.

 Asynchronous Transfer Mode (ATM): This describes an extremely high-bandwidth technology. It's the WAN technology of choice for phone and other communications companies, and comes in a variety of implementations that range from 155 Mbps to 2.48 Gbps. Windows Server 2003 includes support for various ATM implementations.

This limited interpretation of the word *network* made it necessary to invent the term *internetwork*. An internetwork is what happens when some devices (such as repeaters, bridges, routers, and gateways) are attached to two or more cable segments to create a network of networks. In internetworks, information from one cable segment can flow through one or more of those devices to move from one cable segment to another. The mother of all internetworks is the worldwide Internet itself, which is a network of more networks than you (or we) want to think about for too long.

When you're dealing with technical talk about networks, be sure that you understand what the word *network* means in the context of whatever discussion is underway. In most cases, it doesn't matter that what may commonly be referred to as a network is really an internetwork, but when it does matter, it matters a lot. So pay attention!

Beyond Local Networks

Just as talk about backbones leads to talk about the Internet, talk about networks of networks leads inevitably to talk about wide area networks, or WANs. In days of yore, only companies with deep pockets could afford WAN links. Today, with high bandwidth connections to Internet Service Providers (ISPs) becoming increasingly common, small- to medium-sized outfits now have to worry about linking their internetworks to other networks using a variety of long-haul digital links.

For most Windows Server 2003-based networks, understanding how to connect to your local ISP is all the WAN linking you'll ever need to do. Most situations require T1 or slower technologies. In such situations, Windows Server 2003 performs creditably as a router or works admirably with an external routing device to help you make the outside connections your network needs.

Part III
Servers, Start Your Engines!

The 5th Wave   By Rich Tennant

"I'm not saying I believe in anything. All I know is since it's been there our server is running 50% faster."

In this part . . .

When the networking basics are covered, you can jump into the details involved in installing and configuring Windows Server 2003. That's precisely what this part of the book is all about. It begins with coverage of the Windows 2003 product family (there's more than just plain Server going on here) and continues with detailed coverage of the installation and configuration of the Windows Server 2003 software itself. Connections to the outside world are covered next as well as how to provide dial-in and dial-out access to your users.

After that, it's on to Active Directory — also known as the nerve center of Windows Server 2003 — for a couple of bracing chapters that discuss how to install, configure, and use this powerful feature of the Windows 2000 and Server 2003 families. From there, it's on to working with printers and print services in the Windows 2003 environment. This part ends with a refreshing discussion of TCP/IP addressing and configuration details that anyone who works with Windows Server 2003 should find interesting, if not downright informative.

In short, Part III takes you through just about everything you need to know to install Windows Server 2003 and make it useful for your users . Although some of its more exotic and outlandish services are not covered in this part, what is included will get your network up and running with minimal muss and fuss.

Along the way, you find out how to build a powerful networking environment around Windows Server 2003, including basic system configuration, network configuration, printing services, and directory services. You also discover how to use Windows Server 2003 to deliver the goods across a network, be it for file or print services or something a bit more exciting.

Chapter 8

Meet Windows 2003

*W*indows Server 2003 is part of Microsoft's new outlook on life, which focuses on establishing an infrastructure that companies can use to bring rich e-commerce Web applications to clients swiftly and efficiently. What this means in non-geek terms is that Microsoft wants to encourage more companies to use their products to create online shopping malls. To sweeten the deal, Microsoft has added several improvements to their Web development and deployment technologies.

However, we think this is more hype than gold. As you explore Windows Server 2003 on your own and through this book, you'll find little difference between Windows 2003 and its Windows 2000 Server predecessor. Yeah, there are some bug fixes, feature improvements, and stronger security defaults. But Windows Server 2003 can participate in Windows 2000 domains; it can even serve as a domain controller without problems. And all the user controls and administrative tools are the same.

So, what do you get with Windows Sever 2003? You get an improved user experience, which is a bit of a hybrid between the user interface and desktop of Windows 2000 and Windows XP. You also get a few new tools, such as Remote Desktops, Remote Assistance, Microsoft .NET Framework Configuration, and Microsoft .NET Framework Wizards. You might recognize the first two of these from Windows XP. The last two items are something new to the Microsoft world. We talk about all these tools in later chapters.

One last item: Like Windows XP, Windows Server 2003 requires that you activate the operating system within 30 days of installation. If you don't, you get cut off — the OS stops letting you in and won't let you do anything. Activation is a new headache for Microsoft product users; we talk about it in Chapter 9.

The Very Basics of Windows 2003

Windows Server 2003 is built on Microsoft's time-tested Windows NT architecture. From Windows NT's humble beginnings in the early 1990s, Microsoft's premier network operating system server product has come quite a long way.

Today, Windows Server 2003 offers a reliable and scalable platform for deploying complex intranet solutions by integrating Internet and local network capabilities. In other words, this product will let you play Doom with people across the office or across the globe.

All the features and benefits you enjoyed with Windows 2000 Server are still in Windows Server 2003. We can't think of anything that you're giving up (at least, anything you'd actually miss). Most of the improvements in Windows Server 2003 are found under the hood, such as changes to how Active Directory works, an expansion of command-line management tools, improvements to how domains are managed, improved security mechanisms, improved Terminal Services, improved Remote Access, and enhanced Internet Information Services.

A can't-miss interface change is the Manage Your Server window, which appears automatically when you log on. In the Manage Your Server window, you can manage server roles and access Administrative Tools, Windows Update, the Help and Support Center, and much more. It's up to you whether you want to use Manage Your Server or start programs and utilities the old-fashioned way (by choosing Start). We chose to bypass the Manager Your Server window by selecting the Don't Display this Page at Logon check box at the bottom of the window.

The entire 2003 platform does offer some interesting promises that just might come true. The most important of these promises is the reduced effort required to develop and deploy complex e-commerce Web sites. Windows Server 2003 (as well as the rest of the .NET OS family) is tuned to provide better Internet and network service support to clients. When used with the .NET editions of Microsoft programming languages and networking services, you can create an online presence that would impress Hugh Hefner.

The Windows 2003 Family

Windows 2003 is not just a single product, it's a family of servers and a whole gaggle of relatives. The Windows 2003 family has the following four core members:

✔ **Windows Server 2003, Web Edition:** This is a new type of server for Microsoft. This server is optimized for hosting Web sites and is the only Windows Server 2003 that installs IIS 6.0 as a default component.

✔ **Windows Server 2003, Standard Edition:** This server is the same level of server as Windows 2000 — just a normal network server capable of establishing and managing a domain. According to Microsoft, "this flexible server is the ideal choice for the everyday needs of businesses of all sizes." And if that doesn't say it all, nothing will.

✔ **Windows Server 2003, Enterprise Edition:** This server is a bit more robust. It demands more computing horsepower, but can return it in spades. Enterprise Edition is designed to support infrastructure servers that require high reliability and superior performance.

✔ **Windows Server 2003, Datacenter Edition:** This is the granddaddy of all servers from Microsoft. It's designed to offer mission-critical fault-tolerance for demanding applications by providing a scalable clustering architecture that offers high availability. In other words, this is one super-powerful beast that you wouldn't want to meet in a smack-down fight.

You might be thinking, "Wow, what a group of systems! You can't possibly get any better than that!" Well, that's what Microsoft was aiming for. To expand and proliferate the new 2003 platform, Microsoft has repositioned many of their top products as 2003 Enterprise Servers, including the following:

✔ Windows 2000 Server family (yeah, they repositioned their old product in the new hype)

✔ Application Center 2000

✔ BizTalk Server 2000

✔ Commerce Server 2000

✔ Content Management Server 2000

✔ Exchange Server 2000

✔ Host Integration Server 2000

✔ Internet Security and Acceleration Server 2000

✔ Mobile Information 2001 Server

✔ SharePoint Portal Server 2000

✔ SQL Server 2000

If you want to get a head full of info about Windows 2003, check out `www.microsoft.com/net`. Everything you'd ever want to know about the new 2003 platform is there just waiting for you.

Why Use Windows Server 2003?

Any time a vendor introduces a new version, such as Windows 2003, of a popular product, it has to create inducements for users of the previous version to upgrade. Likewise, the company has to attract new buyers to the new version to keep ramping up sales.

Where Windows Server 2003 is concerned, those inducements can be powerful. Windows Server 2003 systems can function alongside Windows 2000 Server systems as members of the domain or even as domain controllers. Windows Server 2003 also plays well with older Microsoft servers, such as Windows NT 4.0 Server, but note that Microsoft claims that Windows Server 2003 shines best when it plays by itself (in other words, when it's the only server type on the network).

Lowered TCO

Total cost of ownership (TCO) measures what it costs to acquire, install, configure, manage, and maintain a system during its entire productive life. In a magnificent case of making a virtue out of necessity, Microsoft stresses all the ways that Windows 2003 has been engineered to help lower its TCO. In effect, what's happened is that numerous problems with or deficiencies in Windows NT and Windows 2000 have been remedied in Windows 2003.

Here's what falls under this "remedied" umbrella (much of which is sure to be appreciated by systems administrators and users alike, so we don't mean to suggest that these improvements aren't valuable or significant):

 ✔ **IntelliMirror management technologies:** IntelliMirror is alive and well in Windows 2003. IntelliMirror is not a product in and of itself; rather, it's a term used to describe the overall benefits gleaned from Windows 2000 or Windows 2003 when several of its key features are used in concert. IntelliMirror is possible through the use of Active Directory, Group Policy, roaming profiles, and Remote Installation Services (RIS). IntelliMirror sets up a mechanism to capture updates made to any suitable client machine (which can be on Windows 2003, Windows 2000, or Windows XP) and save those updates to a network server. This technology not only allows the original desktop to be rebuilt or repaired on an as-needed basis, but also allows users to rove from desktop to desktop, taking their applications, data, preferences, and desktop settings with them wherever they go. Because it reduces the need to re-create complex configurations and setups, IntelliMirror should greatly help reduce the cost of ownership for maintaining complex modern systems.

✔ **Support for broad and varied management tools:** Windows 2003 includes an improved and expanded set of built-in remote management tools for networks, desktops, servers, and other key network components. Windows 2003 also works with management agents and software from other vendors, such as Tivoli Systems, Hewlett-Packard, NetIQ, and Microsoft's own Systems Management Server (SMS). Because the Windows 2003 system works with these other vendors, the cost of ownership for maintaining complex modern systems should be significantly reduced. Plus, many new command-line administration tools can be used to create powerful scripts that automate many tasks.

✔ **Easy to learn and easy to use:** By making Windows 2003 much like a Windows 2000 and Windows XP hybrid, Microsoft hopes to leverage the learning curve for those who have worked with previous versions of Windows. Even better, Windows 2003 includes numerous wizards and other automation tools that store frequently used fields (such as username and password) and can supply them on demand when input context indicates that such data might be helpful. The Windows 2003 desktop is also quite friendly, shows Start menu items based on usage patterns, and is easy to reconfigure and customize. By shortening the learning curve and increasing usability, the overall cost of ownership should be reduced at the user level, which is where costs are typically highest.

✔ **Remote computing to boost productivity:** With its inclusion of terminal server technology, plus Web-based remote management and administration tools that can work on any desktop with a suitable Web browser installed, Windows 2003 is easier to set up, configure, and manage than earlier versions of Windows. This should help manage the cost of ownership for networks; especially for those networks in which local expertise may be missing or low, but in which global expertise can be applied remotely to handle situations and solve problems that may be beyond the abilities of branch office workers.

✔ **Network-wide availability and access:** The combination of Active Directory — with its globally available window on network resources, access controls, security, and administration — and the Web-based capabilities of Windows 2003's configuration and management tools makes Windows 2003 networks easier to install and maintain for administrators. In addition, it's easier for end users to navigate and use. By lowering the human costs of networking, Windows 2003 promises to significantly lower the costs of ownership and the costs of the equipment and software that make networks work.

There's even more to the capabilities of Windows 2003 to help control TCO than what we cover in the preceding list. By addressing user concerns stemming from earlier implementations and working to improve ease of installation, configuration, and everyday use of Windows 2003, Microsoft has come up with a truly impressive benefits package. Although such benefits can sometimes seem subtle and elusive, they're quite real when it comes to making the job of a network or systems administrator easier and more straightforward.

Faster and more reliable

Faster and more reliable covers a multitude of Windows 2003 features — all of which contribute to improved system performance, availability, or reliability. Among the many items that belong to this category, the following are the most noteworthy:

- ✔ **Increased levels of system test:** Microsoft has performed more in-house testing — with more hardware configurations — for Windows 2003 than for any previous version. Likewise, it's released many more beta copies (including several to large production network environments) to take advantage of pre-final-release user feedback.

- ✔ **Hardened memory management:** The Virtual Memory Manager (VMM) in Windows 2003 is more robust than in earlier versions and handles illegal memory references from applications, system components, or device drivers better than ever before. Windows 2003 also includes a signing mechanism for device drivers, so administrators can configure systems to run only those device drivers with valid digital signatures.

- ✔ **Fewer reboots and faster restarts:** Windows 2003 needs to be rebooted only after completing about seven system-configuration tasks; Windows NT had to be rebooted after running any of forty-odd system configuration tasks. Also, reduced memory dump requirements, safe mode startup options, a faster CHKDSK utility, and automated system recovery tools make it much easier to restart (or rebuild) Windows 2003 systems.

Exploit the full advantages of Active Directory

It's true that Active Directory can emulate the Windows NT domain model to the point of supporting Windows NT-based backup domain controllers (BDCs) in hybrid Windows Server 2003 and Windows NT Server domains. Don't forget that Windows 2000 Server has the capability to emulate a NT PDC as well. Active Directory can also support old-style, NetBIOS-based Windows networking client software and LAN Manager-style authentication models.

Using these features in a hybrid network, however, means that you can't use native Windows 2003 Kerberos- and certificate-based security to their fullest extent. Using these features means also that the complete structure that a forest of Active Directory trees can support won't be available to older clients. (Forests, trees, domains, sites, and organizational units are defined and discussed in Chapter 11.)

After a network switches all its servers from Windows NT to Windows 2003 and Windows 2000, and clients are upgraded to include Active Directory support, the capabilities of Windows Server 2003 can be much more fully exploited. Administrative controls can be defined for individual machines, groups of machines, single domains, or multiple domains. (In Windows NT, domain administration is more an all-or-nothing proposition.)

In fact, Active Directory-enabled applications can use directory data to find network resources (such as files and printers) without requiring any user direction on a pure Windows 2003 network. Best of all, much more powerful, multileveled security controls can be imposed upon resources at the domain, machine, or individual resource level. In addition, Windows 2003 can enforce more rigorous authentication to make sure that the user ID used to request a resource matches the true identity of the actual requester of that resource.

More networking

Windows 2003 supports improved networking access and reliability in a number of ways. Right off the bat, Windows 2003 supports the use of multiple NICs, where one or more NICs function in a *hot-standby capacity.* This means that failure of the primary interface causes failover to a secondary interface, which helps guarantee the continued availability of important network resources in the event of NIC or media failures. Windows 2003 also shares a common driver model with Windows 2000, XP, and 98, which instantly makes a vast array of high-speed networking technologies and devices available for Windows 2003 to use. This approach also helps assure system administrators that drivers for the latest, fastest, newest networking technologies will be readily available for Windows 2003 when they're released.

Windows 2003 also includes support for high-bandwidth storage area networking technologies, such as Fibre Channel devices. These technologies allow data to be located almost anywhere on a network and still be instantly available to whatever server might be called on to either use that data or provide it to satisfy a client service request.

Windows Server 2003 also includes improved remote access, a better implementation of NAT, and enhanced Terminal Service capabilities.

Improved Internet and network access

Windows Server 2003 includes the latest release of Internet Information Services (IIS), version 6.0. This software takes advantage of the improved performance and reliability of Windows 2003 to provide more uptime for Web-based services. In addition, improved support for Active Server Pages (ASP) technology makes it easy for Windows 2003 to support powerful, Web-based applications. IIS 6.0 has many improvements, including improved authentication, ASP management, Common Gateway Interface (CGI) controls, fault tolerance, command-line administration, resource handling, security, and load balancing.

Windows 2003 also includes an improved set of application services, including interfaces that already support advanced server functions, such as clustering, load balancing, and transaction processing. In plain English, Windows 2003 makes it easier than ever before to create powerful, reliable applications that share data and code across the network. In fact, all Windows 2003 applications services are Internet-ready, which means you can deploy them with equal success on an in-house LAN, across an intranet or extranet, or across the Internet itself.

Chapter 9

Ready, Set, Install!

*I*nstalling Windows Server 2003 is relatively easy, but it can take more than an hour from start to logon. You can, however, reduce many of the delays with just a little planning. And by following our suggestions in this chapter, we hope that you can avoid some common installation problems, many of which relate to a lack of correct equipment. We also provide a troubleshooting section to smooth out any ruffles you encounter along the way.

Installation: Upgrade or New?

Whether you're installing Windows Server 2003 from scratch or upgrading from a previous version, planning can help ensure a smooth installation.

Upgrade, as the term implies, means that you currently have an operating system installed on your computer and you want to install Windows 2003 over the existing operating system while retaining as many settings as possible. Windows 2003 provides upgrade paths from Windows NT 4.0 with SP5 or greater and Windows 2000.

Note that there's also an upgrade path from beta versions of Windows 2003. If you select to perform an upgrade installation of Windows Server 2003 from a beta, we strongly recommend that you begin by backing up all the data on every machine that you plan to upgrade. (We cover backups in Chapter 17.) Although you can upgrade to Windows 2003 without losing current data, hardware and software sometimes have minds of their own and can mess things up. A smidgen of prevention can save you some real headaches!

Installing means you're adding Windows 2003 to a computer that may or may not have an existing operating system. On systems with existing operating systems, you can select to replace the current one or create a multiboot system. A multiboot system is a computer hosting two or more operating systems. You're given a choice on bootup as to which operating system will be loaded. In some multiboot configurations, data from one operating system will not be accessible from other operating systems (for example, NTFS partitions from Windows Server 2003 can't be accessed from Windows 95 or Windows 98).

If you're installing Windows Server 2003 for the first time, you need to make some decisions about how you're going to set up the server before you install the software. You can install Windows Server 2003 in the following three basic ways:

- ✔ **CD-ROM:** This type of installation requires that you have a computer with a local CD-ROM drive installed. CD-ROM installations don't require a network interface card (NIC), but if you plan on connecting the system to a network, it's best to have the NIC in place during installation. We focus on this type of installation in this chapter.

- ✔ **Across the network:** This type of installation requires network access and that the CD-ROM files be available on the network. Network access can be gained either from an existing operating system or a boot floppy.

- ✔ **Automated:** This type of installation requires you to input installation information into a data file that you can then merge into a script file for execution.

You can launch the installation of Windows Server 2003 in several ways:

- ✔ **CD-ROM boot installation:** If your computer allows the CD-ROM drive to participate in the boot sequence, you can boot the Windows 2003 installation program from the CD.

- ✔ **Floppy boot disks:** If you don't have a bootable CD-ROM drive, don't fret; you can launch the installation from floppy disks. However, the setup boot floppy creation tool is no longer included on the CD; you'll have to download it from the Windows 2003 area of the Microsoft Web site. To locate the setup disk creation tool, go to `www.microsoft.com/ windowsserver2003/` and search for *setup disks*.

- **CD-ROM from operating system installation:** If the existing operating system on your computer gives you access to the CD-ROM drive, you can launch the Windows 2003 setup without the boot floppies. (See the "Step-by-Step: Installing Windows 2003" section later in this chapter for details.)

- **Across the network installation:** You can perform this if the Windows 2003 installation files are available on some other computer on the network. The files can be on a shared CD-ROM drive, or a copy of the contents of the distribution CD can be on a shared network drive. See the "Installing across a Network" section later in this chapter for details.

- **Remote installation:** Microsoft has a remote OS installation procedure named Remote Installation Services (RIS) that enables network administrators to push a Windows 2003 installation out to network systems. (_Pushing an installation_ means that an administrator can deploy Windows 2003 on a network without going to every client to launch the setup.)

Preparing for the battle

We offer the following pre-installation list to help you gather the information and equipment that you need for your setup. The Setup program in Windows 2003 doesn't require all the items that we list in the following sections, but we like to have everything handy when we perform an installation so that we don't need to run around looking for things during the process.

Manuals

The following is a list of books that you may want to have within arm's reach (this book, of course, is the most important):

- **Windows 2003 manuals:** In some cases, the manuals you receive with Windows 2003 are in print form; in others, they're available only in electronic form from the distribution CD or online at the Microsoft Windows Web site at www.microsoft.com/windowsserver2003/.

- **Computer hardware manuals:** These are the manuals for the base machine and all additional components or peripherals on which you plan to install Windows 2003. You especially want to have the manuals for your NIC(s) and video cards.

- **Modem manual (optional):** Grab this manual only if you plan to install one or more modems on the server.

Software

If you don't want to hunt around halfway through the installation, make sure that you have the following software handy:

- ✔ **Windows Server 2003 CD-ROM:** This disc is the CD-ROM that ships with **Windows Server 2003.** You also need the CD key from the sticker on the jewel case.

- ✔ **Windows Server 2003 Service Pack CD-ROM or downloaded file:** Don't expect a service pack for Windows 2003 for at least three months after it's officially released. Until then, you can skip the "Windows 2003 Service Packs" section later in this chapter.

- ✔ **NIC driver:** Windows 2003 Setup should find the NIC in the server, but keep a floppy with the necessary drivers handy in case it doesn't.

- ✔ **Small Computer System Interface (SCSI) drivers:** Windows 2003 Setup should recognize all SCSI devices if they're listed in the Hardware Compatibility List (HCL) at `www.microsoft.com/hwdq/hcl/`. Again, keep the drivers handy just in case.

Hardware

Of course, setting up Windows Server 2003 also requires some hardware, particularly the following:

- ✔ **Computer:** Make sure that the computer complies with the HCL. Remember that you'll need at least a 133-MHz CPU, but we don't think you'll be satisfied with anything slower than 550 MHz. You also want to have a mouse attached to the computer — it just makes life easier!

- ✔ **RAM:** The more memory that you can afford, the better. You must have at least 128MB, but you'll get better results with 256MB or even 512MB.

- ✔ **CD-ROM drive:** If you're installing Windows Server 2003 from a CD-ROM, you need a CD-ROM drive. Later model computers allow this drive to participate in the boot sequence, and this enables you to start your Windows 2003 installation directly from the CD.

- ✔ **Hard disk:** You must have at least 1.5GB of free space, but we think you shouldn't even begin with less than 4GB of available disk storage space.

- ✔ **Modem:** If the server connects to the Internet or provides access to remote users, a modem (either internal or external) is one way to provide this connection. We prefer at least a 56 Kbps modem.

- ✔ **Video:** You need a Video Graphics Array (VGA) or higher resolution video adapter and monitor. We recommend Super Video Graphics Array (SVGA) as a minimum.

- ✔ **Cables:** Depending on the components you install, you may need modem cables, telephone cables, power cords, monitor cables, and more.

Information

You need to make several choices as you go through the setup routine. You're better off if you already have an idea of what you're going to answer before you begin the installation. Consider the items in the following list:

✔ **SERVER1.TXT — SERVER4.TXT files:** The Windows Server 2003 installation CD provides several files in the \docs subdirectory for some last-minute information and installation details gathered too late to include in the printed manuals. Check there for a lot of good information.

✔ **NTFS:** NTFS is the Windows 2003 native file system and is much more secure than the File Allocation Table (FAT) file system. Unless you need backwards compatibility with older Microsoft operating systems on the same machine in a multiboot configuration, there's really no need to use FAT.

✔ **Licensing:** You need to know how you purchased your Windows Server 2003 and client licenses because the Windows 2003 Setup program asks you whether you want per-seat or per-server licensing.

✔ **Computer name:** Each computer needs a unique name that you can identify easily on the network.

✔ **Workgroup/domain name:** If this is the first domain controller installed in a network, you must create a domain name. If this computer joins a current domain where a domain controller already exists, you're better off connecting this computer to a network with access to that domain. If you're installing Windows 2003 in a workgroup, you need the workgroup name. Remember it's an either-or setting, but you can always change your mind later.

✔ **Protocols:** Determine which protocols the computer uses (or will use) to communicate. If you're planning to use the Transmission Control Protocol/Internet Protocol (TCP/IP), see Chapter 14 for more details. Decide whether you must configure TCP/IP manually or automatically through a Dynamic Host Configuration Protocol (DHCP) server. If this server connects to the Internet, make sure that you have a valid IP address.

✔ **Remote connectivity options:** Determine whether the server connects (or will connect) to the Internet or will host a Web server. If so, you can install Internet Information Services (IIS) to provide Web services and Remote Access Services (RAS) for the connectivity. RAS can also enable your users or customers to dial into the network. You can always install RAS and IIS later. In either case, you need a working Internet connection.

✔ **Server roles:** The game has changed in regard to the roles that servers can play when maintaining a domain. The function of your server may affect how you install Windows Server 2003, but it's no longer a life-threatening decision because the server is not configured until after the initial installation is complete. See Chapters 11 and 12 for more details.

Got Enough Horsepower?

Before you install Windows Server 2003 (whether you are just upgrading or performing a new installation), you need to know Microsoft's minimum hardware requirements. If your server doesn't match these requirements at the barest minimum, your installation can halt midway and leave you stuck in the mud.

Microsoft goes easy on its minimum requirements, so we provide some more realistic numbers to match real-world needs. If you follow Microsoft's numbers, you can expect to end up with a doo-dah server that lacks the zip-a-dee part. Table 9-1 shows a comparison between Microsoft's numbers and our real-world numbers.

Table 9-1	Minimum Requirements: Microsoft versus For Dummies	
Item	*Microsoft Says*	*Real World Says*
Processor	133 MHz	550 MHz or better
RAM	128MB	256MB or better
Monitor	VGA	SVGA or better
NIC	None*	One (at least 32 bit)
CD-ROM	None	CD-ROM (12X or better) or DVD
Hard disk	1.5GB+	4GB or better
Floppy disk	3.5"	3.5" high density

Note: A NIC is required for direct network access. If a NIC is not present at the time of installation, you can install it later.

You can squeak by with Microsoft's minimum requirements, but many of your server's capabilities end up terribly slow or intractable. For example, even though Windows Server 2003 supports low-resolution monitors, you should use a higher-resolution monitor (SVGA or better) because of the Windows Server 2003 graphical user interface (GUI). In many cases, more (disk space, RAM, processor power, and so on) is better. Buy as much as your budget allows so you don't need to upgrade too soon.

Take a trip to Microsoft's Web site, particularly the Windows Server 2003 pages at www.microsoft.com/windowsserver2003/. There you can find white papers and Frequently Asked Questions (FAQs) that answer common questions to many issues, such as licensing, minimum requirements, and upgrades. If you don't find enough answers there, head to www.ntfaq.com for a searchable Windows FAQ site — it includes Windows 2003 information.

TIP

Windows 2003 utilities aplenty

No single operating system can do everything that users want. Programmers and others adept at computing typically develop small scripts or programs to perform functions that the basic operating system doesn't include. Utilities for Windows 2003 abound because of its popularity. You can find many of these utilities, especially installation tools, on the Internet at popular Windows 2003 and NT Web sites, such as http://windowsnt.about.com or www. bhs.com.

In some cases, the same tool used on Windows 9x, NT, or 2000 will work on Windows Server 2003. However, this is not always the case. You should test applications on Windows 2003 before you actually use them in situations where data loss is possible.

Microsoft sells a Windows Server 2003 Resource Kit that you can purchase on the Internet or at a bookstore. The package includes utilities for installation, file management, troubleshooting, and planning.

Another important item to check is whether your server appears on Microsoft's HCL. Microsoft's test lab spends its time testing products for compatibility with Windows 2003. Obtaining Microsoft lab certification means that an organization can display Microsoft's logo on its product or products. Similarly, Microsoft places listings for certified products in its HCL.

Selecting a network server from the ones listed in the HCL helps ensure the smoothest installation possible, because you know Microsoft has already tested and certified that product. Certifying products for the HCL is an ongoing task at Microsoft, and the company maintains an updated HCL for all of its current operating system releases on its Web site at www.microsoft. com/hwdq/hcl/.

If you're unsure about the compatibility of an entire system or a specific component, you can either look it up on the HCL or employ the automatic system compatibility checker right off the CD. Just insert the CD into a system with an existing Windows OS (if the Welcome screen does not appear automatically, run setup.exe from the root of the CD). Choose the Check System Compatibility option, and then choose the Check My System Automatically option. The test wizard loads and prompts you whether or not to download updated files. If you have Internet access, this tool can always update itself with the latest and greatest HCL before scanning your system. If any problems or incompatibilities are found, a list of problems will be displayed.

Step-by-Step: Installing Windows 2003

In this section, we walk you through an entire Windows Server 2003 installation — screen by screen. We don't have enough space in this book to present screens for every possible type of installation, so in this section, we provide instructions on one type of installation: from a bootable CD-ROM drive.

Server: Are you ready?

The first major task in getting the software onto a system is to make the server ready for the process. Generally, these are the issues you must resolve before traveling into the Windows Server 2003 installation process:

1. **Ensure that all hardware is HCL compatible.**

   Although It's possible to install Windows 2003 on a system with some components not on the HCL, it's not always easy. In short, if it's not HCL compatible, you don't want to keep it in your system.

2. **Install the NIC in the server.**

   Fortunately, Windows 2003 supports Plug and Play, so most card changes can be made on the fly — unless you have a card so old it still uses dual in-line package (DIP) switches or jumpers.

3. **If you need an internal modem and want to connect the server to external sources such as the Internet, install the modem.**

Windows 2003 Setup: A walkthrough

The following steps detail the Windows 2003 installation process from a bootable CD-ROM drive. Throughout this installation, we accept the default options. Ready, set, here are the steps:

Your system must be configured to boot from the CD. This is accomplished by editing the CMOS. Consult your motherboard documentation on how to enter, edit, and save the CMOS settings.

1. **Insert the Windows Server 2003 CD-ROM into the CD-ROM drive and boot the computer. If prompted to press a key to boot from the CD, do so.**

A gray GUI screen appears that lists the five main installation processes: Collecting information, Dynamic Update, Preparing installation, Installing Windows, and Finalizing installation. In addition, the Windows Setup Wizard starts automatically.

2. **Choose the default installation type, which is New Installation (Advanced), and click Next.**

   The License Agreement screen appears.

   Use caution when working through the GUI wizard. Often, after you click the Next button to continue, the system takes several seconds (sometimes up to a minute) to change the display. Do *not* try to click the Next button again — even if you suspect that you missed the button by accident. If you click the Next button twice, you skip screens and the Back button does not always work; in some places the Back button is grayed. If you wait two to five minutes and the system doesn't change the display, try clicking Next again.

3. **Read the license agreement, click the I Accept this Agreement option, and then click Next.**

   The Your Product Key screen appears.

4. **Enter the 25-character product key and click Next.**

   The Setup Options screen appears, which allows you to choose installation and accessibility options, as well as set the language and region.

   The Product Key is usually found on a sticker on the CD case.

5. **Use the default options for copying and installing files. If you require special accessibility features during installation, such as Magnifier or Narrator, click the Accessibility Options button and make your selections. If the default language/region is incorrect, make a new selection from the drop-down list. Click Next to continue.**

   The Get Updated Setup Files screen appears.

6. **If you have Internet Access, click the Yes, Download the Updated Setup Files option and then click Next. If you don't have Internet access, click the No, Skip this Step and Continue Installing Windows option and then click Next.**

   If you chose Yes, Dynamic Update downloads updated installation files.

   Setup copies the installation files and restarts your computer in text mode. Eventually, the Windows Server 2003 Setup routine prompts you with the following:

```
Welcome to Setup.
This portion of the Setup program prepares Microsoft (R)
        Windows 2003 (TM) to run on your computer.
```

```
* To set up Windows now, press ENTER.
* To repair a Windows installation using Recovery
     Console, press R.
* To quit Setup without installing Windows, press F3.
```

7. Press Enter to continue.

Setup prompts you to select the drive and partition where Windows Server 2003 will be installed.

8. Use the arrow keys to select a partition hosted by a physical hard drive and then do the following:

- If you want to use all the free space on a drive for the Windows 2003 boot partition, press Enter after selecting the location.

- If you want to use only a portion of the free space on a drive for the Windows 2003 boot partition, press C. Next, you're prompted for the size of the partition to create. Type a value between one and the maximum space available on the drive and then press Enter. The newly created partition appears on the list of drives and partitions as "New (Unformatted)." Select this new partition and press Enter.

- If you need to delete existing partitions, select the partition and then press D. You're prompted to confirm partition deletion by pressing L. After you press L, the partition is destroyed.

Usually, you want to select the first drive on the system and the first free partition for the Windows 2003 boot drive. Also, you should create a partition of at least 1.5GB to host Windows 2003 (but we recommend at least 4GB).

9. When Setup asks for the file system with which you want to format the selected partition, select NTFS and then press Enter.

Setup spends a considerable amount of time formatting the drive, especially if the partition is large. After formatting is complete, Setup inspects your hard drives, builds a file list, and then copies lots and lots of files from the CD to the newly formatted drive. This would be a great time to stretch, change your oil, get coffee, or learn how to cross stitch.

10. When you see a message stating that the system will be rebooted, you can press Enter to immediately reboot or wait 15 seconds for the setup process to reboot automatically.

Be sure there are no floppies in the drive. Also, do not press a key to boot to the CD. If your CD boots automatically instead of requiring a keypress to initiate a CD boot, eject the CD before the reboot.

After the reboot, Windows 2003 Setup re-enters the GUI mode. Setup scans your computer for devices and installs drivers appropriately.

11. **When the Regional and Language Options wizard screen appears, accept the defaults and click Next if you're in the United States. If you live elsewhere, make the necessary changes using the Customize or Details button and then click Next.**

12. **When Setup prompts you for your name as well as your organization's name, type the necessary information and then click Next.**

    If you're using the server for personal use, you can leave the organization's name blank.

13. **When Setup asks you to select the type of licensing you're using, click the Per Server option or the Per Device or Per User option, and then click Next.**

    Check your purchase order to verify which license you purchased before marking this selection. Per-device or per-user licensing is typically used on enterprise networks and per-server licensing on small networks. You can change from per-server licensing to per-device or per-user licensing only once, so you must consider this installation option carefully before continuing.

    If you're not sure which option to choose, select Per Server. Make sure that the Number of Concurrent Connections setting is correct. It defaults to 5.

14. **When Setup prompts you for a computer name and the administrative user account password, type them and then click Next.**

    If your organization employs a naming convention, make sure the computer name you select complies with this policy.

    The administrator account password should be a non-blank, complex password of at least six characters, preferably with upper- and lowercase characters and at least one number or nonalphanumeric character. Well, it should be if you don't want someone to figure it out easily.

15. **If Setup prompts you for dialing information, type the correct dialing information and then click Next.**

    Setup prompts you for dialing information if it detected a modem in your computer. In most cases, you need to provide only an area code.

16. **Enter the correct date, time, and time zone information according to your present location, and then click Next.**

    Setup proceeds to load drivers for the detected network components.

17. **Decide whether you want to accept the default settings or customize the settings for your network.**

    The typical settings set TCP/IP to use DHCP, a dynamic configuration service. If your network offers this service and this system is required to employ it, use the default settings.

If you need to specify an IP address, subnet mask, and default gateway, choose the custom settings.

18. **If you're customizing the settings, do the following:**

     a. **Choose the Custom Settings option and then click Next.**

     Setup displays the name of the detected NIC and lists several installed-by-default network services: Client for Microsoft Networks, Network Load Balancing, File and Printer Sharing for Microsoft Networks, and Internet Protocol (TCP/IP).

     b. **Select Internet Protocol (TCP/IP), and then click the Properties button.**

     The Internet Protocol (TCP/IP) Properties dialog box appears.

     c. **Click the Use the Following IP Address option.**

     d. **Type the IP address, subnet mask, and default gateway.**

     e. **Click OK.**

19. **If you're using the default settings, do the following:**

     a. **Choose the Typical Settings option.**

     b. **Click Next.**

     Setup prompts you for the name of the workgroup or domain that this system will join.

20. **When asked whether your computer will be part of a domain, do one of the following:**

     • **If the system will be joining a workgroup, click the No option, type a workgroup name (the default is WORKGROUP), and then click Next.**

     • **If the system will be joining a domain, click the Yes option, type the name, and then click Next. Type the administrator-level user account and password (if needed) and then click OK.**

Setup copies and configures system components and then fine-tunes the Start menu and Registry. While this goes on, you get to wait. Keep waiting, and waiting, and waiting. (As if you have nothing better to do.)

After Setup completes its work, you'll see a message stating that the system will be rebooted. You can press Enter to immediately reboot or wait 15 seconds for the setup process to reboot automatically. The Welcome splash screen appears after reboot.

21. **Press Ctrl+Alt+Del to display the Log On to Windows dialog box.**

22. **Type your password for the Administrator account, and then click OK to log on.**

    After several moments, the Windows Server 2003 desktop appears — a sure sign that you've successfully installed Windows Server 2003! (Just to keep you on your toes, Windows Server 2003 automatically launches the Configure Your Server Wizard in preparation for your next set of tasks. Jump to Chapter 10 to find out more about this wizard.)

 Copying the \i386 subdirectory from your Windows Server 2003 CD-ROM to your newly installed server makes drivers and other resources immediately available to you if you want to add services and resources later. If you don't take this recommended step, you must insert the CD-ROM every time you want to add resources or services to that machine.

Installing from an Existing OS

If your computer already has an operating system with access to the CD-ROM drive, such as DOS, Windows 3.*x*, Windows for Workgroups, Windows 9*x*, Windows NT, Windows 2000, or Windows XP, you can launch the Windows Server 2003 setup from that OS. This is the only way to accomplish an upgrade install. If you launch an install from a bootable CD, a full install is performed automatically.

 Although you can begin the Windows Server 2003 installation from DOS, Windows 3.*x*, Windows for Workgroups, or Windows 9*x*, you can't upgrade to Windows Server 2003 from these operating systems. Regardless of the existing OS, you must meet the minimum hardware requirements to install Windows Server 2003, which would not ordinarily be found on a system running Windows 9*x* or earlier.

To install from the CD-ROM drive, issue one of the following from a command prompt or a Run dialog box:

- If you're using a 16-bit operating system, such as DOS, Windows 3.1, or Windows for Workgroups, you need to use this command:

  ```
  <CD-ROM drive letter>:\i386\winnt
  ```

- If you're using a 32-bit operating system, such as Windows 9*x*, Windows NT, Windows 2000, or Windows XP, and you don't have autorun enabled, you need to use this command:

  ```
  <CD-ROM drive letter>:\i386\winnt32
  ```

If you try to run the wrong setup program, the tool will tell you — just run the other program.

If autorun is enabled, you see the Welcome to Windows Setup wizard screen.

Manually launching Setup from DOS, Windows 3.*x*, or Windows for Workgroups requires you to do the following after the DOS, text-only display appears, asking for confirmation of the location of the distribution files:

1. **Make sure that the screen shows the correct path to the i386 directory on the distribution CD-ROM, and then press Enter.**

   Setup copies files from the CD to your hard drive.

2. **After Setup informs you that all files have been copied, press Enter to reboot and continue.**

   After the machine has rebooted, the setup resumes at Step 8 of the "Windows 2003 Setup: A walkthrough" section earlier in this chapter.

 If you insert the Windows Server 2003 CD into a CD-ROM drive under an operating system with autorun enabled (for example, Windows NT), the Windows Server 2003 splash screen appears and asks whether you want to upgrade to Windows 2003. By clicking Yes, you don't need to manually locate and execute WINNT or WINNT32.

Launching Setup from Windows 9*x*, Windows NT, Windows 2000, or Windows XP requires you to follow these steps:

1. **On the Welcome to Windows Setup Wizard screen, choose New Installation (Advanced). Click Next.**

2. **Read the license agreement. Choose the I Accept This Agreement option and then click Next.**

3. **Enter your product key and then click Next.**

   The Setup Options screen appears.

4. **Click the Advanced Options button.**

5. **Alter the Windows installation folder if the default is not satisfactory.**

6. **To install Windows 2003 to a partition other than the one currently hosting an operating system (highly recommended), be sure the I Want to Choose the Install Drive Letter and Partition during Setup option is selected.**

7. **Click OK.**

8. **Click the Next button to continue.**

Setup copies files from the CD to your hard drive. It then offers a 10-second delay before automatically rebooting your computer.

After the machine has rebooted, the setup resumes at Step 8 of the "Windows 2003 Setup: A walkthrough" section earlier in this chapter.

Installing across a Network

Installing Windows Server 2003 across a network is almost the same as performing the installation from a local CD-ROM. Both methods require access to the distribution files from the CD (duh!), and you have to manually launch the WINNT or WINNT32 setup tools.

Manually launching setup from DOS, Windows 3.*x*, or Windows for Workgroups over a network requires little change to the process described in the preceding section. However, from these operating systems, you need to map a local drive letter to the network share. (This mapped letter tells Setup where the distribution files live.) Setup automatically copies all of the data files it needs before rebooting.

Manually launching setup from Windows 9*x*, Windows NT, Windows 2000, or Windows XP over a network requires an additional check box. In the Advanced Options dialog box (the one that appears when you click the Advanced Options button on the Setup Options screen during the installation process), be sure that the Copy all Installation Files from the Setup CD option is selected.

Remote Installation

Microsoft has created a new installation process called the Remote Installation Service (RIS). RIS enables network administrators to push a Windows 2003 installation out to network systems. Although this process simplifies multiple installations overall, it's not a simple activity. It requires the installation and configuration of several key services, namely Domain Name Service (DNS), DHCP, and Active Directory, in addition to RIS.

The clients that will have the Windows 2003 installation pushed to them must have a Pre-boot Extension Environment (PXE)-compliant NIC or be booted with a special network client boot disk.

If you want to explore the remote OS installation procedure further, we highly recommend that you check out the RIS documentation in the operating system, TechNet, and the Windows Server 2003 Resource Kit.

Post-Installation Stress Disorder

After you finish the basic installation, you've simply defined a basic server. You need to dress it up with things such as users, groups, domain controllers, Active Directory, applications, services, and printers, as we describe in Chapters 11 through 18. But, before you get excited and flip to those chapters, we want to mention two more issues.

Activation

In an effort to curb pirating of software, Microsoft has implemented an installation control feature (first debuted in Windows XP) called Activation. After the initial installation of a product, such as Windows Server 2003, Microsoft grants you a 30-day period within which you must contact Microsoft and activate that product. If you fail to activate the product, on day 31, the product will no longer function. In fact, the only activity you can perform from that point on is to perform the Activation. After a product has been activated, it functions normally.

The activation process requires that a 50-digit code be generated for your computer system. This code is unique to your system and is used to associate your product key with your computer system. If any other computer attempts to activate the same product key on a different computer, Microsoft will think you've pirated their software or at least attempted to install it on another system without purchasing another package. The gotcha to Activation is this computer ID, which is generated by pulling unique IDs from 10 different parts of your computer, including your motherboard, CPU, and hard drives. If you change six of these parts, the system thinks you've changed computers, and your activated status will be terminated. You have to re-contact Microsoft and explain that you've only upgraded your existing system and that you're not just installing the product onto a completely new second system. Can we say major headaches ahead?

Activation can occur over the Internet, in which case it takes only a few seconds. Activation can occur also over a phone line, whereby you must read off the 50-digit computer ID to the customer service representative and he or she will read you a long confirmation key you have to type in.

To activate your system, you can click on the reminder pop-up bubble that appears over your *notification area* (previously known as the *icon tray* or *system tray*), which is right beside the clock. Until you activate, the operating system will remind you every day or every time you log on about activating. You can initiate the activation process also by launching the Activation

Wizard found in the Start menu. It appears in the top-level menu initially; after you activate, it appears only in the All Programs⇨Accessories⇨System Tools section.

Windows 2003 Service Packs

A *service pack* is a release of updates and patches for a software product. Microsoft is famous for releasing service packs to repair its software. This reveals the fact that Microsoft is concerned enough about its user community to maintain a product but not concerned enough to get it right the first time. Be that as it may, Windows 2003 will probably have a service pack released about three months after the release of Windows Server 2003.

Microsoft has integrated two capabilities into Windows 2003 to ease the burden of maintaining an up-to-date version. First, the Windows Update tool can be configured to regularly check for new updates and prompt you to download and install them. Second, service packs can be slipstreamed into the distribution files so that an initial setup will result in the service pack being automagically applied. In other words, service packs can be applied to a distribution point so that new systems automatically get installations with the service pack applied. After service packs are available for Windows 2003, you can read the accompanying documentation to learn exactly how to slip-stream them.

Windows 2003 service packs will not entangle you in the Catch-22 of installing files from the original distribution CD after a service pack is applied. In other words, adding new services will not require the reapplication of service packs, and the application of service packs will not require the reinstallation of services from the distribution CD.

Microsoft advertises the releases of its service packs, thus making it much easier for the typical user to locate, download, and apply these jewels. You'll usually find a link on the product-specific Web page at www.microsoft.com/windowsserver2003/.

Automated System Recovery

Automated System Recovery (ASR) is partially designed to replace the function of the previous ERD repair process (remember that from Windows NT?). ASR can be used to restore a system back to its stored configuration settings in the event of a complete system failure. The only drawback to ASR is that it restores files found on only the system partition. Therefore, if you have applications or user data files on other partitions, ASR will not offer you a safety net for these items.

To use the ASR restore process, you must first create an ASR backup set. Creating an ASR backup set is accomplished from the Welcome tab of the Backup utility (Start⇨All Programs⇨Accessories⇨System Tools⇨Backup). The ASR backup set will consist of a single floppy and one or more backup tapes (depending on the amount of data stored on your system partition). To restore a failed system, you must boot to the original setup program either from a bootable CD or using the setup boot floppies, and then press F2 when prompted to initiate the ASR repair process. You'll then be prompted for the floppy and your backup tapes.

If you want to protect all your data, you have two options. You can use the full backup capabilities (which includes the System State) of the native Backup utility. Or you could spend the money for a quality third-party backup solution that offers restoration from tape after simply booting from a floppy instead of requiring that the entire operating system be reinstalled before a restoration can be performed.

Oops, My Installation Didn't Take

In most cases, as long as your hardware is on the HCL, installation will be a breeze. (Well, how about a long, continuous gust?) For those other cases, here are some common problems and how you can resolve them:

✔ **CD-ROM problems:** The entire Windows 2003 installation ships on a CD-ROM, so if you can't read the CD, you can't install Windows 2003 (unless you're installing over a network, but even then, the distribution files have to come from a CD at some point). CD-ROMs are similar to music records or CDs in that one little scratch or speck of dust on the surface can cause problems. On the other hand, the CD may be okay, but the drive may not be functioning correctly or Windows 2003 may not recognize the drive. We hope that your drive appears on the HCL. To determine whether the drive or the CD isn't functioning, take the CD to another CD-ROM drive and see whether you can read it there. After you determine which element is the culprit, you can replace it and retry your installation.

✔ **Hardware problems:** If Windows 2003 Setup doesn't recognize a server's hardware, it's likely to stop. Make sure that the machine's hardware appears in the HCL and that you configured all devices correctly. If you have more than one SCSI device, for example, make sure that they are chained (connected) correctly.

✔ **Blue screen of death:** Sometimes, Setup simply crashes and gives you a blue screen; other times, it gives you a display of error codes that only a propeller head can understand. By itself, the blue screen simply means that you must reboot. If you get a fancy stop screen, however, you can look at the first few lines to determine the error code and then use it to look up the error message in the error-message manual. Stops typically occur if a driver problem occurs; if you look beyond the first few lines of the error-message screen, it tells you which drivers were loaded at the time the crash occurred. A good idea is to write the first few lines of the stop screen down before attempting to reboot.

✔ **Connectivity problems:** Installing a machine into an existing domain requires that the new system be capable of communicating with a domain controller to create a domain computer account. If communication is not possible for any reason (such as a wrong NIC, a wrong driver, a bad or missing cable, a domain controller offline, or too much network traffic), you won't be able to join the domain. In some cases, you can resolve the problem by quickly replacing a cable or allowing the system to try the connection a second or third time. In other cases, you can delay confronting the problem by joining a workgroup instead. Then you can resolve any problems (such as NIC, driver, and configuration problems) with a functioning system.

✔ **Dependency problems:** Some services in Windows 2003 depend on other services loading correctly. If service A doesn't load, service B doesn't work, and you get error messages if service B is set to automatically start at bootup. For example, if a NIC isn't installed correctly, all services that use that NIC also fail to start. Your first order of business, therefore, is to get the NIC to function correctly. If you get this far in the installation process, you can view the error logs (Start⇨Administrative Tools⇨Event Viewer) to see which service did not start and then work your way from there.

✔ **Script file errors:** The Windows 2003 automated installation program (see the next section) is not forgiving if you mistype a script. If a script stops midway and the Windows 2003 Setup program asks you for manual input, you entered something incorrectly. Check the input file to look for transposed letters or anything else that may be out of place. Scripts expect to feed the computer exactly what you put in the script file. If you don't enter the right information, Setup doesn't receive the information it expects.

✔ **SERVER1.TXT-SERVER4.TXT files:** If you encounter driver problems or other problems missing from the preceding list, obtain and read these files to see whether some late-breaking news that Microsoft couldn't get into the manuals may have affected your installation. The file is in the \docs subdirectory.

About Automated Installation

An unattended installation feature enables you to install Windows 2003 without keyboard interaction. Just start the process and walk away. Unattended installation uses a script file that pipes in information and keyboard strokes from a data file that you compose in advance. If you already know all the answers to the questions that the installation program asks, you can answer these questions and place them in a data file. You can use more than one data file for different types of installations.

Unattended installation is great for organizations that install Windows 2003 over and over on machines with the same hardware configurations. Large enterprise networks that include remote offices can also take advantage of unattended installation, because home office administrators can customize script files and transmit them to remote offices. The caveat here is that you must test the script files for accuracy thoroughly in the central office; otherwise, the folks in the remote office may soon be screaming for help!

Details on creating the automation scripts are contained in the Windows Server 2003 Resource Kit.

Chapter 10

Configuring Connections to the Universe

In This Chapter

▶ Configuring your server

▶ Configuring domain controllers

▶ Understanding server roles

▶ Using remote access

*E*ven after you complete the installation of Windows Server 2003, you're still faced with a number of decisions you have to make before you can safely say, "mission accomplished." What role will the server play in the network? Will it host multiple network interfaces? Will you need remote access? In this chapter, you look into the answers to these questions and see the steps you can take to implement your decisions.

Before you get too excited, we want to warn you that certain topics brought up in this chapter are just flat-out complicated. We try to give a general overview of each topic, but in some cases, these issues are beyond the scope of this book. When this happens, we refer you to other resources and materials where you can find meaningful, reliable, more detailed coverage of the topics.

Meeting the Configure Your Server Wizard

In this section, you go through the steps needed to get your Windows Server 2003 up and running. Starting at square one, you see that the first time you log on to Windows Server 2003 after completing the initial installation, you're confronted with the Configure Your Server Wizard. This wizard appears by default when you first log on. You can always access it again by choosing Start➪All Programs➪Administrative Tools➪Configure Your Server.

This wizard has a new look and functions completely differently than the Configure Your Server wizard in Windows 2000. If you're used to a Windows 2000 environment, brace yourself for a bit of newness.

First, from the Welcome page of the Configure Your Server wizard, click Next to move to the Preliminary Steps page. The Preliminary Steps page informs you that the computer must have the following:

✔ Network connectivity

✔ Internet connectivity

✔ Peripherals (such a printers and external drives) that are properly attached and powered on

✔ The distribution files for Windows Server 2003 (if not the entire CD) available

If you can curtsey to these stipulations, click Next.

You can use the Server Role page in Figure 10-1 to install a wide range of networking services, including the following:

✔ Dynamic Host Configuration Protocol (DHCP) — see Chapter 14

✔ Domain Name Service (DNS) — see Chapter 14

✔ Active Directory — see Chapters 11 and 12

✔ File services — see Chapter 16

✔ Print services — see Chapter 13

✔ Remote Access service — covered later in this chapter

✔ Internet Information Services (IIS) — covered later in this chapter

✔ Windows Internet Naming Service (WINS) — see Chapter 14

As for the more advanced network services, such as Terminal Services, Streaming Media server, SharePoint Team Services, and Real Time Communication server, you'll need to consult other documentation, such as the Windows Server 2003 Resource Kit.

Figure 10-1:
The server
roles that
can be
installed
through the
Configure
Your Server
Wizard.

Planting your first forest

To get your Windows Server 2003 system up and running, the first bit of information you need to feed it is whether it's the first server in your domain. If it
is the first server, the Configure Your Server Wizard helps you install the core
services required to maintain a domain. If it's not the first server on the network, you can set the server up as another domain controller or as just a
member server. You can also elect to make the server a stand-alone server.

If you're setting up the first domain controller in the first domain for your
entire organization, you're setting up more than just a domain; you're also
defining the root of your first tree and the root of your first forest. In Active
Directory domain lingo, a group of computers that shares a single namespace
and DNS structure is called a *domain.* A group of domains linked in parent-
child relationships (also like the roots of a tree) is called a *tree.* A domain tree
is a set of domains connected through a two-way transitive trust, sharing a
common schema, configuration, and global catalog. The domains also form a
contiguous hierarchical namespace with one domain being the domain root.

The first domain installed in a tree is considered the *root domain* of that tree.
It would be considered the forest root domain only if it was also the first
domain in the forest, which is discussed next.

Groups of trees are linked together as a forest. The capability to organize a
network into complex logical namespace structures gives Windows 2003 (and
Windows 2000) its scalability and versatility as an enterprise-capable network operating system.

A *forest* is the collection of one or more domains that share a common schema, configuration, and global catalog. A forest may or may not have a common domain namespace. If the forest has only a single tree, it will have a common domain namespace because it is the only tree. Because a forest can have more than one domain tree (it is not a requirement, but it is allowed), these different domain trees will have their own individual, contiguous namespaces.

All the domains in a domain tree and all the trees in a single forest have the connectivity benefit of the two-way, transitive trust relationship, which is the default trust relationship between Windows 2000 and 2003 domains. A two-way, transitive trust is the combination of a transitive trust and a two-way trust. This complete trust between all domains in an Active Directory domain hierarchy helps form the forest as a single unit through its common schema, configuration, and global catalog.

The first Windows 2000 or 2003 domain installed in the forest is considered to be the *forest root domain*.

The first domain controller you create also defines the domain. If it's the first domain on your network, it's also the root of the first tree and the first tree in the forest. For more detailed information on the logical structure of domains, trees, and forests, please consult the Windows Server 2003 Resource Kit.

For now, we assume that your server is the first server on the network. To set up your server, follow these steps:

1. **On the Configure Your Server Wizard, click Next. Then, on the Preliminary Steps page, click Next.**

    The Configure Your Server Wizard appears automatically the first time you log on to your Windows Server 2003. If it's not already open, launch it from the Start menu by choosing Start⇨All Programs⇨Administrative Tools⇨Configure Your Server.

2. **Select the Domain Controller (Active Directory) option and then click Next.**

    A summary of the changes to be made is displayed.

3. **Click Finish.**

    The Active Directory Installation Wizard is launched.

    During this configuration process, you may be prompted for the Windows Server 2003 distribution CD. If so, place the CD in the local CD-ROM drive or provide a path to a local or network copy of the distribution files.

4. **Click Next.**

    The Domain Controller Type page appears.

5. **Assuming that this is the first domain controller in your new domain, select the Domain Controller for a New Domain option. Click Next.**

   The Create New Domain page appears.

6. **Assuming that this is the first domain in a new forest (which implies that it's also a new tree), select the Domain in a New Forest option. Click Next.**

   The New Domain Name page appears.

7. **Type the name of your new domain.**

   The name must be in fully qualified domain name (FQDN) format, such as mycompany.local or googleplex.com. This is not the name of your server; you defined that when you first installed Windows Server 2003. Instead, this defines the top-level domain name.

   You can use the same name that will be used on the Internet to access your organization (such as googleplex.com), or you can use an internal, network-only domain name that will not be Internet capable (such as mycompany.local or mycompany.ad).

8. **Click Next.**

   The NetBIOS Domain Name page appears, with an automatically generated name for the domain. This name is used by systems and applications that are not Active Directory compliant. In most cases, this name is just the first 15 characters before the first period of your domain name, such as googleplex or mycompany.

9. **If the suggested name is satisfactory (it usually is), click Next. Otherwise, provide a new name and then click Next.**

   The only restrictions on the NetBIOS domain name are that it must be 15 characters or less, use only NetBIOS- and DNS-approved characters (*Aa–Zz,* 1–9, and hyphen), and be unique within the domain in which it resides.

   The Database and Log Folders page appears, requesting the paths for the storage folders for the main directory and log files. Defining paths to hard drives other than the one hosting the system partition improves overall performance, but the default suggested locations is sufficient for most purposes.

10. **Click Next.**

    The Shared System Volume page appears, requesting the path to store the SYSVOL folder. This can be defined on a separate hard drive to improve performance or the default suggestion can be accepted.

11. **Click Next.**

    Unless you already have DNS installed, the DNS Registration Diagnostics page appears. This indicates that no DNS server was located to service the new zone being created for the new domain.

12. **Select the Install and Configure DNS Server on This Computer option and then click Next.**

    The Permissions page appears, asking whether to use permissions that are compatible with pre-Windows 2000 systems. In most cases, it's a good idea to use permissions compatible with pre-Windows 2000 Servers only when you're sure you'll be using legacy systems, such as Windows 9x or Windows NT Workstation, because this affects the security of the domain and possibly the forest and is required only when using these legacy systems in the domain.

    When you elect to use permissions compatible with pre-Windows 2000 Server operating systems, you allow the Active Directory Installation Wizard to configure the domain (and possibly the forest if this installation is the first one in the forest), so the Anonymous Logon group and the Everyone security groups are added to the Pre-Windows 2000 Compatible Access group.

    If you do not want the Anonymous Logon group to be able to read user and group information for the domain and no legacy clients are involved, you should choose the Permissions compatible only with Windows Server 2003 Operating Systems option.

13. **Select the desired option for a permissions preference and then click Next.**

    The Directory Services Restore Mode Administrator Password page appears, requesting a unique password to be used to enter into Directory Services Restore mode if a system failure requires an Active Directory restore.

14. **Type a password and then click Next.**

    The Summary page appears, listing the changes that will be made to the system.

15. **Click Next.**

    The installation and configuration process takes a considerable amount of time (up to an hour on some systems), so hurry up and wait.

16. **If your system was using a DHCP assign (dynamically or automatically assigned) IP address, you may see a warning pop-up stating that you need to define a static IP address for reliable DNS services. Click OK in this dialog box.**

17. **In the Local Area Connection Properties dialog box, select the Internet Protocol (TCP/IP) component, and then click Properties.**

    The Internet Protocol (TCP/IP) Properties dialog box appears.

18. **Choose the Use the Following IP Address option. In the IP Address and Subnet Mask boxes, type your preferred settings. Click OK.**

If you don't have or don't know an IP address to assign, use the following: 192.168.0.1 and 255.255.255.0. For more details on managing, assigning, and configuring the Transmission Control Protocol/Internet Protocol (TCP/IP), please see Chapter 14.

19. **Click Close to close the Local Area Connection Properties dialog box.**

20. **When the installation complete message is displayed, click Finish.**

21. **When you're prompted to reboot your system, click Restart Now.**

22. **After the system reboots, log back in. You're finished!**

At this point, you can decide which network or application components you want to install on the new server. The second, third, and fourth servers installed on a network can each have a different network role, including serving as one of the following:

- ✔ A peer domain controller hosting Active Directory

- ✔ A network management server hosting DHCP, DNS, WINS, Routing and Remote Access, or any other of a myriad of network services

- ✔ A file or print server

- ✔ A Web, media, or application server

We cover Active Directory in Chapters 11 and 12, file servers in Chapter 16, and print servers in Chapter 13. All you need to know about these Configure Your Server options appears in these chapters.

A Windows Server 2003 is just a stand-alone system that acts like a workstation until you employ the configurations offered through the Configure Your Server Wizard. After you do that, your Windows Server 2003 machine can take on almost any role you want. Unlike Windows NT, in which you have either primary or backup domain controllers, all domain controllers on Windows Server 2003 are essentially the same. Each and every domain controller shares the responsibility of maintaining the domain, updating changes to the Active Directory, and distributing the authentication and communication load.

Getting the word out

Windows Server 2003 includes Internet Information Services (IIS) 6.0 and supports Streaming media server, also known as Windows Media Services (WMS). IIS allows you to host Web and File Transfer Protocol (FTP) sites to intranet and Internet users. With WMS, you can create stunning multimedia presentations, combining audio, video, slides, interactive media, and more — all delivered by means of streaming connection.

You can use the IIS and WMS items on the Configure Your Server Wizard to jump directly to the administrative tools for IIS 6.0 and Media Services. You can also access Internet Information Services Manager (also known as the IIS MMC snap-in), shown in Figure 10-2, by choosing to Start⇨Administrative Tools⇨Internet Information Services (IIS) Manager.

Figure 10-2:
Internet
Information
Services
Manager for
IIS version
6.0.

To host Windows Media Services on your Windows Server 2003 system, you first need to configure it as a streaming media server by choosing Start⇨ Administrative Tools⇨Configure Your Server Wizard. Next, choose the Streaming media server role, which allows you to complete the setup of your server to stream audio and video content to clients over the Internet or your company's intranet.

IIS 6.0 is its own application, and its features are far beyond the scope of this book. If you really want to set up this service on your server, see the Windows Server 2003 Resource Kit or TechNet.

Organizing the neighborhood

The Configure Your Server Wizard's Networking option offers you quick access to the configuration tools used to manage DHCP, DNS, Remote Access, and Routing.

DHCP is a method of automatically configuring TCP/IP settings of clients and non-critical servers upon bootup. *DNS* is a method of resolving host names into IP addresses. We cover both DHCP and DNS in Chapter 14.

Although DHCP and DNS qualify as neat stuff, they're fairly complex topics that are not covered in detail in this book. Please look in the Windows Server 2003 Resource Kit for complete instructions on configuration and management of these services.

Routing and Remote Access is the service that combines two functions: routing and remote access (duh!). Routing is the capability to direct network communications in a local area network (LAN) or — with the help of a remote access link — across a wide area network (WAN). Remote Access is the capability to establish network connections over either telephone or Integrated Services Digital Network (ISDN) lines. Windows Server 2003 can act as a client to connect to remote systems, or it can act as a server to accept inbound calls. The Remote Access and Routing selections under the Networking option (in the Configure Your Server Wizard) offer a link to the Routing and Remote Access management console shown in Figure 10-3. With this console, you can install and configure Routing and Remote Access.

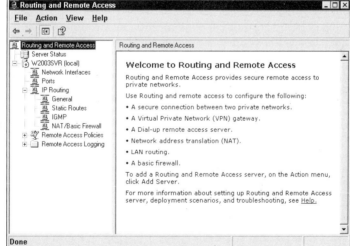

Figure 10-3:
The Routing and Remote Access management console.

Here are the basic steps to enable this service:

1. **Open the Routing and Remote Access management console (Start⇨Administrative Tools⇨Routing and Remote Access).**

2. **Click the Routing and Remote Access item in the left pane.**

   The list of servers on the network is displayed.

3. **Right-click your server and choose Configure and Enable Routing and Remote Access.**

   The Routing and Remote Access Server Setup Wizard appears.

4. **Click the Next button to continue.**

   The wizard provides a selection list of common configurations and the option to manually define settings. The options available in the Common Configurations windows are as follows:

   • Remote access (dial-up or VPN)

   • Network address translation (NAT)

   • Virtual private network (VPN) access and NAT

   • Secure connection between two private networks

   • Custom configuration

5. **Choose the option that best matches your needs, or choose Custom Configuration and set things up manually.**

6. **Click Next.**

   Each of the four common configuration suggestions prompt you for further details to fine tune the system. For more information on these selections, consult the Windows Server 2003 Resource Kit.

7. **Just follow the prompts through the rest of the wizard to complete the configuration.**

Keep in mind that to enable routing, you need at least two network interfaces. These can be NICs, specialized connections to the Internet, or even modems.

Although it looks like everything has been enabled, we recommend that you reboot before you make any further modifications.

After the reboot, Routing and Remote Access is configured and functioning. All it needs now are network interfaces and a bit of configuration. The Routing and Remote Access interface is a Graphical User Interface (GUI), which — compared to the previous command-line, text-only control and display — is a great improvement. Furthermore, this management tool allows you to install routing protocols, monitor interfaces and ports, watch dial-up clients, define access policies, and modify logging parameters. You'll never want to use the ROUTE command again!

However, routing is not a subject for the timid. For this reason, we recommend that you consult the Windows Server 2003 Resource Kit for more information. We don't want to leave you completely in the dark, so we list a few more features of Remote Access in the "Other frills" section a little later in the chapter.

Remote Connections

Remote communications consist of two distinct elements: the client and the server. Windows Server 2003 can either establish a connection to a remote system (as a dial-up client) or accept connections from remote clients (as a dial-up host). For more information on using Windows Server 2003 as a dial-up host, please see the Windows Server 2003 Resource Kit.

Getting connected

Using Windows Server 2003 as a dial-up client is not terribly difficult. In most cases, you dial out to an Internet Service Provider (ISP) to make an Internet connection. We can take you step-by-step through the process of establishing such a connection if you have the following pieces of information at hand:

- ✔ Phone number of the ISP
- ✔ Logon name
- ✔ Logon password

For this type of connection, we assume that you have a modem, not an ISDN line or other connection device. If you don't have a modem, you definitely need one for this exercise. You can install a modem using the Add/Remove Hardware applet from the Control Panel. If you follow the prompts, you'll be amazed at how easy it is to do the installation.

We also assume that your ISP has a simple logon procedure. If you require special characters prefixed to your logon name, must traverse a logon menu, or must execute a logon script, you need to consult the ISP for instructions on how to configure Windows Server 2003 to properly establish a connection. Fortunately, most ISPs have a simple logon.

Here's how to get things rolling:

1. **Choose Start➪Settings to display the Network Connections screen, as shown in Figure 10-4.**

   You should have a modem installed before you follow these steps.

Figure 10-4:
The
Network
Connections
manage-
ment
console
(after a
dial-up
object has
been
defined).

2. **Double-click the New Connection Wizard and then click Next.**

3. **Choose the Connect to the Internet option and then click Next.**

4. **Choose the Connect Using a Dial-up Modem option and then click Next.**

5. **Provide a name for this connection object, such as the ISP name, and then click Next.**

6. **Provide the phone number and then click Next.**

7. **Select whether this object can be used by anyone logged on to this system or only you and then click Next.**

8. **Provide the login name and password for the ISP account and then click Next. Click Finish.**

That's it! An icon now appears in the Network Connections window with the name you provided. Double-click this icon to display the Connection dialog box. Click the Dial button to establish the connection. After a few noisy moments, you'll establish a connection and be ready to surf!

You can view the status of the connection by placing your mouse cursor over the connection icon (the one with the two overlapping computers) in the icon tray. You can also double-click the icon to display a dialog box with more information.

You can change the parameters of the dial-up connection by right-clicking the icon in the Network Connections window and choosing Properties. In the dialog box for the Network Connections Property page, you can change every aspect of the connection.

To end the connection, right-click the connection icon in the icon tray and choose Disconnect — or double-click the connection icon to display the Details box and then click Disconnect.

Other frills

Windows Server 2003 includes all the latest capabilities that you would expect in a Windows-based remote access server. You'll recognize most of these from Windows 2000 and some from Windows NT. But even with the latest enhancements, Windows Server 2003 has retained nearly all of its old capabilities and functions. That means if you could accomplish something using Windows NT 4.0 or Windows 2000 RAS, you can do it better using Windows Server 2003 Remote Access.

These features include but are not limited to the following:

- ✔ Point-to-Point Protocol (PPP) for dial-out and dial-in connections. Serial Line Internet Protocol (SLIP) is still retained for outbound connections to non-PPP systems. (Windows XP Professional doesn't support SLIP for incoming connections; only Windows Server 2003 can use TCP/IP to connect through SLIP.)

- ✔ Multilink PPP for aggregating similar connections into a single pipeline.

- ✔ Point-to-Point Tunneling Protocol (PPTP) for link establishment over the Internet for secure communications.

- ✔ Authentication encryption to secure logon passwords.

- ✔ VPN security features: IPSec and L2TP (see the Windows Server 2003 Resource Kit or TechNet for more information).

- ✔ Support for smart cards (which are small cards added to the system to store security information).

- ✔ Full Remote Authentication Dial-in User Service (RADIUS) support.

- ✔ Shared connections (a single computer sharing its connection with other network clients).

For an in-depth discussion of Remote Access, check out the Windows Server 2003 Resource Kit.

Chapter 11

Doing the Directory Thing

*I*n this chapter, you look at the updates made to the directory service known as Active Directory. You find out what a directory service is, why it's required for a Windows domain and forest structure, and how to plan for and install the Windows Server 2003 Active Directory. It may not be the greatest thing since sliced bread, but it's at least as good as cracked pepper crackers!

What Is a Directory Service?

You may not know it, but you use directory services all the time. When you get hungry and crave pizza, you open your telephone directory and look under *P* for this peerless paragon of sustenance. That telephone book is a kind of directory service — namely, it contains the information you need, along with a way to locate the information you require. (In this case, it's in alphabetical order.) A computerized directory service works pretty much the same way: It contains information about numerous aspects of your company, organizes that information, and provides one or more tools to help you explore the information it contains.

The first operating system from Microsoft to offer directory services was Windows 2000. Novell NetWare has its own native directory service — Novell Directory Services (NDS) or eDirectory in NetWare 6 — and it's been offered in all the released Novell versions of Network Operating System (NOS) since 1993. Microsoft bases the entire Windows Server 2003 domain structure (which started with Windows 2000) around its directory services, rather than simply offering them as an add-on to previous domain implementations. Microsoft's directory service is called *Active Directory.*

Although Active Directory and Novell Directory Services do not interact directly, the capability to synchronize Active Directory with Novell Directories is possible through the Microsoft Directory Synchronization Services (MSDSS). MSDSS, which is included with Services for NetWare 5, allows Active Directory synchronization with NDS and NetWare 3.*x* binderies so that system administrators can reduce their overall directory management tasks by administering one, rather than two, separate directory services.

When it comes to its names, Microsoft has an obsession with the word *active.* There's Active Desktop, Active X, and now Active Directory. However, the term is accurate — after all, Active Directory *is* active (when it's used correctly).

Meet Active Directory

To do its job properly, a directory service must meet three primary requirements:

- ✔ It must include a structure to organize and store directory data.
- ✔ It must provide a means to query and manage directory data.
- ✔ It must supply a method to locate directory data and the network and server resources that might correspond to such data. (For example, if the directory data includes a pointer to a file and a printer, the directory service must know where they reside and how to access them.)

Windows Server 2003's Active Directory fulfills all these requirements using various technologies. For more information about Active Directory, pick up a copy of *Active Directory For Dummies* by Marcia Loughry (published by Wiley Publishing, Inc.).

Organizing and storing data

The structure of Active Directory follows the formatting guidelines of the *ISO X.500 protocol.* (ISO stands for International Organization for Standardization.) Figure 11-1 shows the hierarchical structure of an X.500 directory. This is a common standard used in nearly all directory services, including not only Microsoft's Active Directory but also Novell Directory Services (NDS), Netscape products, and other implementations. X.500 has proven to be useful for this application because it organizes data in a hierarchy that breaks directory information into a variety of useful containers, such as countries, organizational units, subunits, and resources. The example in Figure 11-1 organizes the directory down to the user objects.

The two X.500 standards commonly used today are the 1988 and 1993 X.500 standards. The 1993 version includes a number of advances over the older 1988 version. Happily, the 1993 version is the standard upon which Windows Server 2003 built Active Directory.

Managing data

A special-purpose protocol known as the *Lightweight Directory Access Protocol* (LDAP) provides the second ingredient for the Active Directory service. LDAP normally utilizes TCP port 389 as its main network transport connection. As the latter part of its name suggests, LDAP is designed specifically to retrieve and access directory data. (The *Lightweight* part of its name stems from the fact that it's a stripped-down version of an older, more cumbersome X.500 DAP.)

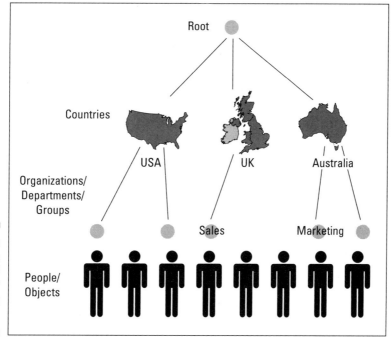

Figure 11-1:
The hierarchical structure of an X.500 directory.

The terminology used in this chapter may seem familiar to those of you who are acquainted with Microsoft Exchange Server's directory service. This is because the Active Directory service in Windows Server 2003 shares a common heritage (and common technology) with the Exchange Server directory service. In fact, an Exchange connector is supplied with Windows Server 2003 to link the two directory services and to replicate data between them. Not surprisingly, this software component is called the *Active Directory Connector.*

Additional information on LDAP can be found at the RFC #1777 (Request For Comments) page at `www.ietf.org/rfc/rfc1777.txt`.

Locating data and resources

If Windows Server 2003 directory data is structured using the X.500 protocol and this data is accessed using LDAP, there still must be a way to locate directory data. Time for the missing third ingredient! How does Active Directory meet the third and final requirement for a working directory service? We're glad you asked. Active Directory relies on the well-known and widely used Internet standard called the *Domain Name Service* (DNS) as its locator service.

Of Domains and Controllers

Behind every great domain is a great domain controller (so the Aretha Franklin song goes), but before you look at how Windows Server 2003 and Windows 2000 use domain controllers, a quick recap of Windows NT 4.0 usage is in order.

The Windows Server 2003 and Windows 2000 way of doing the domain controller thing is quite different from the Windows NT 4.0 way — mainly because of Active Directory. Okay, so I don't have to repeat it over and over, Windows Server 2003 and Windows 2000 both support Active Directory in the same way, so what you see here for Windows Server 2003 is also true of Windows 2000. (The few small differences, mainly in high-level schema control and naming management, are too detailed for this book.)

In the beginning . . .

In Windows NT 4.0, 15-character NetBIOS (Network Basic Input-Output System) names represent domains. Such domains revolve around a single user/group/policy database called the Security Accounts Manager (SAM) database, stored in writable format on a single, primary server known as the *primary domain controller* (PDC).

NetBIOS names can be a total of 16 characters. On Microsoft operating systems, the NetBIOS name is limited to 15 characters. The 16th character is hidden from view and is used as a NetBIOS suffix by Microsoft Networking software to identify services installed on the given system. Additional information on NetBIOS suffixes in the Microsoft environment is available at `http://support.microsoft.com/default.aspx?scid=KB;en-us;q163409`.

Access to the domain database is required to access a domain's resources, so any model that depends on a single domain controller introduces a single point of failure. To improve availability and reliability of the domain database, Microsoft added a second type of server to this mix, known as a *backup domain controller* (BDC), which stores a read-only version of the SAM database. Users can access the BDC to log on to a domain and to investigate user, group, or account information, but changes to the database can be applied only to the PDC.

In this kind of domain environment, the PDC must periodically update the SAM database on all BDCs in its domain to keep them synchronized. Should a PDC ever fail, a BDC can be promoted to become the PDC and write-enable its copy of the SAM database. However, there's an unbreakable master-slave relationship between PDCs and BDCs, because changes to the SAM database must be applied to the PDC and copied from the PDC to all BDCs. Therefore, if the PDC goes down, no changes can be applied to the SAM database unless the PDC is brought back up or a BDC is promoted to become the new PDC instead. Phew! Got all that?

Although this sounds like a form of subjugation, a master-slave relationship is computerese for "everything that changes on the master is copied to all slaves" and "only a master can accept changes and copies all changes to its slaves."

Windows Server 2003 no longer uses NetBIOS to name its domains; instead, it uses DNS domain names. (See Chapter 14 for more information on DNS domain names.) For example, rather than a `Dummies` domain, you might have `sales.dummies.com` as a legal domain name. However, you can still use a NetBIOS name to refer to a domain, which is a requirement for all non-Active Directory systems, such as the Windows 98 and Windows NT client operating systems, which are sometimes referred to as legacy clients. (That's why you define one when you install Active Directory in Chapter 10.) Likewise, the concept of a SAM is no longer used in a Windows Server 2003 domain. All information about users, passwords, and groups is stored in Active Directory. Therefore, instead of servers that can read from or write to the SAM, servers must supply the LDAP service that's needed to interface with Active Directory.

On Windows Server 2003, network servers that host the LDAP service are the domain controllers. As in Windows NT-based networks, these servers are responsible for authentication and other domain activities. In Windows Server

2003-based networks, however, servers use Active Directory to provide the services that their older counterparts delivered using the SAM database.

Wherefore art thou, BDC/PDC?

The concept of PDCs and BDCs is not used in the Active Directory domain structure of Windows 2000 and Windows Server 2003. In this brave new world, all domain controllers are equal (though some are, indeed, more equal than others). How is this equality maintained? A process known as *multi-master replication* ensures that when changes occur on any domain controller in a domain, these changes are replicated to all other controllers in that domain. Therefore, instead of the older master-slave relationship between PDC and BDCs, you have a peer-to-peer relationship among all domain controllers in a Windows Server 2003 domain (and beyond) where trust relationships exist. (A *trust relationship* is a special interdomain access arrangement that you define when users in one domain require access to resources in another domain.)

Because you won't be able to upgrade all your domain controllers from Windows NT 4.0 to Windows Server 2003 in one fell swoop, Windows Server 2003 allows you to operate your domains in a *mixed* mode. This allows Windows NT 4.0 BDCs (but not PDCs) to participate in a Windows Server 2003 domain. The idea is that you begin by upgrading the NT4 PDC to Windows Server 2003 and then proceed on other server-based systems in the enterprise. This will often include the upgrading or total demotion of all existing NT4 Server class BDCs.

For a Windows NT 4.0 BDC to function properly, it needs to obtain updates from a PDC. Therefore, a single Windows Server 2003 domain controller impersonates a Windows NT 4.0 PDC, which allows changes to be replicated to any Windows NT 4.0 BDCs in that domain. This capability of a Windows Server 2003 domain controller is known as a *Flexible Single Master Operations* (FSMO) *role* (also known as operations master role). This specific server role is called *PDC emulator.*

Even in a full-fledged, Windows Server 2003-only environment, the PDC Emulator Operations Master still plays an important part in the scheme of things. It performs certain duties that no other DCs in the domain handle. The PDC emulator receives preferential replication of password changes performed by other domain controllers in the domain. When passwords are changed, it takes time to replicate the change in every domain controller in the domain. That synchronization delay might cause an authentication failure at a domain controller that hasn't yet received the change. Before that remote domain controller denies access to whatever is trying to perform the access, it forwards the authentication request to the PDC emulator because the PDC emulator may have different information (for example, a new password).

In a mixed-mode domain operation, clients can use NetBIOS names to access old-style domain services, or they can use Active Directory to access Windows Server 2003 domain services. To find a Windows Server 2003 domain controller, clients must query a DNS server for a service record that takes the general form

```
_ldap._tcp.<domain name>
```

where `_ldap._tcp.dummies.com` represents the domain controllers for the `dummies.com` domain, for example.

Windows Server 2003 domain controllers do not have to run the DNS service locally. The only requirement is that the DNS servers support the service record types required so that those domain controllers can be located.

What Makes Active Directory Tick?

Putting things in a technobabble nutshell, Active Directory is implemented using an X.500 structure for directory data, an LDAP interface to access directory data, and Dynamic DNS as a locator mechanism for directory data. So, now that you know all this stuff about Active Directory, what does it give you? The following list recounts some of the main features and advantages of Active Directory:

✔ **Security:** Information is stored in a secure form. Each object in Active Directory has an *Access Control List* (ACL) that contains a list of resources that may access it and what access privileges are granted to each such resource.

✔ **Query capabilities:** Active Directory generates a *global catalog* to provide a flexible mechanism for handling queries. Any client that supports Active Directory can query this catalog to request directory data.

✔ **Replication:** Replication of the directory to all domain controllers in a domain means easier access, higher availability, and improved fault tolerance.

✔ **Extensible:** Active Directory is *extensible,* which means that new object types can be added to a directory or existing objects can be *extended.* For example, you could easily add a salary attribute or an employee ID to the user object. (An *attribute* is extra information about an object.)

✔ **Multiple protocols:** Communication between directory servers or across directories from multiple vendors can use numerous networking protocols because of Active Directory's X.500 foundation. These protocols currently include LDAP Versions 2 and 3 and the *Hypertext Transfer Protocol* (HTTP). Third parties can extend this capability to include other protocols as well, if needed.

✔ **Partitioning:** In an Active Directory environment, information may be partitioned by domain to avoid the need to replicate large amounts of directory data. Each such domain is called a *tree* because of the way that X.500 structures directory data into an interlinked hierarchy with a single root. In a large and complex network, a collection of domains forms a group of trees that is — you guessed it — called a *forest!*

When you partition Active Directory data into different trees, it does not mean that Active Directory cannot be queried for information from other domains. *Global catalogs* contain a subset of information about every object in an entire domain forest, which allows such searches to be performed on the entire forest through the agencies of your friendly local domain controller.

What replication means

In a Windows Server 2003 domain, all domain controllers are equal. Therefore, if you apply changes to any domain controller, the complete domain directories of all other domain controllers must be updated (through a process called *multi-master replication*) to record those changes.

Here's how multi-master replication works: Active Directory uses an Update Sequence Number (USN) to track changes and updates made to Active Directory objects. As changes are made to the objects, this number is incremented by 1 on each object affected by the change. For example, a user account object that was updated to include a home telephone number would have its USN incremented by 1 to reflect that it had been modified. This modification is then sent to the other domain controllers in the domain. The object with the higher USN — that is, the updated object — overwrites the object with the lower USN.

USN increments are *atomic operations;* in English, this means that the increments to the USN's value and the actual change to directory data occur at the same time. If one part fails, the whole change fails; therefore, it's not possible to change any Active Directory object without its USN being incremented. Thus, no changes will ever be lost. Each domain controller keeps track of the highest USNs for the other domain controllers with which it replicates. This allows the domain controller to calculate which changes must be replicated during each replication cycle. In the simplest terms, the highest-numbered USN always wins!

Domain trees

A *domain tree* is a set of Windows 2000 domains or Windows Server 2003 domains (or both) connected by a two-way, transitive trust and sharing a common schema, configuration, and global catalog. To be considered a true domain tree, the domains must form a contiguous hierarchical namespace. A single domain all by itself with no child names is still considered a tree.

The first domain installed in a domain tree is the *root domain* of that tree. It is considered the *forest root domain* if it is also the first domain in the forest. An *Active Directory forest* is a collection of one or more Windows 2000 domains or Windows Server 2003 domains (or both) that share a common schema, configuration, and global catalog. Active Directory forests have a non-contiguous namespace.

All domains in a domain tree and all trees in a single forest have the connectivity benefit of the two-way, transitive trust relationship, which is the default trust relationship between Windows 2000 and Windows Server 2003 domains. This complete trust between all domains in an Active Directory domain hierarchy helps to form the forest as a single unit through its common schema, configuration, and global catalog.

At the start of each replication cycle, each domain controller checks its USN table and queries all other domain controllers with which it replicates for their latest USNs. As an example, the following represents the USN table for Server A.

Domain Controller	USN
DC B	54
DC C	23
DC D	53

Server A then queries the domain controllers for their current USNs and gets these results:

Domain Controller	USN
DC B	58
DC C	23
DC D	64

From this data, Server A can calculate the changes it needs from each server:

Domain Controller	*USN*
DC B	55, 56, 57, 58
DC C	Up-to-Date
DC D	54-64

It would then query each server for the updates it needs.

Up-to-Date Vectors are two different segments of data that contain a Globally Unique Identifier (GUID) and the Update Sequence Number (USN). The Up-to-Date Vector is made up of server USN pairs held by the two domain controllers containing the highest originating updates. (This is usually the domain controller in which the originating update occurred and then its immediate replication partners.) The High Watermark Vector contains the highest attribute USN for any given object. By using both of these vectors, domain controllers can calculate the fact that a given replication of data has already been received to prevent further replication of that particular update.

Because objects have properties, they also have Property Version Numbers (PVNs). Every property of an object has a PVN, and each time a property is modified, its PVN is incremented by 1. (Sound familiar?) These PVNs are used to detect collisions, which happen when there are multiple changes to the same property of an object. If a collision occurs, the change with the highest PVN takes precedence.

If those PVNs match, a *time stamp* is used to resolve any such conflicts. Time stamps are a great second line of defense in avoiding collisions. They explicitly mark when each change to the directory data has been made, thus enabling the system to determine whether one change does in fact take precedence over another.

In the highly unlikely event that the PVNs match *and* the time stamp is the same, a binary buffer comparison is carried out and the larger buffer size takes precedence. PVNs (unlike USNs) are incremented only on original writes, not on replication writes. PVNs are not server specific but travel with the object's properties.

A propagation-dampening scheme is also used to stop changes from being repeatedly sent to other servers. The propagation-dampening scheme used by Windows Server 2003 prevents logical loops in the Active Directory structure from causing endless proliferation of updates and prevents redundant transmission of updates to already current servers.

The grand schema things

Every object in an Active Directory forest is part of the same schema. The schema defines the different types of information that active directory objects can have and store in Active Directory. The two main data definitions outlined in the schema are attributes and classes.

For example, a user object has attributes such as name, address, and phone number. The collection of these attributes and their definitions is called the schema. You may think of an object's schema as a laundry list of its attributes or a checklist of its capabilities. The default schema supplies definitions for users, computers, domains, and more. You can have only one schema per domain per object because you can't have multiple definitions for the same object.

The default schema definition is defined in the SCHEMA.INI file, which also contains the initial structure for the NTDS.DIT file that stores Active Directory data. The SCHEMA.INI file is located in the `%systemroot%\ntds` directory, it's an ASCII file, and it can be viewed on the screen or printed.

By default, the Active Directory schema cannot be easily edited. For example, you could easily add a salary attribute or an employee ID to the user object. In most cases you should leave schema editing up to the most senior programmers or system administrators, because changes made to the schema can't be undone and incorrect edits can severely damage your Active Directory and affect the entire forest. Some applications, such as Exchange, will edit the schema for you when they're installed. If you feel the need to edit the schema for whatever reason, lie down and wait for that feeling to go away. If it comes back, hire a professional Active Directory programmer.

An entire enterprise forest (a collection of Active Directory trees in a single organizational container) shares a single schema. If you change that schema, it affects every domain controller in every linked domain. Therefore, you'd better be sure that any changes you make are both correct and desirable. The schema should be changed only by experienced programmers or schema administrators. For more information on extending the schema, search the Microsoft Web site (`www.microsoft.com`) for "Active Directory Programmer's Guide."

Global catalogs

The *global catalog* contains entries for all objects in a single Active Directory forest (which is a collection of domain trees that may or may not explicitly share a single, contiguous namespace). It contains all the properties for all the objects in its own domain, and it contains a partial subset of properties from all the remaining objects in the forest. The entire forest shares a single global catalog. Multiple servers hold copies of the entire catalog; these servers are domain controllers called *global catalog servers.* To hold a copy of the global catalog, a server must maintain a copy of the Active Directory, which automatically makes the server a domain controller.

Searches across the entire forest are limited in scope to the object properties that appear in the global catalog. Searches in a user's local domain can be for any property when you perform a so-called *deep search* on properties not in the global catalog.

Do not configure too many global catalogs for each domain, because the replication needed to maintain such catalogs can be a burden on a network. One global catalog server per site is usually sufficient.

Although any given search can encompass a specific container or OU in a domain, a specific domain, a specific domain tree, or the entire forest, in most cases full searches involve querying the entire Active Directory forest through the global catalog.

Planning for Active Directory

If you're running some version of Windows NT, you may have multiple domains with several trust relationships between individual pairs of domains. Theoretically, you could just upgrade each domain, keep existing trust relationships, and make no changes. If you did that, however, you'd lose the advantages of Active Directory.

If you're running a Windows 2000 domain, a bit of planning is still necessary. Even though Windows Server 2003 and Windows 2000 can both be domain controllers of the same domain, we generally don't recommend using two versions of a product to perform a single function. In most cases, having the exact same version of operating system (including upgrades and patches) will keep unexpected hiccups from corrupting your domain and bringing down your network.

With that said, you can deploy Windows Server 2003 systems into a domain as domain controllers. You can even perform an upgrade installation on a Windows 2000 domain controller to convert it to a Windows Server 2003 domain controller. Just be careful. Don't upgrade every system at once. Upgrade one or two, and then test everything to make sure your network still performs as you expect it to. Always leave yourself an out — the ability to roll back to a previous configuration, when things were working properly.

In most cases, businesses already using Windows 2000 will not be moving to Windows Server 2003 in a hurry. The most likely candidates for Windows Server 2003 migration are Windows NT shops that have been waiting for the second generation of Active Directory servers from Microsoft before jumping on the bandwagon. Therefore, the remainder of the discussion of Windows Server 2003 migration focuses on upgrading from Windows NT. If you need to upgrade from Windows 2000, some of the following applies, but it's almost a no-brainer.

Before you upgrade a single domain controller, you should create a plan for your domain. Then, you should use this plan to govern the order and method for your migration from Windows NT domains to Windows Server 2003 Active Directory.

What's in a namespace?

A *namespace* is a logically bounded region that contains names based on a standardized convention to symbolically represent objects or information. Specific rules guide the construction of names within a namespace and how a name can be applied to an object. Many namespaces are hierarchical in nature, such as those used in DNS or Active Directory. Other namespaces, such as NetBIOS, are flat and unstructured.

In Windows Server 2003, domains use full-blown DNS names rather than NetBIOS names. This creates interdomain parent-child relationships — where one domain may be created as a child of another — that Windows NT could not support. For example, sales.dummies.com is a child of the dummies.com domain. (A child domain always contains the full parent name within its own name.)

It's important to remember that parent-child relationships can be created only from within a parent domain using DCPROMO, the Active Directory Installation Wizard. The parent domain must exist before you create a child of that parent. Therefore, the order in which you create or upgrade your domains is crucial!

In the next section, you find out more reasons why it's important to create your domains in a certain order. But even before you concern yourself with site issues, you need to be aware that you should always create an enterprise root domain before creating any other domain. For example, if you begin by creating the dummies.com root domain, the sales.dummies.com domain and all other dependent domains can then be created as children of the dummies.com root domain. This structure helps when searching other domains and enables the possibility of moving domains around in future versions of Windows Server 2003.

Making sites happen

Sites in Active Directory are used to group servers into containers that mirror the physical layout of your network. This organization allows you to configure replication between domain controllers. Actually, sites are primarily used for replication control over slower wide area network (WAN) links between separate sections of the same network. A number of TCP/IP subnets can also be mapped to sites, which allows new servers to join the correct site automatically, depending on their IP address. This addressing scheme also makes it easy for clients to find the domain controller closest to them.

When you create the first domain controller, a default site called Default-First-Site is created, and the domain controller is assigned to that site. Subsequent domain controllers are added to this site, but they can be moved. You can also rename this site to any name you prefer.

Sites are administered and created using the Active Directory Sites and Services Microsoft Management Console (MMC) snap-in. To create a new site, do the following:

1. **Start Active Directory Sites and Services (Start⇨Administrative Tools⇨Active Directory Sites and Services).**

2. **Right-click the Sites branch and choose New Site.**

   The New Object — Site dialog box appears.

3. **Type a name for the site (for example, NewYork).**

   The name must be 63 characters or less and cannot contain '.' or space characters. You must also select a site link from the list. By default, DEFAULTIPSITELINK is created during the DCPROMO process. If you haven't created additional sites manually, this will be the only one listed.

4. **Select a site link to contain the new site, and then click OK.**

5. **Read the confirmation creation dialog box, and then click OK.**

Now that the site is created, you can assign various IP subnets to it. To do so, follow these steps:

1. **Start Active Directory Sites and Services (Start⇨Administrative Tools⇨Active Directory Sites and Services).**

2. **Expand the Sites branch.**

3. **Right-click Subnets and choose New Subnet.**

   The New Object — Subnet dialog box appears.

4. **Type the name of subnet in the form `<network>/<bits masked>`.**

   For example, 200.200.201.0/24 is network 200.200.201.0 with subnet mask 255.255.255.0.

5. **Select the Site with which to associate the subnet, for example, New York.**

6. **Click OK.**

You now have a subnet linked to a site. You can assign multiple subnets to a site if you want. For more information on subnets, see Chapter 14. For even more detailed information, search the Windows Server 2003 Help menu for subnets.

Oh, you organizational unit (OU), you

The *organizational unit* (OU) is a key component of the X.500 protocol. As the name suggests, organizational units contain objects in a domain that are organized into logical containers, thus allowing finer segregation and control within a domain. Organizational unit containers can contain other organizational units, groups, users, and computers.

OUs can be nested to create a hierarchy that closely matches the structure of your business or organization. Using OUs, you can eliminate the need for the cumbersome domain models developed for Windows NT Server-based domains (the master domain model, for example, in which several resource domains use accounts from a central user domain). Using Active Directory, you can create one large domain and group resources and users into multiple, distinct OUs.

The biggest advantage of OUs is that they allow you to delegate authority. You can assign certain users or groups administrative control of an OU, which allows them to change passwords and create accounts in that OU but does not grant them control over the rest of the domain. This capability is a major improvement over Windows NT domain administration, which was an all-or-nothing situation.

Installing Active Directory

In Windows NT, you set up each server's type during installation. The server's function could be in one of the following roles:

- Stand-alone/member server
- PDC
- BDC

With the exception of PDC/BDC swapping, a server's role could not be changed without reinstalling the software. For example, it wasn't possible to change a member server to a domain controller without reinstalling Windows NT.

Windows Server 2003 has left all that behind by allowing you to install all servers as normal servers. You can use a wizard (covered in the following section) to convert normal servers to domain controllers, or domain controllers to normal servers. This facility also gives you the ability to move domain controllers from one domain to another by demoting a domain controller to a member server and then promoting it to a domain controller in a different domain. In the Windows NT environment, demoting and promoting domain controllers typically requires reinstalling the operating system or jumping through some pretty major hoops.

Promoting domain controllers

Windows Server 2003 allows you to convert servers from normal servers to domain controllers and vice versa. To do this, you use the Active Directory Installation Wizard. This wizard can be accessed through the Configure Your Server tool (Start⇨All Programs⇨Administrative Tools⇨Configure Your Server — see Chapter 10) or by executing DCPROMO from the Run command (or Command Prompt). The Active Directory Installation Wizard can be used also to remove Active Directory from a domain controller; this returns the system to a member server state. For the step-by-steps to installing Active Directory and creating a domain controller, go to Chapter 10 and review the "Planting your first forest" section.

Active Directory's database and shared system volume

Although you should think of Active Directory as an information bubble, it's stored in file form on each domain controller in the file named `%systemroot%\NTDS\ntds.dit`. This file is always open and cannot be backed up using a simple file copy operation. However, like old methods for backing up SAM in Windows NT 4.0, the new NTBACKUP program included with Windows Server 2003 includes an option to take a snapshot of Active Directory and back up that information (this option is called System State). There's even a special *directory restoration mode* you must boot into to restore an Active Directory backup! (Chapter 17 covers backups in detail.)

The *share system volume,* or SYSVOL, is the replication root for each domain. Its contents are replicated to each domain controller in the domain using the File Replication Service. The SYSVOL must reside on an NTFS 5.0 volume, because that's a File Replication Service requirement.

SYSVOL is also a share that points (by default) to `%systemroot%\SYSVOL\sysvol`, which contains domain-specific areas, such as logon scripts. For example, the logon share NETLOGON for domain `savilltech.com` points to `%systemroot%\SYSVOL\sysvol\savilltech.com\SCRIPTS`. You can simply copy files used for logging on to or log off this directory, and the change will be replicated to all other domain controllers in the next replication interval (which by default is set to 15 minutes).

Modes of domain operation

Windows Server 2003 domains operate in four modes: mixed, native, .NET, and .NET interim. *Mixed-mode domains* allow Windows NT 4.0 BDCs to participate in a Windows Server 2003 domain. In *native mode,* only Windows Server 2003-based and Windows 2000-based domain controllers can participate in the domain, and Windows NT 4.0-based BDCs can no longer act as domain controllers. In *.NET mode,* only servers running Windows Servers 2003 can act as domain controllers. The *.NET interim mode* is used when upgrading a Windows NT 4.0 domain to the first domain in a new Windows 2003 forest.

The switch from mixed to native mode or native mode to .NET mode can't be reversed, so don't change the mode until all domain controllers are converted to Windows Server 2003 or Windows 2000 for native mode or just Windows Server 2003 for .NET mode. Also, note that you can't add any Windows NT 4.0-based BDCs after the mode of the domain is switched.

In addition, the switch to native mode allows the use of *universal groups,* which, unlike global groups, can be nested inside one another. Older NetBIOS-based clients will still be able to log on using the NetBIOS domain name even in native mode. Universal groups are supported also in .NET mode.

Changing the domain's mode is known as raising a domain's functionality. You can choose to step up to native mode from mixed mode, step up to .NET mode from native mode, or jump directly to .NET mode from mixed mode. Just be careful: This is a one-way switch. After you raise the functionality, you'll have to reinstall to return to a lower functionality.

To raise a domain's functionality, perform the following steps on a Windows Server 2003 domain controller:

1. **Start Active Directory Domains and Trusts (Start⇨Administrative Tools⇨Active Directory Domains and Trusts).**

2. **Select the domain you want to change.**

3. **Choose Action⇨Raise Domain Functional Level.**

    The Raise Domain Functionality dialog box appears.

4. **Use the pull-down list to select Windows 2000 native or Windows .NET Server 2003 mode, and then click Raise.**

   A confirmation message is displayed.

5. **Click OK.**

   A warning is displayed stating that the domain mode change can take up to 15 minutes.

6. **Click OK.**

You also need to check all other domain controllers in the domain. Make sure each domain lists the correct mode on its properties dialog box (right-click the domain and select Properties). If any domain controller is not reflecting the change after 15 to 20 minutes, reboot it. This forces a replication.

If a domain controller can't be contacted when you make the change (for example, if it's located at a remote site and connects to the main site only periodically), the remote domain controller will switch its mode the next time replication occurs.

When Domains Multiply

In this section, you look at new methods available in Windows Server 2003 to interconnect domains. In Windows NT 4.0 domains, you're limited to simple unidirectional or bidirectional trust relationships to interconnect two domains explicitly at a time. Windows Server 2003 has many more sophisticated, functional models to create relationships and connections among its domains.

Trust relationships across domains

Windows NT 4.0 trust relationships are not transitive. For example, if domain A trusts domain B, and domain C trusts domain B, domain C does not automatically trust domain A (see Figure 11-2).

This lack of transitivity is no longer the case with the trust relationships used to connect members of a tree or forest in Windows Server 2003 or Windows 2000. Trust relationships used in a Windows Server 2003 or 2000 tree are two-way, transitive trusts. This means that any domain in the forest implicitly trusts every other domain in its tree and forest. This removes the need for time-consuming administration of individual trusts between pairs of domains, because such trusts are created automatically whenever a new domain joins a tree.

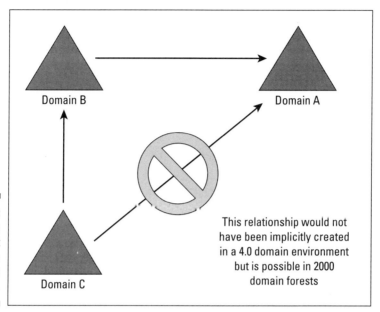

Domain B

Domain A

Domain C

This relationship would not
have been implicitly created
in a 4.0 domain environment
but is possible in 2000
domain forests

The security of Windows Server 2003 trusts is maintained by employing Kerberos. *Kerberos Version 5.0* is the primary security protocol for Windows Server 2003, but it's not a Microsoft protocol. Kerberos is a security system developed at the Massachusetts Institute of Technology (MIT). It verifies both the identity of the user and the integrity of all session data while that user is logged in. Kerberos services are installed on each domain controller, and a Kerberos client is installed on each workstation and server. A user's initial Kerberos authentication provides that user with a single logon to enterprise resources. For more information about Kerberos, see the Internet Engineering Task Force's (IETF's) Requests for Comments (RFCs) 1510 and 1964. These documents are available on the Web at www.rfc-editor.org.

Building trees

In Windows Server 2003, one domain can be a child of another domain. For example, legal.savilltech.com is a child of savilltech.com (which is the root domain name and therefore the name of the tree). A child domain always contains the complete domain name of the parent. As shown in Figure 11-3, dev.savillCORP.com can't be a child of savilltech.com because the domain names do not match. A child domain and its parent share a two-way, transitive trust.

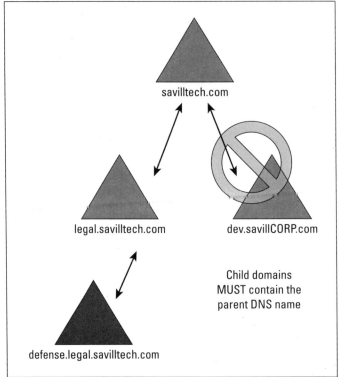

Figure 11-3:
Parent/child
relationship
example.

savilltech.com

legal.savilltech.com   dev.savillCORP.com

Child domains
MUST contain the
parent DNS name

defense.legal.savilltech.com

When a domain is the child of another domain, a *domain tree* is formed. A domain tree must have a contiguous namespace (which means all namespaces share a common root, that is, have the same parent).

Domain trees can be created only during the server-to-domain-controller-promotion process with DCPROMO.EXE.

There are a number of advantages in placing domains in a tree. The first and most useful is that all members of a tree have Kerberos transitive trusts with their parent and all its children. These transitive trusts also mean that any user or group in a domain tree can be granted access to any object in the entire tree. In addition, a single network logon can be used at any workstation in the domain tree.

Understanding forests

You may have a number of separate domain trees in your organization with which you would like to share resources. You can share resources between domain trees by joining those trees to form a forest.

A *forest* is a collection of trees that does not explicitly share a single, contiguous namespace (however, each tree still has to be contiguous). Creating a forest may be useful if your company has multiple root DNS addresses.

For example, in Figure 11-4, the two root domains are joined via transitive, two-way Kerberos trusts (like the trust created between a child and its parent). Forests always contain the entire domain tree of each domain, and you can't create a forest that contains only parts of a domain tree.

Forests are created when the first server-to-domain-controller-promotion process using DCPROMO is initialized and cannot currently be created at any other time.

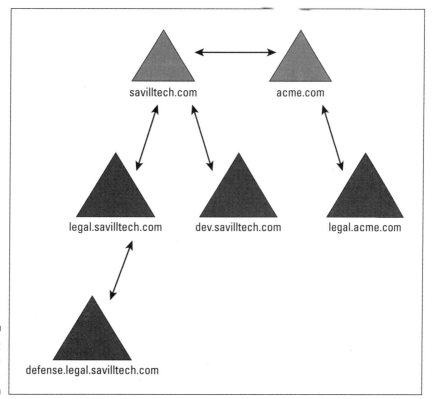

Figure 11-4:
An example
of a forest.

You're not limited to only two domain trees in a forest. (You can have as few as one, because a single domain by itself is technically considered both a tree and a forest.) You can add as many trees as you want, and all domains in the forest will be able to grant access to objects for any user in the forest. Again, this cuts back the need to manage trust relationships manually. The advantages of creating forests are as follows:

✔ All trees have a common global catalog containing specific information about every object in the forest.

✔ The trees all contain a common schema. Microsoft has not yet confirmed what will happen if two trees have different schemas before they're joined. We assume that the changes will be merged.

✔ Searches in a forest perform deep searches of the entire tree of the domain from which the request is initiated and use the global catalog entries for the rest of the forest.

Chapter 12

Working with Active Directory, Domains, and Trusts

In This Chapter

▶ Understanding domains

▶ Controlling domains and directories

▶ Handling directory permissions

▶ Managing trusts

*A*ccess to Active Directory's sheer power is useless unless you can manipulate and configure its content. Only then will you be able to get the most out of its powerful (but cryptic) environment. In this chapter, you take a long hard look at Active Directory. Before you enter into this staring contest with your computer screen, however, we want to show you how manipulating and configuring content is tied to manipulating and configuring domains. That's right; you get to tackle domains one more time. So once more into the breach, dear friend, so that you too can become a master of your own domain.

For details on domain controllers and their changing role in Windows 2003, see Chapter 11. We also suggest you pick up a copy of *Active Directory For Dummies* by Marcia Loughry (published by Wiley Publishing, Inc.).

Master of Your Domain

Domain controller roles are not defined during the installation of Windows Server 2003 but rather by running the Active Directory Installation Wizard. (For a little more information about the Active Directory Installation Wizard, see Chapter 11.) Windows Server 2003 does borrow the concept of a primary domain controller (PDC) from Windows NT through the use of the PDC emulator domain controller for certain domain functions, but it has jettisoned

Windows NT's concept of a backup domain controller (BDC). In Windows 2003, all domain controllers are equal and share peer-to-peer relationships, rather than acting either as a master (PDC) or a slave (BDC) in a master/slave relationship.

To support older Windows NT Server 4.0 and 3.51 BDCs in a mixed-mode environment, one of the Windows Server 2003 domain controllers must emulate the actions of a Windows NT Server 4.0 PDC. Then it has to replicate changes to those old-fashioned BDCs so that they can make the necessary changes, such as password modifications.

Having all these peers around can cause problems if you don't watch out. (Ever hear the expression, "Too many cooks spoil the broth"?) Windows Server 2003 utilizes five special roles to keep all these peers in line. One role was specifically designed to support any Windows NT vintage clients and domain controllers. The other four roles work to eliminate the risk of multiple domain controllers making changes to the same object and losing attribute modifications.

These roles are called *Flexible Single Master of Operations* (FSMO) roles, where each of the five roles manages a particular aspect of a domain or forest. Some of the Flexible Single Master of Operation domain controllers, sometimes referred to as Operations Masters, have a role that is domain wide, so their effect is throughout the given domain. When a forest has multiple domains, each domain has a domain-wide FSMO domain controllers. Other FSMO domain controllers have a forest-wide role. Each forest-wide FSMO domain controller is the only one of its type in the entire forest, regardless of how many domains are within the forest.

The *flexibility* of the Flexible Single Master of Operation domain controllers comes from the fact that these roles can be moved between domain controllers within a domain if the role of the original FSMO DC was domain wide, or between other domain controllers in the forest if the role of the original FSMO DC was forest wide. However, it does take a bit of effort on your part to move them.

You assign the FSMO roles using the NTDSUTIL utility. For more information on the NTDSUTIL utility, see the Windows Server 2003 Server help files or the Resource Kit.

The following list gives you an idea how these five roles work with domains in Active Directory:

> ✓ **Schema master:** At the heart of Active Directory, the *schema* is a blueprint for all objects and containers. Because the schema has to be the same throughout an entire forest, only one domain controller can be used to make modifications to the schema. If the domain controller that

holds the role of Schema Master can't be reached, no updates to the Active Directory schema are performed. You must be a member of the Schema Administrators group to make changes to the schema. (See Chapter 11 for a more detailed definition of the schema.)

✔ **Domain naming master:** To add a domain to a forest, its name has to be verifiably unique. The domain naming master of the forest oversees the domain name operation and ensures that only verifiably unique names are assigned. It also functions to add and remove any cross-references to domains in external directories, such as external Lightweight Directory Access Protocol (LDAP) directories. Only one domain naming master exists per forest, and you must be a member of the Enterprise Administrators group to make changes to the domain naming master, such as transferring the FSMO role or adding domains to or removing domains from the forest.

✔ **Relative ID (RID) master:** Any domain controller can create new objects (such as user, group, and computer accounts). The domain controller contacts the RID master when fewer than 100 RIDs are left. This means that the RID master can be unavailable for short periods of time without causing object creation problems. This ensures that each object has a unique RID. There can be only one RID master per domain.

✔ **PDC emulator:** The PDC emulator domain controller acts as a Windows NT primary domain controller when there is a domain environment that contains both NT4 BDCs and Windows 2000 DCs or Windows 2003 DCs (or both). It processes all NT4 password changes from clients and replicates domain updates to the down-level BDCs. After upgrades to the domain controllers have been performed and the last of the BDCs are upgraded or removed from the environment, the Windows 2000 domain or Windows Server 2003 domain (or both) can be switched to native mode. After the domain is in native mode, the PDC emulator still performs certain duties that no other DCs in the domain handle.

Each domain in the forest, including child domains, has only one PDC emulator domain controller.

✔ **Infrastructure master:** When a user and a group are in different domains, there can be a lag between changes to the user profile (a username, for example) and its display in the group. The infrastructure master of the group's domain is responsible for fixing the group-to-user reference to reflect the rename. The infrastructure master performs its fix-ups locally and relies on replication to bring all other replicas of the domain up to date. (For more information on replication, see the "When replication happens" section, later in this chapter.)

Trusts Are Good for NT 4.0 and Active Directory Domains

In the good old days before the need for FSMO roles (that is, during Windows NT's prime), you had one main domain controller (a primary domain controller, or PDC) that could make changes to the Security Accounts Manager (SAM) database. Those changes were then replicated to other backup domain controllers (BDCs). In this model, the SAM database was simply a file stored on each PDC that contained information about the domain's security objects, such as users and groups. To support authentication across domains (and thus hinder unauthorized access to the network), you created one-way trust relationships between domains that would allow users and groups from the trusted domain to be assigned access to resources in the trusting domain.

The concept of trusting and trusted is confusing, so we're going to try to shed some light on the subject. Imagine a trust between two domains: A and B. Domain A trusts domain B, so domain B is the trusted domain and domain A is the trusting domain. Because domain A trusts domain B to correctly authenticate its users, users from domain B can be assigned access to resources in domain A. (You could create a bidirectional trust relationship, where domain A trusts domain B with its resources and domain B trusts domain A with *its* resources. However, what you really have with a bidirectional trust is two unidirectional trusts that have been joined.) Before you get the idea that we're all one happy, trusting family, don't forget that Windows NT 4.0-based trusts are not transitive; therefore, if domain C trusts domain B, and domain B trusts domain A, domain C does not implicitly trust domain A. For domain A to trust domain C, you must establish an explicit trust relationship between domain A and domain C. Got all that? Remember it; we'll come back to it later.

Windows Server 2003 makes use of Active Directory to keep domains in line when it comes to trust relationships. Windows Server 2003 domain controllers store the directory service information in a file (NTDS.DIT), and trust relationships are still needed to authenticate across multiple domains. Windows Server 2003 automatically creates trust relationships between all domains in a forest just as it did under Windows 2000, but the real change from the older NT4 model to the Active Directory approach lies in how modifications are made and replicated to the domain database and how all automatically created trusts are two way and transitive by default. Now if A trusts B and B trusts C, A trusts C — and the reverse is true as well.

Before you get too flabbergasted, don't forget that Windows 2000 and Windows Server 2003 use trusts in the same way. Both operating systems create two-way and transitive trusts.

How domain controllers work together

In the days of Windows NT, domains had it easy. You made changes at only one domain controller, and the changes were copied at regular intervals to any other controllers for the domain.

Now, with Windows Server 2003, you can make changes at any domain controller and remain confident that Windows Server 2003's left hand will always know what its right hand is doing. How does this work, you ask? The answer, dear friend, is multi-master replication. (And you thought we were going to say "blowing in the wind.") How multi-master replication works is discussed in Chapter 11, but here you look at the concept at a higher level.

With multi-master replication, any domain controller can make changes to the Active Directory database. Those changes are then replicated to all other domain controllers in that domain.

Replication between domain controllers in a Windows NT 4.0 domain is configured using a couple of Registry settings — that's it — fairly useless really. Windows Server 2003 is *much* cooler!

A *site* is a collection of machines and domain controllers connected by means of a fast network and grouped by IP subnets. What do sites have to do with replication, you ask? Well, everything. They allow us to define different replication schedules depending on the domain controllers' site membership.

There are essentially two types of replication: *intra-site replication* (between domain controllers in the same site) and *inter-site replication* (between domain controllers in different sites).

Intra-site replication

When a change is made to the Active Directory, such as adding or deleting a user or changing an attribute of an object (say, adding properties to a printer), this change must be replicated to other domain controllers in the domain. The change is called an *originating update*. The domain controller where the originating update was made sends a notification to its replication partners (other domain controllers in the site) that a change is available. After replication occurs, the replication partners will have a copy of the change that was made on the other domain controller. This updating of the Active Directory on the partner domain controller is called a *replicated update* because it originated elsewhere.

Replication is initiated between domain controllers at a defined regular interval (five minutes, by default) and urgent replication using notification can be initiated for any of the following:

✓ **Replication of a newly locked-out account:** Prevents users from moving to another part of a domain to log on with a user account that has been locked out on a domain controller.

✓ **Modification of a trust account:** Enables all members of a domain to take advantage of a new trust with another domain.

This replication methodology has some problems. In the good ol' days (in other words, with Windows NT 4.0), you changed your password at the PDC to avoid the problem of the new setting not being replicated for a long time. With Windows 2003, the password changes are initially changed at the PDC FSMO; in the event of password failure, the PDC FSMO is consulted in case the password has been recently changed but has not yet been replicated.

If replication partners do not receive any change notifications in an hour (the default setting), they initiate contact with their replication partners to see whether any updates were made remotely and whether the subsequent change notifications were missed.

Inter-site replication

Inter-site replication takes place between particular servers in one site to particular servers in another site. This is where Windows Server 2003 shines. You can configure a timetable of how often to replicate for every hour of every day. All you need to do is go through the Active Directory Sites and Services MMC snap-in (Start➪Administrative Tools➪Active Directory Sites and Services). Go to the Inter-Site Transport branch and select IP. In the right-hand pane, select a site link (for example, a remote domain), right-click, and choose Properties. Make sure that the General tab is selected and then click Change Schedule. The dialog box used to change replication times appears, as shown in Figure 12-1.

In Figure 12-1, replication is set to occur from 12 a.m. to 5 a.m. Sunday through Saturday. You can change this to any schedule you like. For example, you can set it to replicate only on Sundays from 6 p.m. to 7 p.m.

Figure 12-1:
This is where you change replication times.

You can have different replication schedules for every pair of sites, so depending on the network connectivity and geographical location, different schedules may be appropriate. For example, if a slow WAN link exists between two sites, a replication with less frequent updates may be necessary to prevent bandwidth consumption.

One other area of replication crosses domains: Global Catalog information. The Global Catalog contains all the information about all the objects in its own domain and a subset of information for every object in the forest. However, Windows Server 2003 performs all the calculations needed to optimize this replication, so mere mortals like us don't need to worry about it.

Know your database limits

In Windows 2003, there's really no limit to the number of objects per domain — you're organization will never get that big! Windows NT 4.0 domains are limited to around 40,000 objects per domain. This forces some companies to require multiple master domains joined by bidirectional trust relationships.

Windows 2003, on the other hand, extends this to around 10,000,000 objects per domain. Compaq has performed tests and created 16,000,000 user objects in a single domain with no significant performance problems. However, it had some *very* powerful hardware — probably much more powerful than your home PC or even your company's primary server!

These objects have to be replicated at some point. Windows Server 2003 uses *property* rather than *object* replication, which means that only the property change is replicated, not the entire object. In other words, if you change just one property of an object (a user's phone number, for example), only the property change (the new phone number) is replicated — not the entire user object.

Your database size is governed by your domain controller hardware and the physical network infrastructure. But if you have enough money to invest in the proper hardware, we doubt that you would need more than a single domain (unless your company is really big). There are, however, other reasons for needing multiple domains and forests, such as needing different schemas. (See Chapter 11 for more on schemas.)

The backup and restoration needs of your enterprise may govern database size because a huge directory database is no good if it takes days to back it up.

Administrivia Anyone? (Controlling Domains and Directories)

If you don't have sufficient tools available to manipulate and manage Active Directory, its power won't do you much good. Fortunately, not only does

Windows Server 2003 come with a complete set of ready-made tools, but you can also write your own tools and scripts using the Active Directory Scripting Interface (ADSI).

The directory management console

As with everything else in Windows 2003, management of Active Directory is accomplished using a Microsoft Management Console (MMC) snap-in. The snap-in you'll use most often is the Active Directory Users and Computers snap-in (shown in Figure 12-2), which is what you use to create, manage, and delete everything from users to computers. It includes some of the features of the old User and Server Manager from Windows NT.

To access the Active Directory Users and Computers snap-in, choose Start⇨ Administrative Tools⇨Active Directory Users and Computers. When you first start the snap-in, you see your domain name (represented as a DNS domain name) at the top of the directory. You'll also notice several containers (known more commonly as folders). Some of these containers are built-in organizational units (OUs), which contain objects in a domain that are organized into logical containers, thus allowing finer segregation and control in a domain. Certain container objects appear in all typical Active Directory installations:

- **Builtin:** By default, the details of the old Windows NT 4.0 groups, such as Administrators and Backup Operators.
- **Computers:** The computer accounts that were managed using Windows NT's Server Manager. Computer objects in other organizational units are not listed in this container.
- **Domain controllers:** A built-in organizational unit that contains all domain controllers.
- **Users:** The default store for all domain users. Again, users in other organizational units are not listed.

In a fully functional domain, you'll find various organizational units, depending on the services you have installed and the organizational units you create.

Everything is *context driven* in Windows Server 2003. This means that if you right-click an object or container, a menu specific to that object or container is displayed. This is much better that hunting through huge standard menus for options relevant to the chosen object.

Figure 12-2:
The Active
Directory
Users and
Computers
MMC
snap-in.

Creating directory objects

Windows Server 2003 has tons of objects, such as computer, user, group, and shared folder objects. In this section, we concentrate on the creation of only the first two (computer and user objects) because the others are fairly intuitive and don't support many configuration options.

In a Windows NT 4.0 domain, it never took too much planning to create new user or computer objects. You just did it. In Windows Server 2003, however, you can't be quite so spontaneous. You first need to think about where you want to create such an object. Placement is important because, although you can still move objects around, it's much easier in the long run if you create an object in the correct location from the get-go. However, because you may not always have the time to plan and do it right the first time, you can always move the object later if you have to (just don't say we didn't warn you).

Use OUs to help you organize your data into logical containers. First you create an OU for the various departments in your organization (for example, one for accounting, one for engineering, one for personnel, and so on). Then you can put all user and computer objects in a particular department in its OU. In addition, you can lighten your administrative load by assigning a person in each department the rights necessary to manage his or her OU and that OU only. Pretty nifty, huh?

You can create a user object in one of two places: in the default User/Computer container or in some organizational unit they or someone else has already created. If you delegate the ability to create objects, you can set it up so that the delegated users will be able to create objects in only one location or certain selected locations.

To create a user object, perform the following steps:

1. **Start Active Directory Users and Computers (Start⇨Administrative Tools⇨Active Directory Users and Computers).**

2. **In Active Directory Users and Computers, right-click the container (such as Users) in which you want to create the user object and then choose New⇨User.**

   The first page of the User Creation Wizard (the New Object — User dialog box) is displayed, as shown in Figure 12-3.

Figure 12-3:
The first page of the User Creation Wizard.

3. **Type the user's name and a logon name, and then click Next.**

   The next page of the Wizard allows you to set the new password and the following options:

   • User must change password at next logon

   • User cannot change password

   • Password never expires

   • Account is disabled

4. **Make the appropriate selections, and then click Next.**

   A summary of the proposed addition is displayed.

5. **Click Finish.**

That's it; you've created a new user. You're probably thinking, "What about all the other user attributes, such as security features?" Well, you no longer define those settings during the creation of the user. After you create the user object, you right-click it and select Properties. The Properties dialog box for the user appears (as shown in Figure 12-4).

Figure 12-4:
The Elvis A.
Presley user
object.

Each tab pertains to various aspects of the selected user object. These tabs vary depending on the Windows Server 2003 subsystems in use, on other back office applications such as Exchange Server or SQL Server, and even on what third-party software you might have installed.

Computer account creation is much simpler and doesn't bombard you with quite so many tabs. Again, in Active Directory Users and Computers, right-click the container in which you want to create the new computer object (such as computers) and choose New⇨Computer. The New Object — Computer dialog box appears, as shown in Figure 12-5. You have to only type a computer name and select who can add the computer to the domain.

Finding directory objects

Finding objects is one of Active Directory's greatest pluses. Using the Global Catalog, you can find an object anywhere in an enterprise forest by querying Active Directory.

Figure 12-5:
We're
creating a
new
computer
object
named
Fried-
Banana-
Sandwich.

You can search for anything — a user, a computer, even a printer — and you can search for many attributes. (The attributes presented vary depending on the type of object you're searching for.) For example, you can ask Active Directory to find the closest color-capable, double-sided printer at your site. You don't even have to tell Active Directory where you are. It figures that out automatically.

On a Windows Server 2003 system, there's a Search component that you can access from the Start menu (Start⇨Search). Under this menu, a number of options can be used to search for users, folders, and printers. The available options are as follows:

- ✔ For Files or Folders
- ✔ On the Internet
- ✔ Find Printers
- ✔ For People

For example, if you want to search for a color printer, you would choose Start⇨Search⇨Find Printers. There are three available tabs: Printers, Features, and Advanced. You would choose the Advanced tab because it allows you to specify that you're searching for a color printer. After you enter all your details, click Find Now and your results appear. In a large enterprise, many listings that meet your requirements may appear, so always try to be as specific and detailed as possible when performing a search.

A word on ADSI

Active Directory Scripting Interface (ADSI for short) allows you to manipulate the directory service from a script. You can use Java, Visual Basic, C, or C++

scripts. With ADSI, you can write scripts that automatically create users, including their setup scripts, profiles, and details.

If you need to manage a medium or large domain, you should learn ADSI. In the long run, it will save you a great deal of time and aggravation.

Search the Microsoft Web site at `www.microsoft.com/windows/` for ADSI, and you'll find loads of great information (more than you would want!). Also check the Windows Server 2003 Resource Kit for details.

Permission to Proceed? Handling Directory Permissions

The old concept "you're the administrator, administrate no longer" does have some truth to it in Windows Server 2003. Although some tasks still require a full-fledged domain administrator, the common management of a domain may be more easily accomplished when you grant different sets of users permissions to manage different sets of users and user properties. In English, this means you can delegate the responsibility for managing low-level users to slightly higher-level users, and so on, until you, as the administrator, only need to get involved to manage more weighty constructs, such as domain forests and trees or intra-site access.

About Active Directory permissions

If you're familiar with the Windows NT security model, you probably know all about Access Control Lists (ACLs). *ACLs* allow a set of permissions to be applied to a file, directory, share, or printer (and more), thus controlling which users can access and modify these particular objects.

Windows Server 2003 takes this to the next level by assigning an ACL to every single attribute of every single object. This means you can control user access to such a fine degree that you can micromanage your users into the nearest insane asylum. You could insist, for example, that "User group Personnel Admin may change the address, phone number, and e-mail attributes of all users but nothing else."

Assigning permissions

You can assign permissions to Active Directory objects in a number of ways. Here, we show an extreme case, so that everything else will look like a piece of cake!

Remember Active Directory Users and Computers? Well, earlier in this chapter, in "The directory management console," you saw a nice, basic view of this utility. However, it has other options that are shown only when it's in Advanced Features mode. To turn on Advanced Features, start Active Directory Users and Computers (Start⇨Administrative Tools⇨Active Directory Users and Computers), and then choose View⇨Advanced Features.

Some new branches are added to the basic domain root: LostAndFound and System. We don't care about that, though. Instead, we're interested in the new tab added to the objects — the Security tab.

In Active Directory Users and Computers, find a user, any user. Right-click the user and then select Properties. In the user's Properties dialog box, click the Security tab, and then click the Advanced button. You see a list of permission entries that consists of a type (Allow/Deny), a user or group, and the permission and its scope (Figure 12-6). Notice the size of that scroll bar. Ouch!

Figure 12-6:
The
Advanced
Security
Settings
dialog box
for an object
used to
control user
access.

Obviously, assigning permissions explicitly to every object takes forever. Thankfully, Active Directory uses an inheritance model so that you need to make changes only at the root; the changes propagate down from there. The following section spells out how this works.

Permissions inheritance

There are two types of permissions: explicit and inherited. *Explicit* permissions are assigned directly to an object, and *inherited* permissions are propagated to an object from its parent (and so on). By default, any object in a container inherits permissions from its container.

Sometimes, you don't want permissions to be inherited. For example, when you're working with a directory structure in which different permissions are defined on each contained object, such as with a multiuser File Transfer Protocol (FTP) site or a shared folder that contains user home directories. The default setting in Active Directory specifies that permissions are inherited, but you can change this default behavior.

Remember the Advanced Features view for Active Directory Users and Computers? Well, you need it again. When you turn on the Advanced Features from the View menu and check out the advanced security properties of a user (right-click the user, choose Properties, click the Security tab, and then click the Advanced button), notice the small box that says "Allow inheritable permissions from parent to propagate to this object and all child objects." This box was easy to miss, wasn't it?

The Allow Inheritable Permissions from Parent to Propagate to This Object and All Child Objects box is checked by default. If you uncheck it, any changes made to the parent container no longer propagate to the objects it contains. You have disabled inheritance for the object.

If you do disable inheritance, you're given the following options:

- ✔ Copy previously inherited permissions to this object
- ✔ Remove inherited permissions
- ✔ Cancel (disable) the inheritance

Of course, you can enable this later if you want. It's not a one-way operation, so don't panic!

Delegating administrative control

Delegating administration over certain elements of your domain is one of the great things about Active Directory — no more administrator or non-administrator. Different people or groups can be delegated control over certain aspects of a domain's organizational unit. The following steps can be employed to delegate administration on objects:

1. **Right-click a container (an organizational unit or domain) in Active Directory Users and Computers, and choose Delegate Control.**

   The Delegation of Control Wizard starts up and the welcome screen is displayed.

2. **Click Next to start delegating!**

3. **Select the group of users to whom you want to delegate control.**

   This is accomplished by clicking the Add button to access the Active Directory search tool to locate users and groups. Make your selections (hold down Ctrl to select multiple users at the same time).

   The users are now displayed in the selected user's area. The people you have selected are the ones who can perform the tasks you're about to choose.

4. **Click Next.**

   A list of common tasks is displayed for which you can delegate control (reset passwords and modify group membership, for example).

5. **Make your selections, and then click Next. If you choose to create a custom task to delegate, follow the steps presented by the Wizard.**

   A summary screen is displayed (as shown in Figure 12-7), giving you the option to change your mind.

6. **When you're happy with the changes you have made, click Finish.**

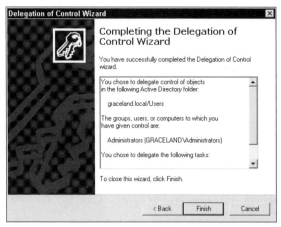

Figure 12-7: The summary screen of the Delegation of Control wizard.

That's it; a few mouse clicks and you've delegated control of a container to a specific person or groups of people.

Managing Trusts

In Windows NT 4.0, trust management was a big problem in a large enterprise. In Windows Server 2003, however, trust management is simple because all trusts are set up by default between all domains in a forest and these trusts are two-way transitive trust relationships.

Two-way transitive trusts are created automatically between all domains in a forest when you run DCPROMO. You can, however, still create the old-style Windows NT 4 trusts for any domains that are not part of the same enterprise forest.

Establishing trusts

Old-style trusts are created using Active Directory Domains and Trusts, which is accessed by choosing Start➪Administrative Tool➪Active Directory Domains and Trusts. Right-click the domain of choice in the Active Directory Domains and Trusts interface and then choose Properties. Click the Trusts tab (see Figure 12-8) to create one-way trusts. (*One-way external trusts* are not transitive in nature and work the same as the old Windows NT 4.0 trusts.) You can delete a trust by selecting the trust and choosing Remove.

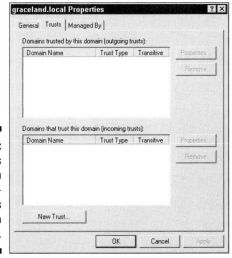

Figure 12-8:
This is where you create one-way trusts between domains.

If you open the door to trusts, who gets to come through?

In a forest, when you open the trust door (which happens automatically between all domains in the same forest), anyone gets to come in. All trusts are transitive, so anyone in any domain in the forest can be granted permission to any resource.

For old-style trust relationships (which are created manually between domains in different forests or in a Windows NT domain), the trust is not transitive. Only users in the two domains for which the trust is defined can be assigned access to resources and only in the direction of the trust.

There's no need to panic, though, because users can't access resources without permission. Therefore, although they *can* be given access, they won't be able to gain access until specifically given permission to do so.

Chapter 13

Printing on the Network

. . . .

. . . .

*N*ext to not being able to access network resources, nothing freaks out users more than not being able to print their work. We bet you can't find a network administrator who can say that he or she hasn't struggled with print devices at one time or another. (If you've seen the movie *Office Space,* you can imagine the kind of frustration we're talking about.)

We think that Microsoft designed Windows 2003 with a good printing system. In this chapter, you find out the specifics on setting up print devices on your network and avoiding some common printing problems.

Throughout this chapter, we use the Microsoft terminology *print device* and *printer,* which may be confusing in the real world. Microsoft defines a print device as the physical printer, such as an HP LaserJet 1200, and a printer as the software on the server where you configure settings for the physical print device. We use Microsoft's terms in this chapter to be technically accurate. However, this terminology may be confusing if this is your first time working with Windows 2003.

Windows 2003 Has a Print Model

When a user prints, the print data follows a particular path from the user to the print device. In Windows Server 2003, the basic pieces of this print scheme are as follows:

- **Print users:** Print users are the people who want to send print jobs to a print device located on the network, on the Internet, or attached to their workstation. To actually print, users must have a *print device driver* (called a *print driver* in non-Microsoftspeak) installed on their workstation.

- **Graphics Device Interface (GDI):** The already expanded GDI is a software program that finds the appropriate print device driver and works with the driver to render the print information into the appropriate printer language. After the information is rendered, the GDI sends it to the client-side spooler. (A Windows client application would call the GDI the *print process*.)

- **Print device driver:** This software piece is either provided by the manufacturer (for the latest version) or by Microsoft (not always the latest) and corresponds directly to a particular make and model of a print device. It's the interface between the software application and the print device. Again, this is called a *print driver* in non-Microsoftspeak. You may also hear it referred to as a *printer driver*. The print device driver need not be installed directly on the client. Instead, if the client is a Windows 98, SE, ME, NT, 2000, or XP system, it can download the print device driver from the print server when a document needs to be printed. However, this does require that the print server be configured to host the print device drivers for these operating systems.

- **Printers:** This is also called a *logical printer,* and it's not the physical piece of machinery you sometimes want to kick, but rather the bundle of settings you need to make the print device run. It exists as the software on the server that you use to configure settings for print job processing and routing for the physical print device.

- **Print jobs:** Print jobs are file(s) you want to print. Print jobs are formatted at the workstation by the GDI and a print device driver and submitted for output on a local or networked print device. If the print device is local (attached to the workstation), the output is printed right there and then. If a network print device and print server are involved, the output is sent (spooled) to a queue on the print server until a print device is available to service the request.

- **Print servers:** Print servers are computers that manage the network print devices attached to them. A print server can be any computer located on a network (or the Internet) that has a print device attached and runs some flavor of a Microsoft operating system, such as Windows 2003, 2000, NT, or 9*x*. (Even a user workstation can function as a print server — but we don't like this approach because it typically brings too much traffic to the user's workstation.) When a user submits a print job, the print server stores the job in a queue for the print device and then polls the print device to check for its availability. If the print device is available, the print server pulls the next job out of the queue and sends it to the print device.

Any network administrator or user with appropriate access rights can manage print servers from anywhere on the network. By default, in Windows 2003, all members of the Everyone group can *print* to a device, but only those members specifically given rights can *manage* the device.

✔ **Print queues:** A print queue is a location on the hard disk where spooled files wait in line for their turn to be printed. Each print device has at least one corresponding print queue (though additional queues are possible). As users submit print jobs, the jobs go into the queue to wait to be printed. You define a queue for a print device when you add the printer to the Printers and Faxes folder and assign it a name. Print jobs enter the queues on a first-come, first-serve basis.

Only someone with the appropriate access rights to manage queues (Administrators, Print Operators, and Server Operators) can alter the print order in a print queue. You can assign users on your network the permission to manage the print queues for you. Windows 2003 has a built-in user group called Print Operators, and you can add users to this group to give them the proper access rights for the task by choosing Start➪Administrative Tools➪Active Directory Users and Computers, selecting a domain, and opening the Builtin folder.

Giving some users print-queue management rights rather than other users could be seen as playing politics if you don't exercise great caution in making the assignments. Some folks may accuse others of playing favorites when print jobs are rearranged in the queue. We've seen this happen a lot. If you choose people who are neutral, your life will be easier!

✔ **Print devices:** Print devices are physical devices or physical printers, such as HP laser printers. You can walk up to them and touch them. Print devices can be attached locally to a workstation or server or directly to the network. In the real (non-Microsoft) world, this is what we normal people call a printer!

Physical print devices

We call print devices *physical print devices* because you can walk up to these devices and touch them. Print devices come in different categories, including laser, plotter, ink jet, and bubble jet. You can attach a physical print device locally to a workstation, server, or print server or directly to the network (as shown in Figure 13-1).

Figure 13-1:
A network
showing
different
ways to
connect
print
devices on a
network.

A print server is just a network-attached workstation that services print jobs — so, technically, we could lump workstations and print servers in the same category. We list them separately in this case because we want to distinguish between a workstation where a user does work and a dedicated print server workstation located on the network.

Logical assignments

A *logical printer assignment* isn't a print device — it exists intangibly, in the form of a Windows 2003 definition. It's sort of like a name that Windows 2003 uses to identify a physical print device (or a group of physical print devices, as you see later in this section). Each time you define a print device and its properties in Windows 2003, the operating system assigns a logical printer definition to the physical print device so that it knows to which physical print device you want to send your jobs.

When you first install a print device, a one-to-one correlation exists between the physical print device and the logical definition. You can expand the use of logical printer assignments, however, so that one logical printer assignment serves as the definition for several physical print devices. This use is known as *print device pooling,* and you set it up through print device properties by adding ports to the print device's definition.

You don't need to be too concerned about defining logical printers unless you intend to pool print devices. This happens whenever you attach a print device to the server (as explained later in the "Attaching print devices to servers" section). Just understand that Windows 2003 correlates a logical printer definition to one or more physical print devices attached to your network.

For example, you're likely to have several print devices connected to your network, and all or many of them may be the same type, such as HPLJ1200. If you don't define a logical printer definition for Windows 2003, how does it know to which HPLJ1200 print device to send your jobs? You could be running all around the building looking for your expense report! Defining a logical printer definition keeps order in your world. You could name one logical printer *2FLWest,* and you would know that your report is sent to the HPLJ1200 on the second floor of the west wing of your building.

Another bit of magic that logical assignments can help you with is balancing print jobs. Suppose that you have three physical laser print devices (A, B, and C) located on your network in close proximity. If a user chooses to send a print job to printer A, which is printing a large print job, a lot of time and resources are wasted if printers B and C are sitting idle.

You can help your users in this regard by setting up one logical printer definition and assigning it several different physical print devices to which to print. Therefore, your users print to the one logical assignment, which then figures out which physical print device is available. This takes the decision making and worrying from the user and transfers it to the operating system. The only caveat here is avoiding too much physical distance between print devices. Try to make sure that all physical print devices in the logical printer definition are in the same general area so your users don't have to run around the building looking for their printouts.

When setting up logical assignments to service more than one physical print device, the physical print devices must be identical. The only changes you can make are to properties, such as the bin number and paper size of each print device.

Conversely, you can assign several printer assignments to service one physical print device. You want to do this if users are printing special items, such as envelopes. Define one printer assignment to print to the envelope bin on the physical print device and define another printer assignment to print letter-size paper on the same print device.

If you name the logical assignments something descriptive, users will know where the print device is and what type of function it performs. For example, naming two logical assignments *2FLWestEnv* and *2FLWest* tells the user that

2FLWestEnv is on the second floor of the west wing and it prints envelopes, whereas the other is a normal print device on the second floor of the west wing. Both printer assignments service the same physical print device, but they may print to different bins on the print device, or one may pause the print device between pages, and so on. Here, you don't need to do anything other than define separate print devices that all print to the same port.

Installing on the Server's Side

Before you set up clients to print on your network, first make sure to go to the server and install all the print device definitions, drivers, and hardware, and then go to the client side. Doing so ensures that when you finally get to the user's workstation, you can submit a test print job right away because all the components are in place. If you start at the user's side first, you have to go back later to test.

Meet the Printers and Faxes folder

Nearly everything you want to do with print devices can be found on the server in the Control Panel's Printers and Faxes folder. (This information is more quickly available by choosing Start➪Printers and Faxes.) We say *nearly* everything because the print device drivers are stored outside the print devices folder. (Most of the drivers are found on the Windows Server 2003 CD-ROM.)

When you install Windows Server 2003 for the first time, the Printers and Faxes folder contains only an Add Printer icon, which is designed to help you install a physical print device (or logical printer definition). Each time you install a new print device by clicking the Add Printer icon (we cover installation later in this chapter), Windows 2003 assigns it a separate folder in the Printers and Faxes folder, as shown in Figure 13-2.

When you click the Add Printer icon, the Add Printer Wizard appears, bringing with it a set of default policies that it uses to guide you through the process of adding each new print device to the Printers and Faxes folder.

After you've installed the print devices you want, you can still make changes to print devices by visiting the Printers and Faxes folder. Right-click the print device you added and choose Properties from the pull-down list that appears. A window with numerous tabs appears. You make all the changes to the particular print device in this Properties dialog box, so take some time to familiarize yourself with the available settings.

Figure 13-2:
The Printers
and Faxes
folder
showing an
installed
print device
and the Add
Printer icon.

Add a networked printer

In an ideal world, your network and users would allow you to set up one type
of print device in one manner (such as all laser print devices of the same
make and model with network interface cards). In the real world, however,
things don't pan out like that. Therefore, the engineers at Microsoft designed
Windows Server 2003 to provide you with four ways to attach print devices
to your network:

- Windows Server 2003
- Print server
- Networked (as shown in Figure 13-1)
- Workstation

In the following sections, we show you the four approaches to installing print
devices on your network. Three of the four installations are similar; they're
just performed on different machines. For example, the steps for installing
print devices attached to networks and for installing print devices attached to
workstations are very similar. Both machines have print devices connected to
their local ports, and they both share print devices on the network.

Attaching print devices to servers

You may find a need to attach a print device directly to your server. We don't
recommend that you use this method unless your organization can't afford to
spare a machine for you to use as a dedicated print server. Why? Because any
time you attach a device to a file server, you run the risk that it may get hosed
and crash the server — and we've seen this happen often.

To attach a print device to a Windows Server 2003, you need a print device, a Windows Server 2003 computer, a cable, the Windows Server 2003 installation CD (if you didn't copy it to your server's hard disk), and any print device drivers you want automatically downloaded to the clients.

Connect the print device directly to one of the ports on the server (for example, LPT1) and install the print device on this machine in its Printers and Faxes folder by choosing Start➪Printers and Faxes. Then, follow these steps:

1. **Double-click the Add Printer icon, which invokes the Add Printer Setup Wizard. Click Next.**

2. **Choose Local Printer, then choose Automatically Detect My Printer, and then click Next.**

   The New Printer Detection window of the wizard appears and searches for and installs attached Plug-and-Play print devices. If the print device is not Plug and Play, you must follow the rest of the steps in this section.

3. **In the Use the Following Port pull-down list, select the port to which you attached this print device (such as LPT1). Click Next.**

   A window appears for choosing the manufacturer and model of the print device.

4. **In the Manufacturer area, highlight the print device manufacturer. In the Printers area, highlight the model of the print device. Click Next.**

   If you don't see your print device listed here, it means you have to provide the Add Printer Wizard with the driver. Click the Have Disk button and point the wizard to the location and path where the driver resides.

5. **On the Name Your Printer screen of the wizard, Setup suggests a name for this printer. Accept this name or type a new name for this printer. Click Next.**

6. **On the Printer Sharing screen of the wizard, type a share name for this printer if you want to share it. If you don't want to share it, choose the Do Not Share This Printer option. Click Next.**

   The share name is the name that your users will see when they print to this printer, so make it meaningful (for example, 2ndFLWestEnv).

7. **On the Location and Comment screen of the wizard, type a location and description for this print device.**

   Your users can use this information when determining to which printer they want to print. The more information you give here, the less your head will hurt later!

8. **Choose whether you want to print a test page (always a great idea) and then decide whether you want to install drivers for the other client operating systems that will access the printer. Click Next.**

Setup copies files from the Windows 2003 installation CD to the Windows Server 2003 computer's hard disk. Also, if you chose to share the printer in Step 6, you need to have the operating system print drivers handy to install (see Step 9) so that Windows Server 2003 can automatically download the drivers to the client.

9. **If you chose to install additional drivers in Step 8, Setup begins copying drivers for this print device and, if need be, pauses to ask you for the location and path of the appropriate printer drivers. Type the path information and click OK.**

   You can go to the Printer's Properties under the Sharing tab to modify any drivers you've installed. See the section "Managing Windows 2003-Based Printers," later in this chapter, for further information.

10. **If you chose not to print a test page and not to install additional drivers, Setup presents you with a summary page of your choices. Click Finish if your choices were correct. Otherwise, use the Back and Next buttons to correct the information.**

If you're familiar with setting up printers on previous versions of Windows, you probably whipped through these steps because the print device setups are similar. At this point, you have set up the following:

- ✔ **One basic logical printer assignment that points to one physical print device on Windows Server 2003:** We say *basic* because you haven't customized any options, such as paper bins, dots per inch, and separator pages, for this print device yet. You probably weren't aware that as you defined this physical print device, you also assigned it a logical printer assignment. Remember that there's a one-to-one correlation between the two each time you install a physical device and define it unless you add more physical devices.

- ✔ **A print queue for this print device:** Windows 2003 does this for you when you define the print device. To view the queue, double-click the print device icon. You won't see anything in the queue just yet.

- ✔ **Shared access to this print device by everyone on the network:** When you define a share name on the network for a print device, Windows 2003, by default, assigns the Everyone group access to this print device. You have to change this default policy if you don't want "everyone" to have access to this print device. If you have Active Directory installed, the print device is published to the Directory.

You can have multiple logical printer assignments pointing to one physical print device. If you want to assign another logical printer assignment that services this physical print device, you repeat the previous steps but assign a new computer and share name. You can assign different properties to this physical print device for each logical printer definition.

Attaching print devices to print servers

In the preceding section, we show you how to hook up a print device to a Windows Server 2003 computer so that your Windows Server 2003 functions as a print server on your network in addition to its other duties. To help manage the load on the Windows Server 2003, you can offload this printing task to another computer on your network and have *it* function as your print server.

The print server is just another computer on your network with an attached print device that you set up to manage print spooling, print queues, and print jobs. We like this method because it frees up the Windows Server 2003 to perform other tasks. When your clients print to the print server, they bypass the Windows Server 2003.

You can install any Microsoft operating system that you like on the computer that will be your print server. We recommend at least Windows 9x, but we prefer a Windows NT, 2000, or XP workstation because you can download the print drivers to the client workstations from the print server automatically with no intervention on your part. This means that you don't have to install drivers manually on each of the client workstations.

After you've installed an operating system on your soon-to-be print server, repeat Steps 1 through 10 from the "Attaching print devices to servers" section if you're using a Windows NT, 2000, or XP Workstation as the operating system. If you're using Windows 9x, repeat the same steps but exclude the downloadable print device drivers from Steps 8 and 9. Instead, you have to go to each client and install the corresponding print device drivers.

Attaching networked print devices to print servers

Some print devices, such as HP laser print devices, are neat because after you plug a NIC into them, they're almost ready to be placed anywhere on your network where there's an electrical outlet and an available network connection. Almost, but not quite! You still need to make all the physical connections and assign an IP address to the printer. After you do that, perform the following steps to add the networked print device to the print server:

1. **Click Printers and Faxes.**

   The Printers and Faxes window appears.

2. **Double-click the Add Printer icon to invoke the Add Printer Wizard. Click Next.**

3. **On the Local or Network Printer screen, click Local Printer Attached to This Computer, and unmark the Automatically Detect and Install My Plug and Play Printer check box. Click Next.**

   The next screen of the Add Printer Wizard appears.

4. **On the Select the Printer Port screen, click Create a New Port. In the Type of Port drop-down list, select Standard TCP/IP Port. Click Next.**

   The Welcome to the Add Standard TCP/IP Printer Port Wizard screen appears.

5. **Click Next.**

   The Add Port screen appears.

6. **On the Add Port screen, enter the IP address of the networked print device and give the port a name. The wizard will fill in a name for you, but you can change it if you like. Click Next.**

   If your print device is properly configured and set up, and you've entered the proper information in the wizard, the wizard locates your device on the network and displays information for it.

7. **Click the Finish button to complete.**

When installing a printer on a Windows Server 2003 with Active Directory installed, the Add Printer Wizard shares the print device and publishes it in the Directory — unless you change the policy rules. For more information on Active Directory, please read Chapter 11.

Attaching print devices to a workstation

Some users may have print devices on their desks that you want to make available to other users on the network. Attaching a print device to a work-station is the least desirable method because it involves users going to another user's workstation to pick up their print jobs. This can cause a dis-ruption in workflow to the user who's unfortunate enough to have the print device on his or her desk. However, in smaller organizations where budgets are tight, this method is used.

You need to go to the user's workstation desktop and share that print device on the network. You can restrict access to that share so that the entire organi-zation isn't allowed to print there. Where do you find all this? In the Printers and Faxes folder on the user's desktop, of course! Right-click the Add Printer icon if no print device is installed, choose the print device to be a local print device connected to LPT1, and assign it a name. If a print device is already defined, right-click the print device icon and select Properties to give this print device a share name. After you share the print device on the network, other users can see it.

This method causes the user's workstation to manage the printing process. You can define this workstation-attached print device so that Windows 2003 Server will manage the print process instead. Here's how:

1. **Go to the user's computer desktop and define a share for this print device, but limit access to the username of "JoePrinter."**

   See the following section, "Sharing Printer Access," to find out how to define a share.

2. **Mosey back over to the Windows Server 2003.**

3. **Add a user named "JoePrinter" in Active Directory Users and Computers (Start⇨Administrative Tools⇨Active Directory Users and Computers.)**

4. **In the Printers and Faxes folder, double-click Add Printer.**

5. **Follow the same steps as in the "Attaching print devices to servers" section earlier in this chapter, except for the following changes:**

   • Click the Add Printer icon and choose the networked print device instead of the locally attached print device (My Computer).

   • Click the Type the Printer Name or Click Next to Browse for the Printer option. Either type the share name or use the Browse option to select and choose the share name you gave the print device on the client's desktop.

   • Give this print device a new share name that the rest of the users on the network will see.

Again, we don't recommend that you use this method unless your organization is tight on money. It can cause aggravation for the user who has to share the print device with other people on the network and can disrupt that user's work environment.

Sharing Printer Access

After you've installed a printer on your network (as we explain in the previous section), the next step is to create a share on the network for that print device. (See Chapter 16 for more details on Windows 2003 network shares.)

Until you share a print device, your users can't see it on the network. To share a print device, do the following:

1. **Open the Printers and Faxes folder (Start⇨Printers and Faxes).**

2. **Right-click the print device you want to share and choose Sharing.**

3. **On the Sharing tab, choose the Share This Printer option and type a descriptive share name (for example, 2ndFlWest).**

4. **If you want this printer listed in Active Directory, choose the List in the Directory box.**

5. **Click OK and you're finished!**

When you share a printer, it's available to everyone on the network by default. You must specifically restrict groups or users from accessing the printer if that's what you want.

If you have MS-DOS-based clients on your network, make sure that your share names for print devices are only eight characters long.

Bringing Printers and Clients Together

The final step in setting up networked printing involves setting up the print devices on the client side. Fortunately, not much is required in this process. Everything you need is on the Windows Server 2003, the print server, or in the user's Printers and Faxes folder on his or her desktop, depending on which client operating system is used.

If the client operating system is a Windows XP, 2000, or NT system, you need to only add the print device in the Printers and Faxes folder (Add Printer) and choose Networked Print Device. The reason is that the print device is attached to another computer somewhere on the network; it's not local to this workstation. For the port, use the Browse option and find the share name of the print device to which you want to print. That's it!

If your clients have Windows 9x and are printing to a Windows Server 2003 (and you've installed the various client operating system drivers at the server), you simply add the print device in the Printers and Faxes folder (Add Printer) and select it as a networked print device. When you select the port as the share name of the networked print device, Windows Server 2003 automatically downloads the drivers.

Managing Windows 2003-Based Printers

You can view and perform some management of your print servers, queues, and print devices from anywhere on the network, including your Windows Server 2003. From one location, you can view what's going on with all the print devices on your network. The only thing you can't do remotely is install something on the print device itself, such as memory or cables. But you knew that already!

The following list includes some issues to keep in mind as you manage print devices:

- ✔ **Disk space on server:** If you set up spooling on your network, you need to keep a close eye on the hard disk space of the print servers. The spooling process involves sending files from the print user to the print server. Remember that the print server can also be your Windows Server 2003. In either case, if your network has a high volume of print activity, it's possible to fill up a hard disk quickly with the spooling process.

  After files are spooled to the print server, they remain on the hard disk in the queue until an available print device is ready. If there's a problem with the print device, jobs can back up quickly. Remember that queues take up space on the hard disk, so if the queues back up, more and more space is needed. Be careful that you don't run low on disk space!

- ✔ **Memory in the print device:** When your users print graphics on the network, memory becomes an issue on the print devices. Large graphics files require more memory to print. You can find out how much memory is in a print device by performing a self-test on the print device. Some organizations don't have a large budget for adding extra memory to all their networked print devices, so they select one or more in strategic locations and then define logical print device setups that point to the loaded print devices.

- ✔ **Configuring the Printer's Properties:** You can access the Printer's Properties menu by right-clicking a print device's icon in the Printers and Faxes folder. (Figure 13-3 shows the various settings you can alter for any print device on your network.) We go through each of the tabs here to help you understand which print device properties you can change:

  - • **General:** Here's where you add information about the print device, such as comments, location, and whether to use a banner page. We recommend that you add some general comments about the print device and its location. In medium- to large-sized operations, adding a separator page so that print jobs are more easily distinguished from each another is a good idea. The current print driver information is also found here. Change this only if you're going to install a new driver.

  - • **Sharing:** If you want users on the network to see this print device, you define the share name here (remember to make it meaningful). You can also tell Windows 2003 to allow this device to show up in the Directory. This is also where you tell Windows 2003 which client operating systems you have on your network and to which systems you want print drivers automatically downloaded.

  - • **Ports:** This is where you tell the system to which port your print device is attached. If it's a network-attached print device, you define it here using the Media Access Control (MAC) address; if it's a Transmission Control Protocol/Internet Protocol (TCP/IP) print device, you define it here using the IP address.

- **Advanced:** You may opt to have print jobs run at night for this print device. This is where you can schedule the print device's availability, priority, and spooling options.

- **Security:** This is where you set up auditing of your print devices, which enables you to gather information should something go wrong with a device. You may want to use the Security tab for charge-back purposes on a departmental basis (where you audit the usage and charge users or departments for that use) or to limit this print device's availability. You can also define who is allowed to manage this print device.

- **Device Settings:** This is where you define specific properties of the print device, such as paper size, dots per inch, and paper bin.

Figure 13-3:
Print device
Properties
tabs in the
Printers
folder.

Preventing Printer Problems

Printing problems on a network can wreak havoc. Here are a few pointers to help you head off this type of trouble. If you do experience problems, See Chapter 22 for some troubleshooting help.

✔ **Purchase HCL-compatible devices:** Only purchase network print devices listed in the Hardware Compatibility List (HCL). Otherwise, you may spend hours trying to get a print device to work on the network — only to find that the device is not compatible. And always remember to check Microsoft's site for the latest version of the HCL.

✔ **Get the latest print device drivers:** Make sure that you obtain the latest print device driver associated with each print device on your network. Newer drivers correct bugs found in older drivers. If you use an older driver, you sometimes end up troubleshooting a known bug that has already been corrected in the newer driver.

✔ **Purchase a name brand:** We hope that your organization can afford to purchase name-brand print devices, such as Hewlett-Packard and Epson, for your network. We find that the biggest printing problems on networks stem from cheaper models. Even if you're able to hook these cheaper print devices up, sometimes it takes so long to get all the pieces working that investing in more popular brand-name print devices would have been more cost effective.

✔ **Purchase from one manufacturer:** We like to stick with one type (brand name) of print device where possible. Notice we said *brand* and not *model.* We realize that some organizations need to print in both black and white and color. If you can purchase all your print devices from one manufacturer (for example, Hewlett-Packard), your life and your users' lives will be easier. If you have all Hewlett-Packard laser print devices on your network, don't buy another manufacturer's laser print device just because it's on sale that day at your local computer superstore. You can save time by working with one vendor and its equipment and drivers instead of having to hunt all over the Internet for various manufacturers' Web sites. Allow your users to become familiar with the one brand, and they won't have to learn how to use new equipment all the time.

✔ **Buy enough memory:** The influx in graphics software has placed a strain on memory usage in print devices to produce the desired output. Don't wait until print jobs start fouling up before adding more memory. If your budget is too low to do this up front, find a local vendor that stocks memory for your computer and keep their telephone number handy.

Faxing the Windows 2003 Way

Windows 2003, like Windows XP, includes native support for faxing. This means you can now send and receive faxes using your computer without third-party software. The capabilities of Windows 2003 faxing are controlled through (you guessed it) the Printers and Faxes folder.

Faxing is not enabled by default. First, you must have a fax modem already installed and properly configured (that means the driver is installed and things are working properly). Then to enable faxing, open the Printers and Faxes folder from the Start menu or Control Panel, and choose File⇨Set Up Faxing. A wizard launches and installs the necessary components for faxing. After a few moments, you're returned to the Printers and Faxes folder where a new Fax icon appears.

The Properties command for the fax icon reveals a multitabbed dialog box that looks a lot like a printer dialog box. In this dialog box, you can do the following:

- ✔ Define the fax device name and location
- ✔ Share the fax device with the network
- ✔ Define access and control security
- ✔ Set document tracking

In fact, faxing is like printing, but instead of sending the document's print job to a physical print device where the results are on paper, the print job is digitized and sent over the phone line to a receiving fax device (which can be a traditional fax machine or a fax-enabled computer). Other than needing to provide a phone number and the occasional cover sheet, faxing a document is just like printing a document. To send a fax, just select the fax device from the list of printers in the dialog box that appears when you choose File⇨Print.

The first time you attempt to send a fax, the Fax Configuration Wizard is launched. This wizard is used to define information about your fax system, such as the phone number, area code, and sender information.

Double-click the Fax icon to open the Fax Console, which is used to track and manage incoming and outgoing faxes, in much the same way as you might manage e-mail in Outlook. If you want to change your sender information, choose Tools⇨Configure Fax from the Fax Console. To receive faxes, you have to enable incoming faxes and set the answer after rings control.

Keep in mind that you can have only one answering service per modem device. So, if you need a telecommuter to call in to connect to your system, don't set up that modem to wait for faxes. The device that is waiting for incoming faxes can still be used to send faxes or even for normal dial-out connections. If you find that you need more help with the fax capabilities of Windows 2003, check out the help file and the Windows Server 2003 Resource Kit.

Chapter 14

IP Addressing: Zero to Insane in Two Seconds Flat

*T*he *Transmission Control Protocol/Internet Protocol* (TCP/IP) drives the Internet and makes it accessible around the world. However, TCP/IP is a lot more than just a collection of protocols: Many elements in TCP/IP marry protocols to related services to provide more complete capabilities. Important examples include dynamic address allocation and management, known as the Dynamic Host Configuration Protocol (DHCP), plus domain name to address resolution services, known as Domain Name Service (DNS). In this chapter, you find out about TCP/IP names, addresses, and related standard services, as well as some other related services hosted by Windows Server 2003.

Resolving a Name: TCP/IP and NetBIOS

Whenever you issue a command in Windows Server 2003, you're expected to use the proper syntax. Otherwise, your efforts may not produce the desired results. For example, when you issue a NET USE command from a command prompt, you must enter the server name and a share name, as well as the drive to which you want to map. Therefore, a simple command such as

```
NET USE G: \\LANWRIGHTS\APPS
```

associates the drive letter G with a share named APPS on the LANWRIGHTS server. If you use the TCP/IP protocol to convey the data involved, the protocol doesn't know how to interpret the name LANWRIGHTS as the server. Instead, it understands Internet Protocol (IP) addresses, such as 172.16.1.7.

If you use TCP/IP on your network, you need some way to convert IP addresses into names and vice versa. Just as the United Nations requires translators so that everyone can communicate, so too does Windows 2003, which is why understanding naming conventions and name-to-address resolution are such an important part of working with TCP/IP on Windows 2003.

NetBIOS names

If you're like most folks, you freeze like a deer in the headlights when you hear the word *NetBIOS*. Don't worry. Only a small number of people really understand NetBIOS in detail, and figuring out what you need to know is easy.

A NetBIOS name is often called a *computer name*. When you install Windows Server 2003 on a network, each computer that runs Windows 2003 requires a unique computer name. This allows all NetBIOS-based utilities to identify each machine by its name. When you enter a command that includes a computer name, Windows 2003 knows which computer you're talking about.

If you try to give two devices the same name, you run into trouble — like trying to use the same Social Security number for two people. Each time a computer joins the network, it registers its name with a browser service that keeps track of such things. When the second computer with the same name tries to register, it's rejected because that name is already taken. In fact, that machine will be unable to join the network until its name is changed to something unique.

When creating NetBIOS names, you need to work within their limitations, which are as follows:

- ✔ NetBIOS names must be between 1 and 15 characters long. (If you have DOS or Windows 3.*x* machines on your network, they can't recognize NetBIOS names with more than 8 characters.)

- ✔ NetBIOS names may not contain any of the characters shown in the following list:

    "   double quotation mark

    /   right slash

    \   left slash

[	left square bracket
]	right square bracket
:	colon
;	semicolon
		vertical slash
=	equal sign
+	plus sign
*	asterisk
?	question mark
<	left angle bracket
>	right angle bracket

In addition, dollar signs are not recommended because they have a special meaning. (A NetBIOS name that ends in $ does not appear in a browse list.)

✔ Don't use lengthy names or put spaces in names. Windows 2003 doesn't care if you use longer names or include embedded spaces, but other networking clients or systems may not be able to handle such uses.

✔ Choose names that make sense to users and are short and to the point. Don't name machines after their users or locations, especially if users come and go regularly or if machines move around a lot. When it comes to servers, name them to indicate their organizational role or affiliation (for example, Sales, Accounting, or Engineering).

What's in a NetBIOS name, you ask? A NetBIOS name should have a short, clear indication of what's being named so users can recognize what they see. At best, this type of naming convention will make sense without requiring further explanation. At the very least, you can do what we do and put a sticker with the machine's name on each monitor or computer case for identification. You can view a list of your network's NetBIOS names by expanding the My Network Places section of Windows Explorer. See Figure 14-1 for a sample list of NetBIOS names taken from our network (such as W2kpro-1 and Wxppro-2).

TCP/IP names and addresses

TCP/IP uses a different scheme for names than NetBIOS does. TCP/IP uses 32-bit numbers to construct IP addresses (for example, 172.16.1.11). Each host or node on a TCP/IP network must have a unique IP address.

IP addresses are not meaningful to most humans and are difficult to remember. Therefore, it's helpful to have some way to convert IP addresses to meaningful names. On a Windows Server 2003 network, you use computer names (also known as NetBIOS names). The Internet community uses a different naming convention called domain names. Translation methods, such as Windows Internet Name Service (WINS) and Domain Name Service (DNS) maintain databases for converting an IP address to a computer name (WINS) or a domain name (DNS).

If you've ever used a Web browser on the Internet, you know that you can type a Uniform Resource Locator (URL), such as `www.lanw.com/`, or an IP address, such as `206.224.65.194/`, to obtain access to a Web page. You can do so because the Internet uses DNS to resolve IP addresses to domain names and vice versa. If you type the IP address, the Web browser jumps straight to the address; if you type a domain name, your request goes through a DNS server that resolves the name to an IP address, and then the browser jumps to the address.

In the IP world, the naming scheme you can use is limited if you plan to connect your network directly to the Internet. VeriSign (`www.verisign.com`) is one of many domain name registrars in charge of approving and maintaining the database of "legal" Internet top-level domain names. You can request any domain name you want, but if someone else is using it or has a legitimate claim to a trade or brand name, you won't be able to use it. For example, you probably won't be able to use `mcdonalds.com` or `cocacola.com` as domain names. Or if someone else has already registered `xyzcorp.com`, you wouldn't be able to use that name, even if your company is named XYZ Corporation.

The format for a typical IP name is *host.domainname.suffix*. The domain name is something you can't guarantee, but typically represents your organization. The suffix, called a *top-level domain,* sometimes identifies the country

of origin (for example, .ca is Canada and .de is Germany) or the type of organization (.gov is government, .edu is education, .com is a commercial business, .org is a nonprofit organization, and so forth).

Some domain names are more complex; they can take a form such as
host.subdomain.domainname.suffix, as in `jello.eng.sun.com`, where
the host name is `jello`, the subdomain is `eng` (for engineering), and the
domain name is `sun` (the domain name for Sun Microsystems, Inc.), which is
a commercial (.com) entity. The only parts of the name under control of the
various Internet domain name registrars (such as VeriSign and other companies and organizations identified at `www.norid.no/domenenavnbaser/`
`domreg.html`) are the domain name and the suffix — every domain name
must be unique in its entirety to be properly recognized.

Names that include the host part, the domain name, and the suffix (plus any
other subdomain information that may apply) are called *Fully Qualified
Domain Names* (FQDNs). To be valid, any FQDN must have a corresponding
entry in some DNS server's database that allows it to be translated into a
unique numeric IP address. For example, your authors' Web server is named
`www.lanw.com`, which resolves into an IP address of 206.224.65.194.

As long as you're completely isolated from the Internet and intend to stay
that way, you can assign any names and IP addresses you like on your network. If you ever connect your network to the Internet, however, you'll have
to go back and change everything! If your network will be — or simply *might
ever be* — connected to the Internet, you have one of two options for assigning addresses:

✔ **You can obtain and install valid public IP addresses and domain
names now.**

Your Internet Service Provider (ISP) can do this for you. When you obtain
a range of IP addresses for your network — remember, each computer
needs its own unique address, and some computers or devices need multiple addresses (one for each interface) — make sure you get enough to
leave some room for growth.

✔ **You can (and should) obtain a valid domain name from VeriSign or
another domain name registrar, but you can use any of a range of
reserved IP addresses, called private IP addresses, to number your
networks.**

These addresses may not be used directly on the Internet; they've been
set aside for private use. When used in concert with a type of software
called Network Address Translation (or NAT for short), this approach
requires you to obtain only a small number of public IP addresses but
still allows Internet access for every computer on your network. This
topic is discussed in more detail later in this chapter in the section
"Address translation: The new magic."

To find out more about the process of obtaining a domain name, visit VeriSign's Web site at `www.verisign.com`. The form for researching domain names (determining whether a FQDN is already in use) and registering domain names (applying for a new FQDN) is on the main page. You'll find details on name registration services as well as on directory and database services that support the Internet's distributed collection of DNS servers.

Calling Every Node

A unique numeric identification tag, called an *IP address,* is assigned to each interface on a TCP/IP network. Every IP address in a TCP/IP network must be unique. Each device on a TCP/IP network is known as a *host.* Each host has at least one network interface with an assigned IP address. However, a host can have multiple network interface cards (NICs), and even multiple IP addresses assigned to each NIC.

To network ID or host ID, that is the question

An IP address consists of two components: a network ID and a host ID. The *network ID* identifies the network segment to which the host belongs. The *host ID* identifies an individual host on some specific network segment. A host can communicate directly only with other hosts on the same network segment. A *network segment* is a logical division of a network into unique numeric network IDs called *subnets.* A host must use a router to communicate with hosts on other subnets.

A *router* moves packets from one subnet to another. In addition, a router reads the network ID for a packet's destination address and determines whether that packet should remain on the current subnet or be routed to a different subnet. When a router delivers a packet to the correct subnet, the router then uses the host ID portion of the destination address to deliver the packet to its final destination.

A typical IP address looks like

```
207.46.249.222
```

(This matches the domain name www.microsoft.com.) This numeric IP address format is known as *dotted-decimal notation*. However, computers "see" IP addresses as binary numbers. This same IP address in binary form is

```
11001111 00101110 11111001 11011110
```

and is written in collections of eight bits called *octets*. Each octet is converted to a decimal number and then separated by periods to form the dotted-decimal notation format shown at the beginning of this paragraph.

The dotted-decimal version of IP addresses is more human-friendly than the binary version. As you may already know, domain names and NetBIOS names are even more friendly because they use symbolic names that make sense to humans.

An IP address requires 32 binary digits and defines a 32-bit address space that supports nearly 4.3 billion unique addresses. Although this seems like a lot of addresses, the number of available IP addresses is quickly dwindling. Consequently, several plans exist to expand or change the IP addressing scheme to make many more addresses available. For more information on such plans, search for IPng Transition in your favorite search engine.

IP designers carved the entire galaxy of IP addresses into classes to meet different addressing needs. Today, there are five IP address classes labeled by the letters *A* through *E*. Classes A, B, and C are assigned to organizations to allow their networks to connect to the Internet, and Classes D and E are reserved for special uses.

The first three classes of addresses differ by how their network IDs are defined:

  ✔ Class A addresses use the first octet for the network ID.

  ✔ Class B addresses use the first two octets.

  ✔ Class C addresses use the first three octets.

Class A addresses support a relatively small number of networks, each with a huge number of possible hosts. Class C addresses support a large number of networks, each with a relatively small number of hosts, as shown in Table 14-1 (Class B falls in the middle). Therefore, branches of the military, government agencies, and large corporations are likely to need Class A addresses; medium-sized organizations and companies need Class B addresses; and small companies and organizations need Class C addresses.

Table 14-1	Address Classes and Corresponding Network and Host IDs			
Class	*High-Order Bits*	*First Octet Range*	*# Networks*	*# Hosts*
Class A	0xxxxxxx	1–126.x.y.z	126	16,777,214
Class B	10xxxxxx	128–191.x.y.z	16,384	65,534
Class C	110xxxxx	192–223.x.y.z	2,097,152	254

When it comes to recognizing address Classes A through C, the network ID for Class A addresses always starts its first octet with a 0. Each Class B network ID always starts with 10, and Class C network IDs always start with 110. Consequently, you can determine address classes by examining an address, either in binary or decimal form. (See Tables 14-1 and 14-2.)

Table 14-2	Division of IP Address Component Octets According to Class		
Class	*IP Address*	*Network ID*	*Host ID*
A	10.1.1.10	10	1.1.10
B	172.16.1.10	172.16	1.10
C	192.168.1.10	192.168.1	10

Network ID 127 is missing from Table 14-1 because that ID is a loopback address. *Loopback addresses* are used when testing IP transmission — they transmit to themselves.

Subnetting: Quiet time for IP addresses

Subnets represent divisions of a single TCP/IP network address into logical subsets. The motivation for subnetting is twofold. First, subnetting reduces the amount of overall traffic on any network segment by collecting systems that communicate often into groups. Second, subnetting makes it easier for networks to grow and expand, and it adds an extra layer of security controls. Subnets work by "stealing" bits from the host part of an IP address and using those bits to divide a single IP network address into two or more subnets.

Routers move packets among subnets and networks

Only *routers* can transfer packets from one subnet to another, or from one network ID to another, in the TCP/IP world. Routers are specialized, high-end, high-speed devices from companies such as Cisco Systems or Bay Networks. However, any computer with two or more NICs installed (where each NIC resides on a different subnet) can be a router provided that the computer can forward packets from one NIC to another (and thus, from one subnet to another). Right out of the box, in fact, Windows Server 2003 includes the software and built-in capabilities to function as a router. Computer nerds like to call such machines *multi-homed computers* because the machines are "at home" on two or more subnets.

Network administrators typically use subnet masks to divide IP address blocks into smaller subnetworks. A *subnet mask* is a special bit pattern that takes over part of the host ID portion of an IP address, and permits a larger network to be subdivided into two or more subnetworks, each with its own unique network address. The base subnet masks for Class A, B, and C networks are 255.0.0.0, 255.255.0.0, and 255.255.255.0, respectively. You can create additional subset masks by adding extra bits set to 1 in the space occupied by the 0 that appears next to the rightmost 255 in any such number. This transformation is illustrated in Table 14-3, which shows some typical values for usable subnet masks.

Table 14-3	Subnet Masks and Results		
Binary Mask	*Decimal Equivalent*	*Number of New Subnets*	*Number of Hosts*
00000000	A: 255.0.0.0 B: 255.255.0.0 C: 255.255.255.0	A: 16,777,214 B: 65,534 C: 254	1
10000000	A: 255.128.0.0 B: 255.255.128.0 C: 255.255.255.128	A: Not valid B: Not valid C: Not valid	Not valid
11000000	A: 255.192.0.0 B: 255.255.192.0 C: 255.255.255.192	A: 4,194,302 B: 16,382 C: 62	2

(continued)

Table 14-3 *(continued)*

Binary Mask	Decimal Equivalent	Number of New Subnets	Number of Hosts
11100000	A: 255.224.0.0 B: 255.255.224.0 C: 255.255.255.224	A: 2,097,150 B: 8,190 C: 30	6
11110000	A: 255.240.0.0 B: 255.255.240.0 C: 255.255.255.240	A: 1,048,574 B: 4,094 C: 14	14
11111000	A: 255.248.0.0 B: 255.255.248.0 C: 255.255.255.248	A: 524,286 B: 2,046 C: 6	30
11111100	A: 255.252.0.0 B: 255.255.252.0 C: 255.255.255.252	A: 262,142 B: 1,022 C: 2	62
11111110	A: 255.254.0.0 B: 255.255.254.0 C: 255.255.255.254	A: 131,070 B: 510 C: Not valid	126

Because routers are required to communicate across IP subnets, some router's IP address on each subnet must be known to every client on that subnet. This address is called the *default gateway* because it's where all out-of-subnet transmissions are directed by default. (It's the gateway to the world outside each local subnet, in other words.) If no default gateway is defined, clients can't communicate outside their subnet.

Hanging your shingle: Obtaining Internet IP addresses

Deploying your own network or using a stand-alone system with Network Address Translation (NAT) to connect to the Internet requires that you obtain one or more valid IP addresses. For some uses, you may simply contract with an ISP to use a dial-up connection. Each time you connect, you're assigned an IP address automatically from a pool of available addresses. After you disconnect from the ISP, that IP address is returned to the pool for reuse. This works equally well for stand-alone machines and for the servers that might dial into an ISP to provide an on-demand connection for users who have private IP addresses but can attach to the Internet using NAT software.

One way to attach an entire network to the Internet is to lease a block, or subnet, of IP addresses from an ISP. However, leasing IP addresses can be expensive and can limit your growth. Also, many ISPs can no longer lease large blocks of IP addresses, so you may have to limit Internet access to specific machines or subnets.

For more information about taking this approach, you need to contact your ISP to find out what it can offer by way of available addresses and contiguous subnets. For some uses, public IP addresses are required because security needs dictate a true end-to-end connection between clients and servers across the Internet. In plain English, a true *end-to-end connection* means that the IP address that a client advertises to the Internet is the same one it uses in reality. In the section "Address translation: The new magic," you discover an alternate approach in which the IP address advertised to the Internet is different than the private IP address that a client uses on its home subnet.

For some applications, particularly where secure IP-based protocols such as IP Secure (IPSec) or particular Secure Sockets Layer (SSL) implementations are required, network address translation techniques may not work! Make sure you understand your application requirements in detail before you decide whether to lease public IP addresses or use private IP addresses with network address translation.

Address translation: The new magic

If you don't want to pay to lease a range of IP addresses and your application requirements allow you to use private IP addresses, you can employ the IP addresses reserved for private use in RFC 1918 on your networks. When used with network address translation software to connect to an ISP, a single public IP address (or one for each Internet connection) is all you need to service an entire network.

RFC 1918 (which can be found at `www.faqs.org/rfcs/rfc1918.html`) defines special IP addresses for use on private intranets. These addresses, which appear in Table 14-4, will not be routed on the Internet by design. This approach provides improved security for your network as a fringe benefit, because it means that any impostor who wants to break into your network cannot easily masquerade as a local workstation. (Doing so would require routing a private IP address packet across the Internet.) Because all of these addresses are up for grabs, you can use the address class that makes sense for your organization (and for Class B and Class C addresses, you can use as many as you need within the legal range of such addresses).

Table 14-4	Private IP Address Ranges from RFC 1918	
Class	*Address Range*	*# Networks*
A	10.0.0.0–10.255.255.255	1
B	172.16.0.0–172.31.255.255	16
C	192.168.0.0–192.168.255.255	254

Using address translation software to offer Internet access reduces your costs and allows nearly unlimited growth. If you think private IP addresses combined with NAT software makes sense for your situation, consult with your ISP for specific details and recommendations on how to use this technology on your network.

You've probably seen the terms *firewall* and *proxy* thrown about when reading about Internet access. Firewalls and proxy servers are network tools that are little more than special-purpose routers. A firewall may be used to filter traffic — both inbound and outbound.

Firewall filters can be based on a source or destination address, on a specific protocol, or port address, or even on patterns that appear in the contents of a data packet. A *proxy server* is an enhanced firewall, and its primary purpose is to manage communications between an in-house network and external networks such as the Internet. Proxies hide the identity of internal clients and can keep local copies of resources that are accessed frequently (this is called *caching,* and it improves response time for users).

You can check out several great online resources for firewalls, but online information on proxies is limited to product documentation. In addition to consulting the Windows Server 2003 Resource Kit and TechNet (www.microsoft.com/technet/default.asp), here are several online resources you may want to check to discover more about these technologies:

- ✔ Great Circle Associates: www.greatcircle.com/
- ✔ Microsoft's Internet Security and Acceleration Server (ISA): www.microsoft.com/isaserver/
- ✔ Aventail VPN: www.aventail.com/
- ✔ Zone Lab's ZoneAlarm: www.zonealarm.com/
- ✔ Cisco's PIX Firewall: www.cisco.com/univercd/cc/td/doc/pcat/fw.htm
- ✔ Ositis Software's WinProxy: www.ositis.com/
- ✔ Deerfield Communication's WinGate Pro: www.deerfield.com/

In addition to these excellent third-party products, Windows Server 2003 offers a built-in native firewall product known as the Internet Connection Firewall (ICF), which is enabled and configured on the Advanced tab of a connection object. ICF can provide basic protection, but it does not offer the versatility and capabilities that a production network requires in a firewall. If you want to learn more about ICF, check the Help and Support Center and the Windows Server 2003 Resource Kit.

Forcing IP down the Throat of Windows 2003

Configuring TCP/IP on Windows 2003 can range from simple to complex. We review the simple process and discuss a few advanced items. For complex configurations, consult a reference such as the Windows Server 2003 Resource Kit or TechNet.

Three basic items are always required for configuring TCP/IP:

✔ IP address

✔ Subnet mask

✔ Default gateway

With just these three items, you can connect a client or server to a network. The protocol is configured on the Internet Protocol (TCP/IP) Properties dialog box. To access this dialog box, follow these steps:

1. **Choose Start⇨Control Panel⇨Network Connections⇨Local Area Connection.**

2. **Click Properties.**

    The Local Area Connection Properties dialog box appears.

3. **In the list of installed components, select Internet Protocol (TCP/IP).**

4. **Click Properties to open the Internet Protocol (TCP/IP) Properties dialog box (see Figure 14-2).**

If TCP/IP is not already installed, follow these steps:

1. **In the Local Area Connection Properties dialog box, click Install.**

    The Select Network Component Type dialog box appears.

2. **Select Protocol, and then click Add.**

    The Select Network Protocol dialog box appears.

Figure 14-2:
The Internet
Protocol
(TCP/IP)
Properties
dialog box.

3. **Select Internet Protocol (TCP/IP), and then click OK.**

4. **If prompted, provide a path to the distribution CD.**

5. **Provide the configuration details as discussed later in this section.**

The Internet Protocol (TCP/IP) Properties dialog box offers fields for defining the three IP configuration basics. Note the selection to obtain an IP address automatically. This setting configures the system to request IP configuration from a Dynamic Host Configuration Protocol (DHCP) server. Because most servers don't work well using dynamic IP addresses, you may want to define a static IP address for your Windows Server 2003 instead of using DHCP. You'll either obtain a public IP address from your ISP or use a private IP address from one of the reserved address ranges defined in RFC 1918.

You must also calculate a subnet mask for your network (that is, as long as you're not using DHCP). Here again, you may obtain this from your ISP if you're using public IP addresses, or you may calculate your own if you're using private IP addresses. In most cases where private IP addresses are used, the default subnet mask for the address class should work without alteration or additional calculations.

Finally, you must also provide a default gateway address for your server (unless you just don't want this system to communicate with other hosts outside of its subnet). The default gateway should be the address of the router on the local subnet to which the server is attached that can forward outbound traffic to other network segments. On networks using public IP addresses, this is probably a router, firewall, or proxy server that connects the local subnet to other subnets or to the Internet. On networks using private IP addresses, this is usually the machine on which the proxy and NAT software resides, which mediates between the local subnet and an Internet connection.

The Internet Protocol (TCP/IP) Properties dialog box also offers fields to configure Domain Name Service (DNS). For the most part, you can leave these blank . . . at least for now. We talk more about DNS in the "DNS Does the Trick" section later in this chapter.

After you define an IP address, a subnet mask, and a default gateway, click OK, and then close all the windows you've opened and reboot. That's all there is to basic TCP/IP configuration on Windows 2003!

More complex configurations become necessary when your network is larger and, therefore, more complicated. To deal with such complexity, you have to do some advanced work. Click the Advanced button in the Internet Protocol (TCP/IP) Properties dialog box to reveal the Advanced TCP/IP Settings dialog box, complete with its four tabs. The tabs (along with brief descriptions) are as follows:

- ✔ **IP Settings:** This tab allows you to define multiple IP address and subnet mask combinations for a single NIC. You can define also additional default gateways, as well as an interface metric, which is used by routers (or the routing service of Windows 2003) to determine which path to send data to — the path with the lowest metric is used first.

- ✔ **DNS:** This tab allows you to define additional DNS servers — the one or two you defined on the Internet Protocol (TCP/IP) Properties dialog box appears here as well, so don't get confused. In addition, you can specify how to search or resolve issues based on DNS server, DNS domain, and DNS parent domains. The two check boxes at the bottom of the DNS tab allow you to use dynamic registration to automatically add your server's IP address and domain name to your local DNS. For more information about DNS, please consult the "DNS Does the Trick" section later in this chapter.

- ✔ **WINS:** This tab is where IP addresses for Windows Internet Name Service (WINS) servers are defined. WINS servers resolve NetBIOS names into IP addresses. WINS is convenient for Windows 2003 networks with multiple servers and network segments. This tab also offers you control over how or whether NetBIOS operates over TCP/IP. For more information about WINS, please consult the "Everyone WINS Sometime" section later in this chapter.

✔ **Options:** This tab is where you can define alternate settings associated with TCP/IP. This tab offers access to only TCP/IP filtering by default, but the layout of the interface seems to hint that other optional features or services may be configured here if they are installed later. TCP/IP filtering allows you to define TCP, User Datagram Protocol (UDP), and protocol ports that will be allowed to function. In other words, it blocks all traffic except the traffic for the ports that you choose to allow in. This interface is rather limited because it doesn't tell you which ports you need to allow in. We recommend deploying a proxy or firewall to perform TCP/IP filtering, because these devices are more user-friendly and tell you which ports you need.

Everyone WINS Sometime

In a Microsoft Windows network, TCP/IP hosts can be called by NetBIOS names instead of IP addresses or domain names. Because NetBIOS names are more or less unique to Microsoft Networks, there's no current standard for associating NetBIOS names with IP addresses. On a Microsoft Network that uses TCP/IP as its only networking protocol, it's essential to be able to resolve NetBIOS names to IP addresses. This is where Windows Internet Name Service (WINS) comes in.

A glimpse at WINS

Because resolving NetBIOS names to IP addresses is the key to providing access to many of Windows 2003's built-in services and facilities, Microsoft provides two methods to handle this process:

✔ **LMHOSTS:** You can use a file named LMHOSTS to create a static table that associates specific NetBIOS names with specific IP addresses. (LM stands for LAN Manager and points to the network operating system that preceded Windows NT in the Microsoft product world.) Such a file must be present on every machine to provide the necessary name-to-address resolution capabilities.

For small, simple networks, using LMHOSTS files is an acceptable method. On large, complex networks, the busy work involved in maintaining a large number of such files can quickly get out of hand.

✔ **WINS:** Larger, more complex networks are where WINS comes into play. WINS runs on Windows Server 2003 machines as a service that automatically discovers NetBIOS names and manages a dynamic database that associates NetBIOS names with TCP/IP addresses. As networks grow, multiple WINS servers sometimes become necessary to help speed up the time it takes to handle name resolution requests.

A single WINS server can handle an entire network. On networks that include multiple sites or thousands of users, however, multiple WINS servers can distribute the load involved in providing name resolution, and speed users' access to NetBIOS-based resources.

WINS has several advantages over LMHOSTS files. For one thing, it's built on a dynamic database, which means that as networks change and names and addresses come and go, the database changes as the WINS server detects new name and address relationships or finds old names with new addresses. WINS can be especially important on networks where DHCP is used, if clients also share files or printers on their machines. Also, WINS is something like a Spanish-English dictionary that's constantly updated as new words — or in this case, names — are added.

WINS servers

A WINS server maintains a database that maps computer names to their respective IP addresses and vice versa. Rather than sending broadcasts for address information, which eats excess network bandwidth, a workstation that needs a NetBIOS name resolved makes a request directly to a designated WINS server (that's the real purpose of the WINS tab in the Advanced TCP/IP Settings dialog box).

This approach lets workstations take advantage of a well-defined service and obtain address information quickly and efficiently. Also, when workstations with NetBIOS names log on to the network, they provide information about themselves and their resources to the WINS server. Then, any changes automatically appear in the WINS server's database.

Although WINS is much simpler than DNS, it's still not an easy process. You need to install WINS as a network service component through the Network and Dial-up Connections interfaces. We recommend seeking guidance from the Windows 2003 Resource Kit before starting on that journey.

WINS clients

When configuring workstations or servers (at least, those servers that don't play host to the WINS server software) on your network, you'll provide an IP address for one or more WINS servers on your network. When those machines boot, they provide the WINS server with their computer names, share names, and IP addresses. The WINS server handles everything else. If a workstation needs an IP address that corresponds to a NetBIOS name, it asks the WINS server to supply that information.

NetBIOS over TCP/IP

The bane of many security consultants, NetBIOS over TCP/IP is a piggyback application programming interface (API) employed by Windows 2003 for all of its internal and server-to-server communications. Within a secured environment, such as behind firewalls and proxies, NetBIOS over TCP/IP is beneficial because it supports many of the user-friendly features of Windows 2003 networking. But without adequate security, it's a gaping hole that devious individuals can exploit to overtake your network or stand-alone system. The WINS tab offers you the ability to disable NetBIOS over TCP/IP on the current system (meaning NetBIOS will not be transmitted over network links from this computer) or to allow it to mimic its DHCP server (if the DHCP server disabled NetBIOS, this system will as well). You should consider disabling NetBIOS over TCP/IP only if all systems on the network are Windows 2000, Windows XP, or Windows 2003 and no application or service on the network requires NetBIOS to function. In other words, you'll need to live with NetBIOS for a bit longer.

DNS Does the Trick

One way to simplify TCP/IP host identification is to use Fully Qualified Domain Names (FQDNs) instead of IP addresses. An *FQDN* is the type of name used to identify resources on the Internet to make access easier for humans (such as www.microsoft.com). Resolving domain names and FQDNs to IP addresses is a crucial service on TCP/IP networks in general and especially on the Internet, where hundreds of millions of names and addresses can be found. This is where the Domain Name Service — sometimes called the Domain Naming Service or Domain Name System, but always abbreviated as DNS — comes into play.

As with NetBIOS names and IP addresses, the association between FQDNs and IP addresses can also be maintained in two ways:

✔ **HOSTS file:** You can create a HOSTS file on each system. The HOSTS file maintains a local table that associates specific FQDNs with specific IP addresses. When such associations change, the HOSTS file must be updated manually and copied to all machines on a network.

HOSTS files are not suited for interaction with large IP-based networks, especially the Internet. This explains why HOSTS files are mostly relics of an earlier, simpler era of IP networking. Except as a fallback in case access to DNS fails, no one uses HOSTS files anymore.

✔ **DNS:** Access to a DNS server allows network machines to request name resolution services from that server instead of maintaining name-to-address associations themselves. Although DNS servers must be configured manually, a DNS server can handle the name resolution needs of an entire network with ease. DNS servers can also communicate with one another, so a name resolution request that the local server can't handle can be passed up the FQDN name hierarchy until it reaches a server that can resolve the name into an address or indicate that the name is invalid.

The Internet includes tens of thousands of DNS servers. ISPs manage many of these DNS servers; others fall under the control of special top-level domain authorities. To stake out an Internet presence, you must obtain a unique FQDN through the InterNIC (or let your ISP do it for you). After you obtain this name, it's associated with a special root IP address in some DNS server (probably at your ISP, unless you decide to set up a DNS server of your own).

Whether to DNS

Unless you manage a large, complex network, chances are better than average that you'll work with someone else's DNS server — probably your ISP's — rather than managing your own. However, if you have a large network with more than 1000 computers, or if your network spans multiple sites using private wide-area links, a DNS server may be just the thing to help you stake out the right type of Internet presence.

One unique feature of Windows 2003 is that it automatically installs three services on the first server of a domain: Active Directory, DHCP, and DNS. Although you don't actually have to employ DHCP and DNS, they're still installed by default. Installing these services is therefore a breeze (so much so that the Configure Your Server Wizard does it for you automatically). The real headaches come when you try to configure DNS (or DHCP for that matter).

The deans of DNS

If you think you may be interested in setting up a DNS server, you need to consult a technical resource, such as the Windows Server 2003 Resource Kit or TechNet. We also highly recommend *DNS on Windows 2000,* a book by Matt Larson and Cricket Liu (published by O'Reilly & Associates) as the ultimate resource for using Windows 2000 as a DNS server. Even though the title says Windows 2000, this is also a great resource for Windows 2003 because DNS is almost exactly the same. Paul Albitz and Cricket Liu also wrote a general book called *DNS and BIND,* now in its fourth edition (also published by O'Reilly) that is widely regarded as the best general reference on DNS. Both of these books should be updated or revised soon to encompass new material for Windows Server 2003.

DHCP: IP Addressing Automation

DHCP, the Dynamic Host Configuration Protocol, is used to dynamically assign IP addresses and other configuration settings to systems as they boot. This allows clients to be configured automatically at startup, thus reducing installation administration. DHCP also allows a large group of clients to share a smaller pool of IP addresses, if only a fraction of those clients needs to be connected to the Internet at any given time.

What is DHCP?

DHCP is a service that Windows Server 2003 can deliver. In other words, a Windows Server 2003 can run DHCP server software to manage IP addresses and configuration information for just about any type of TCP/IP client.

DHCP manages IP address distribution using leases. When a new system configured to use DHCP comes online and requests configuration data, an IP address is leased to that system (each lease lasts three days by default). When the duration of the lease is half-expired, the client can request a lease renewal for another three days. If that request is denied or goes unanswered, the renewal request is repeated when 87.5 percent and 100 percent of the lease duration has expired. If a lease expires and is not renewed, the client can't access the network until it obtains a new IP address lease. You can initiate manual lease renewals or releases by executing ipconfig /renew or ipconfig /release at the Windows 2003 command prompt.

You can view the current state of IP configuration using the ipconfig command. Issuing the ipconfig /all|more command at the command prompt displays all of a machine's IP configuration information, one screen at a time.

Is DHCP in your future?

We can think of two profound reasons why DHCP is a godsend to Windows 2003 administrators who need to use it:

✔ DHCP enables you to manage an entire collection of IP addresses in one place, on a single server, with little effort beyond the initial configuration of the address pool (the range of addresses that DHCP will be called upon to manage). In the old days (before DHCP), managing IP addresses usually required walking from machine to machine on a far too frequent basis.

✔ DHCP automates delivery of IP addresses and configuration information (including subnet mask and the default gateway addresses) to end-user machines. This makes it astonishingly easy to set up IP clients and to handle configuration changes when they must occur.

To configure IP on a new client, all an end user (or you) must do in Windows Server 2003, Windows NT, or Windows 9*x* is click the single option in the Internet Protocol (TCP/IP) Properties dialog box that reads, Obtain an IP Address Automatically. DHCP does the rest!

When configuration changes occur, these changes are automatically introduced when IP leases are renewed. You can even cancel all existing leases and force clients to renew their leases whenever major renumbering or configuration changes require immediate updates to their IP configurations.

The ultimate reason for using DHCP is because it makes your job much easier. DHCP is recommended for all networks that use TCP/IP with ten or more clients. The first Windows Server 2003 in a domain has DHCP installed automatically, but you still need to enable and configure it properly before it will do you any good. So, if you think you may be interested in setting up a DHCP server, consult a technical resource, such as the Windows 2003 Resource Kit or TechNet, for all the details of installation and configuration.

Enough TCP/IP to choke a hippo

If this chapter whets your appetite for TCP/IP, you can obtain more details and information from the following great resources:

✔ *TCP/IP with Windows NT Illustrated* by Teresa Bisaillon and Brad Werne (published by McGraw-Hill Professional Publishing)

✔ *TCP/IP Illustrated, Volumes 1, 2, and 3* by W. Richard Stevens (published by Addison-Wesley)

✔ *Internetworking with TCP/IP, Volumes I, II, and III* by Douglas E. Comer (published by Prentice Hall)

✔ *TCP/IP For Dummies,* 4th Edition, by Candace Leiden, Marshall Wilensky, and John Landry (published by Wiley Publishing, Inc.)

Ironing Out Problems

Problems that occur on TCP/IP networks are almost always associated with incorrect configurations. The wrong IP address, subnet mask, default gateway, DNS server, WINS server, or DHCP server can bring a system, if not an entire network, to its knees. Therefore, you need to take extra caution to double-check your settings and changes before putting them into effect.

If you connect to an ISP, you should contact the ISP's technical support personnel early to eliminate as much wheel-spinning as possible. You may discover the problem is not on your end, but theirs. If so, your only recourse is to wait it out, and then complain. If problems occur too often for your comfort, take your business elsewhere.

Windows Server 2003 includes a few TCP/IP tools that you can employ to help track down problems. We already mentioned ipconfig; here are the others:

- **PING:** This tool tests the communications path between your system and another remote system. If a PING returns, you know the link is traversal and the remote system is online. If the PING times out, either the link is down or the remote system is offline.

- **TRACERT:** This tool reveals the hops (systems encountered) between your system and a remote system. The results inform you whether your trace route packets are getting through and at what system a failure is occurring.

- **ROUTE:** This tool is used to view and modify the routing table of a multi-homed system.

- **NETSTAT:** This tool displays information about the status of the current TCP/IP connections.

- **NSLOOKUP:** This tool displays DNS information that helps you manage and troubleshoot your DNS server.

- **TELNET:** This tool is used to establish a text-based terminal emulation with a remote system. Telnet gives you access to a remote system as if you were sitting at its keyboard. Windows Server 2003 does not include an inbound Telnet server.

Complete details on these tools are included in the Windows 2003 help files, the Windows Server 2003 Resource Kit, and TechNet.

Part IV
Running Your Network

The 5th Wave   By Rich Tennant

"A centralized security management system sounds fine, but then what would we do with the dogs?"

In this part . . .

After Windows Server 2003 is up and running, the real fun — namely, maintaining the server and network you've just so laboriously constructed — begins. Or at least, so goes the conventional wisdom. In a very real sense, therefore, Part IV begins where Part III leaves off.

First, you begin with managing the users (and their groupings) who will be working on your network and using your server. Then, it's on to a crucial discussion of how to set up and handle NTFS and share permissions, with a heaping order of file systems and related topics. After you have data and users to protect, backing up your system is no longer an option — it's a downright necessity — so it's the next topic on our systems-management agenda. Part IV closes out with an exercise in positive paranoia, wherein you find out about computer and network security in a discussion that covers the bases from physical security all the way up to how to build a solid password.

Therefore, Part IV covers all the important topics related to managing a Windows Server 2003-based network to prepare you to live with one of your very own (or to work on someone else's). Use these chapters to help establish systematic maintenance at regular intervals — not only will your users thank you, but you'll also save yourself some time and effort!

Remember this: Maintenance activities and costs usually represent 90 percent of any computer system's life cycle. That's why establishing a solid maintenance routine and sticking to it religiously are the keys to running a successful network. Do yourself a favor and don't learn this lesson the hard way. . . .

Chapter 15

Managing Users with Active Directory Users and Computers

*U*ser accounts are an indispensable element in the Windows Server 2003 environment. They're the central management and control tools used by the operating system to authenticate users, provide access, and enforce control for the resources on a local system and in the domain and forest as well. If you don't have a defined user account on a Windows Server 2003 stand-alone system or a Windows Server 2003 domain, you can't gain access to that system or to available resources in the forest. This chapter looks at managing domain user accounts and policies through the Active Directory Users and Computers console.

User Accounts Have Properties

Computers are typically used by more than one person. Even systems that workers use exclusively on their desks allow system administrators to log on locally. If these systems have computer accounts in the domain, it is possible for other users with domain accounts to log on to that system as well. The computer distinguishes between one person and another by employing a security device called the *user account object*. Each user on a computer or a network has a unique user account that contains details about the user, such as his or her rights and restrictions to access resources and more.

A Windows Server 2003 domain-based user account contains, is linked to, or is associated with the following items:

- ✔ **Password security:** User accounts are protected by a password so that only the authorized person can gain access to the system.

- ✔ **Permissions:** Permissions are the access privileges granted to a user account. These include group memberships and user-specific settings to access resources.

- ✔ **Identification:** User accounts identify a person to the computer system and the network.

- ✔ **User rights:** A user right is a high-level privilege that can be granted to users or groups to define or limit their actions on a computer system.

- ✔ **Roaming:** You can define user accounts so that a user can log on to any system that is a member of a domain by using a domain user account (certain users may be able to log on to a local account in certain situations), Remote Access Service (RAS), or over a gateway.

- ✔ **Environment layout:** Profiles are user-specific and store information about the layout, desktop, and user environment in general unless they are specifically restricted through the use of mandatory profiles. You can define profiles so that they follow the user account no matter where the user gains access on the network.

- ✔ **Auditing:** Windows Server 2003 can track access and usage by domain user accounts if that level of auditing has been enabled in the domain.

Access to Windows Server 2003 requires that users successfully authenticate themselves with a domain user account. This means that when a user with the proper permission level (not everyone has permission to log on locally to all systems in a domain) sits down at a Windows Server 2003 system, he or she can log on at the local machine with a local account (called an *interactive logon*) by pressing Ctrl+Alt+Del to start the logon process. Then the user must provide a valid username and password. He or she may also log on to a domain user account in the same manner if the server is a member of the domain. After the system verifies this information, the user is granted access. When the user is finished, he or she can log out and leave the system available for the next user to log on.

When Windows Server 2003 is installed, three user accounts are automatically created by default on stand-alone (non-domain member) systems. One of these accounts, the Administrator account, is used to initially configure the system and to create other user accounts. The second account, the Guest account, is a quick method to grant low-level access to any user. The third user account that's created is the HelpAssistant, often named

Support_*<random characters>*, which is the primary account used for Remote Assistance sessions. The Remote Desktop Help Session Manager services manage the HelpAssistant account, which is disabled by default.

Administrators rule!

The Administrator account is the primary means by which you initially configure Windows Server 2003. It's also the most powerful local account on the Windows Server 2003 system; therefore, you should make sure that the password for the Administrator account is complex and secret. The Administrator account has full-control access to almost everything in Windows Server 2003 (the exceptions are a few system processes that the Administrator doesn't own and therefore doesn't have access to), such as managing user accounts, manipulating shares, and granting access privileges.

The Administrator account boasts the following features:

- ✔ You can't delete it.
- ✔ You can lock it out or disable it.
- ✔ You can (and should) rename it (right-click the account and choose Rename).
- ✔ Although defining a blank password on a local Administrator account is allowed, it is actively discouraged as a bad security practice. In certain situations, some services don't function properly if you do not provide a password. Therefore, you should provide a valid, complex password for this account.

 Renaming this account is a good security practice. Would-be hackers (that is, people who want to gain unauthorized access to your system) need only two items of information to gain access to your system: a user account name and a password. Unless you rename this account, they already have half the information they need to gain access to the most powerful account on your system. It ends up being the only thing they need if you don't provide a password for the account.

Guests can wear out their welcome

The Guest account is the second default account created by Windows Server 2003. You can use this account as a temporary public-access method. It has minimal access rights and restricted privileges to resources.

The Guest account boasts the following features:

- You can't delete it.
- You can disable it and lock it out. (It's disabled by default.)
- You can rename it.
- It can have a blank password. (It has a blank password by default.)
- Changes to the environment aren't retained by this user account. (That is, the user profile is mandatory because user changes to the environment are not retained.)

The Guest account can be a security hole. Good security practices suggest that you keep this account disabled, rename it, and assign it a valid password.

Creating Active Directory Accounts

Creating accounts in Active Directory for users to log on to the domain and forest to access resources is a common and simple task. You use the Active Directory Users and Computers console (see Figure 15-1) in Windows Server 2003 to create and manage domain user accounts and domain groups.

Figure 15-1:
Active Directory Users and Computers console is the primary tool that Administrators use to create domain users accounts and groups.

Creating user accounts isn't difficult, but you need to pay attention to lots of details. First, we walk you through creating a quick-and-dirty user account. Then, we talk about all the fine-tuning you can perform on this account:

1. **To get to Active Directory Users and Computers, choose Start⇨All Programs⇨Administrative Tools⇨Active Directory Users and Computers.**

2. **Double-click the domain or organizational unit to which you want to assign this new account.**

   You see all the default settings for this domain or organizational unit, including user accounts. If you're assigning the user account to the Users container, when you initially click it, you see the Administrator and Guest accounts, plus other accounts that Windows Server 2003 set up, depending on the services you installed.

   An *organizational unit* is an Active Directory container that holds other organizational units, computers, user accounts, and groups. For more information on organizational units, see Chapter 11.

3. **You can create a new user account from scratch by highlighting the container in which you want to place it, and then choosing Action⇨New⇨User from the toolbar.**

   (You can also right-click the container and choose New⇨User from the pop-up menu.) This reveals the Create New Object — User Wizard shown in Figure 15-2. When you create a user object from scratch, you should pay attention to every detail of that account.

4. **Fill in the following information:**

   • **First name; last name; initial:** Type the user's first name, last name, and middle initial, if applicable.

   • **Full name:** This is how the name will be displayed on the system. Notice that the Setup wizard has entered the name for you. You can replace what's filled in for you and arrange the display of the full name any way you like. Usually, the first name is displayed, then the last name.

   • **User logon name:** Type the information you want the user to use to validate himself or herself to the network. You should create a company standard such as last name, first initial or something similar. (See the "What's in a name?" sidebar later in this chapter.)

     Pre-Windows 2000, the user logon name is the name given to the user for pre-Windows 2000 systems. Notice that the wizard fills in this information for you. You won't need to change this unless you're a tech head.

5. **Click the Next button to continue setting up this new user account object.**

   In the next screen, you will enter information about the password.

6. **Type a password for this account, and then confirm that password to the system by retyping it.**

7. **Configure the password settings using the options described in the following list:**

   • **User Must Change Password at Next Logon check box:** Forces users to change their passwords.

   • **User Cannot Change Password check box:** Prevents users from changing their passwords.

   • **Password Never Expires check box:** Exempts this account from the policy that can require a password change after a specified time period.

   • **Account is Disabled check box:** Ensures that this account can't be used to gain access to the system. Chances are, if you're creating a new user, you don't want to select this option because you want the user to be able to access the system.

8. **Click the Next button when you're finished marking your selections.**

   You're presented with a confirmation screen about the choices you've made.

9. **Click the Finish button if everything is correct. If you think of something else that needs to be added, press the Back button to add it now. If you need to add data later, you can edit the properties of the account as well.**

What's in a name?

Windows Server 2003 doesn't actually use or even care about the human-friendly name assigned to a user account. Instead, Windows Server 2003 uses a SID, or Security Identifier, to recognize and track user accounts. But, because you're human, you should employ human-friendly names whenever possible. This reduces stress and makes user management easier.

What we're trying to say is that you should employ a naming convention. A naming convention is just a predetermined method for creating names for users, computers, resources, and other objects. The two key features of a naming convention are the capability to always create new names and that the names created provide descriptive information about the named object.

Small networks rarely need complex or even predefined naming conventions. However, when the number of named items on your network exceeds about 100 or so, you may find it increasingly difficult to remember who or what jackal, herbie, and 8675309 actually are. Therefore, starting a small network with a naming convention can ease the growth process later.

Windows Server 2003 doesn't impose or suggest a naming scheme. It just lets you define names as you please. If you decide to use a naming convention, you need to be diligent in enforcing and employing that scheme.

The naming convention you choose or create doesn't matter; as long as it always provides new names and those names indicate information about the objects they label. Here are some general naming-convention rules:

- The names need to be consistent across all element types (user names, computer names, share names, directory names, and so on).

- The names should be easy to understand. (If they're too complex or difficult, they won't be used.)

- The name should somehow identify the type of object.

You can create new names by mimicking the structure of existing names. Here are some examples of partial naming conventions that you can customize for your network:

- Create user names by combining the first and last name of a user (for example, JohnSmith or JSmith).

- Create user names by combining the last name of a user and a department code (for example, SmithAcct and SmithSales5). With Active Directory, this type of design is less needed because, in many cases, the layout of your OU structure reflects the organizational areas of your company.

- Create computer names by combining the user name, a computer type code, and room number (for example, SmithW98 and JS102).

- Create group names by combining resource descriptor, location, project, or department names (for example, Tower12, Planning2, and Conference12).

- Create share or directory names by combining the content or purpose descriptor with a group or project name (for example, Documents, SalesDocs, and AcctSheets).

- Create printer names by combining the model type, location, department, and group names (for example, HP5Sales, CLJRm202, and HP4Acct).

As you can see, each of these suggested partial naming schemes always creates new names and provides enough information about the named object to determine where it is and whether it's a user account, computer, share, or printer.

You've just created a new domain user account object, and you'll see that object in the Active Directory Users and Computers console window. In Step 1, we mention the way the name is displayed, and that's how you should see the object's name listed.

If you right-click the new object and then click Properties, you'll see several tabs, including General, Address, Account, Profile, and many more.

You can use these tabs to enter more information about the new user account object, such as the groups to which it belongs. You may see other tabs, depending on the services installed on your Windows Server 2003 system and whether the server is a stand-alone server, a member of a domain, or a domain controller.

In the following sections, we go through some of the default tabs of a member server individually, so that you'll know what to fill in and why.

General tab

When you click the General tab, you can type more information about the account, such as a description (additional location information, what the account is used for, or whatever you want), office address, telephone number, Web page address, and e-mail address. The more information you can provide at this time, the more you'll be relieved later when you might need this information. The description information shows up in the Active Directory Users and Computers console if you have the detail view selected (View⇨Detail).

Address tab

Click the Address tab to type information about the user's physical mailing address. Although this information is not required, it's good to have handy.

Account tab

Click the Account tab to reveal the logon name, logon name for pre-Windows 2000 systems, logon hours, workstation restrictions (which can be set with the Log on to button), and account expiration information. Most of the options in this tab are self-explanatory — except the logon hours and expiration information, which are described as follows:

  ✔ **Logon hours:** Click the Logon Hours button to reveal the Logon Hours dialog box (see Figure 15-3). In this dialog box, you can define the hours during which a user can gain entry to the system. If this user account attempts to log on during off hours, the logon fails. If the user is already online when the hours expire, the user remains online but can't establish any new network connections (that is, the user can't send a document to a printer or open a new file). You define hours by selecting the day and hour sections and selecting the Logon Permitted or Logon Denied option. This option is mostly used for contractors who are allowed to use the system only during regular working hours.

✔ **Account expiration:** Mark the Account Expires End Of option to define when (if ever) the account expires. This is useful for contract or temporary employees who have been granted access to the system for a specified period of time.

Figure 15-3:
Access
can be set
by time of
day and day
of week.

Profile tab

Click the Profile tab in the Properties dialog box to reveal current information about the user account's profile (see Figure 15-4). In this dialog box, you can define the following:

✔ **User profile path:** The location where the roaming profile for this user is stored. The roaming profile makes a user's working environment available to them on any workstation on the network. (See the "Give Your Users Nice Profiles" section later in this chapter.)

✔ **Logon script name:** The file name of the script file to be executed at logon. Logon scripts are usually batch files that define paths, set environmental variables, map drives, or execute applications. You typically use logon scripts only in Windows Server 2003 for compatibility with older servers or DOS applications or to automatically configure settings for NetWare server access.

✔ **Home directory:** The default storage location for this profile as a local path or as a mapped drive letter to a network drive.

Figure 15-4:
Examples
of a User
Profile and
its profile
path, logon
script
location,
and Home
Folder
designation.

Telephones tab

Click the Telephones tab in the Properties dialog box to enter every imaginable phone number a person can have these days, such as pager, fax, and mobile. There's even a Comments section where you can add whatever you want.

Organization tab

Click the Organization tab in the Properties dialog box to enter information about the user's title in the organization and the names of the people to whom the person reports to directly. If your organization is prone to restructuring, you may opt to leave this tab blank.

Member Of tab

Clicking the Member Of tab in the Properties dialog box reveals information about the account's group membership status. This is where you can add a user account object to a group or remove a user account object from a group (see Figure 15-5). If you want to add this object to another group, click the Add button and select the group. As we discuss later in this chapter, group membership determines the resources to which you grant a user account access.

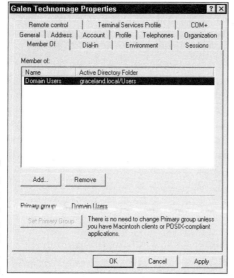

Figure 15-5:
Group
member-
ships are
defined
here.

Dial-in tab

Click the Dial-in tab in the Properties dialog box to enable or disable the account from dialing into the network. This is also where you can set any callback options. *Callback* means that, as users dial into the network, the server dials back a preset telephone number to verify that the users are in fact who they say they are. This number can be preset or set by the user. Callback is often used in security situations but dial back doesn't work particularly well when a user is on the road and staying in different hotels, which all have different telephone numbers. Use this option with caution.

Getting Pushy with Users

At some point during your management lifetime, you may need to disable, rename, or delete user accounts. You can do all this using Active Directory Users and Computers.

Disabling a user account is when you turn off the account so that it can't be used to gain entry to the system. To disable an account, highlight the user account and then choose Action⇨Disable Account. When you create a user using the Setup wizard (see the "Creating Users" section earlier in this chapter), you can select the Account Disabled check box, and the user account is disabled until you enable it.

Renaming a user account changes the human-friendly name of the account. Just select the user account and then choose Action⇨Rename. A dialog box prompts you for the new name. Note that a name change doesn't change the Security Identifier (SID) of the account.

Deleting a user account removes the user account from the system. Highlight the user account you want to delete and then choose Action⇨Delete. You're prompted to confirm the deletion. When you delete an account, it's gone for good. The SID used by the deleted account is never reused. Creating a new account with the same configuration as the deleted account still results in a different account because a new SID is used; therefore, as far as the accounts database is concerned, it's a new account.

When users leave your organization, you need to decide whether you want to retain their old user accounts to use for their replacements. This is your best option because it retains all department and group settings, but it does mean that you have to change all the personal information so that it relates to the new user.

What about Groups?

A *group* is a collection of users who need similar levels of access to a resource. Groups are the primary means by which Windows Server 2003 domain controllers grant user access to resources.

Groups simplify the administration process by reducing the number of relationships that you have to manage. Instead of managing how each individual user relates to each resource, you need to manage only how the smaller number of groups relate to resources and to which groups each user belongs. This reduces the workload by 40 to 90 percent. Windows Server 2003 has a Best Practices section under its Help guide that encourages you to use groups in as many situations as you can.

A group is nothing more than a named collection of users. There are two different types of groups, and each type can have any one of three scopes:

- ✓ **Security groups** are used to assign user rights to objects and resources in Active Directory. A secondary function of a Security group is that it can also be used to send e-mails to all the members of the group.

- ✓ **Distribution groups** are used only for sending e-mail to all the members of the group. Distribution groups can't be used to define permissions to resources and objects in Active Directory.

Both group types can have any of the following scopes:

- **Global groups** exist on a domain level. They are present on every computer throughout a domain and are managed by any Active Directory for Users and Computers tool hosted by Windows Server 2003. When the domain is running in Windows 2000 native mode or Windows Server 2003 mode, members of global groups can include accounts and global groups from the same domain. When the domain is running in Windows 2000 mixed mode, members of global groups can include accounts from the same domain.

- **Domain Local groups** exist only on a single computer. They aren't present throughout a domain. When the domain is running in Windows 2000 native mode or Windows Server 2003 mode, members of Domain Local groups can include accounts, Global groups, and Universal groups from any domain, as well as Domain Local groups from the same domain. When the domain is running in Windows 2000 mixed mode, members of Domain Local groups can include accounts and Global groups from any domain.

- **Universal groups** extend beyond the domain to all domains in the current forest. When the domain is running in Windows 2000 native mode or Windows server 2003 mode, members of Universal groups can include accounts, Global groups, and Universal groups from any domain. When the domain is running in Windows 2000 mixed mode, security groups with a Universal scope can't be created. When the domain is running in Windows 2000 native mode or Windows Server 2003 mode, Universal groups can be created and used to house other groups, such as Global groups, to facilitate the assignment of permissions to resources in any domain in the forest.

The three group scopes simplify the user-to-resource relationship. Using groups greatly reduces the management overhead for medium and large network, but it may seem a bit complicated for a small network. You can use groups like this:

- Local groups are assigned access levels to resources.

- Users are assigned membership to a Global group or a Universal group.

- A Global group or a Universal group is assigned as a member of a Local group.

Therefore, users are granted access to resources by means of their Global or Universal group membership and, in turn, that group's membership to a Local group has access to the resource. Whew, now it's time for a drink!

Here are a few important items to keep in mind about groups:

- ✔ A user can be a member of multiple Global or Universal groups.
- ✔ A Global or Universal group can be a member of multiple Local groups.
- ✔ A resource can have multiple Local groups assigned access to it. Using multiple Local groups, you can define multiple levels of access to a resource from read/print to change/manage to full control.

Although it's possible to add user accounts directly to a Universal group, best practices dictate that you should add them only to Global groups and add these Global groups to Universal groups. When that membership changes in a Universal group, such as the addition or removal of user accounts or groups, the change must be replicated throughout the forest through the Global Catalog Servers. Adding and removing user accounts often from Universal groups will cause a great deal of forest-wide replication traffic on the network.

If you add a Global group to a Universal group, user accounts and nested Global groups can be added to and removed from the Global group without causing a single replication. This is because the membership of the Universal group hasn't changed. It still has the same Global group or groups in it. Only the membership of the Global group changes when you add or remove user accounts or nested Global groups.

Although you can assign a user direct membership to a Local group or even direct access to a resource, doing so subverts the neat little scheme that Microsoft developed to simplify your life. So, just follow this prescription and you'll be vacationing on the beach in no time.

Whereas any other group can be a member of a local group, a Local group can't be a member of any other group when the domain is running in mixed mode. Domain Local groups can be placed in other Domain Local groups from the same domain when the domain is running in Windows 2000 native mode or Windows Server 2003 mode.

You manage groups on Windows Server 2003 using Active Directory Users and Computers. To create a group using Active Directory Users and Computers, follow these steps:

1. **Click the domain to which you want to add the group, and then choose Action⊏>New⊏>Group.**

   The New Object — Group dialog box appears.

2. **Type the new group name.**

   The group name for pre-Windows Server 2003 machines is filled in automatically.

3. **In the New Object — Group screen, select the group scope: Domain Local, Global, or Universal.**

   Universal groups are powerful because they extend to all domains in the current forest.

4. **Select the group type: Security or Distribution.**

   You'll almost never use the Distribution group setting because it does not contain the access control list (ACL) information necessary for security purposes. The Distribution group setting is used mainly for e-mail operations, where you would want to send an e-mail to a collective group of users and don't need security attached to it. We recommend always using the Security type.

5. **Click OK.**

After the group object is created, you can double-click the object to add more attributes to it. You see several new tabs called General, Members, Member Of, and Managed By. These tabs are fairly self-explanatory, but here's a little bit about them:

- ✔ **General:** This tab contains the same information you filled in when you created the group, such as group name, description, e-mail, group scope, and group type.

- ✔ **Members:** This tab shows the users who are members of the group. This is where you add users to the group.

- ✔ **Member Of:** This is where you can add this group to other groups.

- ✔ **Managed By:** This tab allows you to specify who manages the group. You can provide information about the user, such as name, address, and phone number.

You don't have to create your own groups: Windows Server 2003 domain controllers have several built-in Security Domain Local groups that you can use. The groups are in the Builtin container, by default. The following lists just a few of them (the default members are in parentheses):

- ✔ Administrators (Administrator, Domain Admin, Enterprise Admin)

- ✔ Guests (Domain Guests, Guests)

- ✔ Pre-Windows 2000 Compatible Access (anonymous logon, Everyone)

- ✔ Users (Domain Users, Authenticated Users)

Note that your screen may show that these built-in groups have more members than we've listed, depending on which services are installed on your server. For example, if you've installed Internet Information Services (IIS), you'll see more members in the built-in Guests group.

These default, built-in Security Domain Local groups have both predefined built-in capabilities (see Figure 15-6) and default user rights. You can modify the user rights of these groups (see this chapter's section titled "Users Have Properties"), but you can't change the built-in capabilities.

Figure 15-6:
The built-in
security
groups of
Windows
Server 2003.

Windows Server 2003 domain controllers include the following additional security groups as well, which can be found in the Users container by default:

✔ Cert Publishers (Domain Local)

✔ Debugger Users (Domain Local)

✔ HelpServicesGroup (Domain Local)

✔ RAS and IAS Servers (Domain Local)

✔ Telnet Clients (Domain Local)

✔ Domain Admins (Global)

✔ Domain Computers (Global)

✔ Domain Controllers (Global)

✔ Domain Guests (Global)

- ✔ Domain Users (Global)
- ✔ Group Policy Creator Owners (Global)
- ✔ Enterprise Admins (Universal)
- ✔ Schema Admins (Universal)

Other groups may exist, such as DnsAdmins, which would be created if the domain controller hosted DNS services. For the most part, however, the preceding list is inclusive for the forest root domain controller.

Windows Server 2003 has three more groups that it classifies as special identities: Everyone, Network, and Interactive. These are built-in groups that you can modify only indirectly. For example, the Everyone group may reflect a membership of 20 user accounts until you add another account to the domain. The user is automatically added to the Everyone group with no intervention by you. Therefore, although you did not specifically make the new account a member of the Everyone group, you did affect its membership. Guests are also added to the Everyone group, so be careful and modify the Guest account to restrict access to the network. (See the "Guests can wear out their welcome" section earlier in this chapter for more information.)

The Network group is for those who use the network as a means to access resources. When you give users access to resources across the network, they're automatically added to the Network group.

The other group, Interactive, represents users who access resources by logging on locally.

Again, you can't change who is a member of these groups in a direct sense. However, when you set permissions to resources, these groups will appear and you should modify the access levels of these groups to specific resources. For example, when giving users access to the root level of a volume, you can restrict access to the Everyone group so those users have only Read permissions.

You should create groups that make sense to your organizational pattern, method of operations, or just common sense. Groups should be meaningful, and their names should reflect their purposes. Naming a group Sales isn't very useful, but a name such as SalesPrintOnly is very informative. You should create groups so that users are divided by purpose, access levels, tasks, departments, or anything else you consider important. Remember that groups exist for your benefit, so try to get the most out of them.

Give Your Users Nice Profiles

A *user profile* is the collection of desktop, environment, network, and other settings that define and control the look, feel, and operation of the workstation or member server. Windows Server 2003 records profile information automatically for each user. However, unless you make them roaming profiles (which you find out about later in this chapter), these profiles are accessible only locally.

A user profile records lots of information about the user's environment and activities, including the following:

- ✔ Start menu configuration
- ✔ Screensaver and wallpaper settings
- ✔ List of recently accessed documents
- ✔ Favorites list from Internet Explorer
- ✔ Network mapped drives
- ✔ Installed network printers
- ✔ Desktop layout

In addition, a profile includes a compressed copy of the HKEY_CURRENT_ USER Registry key in a file named NTUSER.DAT. To find definitions for all the various Registry keys, you can use the Registry Tools utility in the Windows Server 2003 Resource Kit and access REGENTRY.HLP.

You can turn profiles into roaming profiles. (Note that a nonroaming profile is called a *local profile*.) A *roaming profile* is a profile stored on a network-accessible drive; therefore, no matter which workstation is used to gain access, the user's profile is available. As a result, the user's working environment follows him or her from one computer to the next. (You can also set the profile so that the user can't customize his or her roaming profile, which is called a Mandatory User Profile. See the last paragraph of this section for details.)

To create and enable a roaming profile for a specific user, follow these steps:

1. **On the domain controller, create and share a directory named Users (or whatever name you like best).**

2. **On the workstation where the existing local profile resides, choose System from the Control Panel.**

3. **Click the User Profiles tab.**

4. **Select the profile that you want to make into a roaming profile.**

5. **Click the Copy To button.**

6. **Define a network accessible path for the new storage location for the profile.**

   For example, *domain controller*\users\<*username*>, where *domain controller* is the name of the domain controller, *users* is the share name, and *username* is the name of the user account that is tied to the profile.

7. **On the domain controller (or any domain member that has the ADMINPAK.MSI tools properly installed), launch the Active Directory Users and Computers (choose Start⇨Programs⇨Administrative Directory Users and Computers).**

8. **Right-click the user object you just copied to the domain controller and then choose Properties.**

9. **Click the Profile tab.**

10. **In the Profile Path box in the User Profile section, type the same path from Step 6.**

11. **Click OK.**

The profile for the selected user is now a roaming profile. After a user has a roaming profile, the local profile is no longer used. It remains on the system, but the user account is now associated with the roaming profile.

By default, each time a user logs out, all changes made to his or her profile during that logon session (no matter which workstation he or she uses) are saved to the profile on the domain controller unless you specifically made this a mandatory profile. The next time the user logs on, the work environment is exactly the same as when he or she logged off. Local and roaming profiles should be used only by a single user. If multiple users need to use a single profile, you should employ a mandatory profile.

A *mandatory profile* doesn't save customized or personal changes to the profile when a user logs out. Instead, the profile retains the same configuration at all times. This type of profile is used mainly when system or network administrators want to control or limit the end users' ability to modify their profiles beyond a standard one that may be employed throughout the enterprise.

You create a mandatory profile by simply renaming the NTUSER.DAT file to NTUSER.MAN in either a local or roaming profile. After this change is made, the profile remains consistent no matter who uses it. You can always reverse this process by renaming the NTUSER.MAN file back to NTUSER.DAT.

Where You Find Profiles, Policies Are Never Far Away

Group policies are the collections of rules governing, controlling, or watching over the activities of users. You can set group policies based on sites, domains, or organizational units. In Windows NT Server 4.0, this was known as the System Policy Editor. In Windows Server 2003 (as it was in Windows 2000), you set all these policies using the group policy and its snap-in extensions, such as Administrative Templates, Security Settings, and Scripts.

One way to administer (manage or modify) the group policy from Active Directory Users and Computers is to do the following:

1. **Start Active Directory Users and Computers.**

2. **Right-click the domain or organizational unit for which you want to set a policy and then choose Properties.**

3. **Click the Group Policy tab.**

4. **If you want to modify an existing group policy, select it in the Group Policy Object Links portion of the Window and choose the appropriate option.**

The following options are available on the Group Policy tab (we've listed them in alphabetical order):

- ✔ **Add:** This opens the Add Group Policy Object Link dialog box. If you want to add an existing group policy object to the domain or organizational unit you're viewing, you would do so under this option.

- ✔ **Block Policy Inheritance:** Select this option to prevent the directory object you choose from inheriting the group policy from the parent directory.

- ✔ **Delete:** Use this option if you want to remove the group policy object.

- ✔ **Edit:** Allows you to make changes to the selected group policy.

- ✔ **New:** Allows you to create a new group policy object.

- ✔ **Properties:** Opens the Group Policy Properties dialog box. You can find all sites, organizational units, and domains using the selected policy. In addition, you can set permissions on a user or group basis to this object.

In addition, there's an Options button. When you click it, the following options are available:

✔ **Disabled:** This temporarily disables the group policy from the directory object.

✔ **No Override:** This is similar to a veto. If this is selected, the child directories must inherit the group policy from their parent directory. Not even the Block Policy Inheritance setting can keep this group policy from being forced after No Override is set.

If more than one group policy object is listed, you can use the Up and Down buttons to change the order of the group policies. Policies are enforced from the bottom of the list to the top. The one at the top is enforced last and thus takes priority over any of the others in the list or any of the others processed at higher points in the inheritance scheme, such as at the parent OU or domain or site levels.

A group policy is processed in the following manner:

1. All Windows 2000, XP Professional, and 2003 systems have one local group policy object, and it is processed first when the system is started. In a domain scenario, because the subsequent group policy objects are likely to overwrite these settings, this group policy object will probably have the least amount of effect on the local system when it's in a domain. On a stand-alone Windows system, it's usually the only group policy object processed; in this situation, it will have a large effect if not the only effect.

2. The next set of group policy settings that are processed are the settings for all and any site group policy objects. These group policy objects are processed synchronously (the domain administrator sets the order in which these will execute). They are processed from the bottom of the list to the top, with the one at the top enforced last at this level.

3. After all site group policy objects are run, the next set of group policy objects to be deployed are the ones set at the domain level. These too are executed synchronously, processed from the bottom of the list to the top, with the one at the top enforced last in the event that there is more than one set to be deployed.

4. The final set of group policy objects to be executed are any set at the Organizational Unit level. All group policy objects linked to the uppermost (parent) Organizational Unit in the inheritance tree are executed first, followed by those in the next highest level, and so on, until you reach the local Organizational Unit, which is executed last. At each Organizational Unit in the hierarchy, there may be Several group policies. They are processed in a specific order set by the domain administrator and are executed synchronously. This means that all group policy objects in the highest point of the inheritance tree are executed first in the specific order set by the domain administrator, and then all group policy objects at the next point of the inheritance tree are executed in the specific order set by the domain administrator, and so on all the way down to the local Organizational Unit.

Two rules apply when there are conflicting settings. At any particular group policy object, the computer setting prevails over the user configuration setting. For example, if GPO3 at the bottom of the list set at the domain level has a computer configuration setting set to do one thing and the same group policy object user section is set to do the opposite, the settings outlined in the computer configuration are enabled. The second rule is that anything executed next takes precedence. Following along with the preceding example, if the next group policy object set at the domain level (GPO2) has another setting that conflicts with a previous one, it take precedence.

Here is an example:

1. The local system GPO says to remove RUN from the Start menu. (It's removed.)

2. GPO2 at the domain level (bottom of the list) says to remove RUN from the Start menu. (It's removed.) GPO1 at the domain level (top of the list) says to enable RUN on the Start menu. (It's added.)

3. GPO2 at the Parent OU level (bottom of the list) says to enable RUN on the Start menu. (It's added.) GPO1 at the Parent OU level (top of the list) says to enable RUN on the Start menu. (It's added.)

4. GPO3 at the local OU level (bottom of the list) says to enable RUN on the Start menu. (It's added.) GPO2 at the local OU level (middle of the list) says to enable RUN on the Start menu. (It's added.) GPO1 at the local OU level (top of the list) says to remove RUN from the Start menu. (It's removed.)

You're probably asking, "What does all this mean?" The example policy we create in the next section will guide you through the setup.

Creating a group policy

Suppose you want to set a group policy to apply to all users in the domain. The policy will prevent the users from changing their passwords. Follow these steps to implement this new group policy:

1. **Start Active Directory Users and Computers.**

2. **Right-click the domain where you want to implement the policy and then choose Properties.**

3. **Click the Group Policy tab.**

4. **Click the New button, type a name for this policy, and then press the Enter key.**

5. **In the Group Policy Object Links section, highlight the new policy and click the Edit button.**

6. **Navigate your way down through the left window pane to User Configuration⇨Administrative Templates⇨System⇨Ctrl+Alt+Del Options, as shown in Figure 15-7.**

Figure 15-7: The Ctrl+ Alt+Del options that can be set with the User Config- uration Adminis- trative Template.

7. **Double-click the Disable Change Password object in the right pane.**

8. **In the Policy tab, select Enabled, click the Apply button, and then click OK.**

This new policy affects all current and future user accounts in the domain because it was created and linked to the domain container. However, it does not affect those accounts that are logged in. The effect takes place after they log out and then log back in to the system.

Notice when you went to the Group Policy tab and clicked the Edit button, you saw information relating to computer configuration and also to user con- figuration. If there's a conflict between the two, the computer configuration takes precedence in Windows Server 2003.

The preceding steps allowed you to add a group policy and then edit the policy using the Administrative Templates that were visible to you. Other templates are available but simply not loaded. To add another template for use, go back to the left window pane under User Configuration and right-click Administrative Templates. Next, select Add/Remove Templates to display a list of policies. Click the Add button to view other available templates.

You'll find a lot of useful policies already preconfigured for you in Computer Configuration➪Windows Settings➪Security Settings, as shown in Figure 15-8. For example, there's a template for setting a policy to force unique passwords for accounts.

Figure 15-8: List of group policies that can be applied on a computer configuration basis.

TIP

If you're concerned about security, you should employ an accounts policy that requires regular password changes (a new password every 30 days or so) and locks out accounts that fail to log on successfully after three tries.

Auditing for trouble

To look at the Access Control Information for any given group policy, you can look at which locations are associated with the policy, who has permissions in the policy, and how it's audited (which is what we cover in this section). All this is accomplished by clicking the Properties button in the Group Policy dialog box.

Auditing information on the network allows you to track activities throughout your network. This process can help you locate configuration problems, security breaches, improper activity, and misuse of the system. To enable auditing on your local system, do the following:

1. **In the Group Policy dialog box, click the Properties button.**

2. **From the Administrative Tools area, select Local Security Policy.**

3. **Navigate through the left pane to Security Settings⇨Local Policies, and then click Audit Policy.**

4. **Double-click the option you want to audit.**

   The Security Policy Setting dialog box appears.

5. **Choose to audit either successful attempts or failed attempts.**

   (This dialog box is displayed so that the administrator can choose to audit successful attempts, failed attempts, or both.)

6. **After making your selection, click OK.**

It's beneficial to audit failed attempts for certain objects, such as logon attempts and object access. This can warn you of an impending intruder.

The information obtained through auditing is recorded in the Event Viewer's Security Log. Launch the Event Viewer from the Administrative Tools menu and select Security Log. The right pane displays a list of the items you chose to audit. It's a good idea to check this log regularly, and then clear the log so it doesn't fill up.

Another point to remember is that this example uses the local security policy. If a domain policy is different, it takes precedence. For example, if you set to log all successes and all failures for all local security policy elements and the domain security policy is set to Not Configured, no logging is enabled because the domain security policy is enabled after the local security policy.

When Access Problems Loom . . .

User accounts govern who can access a computer system and at what level of access that person enjoys. Sometimes, though, users run into problems that prevent the normal operation of the logon process.

Most logon problems center on an incorrectly typed password. Therefore, users should take the time to type their passwords correctly. This is good advice only if their accounts haven't been locked out because of failed logon attempts. If your user's account is locked out, it must be re-enabled. This can occur in one of two ways. If the lockout policy is set with a duration, you need to only wait until the time expires and try again. If the lockout policy requires administrative intervention, you have to reset that user's account.

When a user can't log on or communication with the network seems sporadic, check the following:

- ✔ Make sure that the network interface card (NIC) and other physical network connections are solid.

- ✔ On any Windows system — Windows NT Workstation, Windows 2000, Windows XP Professional, or Windows Server 2003 — you must ensure that the computer is a member of the domain to log on to the domain with an account listed in Active Directory to access network resources.

- ✔ If using the Internet Protocol (IP) and a statically assigned IP address, check the configuration settings to ensure that the computer is using the correct IP address, subnet mask, and default gateway and be sure that it has the proper DNS settings for the network.

- ✔ If your network employs Dynamic Host Configuration Protocol (DHCP) to assign IP settings from a small pool to a larger group of computers, you may be stuck as the last person standing when the music stops and all available connection addresses are in use. You can verify whether this would have happened by going to a command prompt, typing IPCONFIG /ALL, and reviewing the settings. If you have an IP address that falls in the 169.254.0.1 through 169.254.255.254 Automatic Private Internet Protocol Address (APIPA) range, it's possible that the DHCP server ran out of available addresses to assign or your system had trouble communicating with the DHCP server.

If users can log on but can't access all the resources that they think they should be able to access, you need to verify several items:

- ✔ Group memberships

- ✔ Physical network connections to resource hosts (that is, check that a server's network cable isn't disconnected)

- ✔ Presence of group policies restricting the user's action

If everything we mention checks out, you may have a fairly esoteric problem. Consult a Microsoft resource (online or through TechNet) to search for a solution. Yeah, that's weak advice, but it's the most valuable thing we can tell you. The Microsoft information database is expansive — if someone else has had the same problem, you can probably find information posted about its resolution.

Chapter 16

Managing Shares, Permissions, and More

. . . .

In This Chapter

▶ Exploring objects, rights, and permissions

▶ Understanding how permissions apply to NTFS objects

▶ Considering FAT and FAT32 partitions

▶ Understanding how permissions apply to file shares

▶ Determining actual permissions

▶ Making access controls work

. . . .

*T*o a large extent, working with Windows Server 2003 means using the Windows NT File System, usually known as NTFS. This file system's advanced features include attribute-level Access Control Lists (ACLs) for objects, so you can control not only which users or groups can access a volume, directory, or file, but also which operations users or groups can perform against a volume, directory, or file.

Windows 2003 also supports the FAT and FAT32 file systems (FAT stands for *File Allocation Table*), which don't include object-level access controls. However, FAT and FAT32 do support so-called *file shares* (shared directories with the files they contain) that do support access controls. Understanding how shares work and how NTFS permissions combine with share permissions is a major focus of this chapter. We show you how to figure out what a user can (and can't) do to your files based on his or her account permissions, the groups to which he or she belongs, and the underlying defaults that apply to Windows Server 2003 itself.

Chapter 12 discusses this information as it applies to Active Directory.

More about Objects, Rights, and Permissions

Before you can revel in the details of the rights and permissions that apply to Windows 2003, you should ponder some technical terminology. That's why we take a brief detour to dictionary-ville — right here, right now.

An object lesson

Windows 2003 treats all user-accessible system resources — including users, groups, files, directories, printers, and processes — as objects. The term *object* has special meaning to programmers and tech-heads: This term refers to a named collection of attributes and values, plus a named collection of methods, which Microsoft calls *services*.

For example, a file object has a variety of attributes that you already know about if you've spent any time at all around computers: Files have names, types, lengths, owners, plus creation and modification dates. For an object, each attribute also has an associated value; therefore, the attributes and values of an object that is a file might be as follows:

- **Name:** BOOT.INI.
- **Type:** Configuration settings.
- **Contents:** Information on how to boot Windows 2003. (Windows 2003 can locate and read the contents using the drive's file directory.)
- **Size:** About 1KB.

Attributes identify individual objects of some specific type — in this case, a type of file — and define what they contain, where they're located, and so on.

On the other hand, it may not be so readily apparent why methods or services are important for objects. If you examine a file object, you can see that its methods describe operations that you would want to apply to a file. Therefore, the methods or services that apply to file objects include things such as read, write, execute, delete, rename, and other typical file operations. In short, methods define the operations that can be applied to a particular object. Among other things, this makes objects pretty much self-defining because they include in their attributes complete descriptions of themselves and include in their methods or services complete descriptions of what you can do to them. Other object types have different associated methods or services that reflect the objects' capabilities and the data that the objects contain.

When you examine the attributes for specific objects in Windows 2003, things start getting pretty interesting. Every single attribute of every single object has an ACL (this is sometimes pronounced *ackle,* to rhyme with *cackle*). ACLs identify those individual user accounts or groups that may access a particular object (or one of its attributes) and also indicate which services each user or group may apply to that object (or one of its attributes). Administrators use ACLs to control access to objects (and, logically, their attributes), giving themselves free rein to troubleshoot objects while limiting ordinary users' abilities to accidentally (or purposefully) harm the system.

When is a file not an object?

Windows 2003 uses objects for just about anything in its operating environment that users can access. In fact, NTFS volumes, directories, and files are Windows 2003 objects with associated attributes and a set of well-defined services that may be applied to those objects. However, because older FAT file systems (and the newer Windows 98 FAT32) do not include built-in support for ACLs, FAT and FAT32 files are *not* objects. Therefore, even though FAT and FAT32 volumes, directories, and files still have attributes similar to those for NTFS files (namely, name, type, creation date, modification date, and so forth), FAT and FAT32 volumes, directories, and files are not Windows 2003 objects, per se. The lack of built-in support for ACLs explains why FAT volumes and their contents are inherently insecure (because normal permissions don't apply to them).

More importantly, this also explains why the default logon behavior for Windows Server 2003 is to deny everyone but administrators, server operators, backup operators, and printer operators the right to log on locally. That's because anyone who can access a FAT or FAT32 volume can do anything they want to it. By denying ordinary users the right to log on to a Windows Server 2003 at its keyboard and requiring them to log on only through the network, Windows 2003 can control access to FAT and FAT32 volumes through shares. Shares function as Windows 2003 objects and therefore have built-in access controls.

Users have rights; objects have permissions

In Windows 2003, the standard terminology is to refer to *user rights* and *object permissions*. Because object permissions is rather vague, you usually hear permissions used in reference to a specific class of object, such as *file permissions* and *printer permissions*.

A user's rights define what he or she can do to objects (or their attributes) in the Windows 2003 environment. A user obtains rights to objects in one of three ways:

- ✔ The rights are explicitly assigned to an individual user account.
- ✔ The rights are assigned to the groups to which the user belongs. This is where users can be granted privileges to perform specific tasks, such as backing up files and directories.
- ✔ The rights are assigned through the Group Policy window. To access that window, open one of the Active Directory Administrative tools, right-click a site, an organizational unit, a domain, or a local computer. Choose Properties, click the Group Policy tab, and then click Edit. You edit user rights in the Group Policy window under Computer Configuration⇨Windows Settings⇨SecuritySettings⇨LocalPolicies⇨ User Rights Assignment.

When a user logs on to a Windows 2003 domain (or a stand-alone system), a special key called an access token is generated. The *access token* represents the user's explicit individual rights and the groups to which the user belongs. It takes some time to generate an access token, which is one reason why logging on to Windows 2003 isn't instantaneous.

Every object (and its attributes) in the Windows 2003 environment includes an attribute called *permissions* (which is found on the Security tab of each object). This permissions attribute includes an ACL that identifies all the users and groups allowed to access the object's attributes as well as the services that each user or group may apply to the object's attributes. Each time a user requests an object, Windows 2003 uses a built-in facility called the *Security Reference Monitor* (SRM) to check the user's access token against the permissions for that object. If the SRM finds that the user has permission, Windows 2003 fulfills the request; otherwise, the user is out of luck. It's possible for users to have access to specific attributes of objects, but not other attributes. For example, Nancy may be granted access to view part of JoAnne's account information, such as her telephone number, but not JoAnne's street address.

Of Windows 2003 NTFS and Permissions

NTFS is a file system just like FAT and FAT32 (the 32-bit File Allocation Table used in Windows 98) are file systems. The difference between NTFS and these other file systems is that NTFS is *an object-oriented file system*. Unlike FAT and FAT32, NTFS sees everything in NTFS partitions as objects of some specific type that have attributes and to which methods and services can be applied. The benefit of using NTFS is that you can set permissions for the volumes, files, and directories that use NTFS.

In fact, NTFS recognizes three types of objects:

✔ **Volumes:** The NTFS-formatted drive partitions that show up as disk drive icons. A volume object may contain files and directories.

✔ **Directories:** Named containers for files that occur in a volume or in some other directory. In fact, Windows 2003 allows you to nest directories however deep you want, which means that you can put as many directories within directories within directories as you like (although nested directories reach a point of diminishing returns fairly quickly).

✔ **Files:** Named containers for data that include type, size, dates, and content among their attributes. Files are where information actually resides in NTFS.

To examine the permissions for any object in NTFS, right-click that object in Windows Explorer, My Computer, or Active Directory Sites and Services. In the pop-up menu, select Properties and then click the Security tab. At the bottom of the Security dialog box, you see the Permissions section (as shown in Figure 16-1). From here, you can investigate the list of available permissions for this object (volume E on our hard drive in this case) through the list that appears in the Permissions section in the lower half of the screen.

Figure 16-1:
The Permissions list shows you all the permissions that apply to the object.

NTFS permissions

The Permissions list shows permissions for files, volumes, and directory objects in NTFS. NTFS file, volume, and directory permissions are similar. The only real differences are that container objects offer child inheritance options and a few permissions apply only to containers. We use the generic term *container* to refer to volumes and directories — in other words, objects that act as parents to child objects.

Windows 2003 has a slightly different method of permission assignments and permission restrictions than what is used in Windows NT, but the same method as what is used in Windows 2000. First and foremost, it does not have the No Access permission. Instead, all permissions are either granted or restricted using an Allow or Deny setting. Selecting Deny for all possible permissions for an NTFS object under Windows 2003 is the same as the No Access setting in Windows NT.

The standard or normal NTFS permissions are

- **Read** grants users the ability to view and access the contents of the folder or file.

- **Write** (folders) grants users the ability to create new folders and files within the folder.

- **Write** (files) grants users the ability to change the contents of a file and to alter its attributes.

- **List Folder Contents** (folders only) grants users the ability to see the names of the contents of a folder.

- **Read & Execute** (folders) grants users the ability to view and access the contents of the folder or file and to execute files.

- **Read & Execute** (files) grants users the ability to view and execute files.

- **Modify** (folders) grants users the ability to delete a folder and its contents, to create new files and folders within a folder, and to view and access the contents of a folder.

- **Modify** (files) grants users the ability to delete a file, change the contents of a file, alter a file's attributes, and to view and access a file.

- **Full Control** (folders) grants users unrestricted access to all of the functions of files and folders.

- **Full Control** (files) grants users unrestricted access to all of the functions of files.

Advanced permissions

Advanced permissions are detailed controls that can be used to create special access rights when the standard compliment of permissions don't properly apply. Advanced controls are accessed by clicking the Advanced button on the Permissions tab of an NTFS object. This reveals the Advanced Security Settings dialog box, which has four tabs: Permissions, Auditing, Owner, and Effective Permissions. The Permissions tab is used to define special-detail permissions. The Auditing tab is used to define the auditing scheme. The Owner tab is used to view the current owner or take ownership of an object. The Effective Permissions tab displays the permissions a user or group has on the current object based on all applicable permission settings.

On the Permissions tab, users or groups can be added and their specific permissions defined. The possible selections are

- Full Control
- Traverse Folder/Execute File
- List Folder/Read Data
- Read Attributes
- Read Extended Attributes
- Create Files/Write Data
- Create Folders/Append Data
- Write Attributes
- Write Extended Attributes
- Delete
- Read Permissions
- Change Permissions
- Take Ownership

If you really must dig up all the details on special access rights, please consult Microsoft's TechNet CD and the Windows Server 2003 Resource Kit.

FAT and FAT32 Have No Permissions

Because the FAT and FAT32 file systems that Windows 2003 supports along with NTFS include no object mechanisms for associating attributes with files and directories, files stored in a FAT or FAT32 formatted volume have no associated permissions. Anybody who's allowed to log on to a Windows 2003 Server with a FAT or FAT32 partition can access any of the files in that partition. This helps explain why you may want to restrict who's allowed to work on your servers, as well as why you should physically lock up your servers.

The reason why FAT partitions are still around is that a dual-boot machine that runs Windows 9x and Windows 2003 together must include a FAT partition from which the other operating system can boot. This might be a FAT32 partition for Windows 98, but we recommend FAT because Windows 2003 can read that partition when it's running and more operating systems can read FAT partitions than any other kind of file system.

Taking ownership of objects in NTFS

An owner of an object can always modify its permissions, no matter which permissions are already set for that object. This permission exists, at least in part, to sidestep the Deny trap that can occur when an object's owner mistakenly sets permissions for a general group, such as Everyone or Authenticated Users. (These two default groups are discussed further in Chapter 18.)

If the Everyone group is assigned Deny for all permissions of an object, that group includes anyone who may want to access that object. Unless an administrator or the object's creator (its owner by default) can reset permissions to be a little less restrictive, no one can access that object — or any objects that it contains.

Full Control is important because it grants the object's owner the power to change access to that object and to change services that apply to the object. In essence, Full Control is your get-out-of-jail-free card!

Only Windows 2003, Windows XP, Windows 2000, and Windows NT can read NTFS partitions, so be careful when reformatting partitions on dual- or multi-boot machines! Plus, Windows 2003, Windows XP, and Windows 2000 all use NTFS version 5. Windows NT uses NTFS version 4 by default, but if you apply Service Pack 4 or later, Windows NT is upgraded to include NTFS version 5.

Share Permissions

When users access files on a Windows Server 2003, they usually do so across the network, especially if you restrict who's allowed to log on to the server and limit physical access to the machine. Therefore, most users who access files on a Windows Server 2003 do so through a *network share,* which is a directory on a Windows Server 2003 that you've shared to the network for public access.

Shares are also objects for Windows 2003, so permissions do apply. The list of applicable permissions consists of the following three entries, which are managed in the same Allow/Deny method as the direct NTFS object permissions:

- ✔ **Read** permits viewing of files in the share, loading of files across the network, and program execution.

- ✔ **Change** includes all Read permissions, plus creating, deleting, or changing directories and files within the share.

- ✔ **Full Control** includes all Change permissions plus changing permissions for and taking ownership of the share.

No Special Access exists for shares. Table 16-1 summarizes the basic permissions for shares.

Table 16-1	Share Permissions and Basic Permissions				
File	Read	Write	Execute	Delete	Change
Read	X		X		
Change	X	X	X	X	
Full Control	X	X	X	X	X

If you want to expose the contents of a FAT partition on a Windows Server 2003 to network users, doing so through a share automatically gives you some degree of access control, which is yet another advantage to using a network!

To create a share, right-click a directory in My Computer or Windows 2003 Explorer, and then choose Sharing and Security. The Properties window for that directory appears with the Sharing tab selected, as shown in Figure 16-2.

Figure 16-2:
The Sharing tab provides easy access to a share's name, user limits, permissions, and caching settings.

The following elements of this window relate to creating and managing shares:

- **Share This Folder:** You must select the Share This Folder option to enable sharing on a directory or folder.

- **Share Name:** By default, a share's name is the same as the directory from which it comes. When creating shares, remember that DOS and

> Windows 3.*x* users can only access shares with names that are a maximum of eight characters long.

✔ **User Limit:** The User limit pane lets you limit how many users can access a share simultaneously. This will usually be a concern only on a heavily loaded Windows 2003 Server; in most cases, you can leave it set to the Maximum allowed default.

✔ **Permissions button:** You control share permissions through the Permissions button at the lower right of the Sharing tab. These permissions work the same way as NTFS permissions.

✔ **Offline Settings button:** This button allows you to enable or disable the ability of remote users to cache the contents of this share on their local systems through Offline Files and Folders. By default, only the files and programs specified by users are available offline.

Calculating Actual Permissions

Users have rights not only as a result of the NTFS permissions explicitly assigned to specific files or directories for their accounts but also by virtue of the groups to which they belong. Because NTFS shares exist, figuring out permissions can get pretty interesting when you have to combine NTFS and share permissions for a particular file or directory while also taking user settings and group memberships into account. To help you figure out what's what, we give you a recipe for calculation, plus a few rules to use, and then walk you through an example to show you how things work.

The rules of calculation

To figure out which permissions apply to a share on an NTFS object, you must first determine which permissions apply to the NTFS object by itself. This could include inheritance features from parent to child object. (See Chapter 12 for a refresher on inheritance.) Next, you must determine the permissions that apply to the share. (The rules for this process appear in the following section.) Whichever of the two results is more restrictive wins and defines the actual permissions that apply to the file or directory in question. This process isn't difficult, but it may produce some counter-intuitive results. You must apply these rules exactly as they're stated, or we can't guarantee the results. Here goes:

1. **Determine the permissions on the object.**

2. **Determine the permissions on the share.**

3. **Compare the permissions between the share and the object. The *more restrictive* permission is the permission that applies.**

Whenever you or your users can't obtain access to a particular file-system object through a share (or NTFS by itself, for that matter), always check group memberships and their associated permissions.

Figure this!

The formal explanation may not completely illuminate the process of figuring permissions, so this section provides a couple of examples.

Betty belongs to the Marketing Dept, Domain Users, and Film Critics groups. She wants to delete the file in an NTFS share named Rosebud.doc. Can she do it? Table 16-2 shows her individual and group permissions.

Table 16-2	Betty's NTFS and Share Permissions		
Type	*Membership*	*Name*	*Permission*
NTFS	User Account	BettyB	Read
Group	Marketing Dept		Read
Group	Domain Users		Change
Group	Film Critics		Change
Share	User Account	BettyB	Read
Group	Marketing Dept		Read
Group	Domain Users		Read
Group	Film Critics		Read

On the NTFS side, Read plus Change equals Change; on the share side, Read is the only game in town. The most restrictive of Read and Change is Read. Read won't allow Betty to delete a file, so Betty's out of luck! Maybe next time. . . .

Let the OS do it for you

Now that you know how to figure permissions manually, we'll show you a shortcut. In fact, we already told you about it earlier in this chapter. If you display the Advanced Properties dialog box from an object's Security tab, you can access the Effective Permissions tab. By selecting a specific user or group, this tab will display the effective permissions for that user or group, as shown in Figure 16-3.

Advanced Security Settings for wnetsvr (E:)

Permissions | Auditing | Owner | Effective Permissions

The following list displays the permissions that would be granted to the selected group or user, based on all relevant permissions.

Group or user name:

Guest   Select...

Effective permissions:

☐ Full Control
☑ Traverse Folder / Execute File
☑ List Folder / Read Data
☑ Read Attributes
☑ Read Extended Attributes
☐ Create Files / Write Data
☐ Create Folders / Append Data
☐ Write Attributes
☐ Write Extended Attributes
☐ Delete Subfolders and Files
☐ Delete
☑ Read Permissions
☐ Change Permissions
☐ Take Ownership

OK   Cancel   Apply

Figure 16-3:
The
Effective
Permissions
tab from the
Advanced
Security
Settings
dialog box.

But What about Access Control with Active Directory Objects?

We've talked about objects and access control, but with Active Directory, you need to be aware of two additional features: delegated access control and property-based inheritance. The following describes these two features in general; turn to Chapter 12 for the gory details.

Delegation of access control

You can enable others to manage portions of your network for you — otherwise, you'd be working 24/7! You can slice up the management by way of the domain, or you can give someone else rights to manage the organizational unit for you, depending on the functions you want them to perform. This is accomplished through the Delegate Administration Wizard, which is in the Active Directory Users and Computers snap-in. (Choose Start➪Administrative Tools➪Active Directory Users and Computers, click a domain, and then choose Delegate Control from the Action menu.)

An organizational unit is an Active Directory container that holds other organizational units, computers, users, and groups. For more information on organizational units, see Chapter 11.

Before you can give others access to manage Active Directory objects, you must first have the proper permissions to delegate that object authority. In addition, you must give the proper permissions to others to manage that object. For more information on this, see Chapter 12.

Property-based inheritance

Just as you might inherit money from a relative, the lower levels of your network structure can inherit access control information set at a higher level of the structure. Inheritance, as its name suggests, always flows in a downward direction. We want to touch briefly on two methods of property-based inheritance. (For more information and detail on how this inheritance works, see Chapter 12.)

The first method is called dynamic inheritance. As the word *dynamic* suggests, the access control information for this type of inheritance is calculated on the fly every time a read/write to the object is requested. This results in some performance overhead (such as extra traffic) that should be considered on a busy network. (Extra traffic on a busy network can slow things down significantly.)

The second method is called the *static model,* also referred to as *Create Time Inheritance.* This means that the access control information for an object is set when the object is created by looking at the parent object permissions and combining those permissions with the new object permissions. Unless the new permissions are set at a higher level, the access control does not change for the object. Therefore, when a request is made to read or write to the object, no recalculation is necessary to determine the permissions. However, if permissions are changed at a higher level, these changes are propagated downward to change permissions or reset combined permissions at lower levels — similar to dominoes toppling over. The only time there's a recalculation is when the permissions at higher levels are set and the propagation is in progress.

Chapter 17

Backing Up for a Rainy Day

. . . .

. . . .

*H*aving a backup recovery scheme for your organization's data is very important because of the critical business applications and functions that typically reside on networks. Without a plan in place to protect data, disruptions to an entire organization's data and workflow process can occur, resulting in loss of revenue.

Unfortunately, many organizations place little emphasis on protecting their data until an actual loss occurs. In this chapter, you find out about different methods for protecting your organization's data to prevent losses.

Why Bother Backing Up?

Backing up is the process of copying data from one location to another — either manually or unattended. Copying data from one directory on a hard disk to another directory on that same hard disk is effective until the hard disk crashes and both copies of the data are inaccessible. In addition, by copying the data to the same drive, you neglect to copy any of the security or account information. This means you have to re-enter that information manually. Don't you think it's a better idea to back up all files, such as system, application, and user data, to another physical medium, such as a tape or other backup device, and then rotate that device off-site periodically?

Many organizations place on a network their critical business functions and data, such as e-mail, accounting information, payroll, personnel records, and operations. Loss of just one segment of that information hinders an organization's operations, even if it's just for a short time. Imagine if the payroll information disappeared from the system, and all or some of the employees did not receive their checks on time. We wouldn't want to be there!

Data loss occurrences can be as simple as one corrupt file or as complex as the entire contents of a server's hard disk becoming unreadable. Organizations can avoid data loss problems almost entirely by backing up their networks on a regular basis.

All types of threats pose danger to data. Everything from fires to computer viruses can obliterate data on a network. Planning for each type of disaster can help you completely secure and restore your organization's data should that disaster occur.

Data loss on a network can occur in many ways. If you know what the potential threats are and plan for them, you can prevent both serious damage to your network and loss of data. We urge you to always back up your network and to rotate a recent copy off-site.

Following are some of the potential threats you and your network can encounter:

- **Hard disk crash:** Even if you've built fault tolerance (such as mirroring or duplexing) into your server, don't expect those methods to always work and recover everything 100 percent. We've seen mirrored drives go out of synch without notice until the hard disk crashes. Without backups, you can lose all your data or segments of it. It's a good idea to complement mirroring and duplexing with regular backups.

- **Ungraceful shutdown:** Every once in a while, you get a smart-aleck employee who hits the on/off switch to the server, causing it to shut down improperly. Most servers today come right back up — but not always. Shutting the server down in this manner can render the hard disks unreadable. You should put your servers in a secure location away from end users. And don't forget to back up on a regular basis!

- **Viruses:** Many organizations connect to the Internet, allowing employees to download all types of data to the local area network that could introduce viruses. Viruses pose a real threat to organizations. One virus can ruin an entire computer and render it useless in a very short time. If this computer happens to be a server on your network, someone's going to be reading the employment classifieds. Installing virus protection software on the server allows you to check for viruses before they're stored on the server. Put a backup plan in place that allows you to restore the data on your network as it was before the introduction of the virus.

✔ **Environmental disasters:** We've seen many organizations lose data during environmental disturbances, such as a bad storm. If lightning can zap the electronics in your home, imagine what it can do to the data on a network.

Some environmental disasters you should plan for include

- **Fire:** One fire in a building or on a floor can annihilate an entire organization. If your organization loses everything in a fire, you'll be the savior if you produce a recent tape of the network that was sitting safely off-site somewhere. If you store your backup tapes on top of your server in the computer room, however, you'll be the one pounding the pavement.

- **Floods:** Placing a computer room, server, or backup equipment in the basement or first floor of a building is a bad idea, particularly in flood-prone areas. One flood can obliterate an entire organization. Even if a flood does occur, you're safe with your backup tapes off-site — away from the flood zone.

- **Hurricanes:** Hurricanes bring high winds and rain with them. Don't put your server or backup equipment in a computer room with outside windows. You could come back and find everything strewn around the computer room and sopping wet — and have no backup tapes to restore.

- **Temperature:** Something as simple as placing a server or a backup machine in an enclosed room without proper air conditioning and ventilation can cause problems. Don't put a server or backup equipment in a small room with other heavy heat equipment, such as a copier, without cool air flowing through it. Buildings do shut down their air systems on weekends and holidays, and the heat can kill servers.

Some viruses have a gestation period; therefore, they can be inserted into your network but go unnoticed until after a set number of days. We've seen disgruntled employees place viruses on networks and then leave a company — 30 days later, a virus appears. Incorporate this thought into your backup plan by always backing up on a 30-day rotation scheme. If a virus like this is introduced onto your network, you can go back at least 30 days in your backup tapes to try to restore the network prior to the virus's introduction. If you have only a week's worth of backup, all the backups you have contain the virus. Virus software from Norton (www.symantec.com/) and McAfee (www.mcafee.com/) tend to have fewer conflicts with Windows 2003 than other brands of virus software.

Just how many types of backups are there?

The computer world has only five types of backup methods, and the same is true with the Windows 2003 backup facility. The five types of backups available in Windows Server 2003 are

- ✓ Normal
- ✓ Copy
- ✓ Daily
- ✓ Differential
- ✓ Incremental

Before you can truly understand these backup methods, you have to understand a little attribute called the archive bit. Files have *attributes,* which are the properties of a file. One of the attributes found in Windows 2003 is the archive bit. After a file is created or modified, its archive bit is automatically reset by the operating system. This *archive bit* indicates that the file needs to be backed up, even if backup software is not installed or configured on the computer. Backup software looks for this bit to identify the status of files. Think of this as a seal on every file on your system. When the operating system, a user, or an application modifies the file, the seal is broken. The backup software then goes through the files and "re-seals" them by backing them up.

Normal

The *normal backup* copies all selected files and sets the archive bit, which informs the backup software that the files have been backed up. This type of backup is performed the first time computer data is backed up. Also, with this type of backup, only the last tape is required to restore all the files. (See the "Local backup" section later in this chapter for more information on tape backups.)

Copy

The *copy backup* is useful because it doesn't set the archive bit and, therefore, doesn't affect normal and incremental backups. It can be used to copy selected files between scheduled normal or incremental backups. (See the "Incremental" section later in this section for more information on incremental backups.)

Daily

The *daily backup* copies selected files that were changed the day the backup job started. A daily backup doesn't set the archive bit. This backup can be used to copy only those files that were changed on that day, and because the archive bit is not set, the regular backup would go on as usual.

Differential

Like the copy and daily backups, the *differential backup* also doesn't set the archive bit. It copies all files that were created or modified since the last normal or incremental backup. One practice is to use a combination of normal and differential backups to configure the backup job for the computer. In this combination, a normal backup is performed weekly, and differential backups are performed daily. If this is the backup job used and a restore is being performed, only the last normal and the last differential tapes are required.

Incremental

The *incremental backup* is similar to the differential backup in that it backs up only those files that have been created or modified since the last normal or incremental backup. Unlike differential backups, however, incremental backups do set the archive bit, which indicates that the files have been backed up. A combination of normal and incremental backups can be used to configure a backup job. In this combination, a normal backup is used once a week and incremental backups are performed on a daily basis. To restore the files using this type of backup combination, the last normal and all incremental sets are required.

Configuring a backup job to use this combination is fast and efficiently utilizes storage space, because only those files that were modified get backed up. However, it's important to note that a restoration is more difficult and takes longer compared to the combination of differential and normal backups, simply because you have to use a whole set of incremental tapes. This type of backup combination or configuration is ideal for an enterprise in which an Automated Tape Library (ATL) can be used. Using an ATL, the backup software controls the entire restore operation, including the decision to load the correct tape sequence using its robotic arm.

An ATL is basically a software-controlled backup system in which loading or changing tapes is not necessary. A typical ATL system is usually designed around a container/library, which can hold from just a few tapes to several hundred, with each tape identified by a unique bar code. Inside the library are one or several tape drives to read and write to tape. An ATL system also includes a mechanism responsible for moving the tape to and from the tape drive. This mechanism can be a robotic arm (in the case of large ATLs) or a simple system similar to those found in a cassette tape recorder. The backup software would control the entire operation by instructing the robotic arm to load a specific tape in a specific tape drive and start the backup or restore job.

Network versus local backup

When backing up information on a network, you have a choice between performing a network backup or a local backup. In this section, we cover the particulars of each option.

Network backup

Network backups are used in large network environments. When you use a network backup, a *host computer* is configured to backup remote computers attached to the host computer through the LAN. In this scenario, data travels from the remote computer over the network to reach the host computer — the one configured with the tape drive. After data is off-loaded from the network interface card (NIC) to the computer's bus, the data is treated as if it were a local backup. (See "The Windows 2003 Backup Facility" section, later in this chapter, for information on how to configure your server to back up a remote computer.)

The transfer rate can be a problem with this type of backup because data must traverse and share the LAN with regular traffic. It's more than likely that the LAN is designed around a 10-Mbps Ethernet or a 100-Mbps Fast Ethernet. In either case, data speed would be greatly reduced compared to the local backup. To deal with this problem and to accommodate the needs of an enterprise in which a large amount of data must be backed up each night, the industry has developed the Storage Area Network (SAN). In this architecture, all computers and storage device(s) are attached directly to the loop using a Fibre Channel Arbitrated Loop (FC-AL), which has a bandwidth of 100 Mbps. Furthermore, only computers and the backup device(s) share this bandwidth. Such architecture is expensive, but its benefits for the enterprise more than justify its high cost.

Local backup

The local backup configuration consists of a local tape drive attached to or installed in the computer by means of an Integrated Drive Electronics (IDE) or a Small Computer System Interface (SCSI) interface. Local backup is fast because when you use these interfaces, the tape drive is directly attached to the computer bus. On some of the new SCSI interfaces, such as the Ultra2 Wide SCSI, the transfer rate can reach 80 Mbps. It's more likely that this transfer rate won't be met, however, because the tape drive can achieve only from 4 to 10 Mbps, depending on the drive type. With today's advances in hardware, it's possible to get close to 15GB per hour.

Local backup is relatively inexpensive because it involves the price of only the tape drive, the tapes, and the price of a SCSI or an IDE interface, if required. Most computers are already configured with an extra IDE or a SCSI interface that can be used for this purpose. One additional cost is the price of a license for the backup software, if third-party software is required. However, Windows 2003 comes with powerful backup software that's free!

The backup tapes we use (Hewlett Packard DDS 3) hold up to 24GB of data. Depending how much data you have to back up and the type of tape you're using, you may need more than one tape to hold all your data.

Understanding the technology

Regardless of whether you choose a network or local backup, and regardless of how often you decide to back up, you need to understand some terminology and technology about the equipment used in backup systems and the different methods.

Online, nearline, offline

You hear a lot of buzz about online, nearline, and offline storage options. Choose the method that suits your organization's retrieval time and effort, depending on how often you find yourself restoring data and how fast you want data retrieved. Descriptions of these three backup types follow:

- ✔ **Online:** This type of backup is typically performed on your server, usually in the form of a second hard disk that is mirrored or duplexed. Data is readily available to users through their desktops with no intervention from you except that you must regularly check the status of this fault tolerance. Drives can go out of synch without notice unless you monitor the drives manually or through software.

- ✔ **Nearline:** This type of backup is performed on a device attached to the network. A nearline backup requires some work on your part because it usually uses some method unknown to the user, such as compression techniques. The data is there, but your users won't know how to perform functions, such as decompressing the files, to access the data.

- ✔ **Offline:** This type of backup involves devices that include their own software and hardware and are separate from the server. You need to know how to operate these devices because the users won't know how or might not have the security access to do so. These devices are typically the slowest because data must go from the server to another device. Many organizations place these devices on the network backbone and connect them through fiber-optic cable for higher transmission rates.

As you progress downward in the preceding bulleted list, options become more expensive, it takes longer for you to retrieve information, and more interaction on your part is required.

What's in the hardware?

Backup systems are composed of backup units, backup media, and software components (oh, and you, the operator). The systems come in all sizes, shapes, and dollar signs, depending on your needs. In this section, we describe the most common ones you encounter so you can talk with your vendor about meeting your network needs.

Backup units

A *backup unit* is hardware that can be as simple as a tape device with one slot or as complex as a jukebox platter system with mechanical arms. If you have small data-storage requirements, a simple tape backup unit that has more capacity than your server will suffice. These units are not that expensive and are available at local computer stores. Some of these units can be daisy-chained if you need more space and don't want to be present to change the tapes.

If your organization has lots of data to back up, you might consider a jukebox approach. A *jukebox* is a device that looks like a little computer tower with a door. Inside, it has several slots plus a mechanical arm that can insert and move around tapes or CDs. With this type of system, you typically can insert a week's worth of backup tapes and let the system back up unattended.

Another option is *magneto-optical (MO) drives,* which use a combination of magnetic and optical technologies for rewritable backups. The advantage of this technology is that it performs random access retrievals, which are faster than sequential retrievals. The units are not expensive, but the medium is. If you have large data requirements and need fast retrieval, look into this technology.

Each type of backup unit will have some sort of slot where the medium is placed. The size of this slot depends on the unit. Some come in 4mm, 8mm, ¼ inch, ½ inch, and more. You must purchase the correct size medium for the backup unit because you can't fit a ½-inch tape in a ¼-inch drive!

Backup media

Backup media mean tapes, cartridges, CD-WORMs (write once, read many), erasable CD-ROMs, diskettes, and more. Any device on which the backup unit stores data becomes the medium. Backup media come in many shapes, sizes, and thicknesses. You want to make sure that you follow the manufacturer's recommendation for purchasing the right medium for your unit.

Great features of Windows Server 2003 NTBACKUP

One of the most frustrating things about the Windows NT Server NTBACKUP program is that it can back up information only to a tape drive. It's not uncommon for you to need to back up information from a system with a tape drive and restore it on one that doesn't have a tape drive. The Windows 2003 NTBACKUP program allows you to back up your information to any media that is available to you, including floppy drives, Zip drives, Jaz drives, a shared drive on a server, or a second hard drive.

Removable Storage Manager (RSM) is an integrated part of the Windows 2003 operating system. This service is responsible for managing tasks such as the mounting and dismounting of storage devices on behalf of Windows 2003 backup software. Relieving the backup software of these tasks and making them part of the operating system, unlike previous versions of Windows NT, makes the software much more reliable and robust.

One of the most amazing features of the Windows 2003 Backup is known as Automated System Recovery (ASR). ASR is a feature that enables you to restore essential system files in the event of corruption, deletion, or other system failure. ASR will not protect installed application settings or any personal data. Instead, it protects only those files necessary for booting and launching the OS. The ASR media set is a bootable floppy and one or more backup tapes. To restore a system using ASR, you need to boot from the original distribution CD for Windows Server 2003 and press F2 when prompted to initiate the ASR restore process. You'll be prompted for the floppy and backup tapes.

Finally, you can back up (and restore) using the Backup Wizard. The Wizard will ask you all the questions that you need to answer for a backup to be completed properly. See the "Scheduling backup jobs" section later in this chapter for more details on the Backup Wizard.

Don't buy video-grade tape cartridges at your local discount store for your backup purposes. Purchase data-grade tapes, which cost more but are designed for more rugged use.

Backup media come not only in different physical sizes but also in capacity. Some tapes store as much as 24GB of data. Erasable CD-ROMs store as much as 650 megabytes in uncompressed mode and gigabytes in compressed mode. Regardless of which unit and medium you select for your needs, get plenty of them so you can work on a rotational scheme without continually using the same medium. We've seen folks who buy just one tape and use that tape over and over until it's time to restore from that tape. And guess what, the tape was defective; therefore, there was no backup! Spread out your backups over multiple tapes to minimize putting all your eggs in one tape basket!

Software

You can use the Windows 2003 built-in backup software on a third-party backup device or you can use the software that comes with the device. We prefer to use third-party software because it's designed to work with certain manufactured devices and the drivers are always readily available. Installation of the devices goes much smoother when you use the recommended software. Always keep a copy of the backup software off-site in case of a fire or other disaster. If you lose all your equipment, you'll need to reload this software on another machine before you can restore data.

Beep! Beep! Planning Backups

One of the most important tasks that you can perform is to plan your backup. Some of the best backup systems and methods can still fail, so it's smart to always test them first.

Store backup tapes off-site

It's not uncommon for companies to store their backup tapes in a fire-proof safe — usually stored in the computer room where the fire might occur. These safes are great for one thing, and one thing only: paper. They're designed to withstand enough heat so paper does not burn. This heat, however, is more than sufficient to melt any tapes that may be stored in them. For this reason, smarter companies store their tapes off-site on a daily, weekly, or monthly basis, depending on how often data changes. Storing data off-site ensures data availability in case of a disaster, such as a fire or a flood. If such a disaster were to take place, a new system could be installed and data could be restored.

There are companies that provide off-site data vaulting for a fee. The tapes are picked up periodically and transferred to an off-site safe facility for vaulting. If needed, customers can call to get the required tapes for a restore. Such companies might have different service contracts. Although it's more costly to have this service 24 hours and 7 days a week, spending the extra funds to ensure access to tapes might be justifiable, depending on the operation and how critical the data is.

Document your hardware and its settings

It's especially important to document your hardware and its setting because it saves time that would be spent guessing and trying different configurations to get the system back up and ready for data to be restored from tape. Document all important settings, such as the size of volumes or drives, the type of file system used, and whether the file systems are File Allocation Table (FAT) or NT File System (NTFS). If you've been using any kind of fault tolerance on your disk subsystem, such as mirroring or some type of Redundant Array of Inexpensive Disks (RAID), it notes these details. Generally, accurate and comprehensive documentation ensures fast and reliable recovery.

You should also have a list of the part numbers of all the components installed in your systems. Include a list of all the vendors and your contacts as well. If the components in your system are from one of the large server manufacturers, such as Compaq or Hewlett Packard, they might loan you a system to recover your data. Finally, have all your device drivers readily available.

Practice disaster recovery for your system

It's wise to practice disaster recovery periodically to ensure its success whenever it's required after a real disaster. In large companies, it's normal practice and, in fact, mandated by management. Whereas it's easy to make this statement, actually implementing this practice is harder than you may think. The problem is that you can't attempt to recover your data on a production system (which is a system already used for another function). If you do and the backup is corrupt, your live data will become corrupt as well. Many organizations purchase a second system with the same specifications as the production system as a backup. These systems tend to get "borrowed" for other pilot projects and come into production.

Windows Server 2003 has a new feature that makes disaster recovery much easier. This feature is similar to a third-party solution in which a total system recovery is possible with a few diskettes. Search for "disaster recovery" in the Windows 2003 Help and Support Center for more information.

The Windows 2003 Backup Facility

Microsoft has always included a backup program called NTBACKUP with its Windows NT operating systems. Windows 2003 continues the tradition. The Windows Server 2003 version of NTBACKUP retains the capability to back up to non-tape media and access network resources, and includes built-in scheduling capabilities. These features were present in the Windows 2000 version of this tool but were blatantly absent from the Windows NT version.

The big picture

Windows Server 2003 ships with a new version of NTBACKUP that includes two methods for backing up your server: a GUI interface (Start⇔All Programs⇔Accessories⇔System Tools⇔Backup) and command-line execution (\WINNT\system32\ntbackup). We prefer the advanced mode of the GUI interface (shown in Figure 17-1) for quick manual backups and the command-line interface for batched and scheduled backups.

These methods are not exactly unattended because you have to start them to run manually — unless you set them up with a scheduler task to run automatically at a preset time. Although somewhat crude and not so fancy, NTBACKUP is better than nothing. If your budget is low and you can't afford to purchase a solution from a third-party vendor that specializes in backup software, this is the way to go. And the best part is that it's free (it's included in the price of Windows Server 2003)!

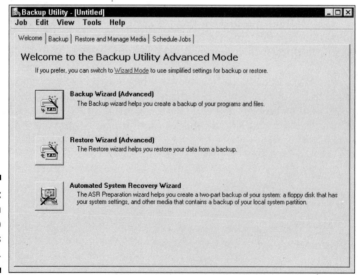

Figure 17-1:
The built-in GUI backup in Windows 2003.

Before purchasing a third-party backup product or using the Windows Server 2003 built-in backup program, search Microsoft Knowledgebase (www.microsoft.com/support/) for known bugs and problems regarding backup issues. Be specific in the search (that is, search for **Windows Server 2003 NTBACKUP**). Also, always install the latest service pack, which will correct most minor bugs known to Microsoft.

Command-line backups

You execute NTBACKUP from the command prompt using the following syntax:

```
ntbackup backup [systemstate] "@bks file name"
/J {"job name"} [/P {"pool name"}] [/G {"guid name"}]
[/T { "tape name"}] [/N {"media name"}] [/F {"file name"}]
[/D {"set description"}] [/DS {"server name"}]
[/IS {"server name"}] [/A] [/V:{yes|no}] [/R:{yes|no}]
[/L:{f|s|n}] [/M {backup type}] [/RS:{yes|no}]
[/HC:{on|off}] [/SNAP:{on|off}]
```

Yikes, that looks complicated! But don't worry, its really not that bad. In most cases, you'll need only a handful of parameters instead of all of them. The best place to get more details on using NTBACKUP from a command line is the Command-line Reference, which you can access by typing **ntbackup /?** from the Run command. This displays a help window that contains the correct syntax for NTBACKUP along with excellent descriptions, restrictions, requirements, and suggested uses of each parameter. Plus, several examples help you figure out how to use the command-line syntax.

However, we really don't see much of a need for command-line operation of NTBACKUP, especially because the GUI tool offers scheduling. But if you're really into batch scripts and would rather do things the hard way, be our guest.

Some files that are hard-coded into NTBACKUP don't get backed up, and you can't change or alter this. Following are some of the files and other things that don't get backed up:

 ✔ **Open files:** Users can't have files open while the backup is running. Those files won't be backed up. Have the users log off the system and disconnect them from any shares.

 ✔ **Temporary files:** No temporary files, such as PAGEFILE.SYS, are backed up.

 ✔ **Permissions:** The account used to perform the backup must have permission to read files.

 ✔ **Registry:** Only the local Registry is backed up. Registries on other servers are not backed up.

Selecting files and folders

In the Windows NT version of NTBACKUP, you could choose the files that you want to back up only through the GUI. The Windows 2000 and Windows 2003 versions allow you to either select a root drive or directory from the command line or use the GUI to define a backup selection file (a .bks file). To create a .bks file, follow these steps:

1. **Choose Start⇨All Programs⇨Accessories⇨System Tools⇨Backup.**

   The Welcome to the Backup or Restore Wizard screen appears.

2. **Click Advanced Mode.**

3. **Click the Backup tab.**

4. **Choose the desired folders and drives that you want to back up. (See Figure 17-2.)**

Figure 17-2:
Selecting files and folders to be backed up.

5. **Choose Job⇨Save Selections.**

6. **Name your .bks file.**

7. **Use the bks filename parameter as part of your command-line syntax.**

If you prefer to use the GUI version of NTBACKUP, just omit Step 7 and read the "Specifying backup destination and media settings" section next for more information on using the GUI version.

Specifying backup destination and media settings

Now that you've selected the files that you want to back up, you can choose the backup destination. If you don't have a tape drive installed on your system, the NTBACKUP program defaults to a file as its backup destination. Otherwise, simply select the backup device to which you would like to back up the information as follows:

1. **Choose Start⇨All Programs⇨Accessories⇨System Tools⇨Backup.**

   The Welcome to the Backup or Restore Wizard screen appears.

2. **Click Advanced Mode.**

3. **Click the Backup tab.**

4. **Choose the backup destination (file or tape).**

   - If you chose to back up the data to a file, choose File in the Backup Destination pull-down list. In the Backup Media or File Name box, type the full path and filename (or click the Browse button to find it).

   - If you chose to back up to a tape, choose a tape from the Backup Destination pull-down list.

5. **Click the Start Backup button.**

Scheduling backup jobs

As mentioned previously, scheduling backup jobs is now a built-in feature of Windows Server 2003. Scheduling backup jobs is now as simple as following these steps:

1. **Go to Start⇨All Programs⇨Accessories⇨System Tools⇨Backup.**

2. **Click Advanced Mode.**

3. **Click the Schedule Jobs tab.**

4. **Click the Add Job button (in the lower-right corner).**

   This starts the Backup Wizard.

5. **Answer the questions presented to you by the Wizard.**

   You'll notice that you're prompted for a username and password. The user performing the backup (probably you) must be either an administrator, a member of the Backup Operators group, or have equivalent rights of these groups.

6. **Specify the frequency of the job and click the Finish button.**

   The calendar in the Schedule Jobs tab changes to reflect the jobs.

Restoring from a Backup

Backing up your data is only half the picture. The other half involves restoring files on the network. We hope that you have to restore only a few files for users from time to time. Making regular backups along the way makes this task friendly and easy. However, in a fire or other disaster, you might lose your data and computer equipment, including the server to which you need to restore. We hope that you heed our advice when we say to rotate tapes off-site each week to plan for this catastrophe. If you also lose the server, we hope that you have a good working relationship with your local vendors so you can get equipment in a hurry.

The most important thing to remember when restoring your network is to practice the restoration process when you're not under the gun. This not only gives you confidence in performing the task, but also periodically tests the integrity of your backup. Although you can examine log files each morning, it's better to perform real restore tests — just like a dress rehearsal. When disaster does strike and you need to perform a real restore, all sorts of people will be looking over your shoulder asking you when things will be up and running. If you confidently know your backup system, you can perform this task under extreme pressure. Don't wait until the last minute to test and learn the system.

Always restore the system files (\SYSTEM32\CONFIG and Registry files) first, reboot, and then take a peek at the system to make sure everything looks like it's in place. Then restore the data files. If you plan your network directory and volume structure to segment system and data files, this task is much easier. Know ahead of time whether certain business departments require that their data be restored first. Sometimes this is not necessary, but in instances where a customer service department exists, they usually want the network back up right away with immediate access to their data. Why? Because they're servicing the external customers that generate the revenue for your organization! Before restores become necessary, try to devise a restoration order plan for your network and practice it.

Note that sometimes you can't restore Windows 2003 system files; you may have to reinstall Windows 2003, and then restore the system files.

Third-Party Backup Options

Because Windows 2003 is such a new operating system, currently no third-party options are specifically designed for it. Rest assured, however, that this will not remain so for long.

We always recommend going with well-recognized, name-brand, third-party companies to ensure good compatibility with Windows 2003 and other network operating systems. Most of the popular packages support the capability to back up several different network operating systems at one time and contain easy-to-use interfaces for backup and restore options.

One easy way to find other third-party backup software is to visit popular search engines on the Internet, such as http://search.cnet.com/, and enter the keywords **Windows Server 2003 Backup**. Discount Internet shops, such as CDW (www.cdw.com/), provide information about various backup devices in one handy location. On the CDW Web site, go to the Hardware section, click the Data Storage option, and look at how much information you have.

The backup market has two types of vendors: small-business backup solutions and enterprise backup solutions. We list the top ones in each category to get your search started:

✔ **Small business:**

- Exabyte, www.exabyte.com/

- ADIC (Advanced Digital Information Corporation), www.adic.com/adicHomePage.jsp

- Hewlett-Packard, www.hp.com/country/us/eng/prodserv/storage.html

✔ **Enterprise business:**

- Veritas, www.veritas.com/

- Legato, www.legato.com/

Search the backup vendors' Web sites for white papers and cost of ownership documents. This information is free, and a lot of research has been compiled. You can use this information to convince management of your backup requirements.

Regardless of which vendor you choose, the following checklist provides some helpful criteria in evaluating tape systems. Determine the requirements for your organization and query the vendor as to whether their product has the features you desire and whether you have to pay extra for some add-on modules.

This list should give you a good idea of what you may need when choosing a tape backup system:

- ✔ **Critical System Files:** An essential feature in any tape system that you purchase is that it can back up the Windows 2003 system files — such as the Registry and event logs, security information, user accounts, and access control lists — in addition to the actual data.

- ✔ **Fast tape index:** When backing up large amounts of data, it's critical that during the restore process you're able to obtain a catalog of the tape's contents within a minute or two. You don't want to wait 30 minutes each time you need to see the contents of a particular tape.

- ✔ **Multiplatform support:** Networks that support multiple platforms, such as Novell, Microsoft, and UNIX, are easier to back up if one backup system can support more than one platform.

- ✔ **Client backups:** Some users simply refuse to store files on the network. In this case, look for a package that automates client workstation back-ups across the network to your tape backup system. Some popular systems already include this option. Ask which client operating systems it supports — for example, Macintosh, UNIX, Windows 98, and OS/2.

- ✔ **Unattended operation:** Some tape systems work like jukeboxes and have a mechanical arm that inserts and removes tapes, so you can go home while the backup runs. These systems are expensive, but if you have a lot of data to back up and don't want to insert tapes all night, look for this feature.

- ✔ **Scheduling features:** If you want to perform incremental and full back-ups on different days, look for a system that is flexible and allows you to automate the scheduling features based on the day of the week.

- ✔ **Open files:** Open files are files in use during the backup operation. Not all backup systems are designed to back up open files, and some even halt when they get to one that's open. Most systems skip over the file and write an exception to a log file. More than likely, you want a backup system that backs up open files.

- ✔ **Security and encryption:** For small operations, this feature may not be as critical. For larger environments, ask the vendor how its system handles passing information through the network, such as passwords and account information.

- ✔ **Hierarchical Storage Management (HSM):** You want to make sure the vendor's product supports online, nearline, and offline storage and can manage using all three at one time.

✔ **Data storage size:** You want to find out how much data you can back up to the system (MB or GB), the size of the tapes the system uses (4mm, 8mm, DLT, or others), and whether it compresses data.

✔ **Remote management:** Getting to monitor backup status and progress remotely instead of being in front of the console is a handy feature.

✔ **Scalability:** Find out whether this system can be scaled to a larger environment should your network grow.

✔ **Security access:** Running an unattended backup means that a device must either log on to the network while you're gone or remain logged on with the keyboard locked. Check with the vendor as to how the product logs on to the network and maintains security.

The Backup Operator

Before a user is allowed to back up or restore the system, he or she must be a member of the Backup Operators group. This group is the same as the Backup Operators group in Windows NT, but Windows 2003 has changed the procedures for adding users to the group and changing the group's policies. Depending on whether or not you're running Windows 2003 with Active Directory, the steps involved in adding a user to the Backup Operator group will be slightly different.

By default, the Backup Operators group does not have any members. It's simply an empty container or a placeholder for when you need to assign backup and restore rights to users.

To modify the membership of the Backup Operators group when Active Directory is not installed (in other words, when your server is configured as a normal server instead of a domain controller), follow these steps:

1. **Choose Start⇨Administrative Tools⇨Computer Management.**

2. **In the left pane, expand the System Tools icon and highlight the Local Users and Groups icon.**

3. **In the right pane, double-click the Groups option.**

   At this point, all the groups that currently exist on your system are displayed in the right pane.

4. **Highlight the Backup Operators group, right-click it, and choose the Add to Group option.**

 5. Click the Add button and choose the user or users that you would like to become members of the Backup Operators group.

 6. Click the Add button again.

 7. Click OK, and then click OK again to close the Backup Operators Properties dialog box.

To modify the membership of the Backup Operators group when Active Directory is installed, follow these steps:

 1. Choose Start➪Administrative Tools➪Active Directory Users and Computers.

 2. In the left pane, double-click the tree to expand it.

 3. In the right pane, double-click the Builtin folder.

 4. In the right pane, right-click the Backup Operators group and choose Properties.

 5. Click the Members tab.

 6. Click the Add button to add users.

Chapter 18

Network Security Management

*I*n the advancing world of information technology, protecting private data from prying eyes is becoming more and more important. Maintaining security to prevent access to internal information is often critical to sustaining a competitive edge. In this chapter, we discuss how to impose tight security on Windows Server 2003.

When you install Windows Server 2003 right out of the box, it does not provide you with a totally secure environment. You must impose security on Windows Server 2003. This process involves executing many steps, careful planning, double-checking your settings, and a few non-computer activities. If you don't care about the security of your data, you can skip this discussion entirely.

The goal of security is not to create a system that's impossible for a hacker or misguided user to compromise. Instead, the goal is to maintain a sufficient barrier against intruders so the difficulty they encounter while attempting to access your system is significantly more than someone else's system. It's kind of like building a brick wall around your yard so tall that it discourages someone from climbing your wall — so they go climb your neighbor's instead. Your goal is to convince the hacker to attack an easier target. By following the prescriptions in this chapter, you can deploy a Windows Server 2003 system that's not only harder to crack than your neighbors' but also nearly watertight!

Protecting proprietary and private electronic property is not only a defense against outside attackers, but it also involves erecting a barrier against inside assaults and taking precautions against other threats to your data.

Network Security Basics

The basics of network security are to keep unauthorized people out of your network, to keep unwanted data out, and to keep wanted data in. Leave it to us to point out the obvious.

Creating a secure environment requires you to pay attention to three key areas:

- ✔ Understanding the operating system (or systems)
- ✔ Controlling physical access to the computer
- ✔ Educating the human users

These three areas are like legs on a barstool. If any one of the legs is weak, the person on the stool will hit the floor.

In this section, we briefly discuss the issues involved with maintaining physical control and education of users. The third leg, the operating system itself, is the subject of the remainder of the chapter.

Getting physical

Controlling physical access means preventing unauthorized people from coming into close proximity of your computers, network devices, communication pathways, peripherals, and even power sources. A computer system can be compromised in several ways. Physical access is always the first step in breaking into a system. Remember that physical access does not always mean a person must be physically present in your office building. If your network has dial-up access, someone can gain access remotely.

Controlling physical access means not only preventing access to keyboards or other input devices but also blocking all other means of transmitting to or extracting signals from your computer system.

Some physical access controls are obvious to everyone:

- ✔ Locking doors
- ✔ Using security badges
- ✔ Employing armed guards
- ✔ Using locking cases and racks

If you address just these items, you leave several other access methods wide open. You need to think about the architecture, structure, and construction of your building. Can ceiling or floor tiles be removed so access can be gained over or under walls? Do ventilation shafts or windows allow entrance into locked rooms? Paranoid yet?

A person getting into your computer room is not the only concern you should have. You also need to think about the environment in which the computers operate. Most computers have a limited range of temperatures within which they operate properly. Therefore, if intruders can gain access to thermostat controls, your system is compromised. What is the one thing that all computers need? Electricity. Is your power supply secure? Can it be switched off outside your security barriers? Do you have an uninterruptible power supply (UPS) attached to each critical system?

Even after preventing entrance into the computer room and protecting the operating environment, you still haven't fully secured your computers physically. You need to think about your trash — yes, the trash! You would be amazed at what private investigators and criminals can learn about you and your network from the information discarded in your trash. If you don't shred or incinerate all printouts and handwritten materials, you may be offering passwords, usernames, computer names, configuration settings, drive paths, and other key information.

Do you think we've covered everything now? *Wrong!* Ponder the following issues:

- ✔ Does the nightly cleaning crew vacuum and dust your computer closet?
- ✔ Is that crew bonded?
- ✔ How often does the crew unplug computer systems to plug in cleaning machines?
- ✔ Is the key that unlocks your front door also the key that unlocks the computer room?
- ✔ How do you know that the cleaning crew is not playing with your computer system?
- ✔ How do you know that the members of the cleaning crew are who you think they are?
- ✔ Are floppy drives installed on servers and other critical systems?
- ✔ Can systems be rebooted without passwords or other authentication controls (for example, smart cards)?
- ✔ Do servers have extra ports ready to accept new attachments?

✔ Are your backup tapes stacked beside the tape drive?

✔ Are your backup tapes protected by encryption and passwords?

✔ Are all backup tapes accounted for? If some are missing, do you know what information was stored on them?

✔ What really happens in your office building after business hours? Are the doors locked every night?

If you can still sleep at night, you probably have most of these items under control. If you can't answer some of these questions with a solid and reassuring response, you have some work to do.

So far, the physical access issues we've discussed have dealt with stationary computer systems. But what about mobile workstations? Remember that expensive notebook system you purchased for the boss, that manager, and that system administrator so they could work while traveling and connect to the network over the phone line? Well, if one of those notebooks were to fall into the wrong hands, someone would have an open door to walk right into your network and take or destroy whatever he or she pleased.

Notebook theft is becoming the number one method of gaining access to a company's network. Most notebooks are stolen at the airport. (We bet you could have guessed that one!) Although most travelers are smart enough not to check their notebooks as luggage, there's a common location where a notebook and its owner are often separated — the metal detector. All it takes is a few moments of delay while waiting to walk through the metal detector after you've placed the notebook on the x-ray treadmill, and *poof* — the notebook is gone by the time you reach the other end.

Controlling physical access is important because without interaction with a computer system, a hacker can't break in. If you fail to prevent physical access to your network, you're relying on your operating-system-supported software security to protect your data. However, there's one problem — if you've failed to properly educate network users, your security may already be compromised.

Informing the masses

The most secure network environment is useless if users don't respect the need for security. In fact, if left to their own druthers, most humans will find the path of least resistance when performing regular activities. In other words, your users will do anything to make traversing the security simple — such as automating the entry of passwords, writing down passwords in plain view, mapping unauthorized drives, installing unapproved software, transferring data to and from work and home on floppies, and attaching modems to bypass the firewall or proxy servers. If you put a software-based or operating-system-based security measure in place, a human can often find a way to get around it or at least reduce its effectiveness.

User education is a two-fold process. First, the users of your network must be thoroughly taught what security is, why it's important, and what security measures are in place on your network. Second, violations of the security system must be dealt with swiftly and strictly.

In most cases, educating your network users requires that an official organization document detailing the security restrictions, requirements, and punishments be created. This document, called a *security policy,* serves as your network's constitution. It's the governing body of regulations. This document allows your network security to remain intact while violators of the law are terminated.

So, what does a user need to know about the security imposed on the organization's network? Here's a brief list of the highlights:

- ✔ Use passwords properly and choose them wisely. (Don't use an obvious name or number, such as a pet's name or your birth date.)
- ✔ Never write down or share passwords.
- ✔ Never share security badges and smart cards or leave them unattended.
- ✔ Restrict network access to authorized employees only.
- ✔ Do not share user accounts with other employees or with anyone outside the organization.
- ✔ Do not distribute data from the network in any form outside the organization.
- ✔ Users should not step away from their workstations while they're logged on to the system.
- ✔ Understand the various levels of security in place on the network and the purpose of the stratification.
- ✔ Do not install unapproved software.
- ✔ Make it clear to all employees that tampering, subverting, or bypassing security measures is grounds for termination of employment.
- ✔ Respect the privacy of the organization and other users.
- ✔ Deal with violations of the security policy in a swift and severe manner without reservation or exemption.

This brings up the issue of punishment. If a user violates a significant issue in the security policy, a severe punishment must be applied. In most cases, firing the individual is the only form of punishment that will effectively control the situation and prevent other users from making the same mistake. The repercussions of violating the security policy must be detailed in the policy itself. And if you spell out the punishment, you must follow through. Even if your top programmer is the culprit, he or she must receive the same severity of punishment as the temporary mail person.

Most analysts have discovered that the deployment of a severe security policy results in a common occurrence — a short-term improvement in security, followed by a brief period of laxness, which results in violations, causing several users to be fired, which immediately results in an overall sustained improvement in security. Companies have reported that the loss of manpower because of violations was negligible in comparison to the prevention of security breaches.

You should create your own security policy that includes details about physical control, user education, and operating-system-level security measures. Remember the adage about the ounce of prevention.

Windows 2003 and Security

Windows 2003 security centers around access control. Access control is dependent on user identity, which is the user's user account. To gain access to a Windows Server 2003 computer or network, you must provide a user with a user account that has a valid username and password. Anyone who knows a valid username and password combination can gain access. Therefore, both the usernames and passwords of user accounts need to be protected.

Usernames are more than just names

Protecting usernames is not always simple, but a little effort can subvert several easy attacks. First, don't create usernames that employ just the first or last name of a person. Combine two or more elements to create the name, such as first name, last name, initials, department code, or division name. You should also avoid using for logon the name that's used as a user's e-mail address. This makes guessing usernames a bit more difficult. Even if a hacker knows your naming convention, making usernames complicated can make brute force attacks more difficult. (See Chapter 15 for more information on naming conventions.)

You should also rename common accounts. These include the Administrator, Guest, and IUSR_<servername> (created by Internet Information Services, or IIS) accounts. Rename these to something descriptive but not easily guessed.

Then, create new dummy accounts with the original name that have absolutely no access, which provides a decoy for hackers, effectively wasting their time and giving you more opportunity to discover who they are.

In your security policy, you should include a restriction to prevent users from employing their network logon username as a logon name anywhere else. In other words, a user's network logon name should not be used as a logon name for Web sites, File Transfer Protocol (FTP) sites, or other external systems. If users don't use the same logon names everywhere, they'll be less tempted to use the same passwords everywhere as well.

Even with these precautions, usernames are often discoverable. The important issue here is to make obtaining any data item needed to log on to your network as difficult to get as possible. After a username is known, the responsibility of protecting your network rests on the strength of the account's password.

Passwords and security

Passwords are the primary method by which unauthorized access to a system is prevented. The stronger the password, the more likely security will remain intact. As part of your security policy, you need to require that strong passwords be used by each and every user. (See the end of this section for guidelines that lead to strong passwords.) A single account compromised can result in the entire system being accessed.

Strong passwords can be enforced using the built-in controls of Windows 2003. By employing all system-level controls that force strong passwords, little additional effort is required to ensure that users comply with the security policy.

Account policies define the restrictions, requirements, and parameters of the Password, Account Lockout, and Kerberos policies. To access the Accounts Policies, follow these steps:

1. **Choose Start➪Administrative Tools➪Active Directory Users and Computers.**
2. **Select the name of your domain.**
3. **Choose Action➪Properties.**

    The domain's Properties dialog box appears.

4. **Click the Group Policy tab.**
5. **Select the Default Domain Policy and then click Edit.**

    The Group Policy Object Editor appears.

6. **Under the Computer Configuration node, expand the Windows Settings item.**

7. **Under the Windows Settings node, expand the Security Settings item.**

8. **Under the Security Settings node, expand the Account Policies item.**

Now you can see the Password, Account Lockout, and Kerberos policies in the right pane of the Local Security Settings window.

The Password Policy

After you've found the Account Policies option, you can access the Password Policy by choosing Account Policies⇨Password Policy. The six options shown in Figure 18-1 allow you to control the requirements for user passwords. The higher you raise the bar in each of the six options, the stronger the password requirements, thus making it less and less likely that a brute-force attack will succeed against your system.

In the following list, we briefly explain each option, spell out the default setting, and recommend the most appropriate settings for general use:

- ✔ **Enforce password history:** The default setting is 3. We recommend a setting of 5 or greater, which means the system will remember the last 5 passwords used by a user so he or she can't reuse any of those passwords.

- ✔ **Maximum password age:** The default setting is 42 days. Use this option to define when passwords expire and must be replaced. We recommend settings of 30, 45, or 60 days.

- ✔ **Minimum password age:** The default setting is 0 days. Use this option to define how long a user must wait before changing his or her password. We recommend settings of 1, 3, or 5 days.

- ✔ **Minimum password length:** The default setting is 0 characters. Use this option to define the smallest number of characters that must be present in a password. We recommend at least 6 characters.

- ✔ **Passwords must meet complexity requirements:** The default setting is Disabled. Complexity requirements are rules such as requiring both capital and lowercase letters, requiring the use of numerals, and requiring nonalphanumeric characters. If the native password requirements are not sufficient for you, we recommend that you research the complexity requirements further by using the Windows 2003 Help and Support feature or the Windows Server 2003 Resource Kit.

- ✔ **Store password using reversible encryption for all users in the domain:** The default setting is Disabled. By enabling this attribute, you can use Shiva Password Authentication Protocol (SPAP), which is a security authentication mechanism for the Point-to-Point Protocol (PPP) developed by Shiva Corporation. Leave this disabled unless SPAP is required by a client.

The Account Lockout Policy

The next policy in Account Policies is the Account Lockout Policy, which governs when user accounts are locked out because of repeated failed logon attempts (choose Account Policies⇨Account Lockout Policy). Lockout prevents brute-force logon attacks (in which every likely or possible password is attempted) by turning off user accounts. The options are as follows:

✔ **Account lockout threshold:** The default setting is 0 invalid logon attempts. Use this option to define how many failed logon attempts result in lockout. We recommend a setting of 3 to 5 invalid logon attempts.

✔ **Account lockout duration:** The default setting is Not defined. Use this option to define how long to lock out an account. A setting of Forever requires an administrator to un-lockout an account. We recommend a setting of 30 minutes or more.

✔ **Reset account lockout counter after:** The default setting is Not defined. Use this option to define the time period after which the count of failed logons for a single account is reset. We recommend a setting of 15 minutes.

The Kerberos Policy

The last policy in Account Policies is the Kerberos Policy, which governs the activity of secured communication sessions (choose Account Policies⇨ Kerberos Policy). Kerberos is an advanced network authentication protocol. Using Kerberos, clients can authenticate once at the beginning of a communications session and then perform multiple tasks during that session without having to authenticate again. In other words, Kerberos is used to prove the identity of a client and a server to each other. After this identity verification occurs, communications can commence without requiring this process again (or at least not until the communications link is broken).

The options for this policy are

- **Enforce User Logon Restrictions:** Enabled
- **Maximum lifetime for user ticket renewal:** 7 days
- **Maximum lifetime for service ticket:** 600 minutes
- **Maximum tolerance for computer clock synchronization:** 5 minutes
- **Maximum lifetime for user ticket:** 10 hours

For more information on Kerberos in Windows 2003, please see the Microsoft Windows 2003 and Security Web site (`www.microsoft.com/net/technical/security.asp`) and the Microsoft Security Web site (`www.microsoft.com/security/`).

A few things we know about passwords

Whether or not you enable software controls to restrict passwords, we recommend that you include the following elements in your organization's security policy regarding passwords:

- Apply a minimum of six characters.
- Prevent the e-mail address, account name, or real name from being part of the password.
- Don't use common words, slang, terms from the dictionary, or other real words.
- Don't write passwords down, except to place them in a vault or safety deposit box.
- Don't use words, names, or phrases that can be associated with you, such as family, friends, hobbies, pets, interests, books, movies, car, or workspace.
- If real words are used, split them with capitalization, numbers, or nonalphanumeric characters, for example, Go7Ril-la.

✔ Use numbers or nonalphanumeric characters to replace letters, for example, 13TT3r.

✔ Use at least three out of four types of characters: uppercase, lowercase, numerals, nonalphanumeric (symbols, punctuation).

✔ Create acronyms to use as passwords from sentences, for example, Fifty-five dollars will pay a parking ticket = 55DwPaPt.

Through a combination of Windows 2003-enforced password restrictions and company security policy rules, you can improve the security of your system through the use of strong passwords.

A Look into the Future: Service Packs

Microsoft regularly releases updates and fixes for its products, called *patch releases*. It did so for Windows NT 4.0 and Windows 2000 and will do so for Windows 2003. Because the patches released by Microsoft correct all kinds of bugs, problems, and other issues, you should assume that some of the patches address problems related to security. Therefore, it's important to keep yourself informed about the release and content of these patches.

Microsoft releases patches in two forms: service packs and hotfixes. A *hotfix* is a patch for a single problem. A *service pack* is many hotfixes combined into a single Band-Aid. There are more significant differences as well. Hotfixes are not fully tested or supported by Microsoft. A hotfix should be applied only if you're actually experiencing the problem it corrects, because a hotfix can sometimes cause other problems. Service packs are thoroughly tested and therefore safer for deployment. However, we recommend that you delay application of a new service pack until it's about two months old. This gives the rest of the Windows 2003 community the time to install and test the patch for you. It's always better to learn from the mistakes of others than to fall into the pit yourself.

Service packs are cumulative, meaning that each new release of a service pack includes the previous service pack plus all hotfixes and other improvements since that time. You need to apply only the most current service pack and any required hotfixes.

Before you apply any patch to Windows 2003, you should read the documentation included with the patches. Then make the following preparations:

✔ Back up the system or at least your data and the Registry.

✔ Reboot the system.

✔ Close all applications and stop any unnecessary services.

If you don't know which level of a service pack you applied, you can check by looking at the Help⇨About page from any native Windows 2003 application (such as Windows Explorer, Control Panel, or My Computer).

In the past, the Microsoft Web site has been secretive about the location of service packs and hotfixes, but recently they've been much more forthcoming. The best place to find service packs is through the Windows Update tool (it's in the All Programs section of the Start menu and appears as a command in the Tools menu of Internet Explorer). You can also check out the download section of the Windows 2003 Web area at `www.microsoft.com/windowsserver2003/`.

Copping an Attitude

To maintain a secure networking environment, you must be a pessimist. View every user as a potential security leak. The key to this philosophy is to grant only the exact level of access that users or groups need to perform their work tasks and absolutely nothing more. To take this to its logical end, you need to deal with the Everyone group and user rights.

The Everyone group

The Everyone group is a default group created by the system that includes all defined users and all anonymous users. Although it's not the catchall group it was in Windows NT 4.0, the expansive nature of the Everyone group can still cause a security problem because Windows 2003 defaults to grant Read access to the Everyone group on new volumes and new shares. This means that you need to keep an eye on where this group appears in your system. You may be granting blanket access where you really don't want any snuggling going on.

The Everyone group can seem hard to track down. It doesn't appear in the list of built-in groups as viewed through Active Directory Users and Computers, for example. However, it does appear in the list of groups when setting security on objects. The Everyone group can't be removed from the system, but it can be effectively managed with a little effort. See Chapter 15 for more information on the Everyone group.

The Authenticated Users group is a standard feature of Windows 2003. It contains all defined users but does not contain anonymous users. Generally, you want to use the Authenticated Users group instead of the Everyone group when you need to grant blanket access. The Everyone group must remain on your system for backward compatibility and system level requirements (such as allowing your system to boot).

Don't set all permissions for the Everyone group to Deny because you'll prevent anyone from accessing resources. Instead, just remove the Everyone group from the list of users and groups granted access.

Each time you create a new drive or a share, remove the Everyone group, and then add only those users or groups that need access to the resource. Just as you don't want everyone gaining access to your computer, you don't want "everyone" to be allowed access to areas where it's not required.

User rights

User rights are system-level privileges that control what types of activities can occur or be performed. The default setting of user rights is reasonably secure, but you can make a few improvements. The User Rights management interface is accessed using the Group Policy editor. (See the "Passwords and security" section earlier this chapter.) The User Rights Assignment is located under Security Settings➪Local Policies➪User Rights Assignments. Through this interface, user rights are granted or revoked. Here are several changes you should consider making:

- ✔ **Remove the Guests group from the Allow Log on Locally right:** Making this change inhibits nonauthenticated users from gaining unauthorized access.

- ✔ **Remove the Everyone group from the Access This Computer from the Network right:** Making this change inhibits nonauthenticated users from gaining access to hosted resources over the network.

- ✔ **Remove the Everyone group from the Bypass Traverse Checking right:** Making this change inhibits nonauthenticated users from jumping into subdirectories for which they do not have access to parent directories.

- ✔ **Remove the Backup Operators group from the Restore Files and Directories right:** Making this change inhibits nonadministrators from restoring files from backup tapes. Because files can be restored to file allocation table (FAT) partitions when Access Control Lists (ACLs) are lost, this is an important security modification.

After you make these changes, double-check that regular users still have the capabilities they need to perform their required tasks. You may need to grant a few users or groups these user rights. For example, if you want users to access resources on a server from across the network, you should add a group, such as the Users group, to the Access This Computer from the Network user right.

Plugging Common Mouse Holes

Windows 2003 has a handful of common security holes that you need to look for and fill. Fortunately, we have crawled around on our hands and knees so you don't have to. Just follow our friendly advice, and you'll be all snug and secure.

Unseen administrative shares

Each time Windows 2003 boots, a hidden administrative share is created for every drive. These shares are backup paths for the system just in case direct access to system files is somehow interrupted. In other words, it's a redundancy you don't need! The administrative shares are disabled by adding AutoShareServer to the following Registry key:

```
HKEY_LOCAL_MACHINE\System\CurrentControlSet\Services\LanMan
        Server\Parameters
```

A value of 0 turns the administrative shares off, and a value of 1 turns them back on. Consult Microsoft TechNet for details about disabling administrative shares.

A hidden share is just like any other share, except it has a dollar sign as the last character in its name. This tells the system not to display the hidden share in standard browser listings of shares. You can use the System Manager to view hidden shares. You can create your own hidden shares just by adding a dollar sign to the end of the share name.

The problem with administrative shares is that they offer unrestricted access to every file on a drive. If the username and password of an administrator account are ever compromised, this share can be used by anyone to map to any administrative share on the network. Therefore, it's a good idea to turn off the administrative shares just as a precaution.

Decoy accounts

Everyone knows the name of the most important user account on your system. Because Windows 2003 creates the Administrator account when Windows 2003 is installed, everyone already knows that you have such an account and exactly what its name is. Therefore, you need to change it!

Don't just change the name. Do one better and create a new dummy account that has absolutely no access or privileges at all and give it the name administrator. This dummy account will serve as a decoy to lure hackers away from real access.

Creating decoys for other common accounts, such as the Guest account and IUSR account (the one created by IIS), is also a good idea.

Last logged on username

By default, when Ctrl+Alt+Del is pressed, the logon dialog box displays the username of the last person to successfully log on. This is not the most secure setting. To prevent the dialog box from appearing, enable the option titled Interactive logon: Do not display last user name policy. This option is in the Security Options area of the Group Policy (see the "User rights" section for details on finding this area).

When good floppies go bad

A nifty tool from System Internals (www.sysinternals.com) enables anyone to read NTFS files after booting from a DOS floppy. The NTFSDOS drivers make possible what Microsoft claimed was impossible. Now, anyone who has physical access to your system can reboot with a floppy and copy files right off your NTFS protected drives. If you value your data (and your job), remove the floppy drives from critical systems.

Security Equals Vigilance

Maintaining a secure environment is an ongoing process. Keeping up with security fixes, system changes, user activity, and a security policy is often a timely task. In your efforts to maintain a protected deployment of Windows 2003, take the time to review the contents of the following Web sites, newsgroups, and other resources:

- ✔ **Microsoft Security & Privacy Web page:** www.microsoft.com/security/
- ✔ **Microsoft Security Partners:** http://members.microsoft.com/partner/partnering/programs/SecuritySolutions/
- ✔ **Windows & .NET Magazine:** www.winntmag.com/

- **Somarsoft:** www.somarsoft.com/
- **@stake:** www.atstake.com/
- **CERT Coordination Center:** www.cert.org/
- **BHS Software:** www.bhs.com/
- **Xtras, Inc.:** www.xtras.net/
- **Microsoft TechNet:** www.microsoft.com/technet/

Here are some books you may find helpful too: (Yes, most of these titles have *Windows 2000* in them. In most cases, the information will still apply to Windows 2003. However, you should keep an eye out for new editions that focus on Windows 2003.)

- *Microsoft Windows 2000 Security Handbook,* by Jeff Schmidt (published by Que)
- *Configuring Windows 2000 Server Security* (published by Snygress Media)
- *Windows 2000 Server Security Little Black Book,* by Edward Austin (published by Coriolis Group)
- *Maximum Security* (published by Sams.net)
- *Firewalls and Internet Security: Repelling the Wily Hacker,* by William R.Cheswick and Steven M. Bellovin (published by Addison-Wesley)
- *Building Internet Firewalls,* by Brent D. Chapman and Elizabeth D. Zwicky (published by O'Reilly & Associates)

Part V
Troubleshooting

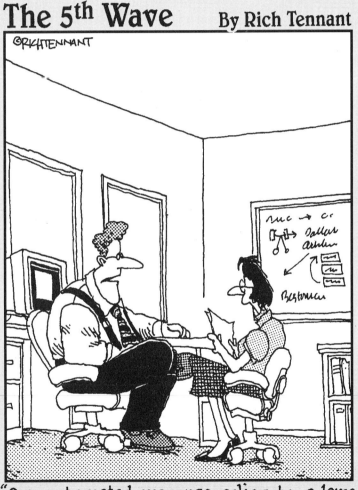

The 5th Wave   By Rich Tennant

"Our automated response policy to a large company wide data crash is to notify management, back up existing data and sell 90% of my shares in the company."

In this part . . .

Despite your best intentions and all the prevention in the world, networks occasionally get weird. Sometimes, they even stop working altogether. That's when troubleshooting is required — when there's trouble to shoot! What you should discover in Part V is that troubleshooting is as much a state of mind as it is any particular set of tried and tested tools, tricks, and techniques for solving problems.

Part V kicks off with a review of key Windows 2003 troubleshooting utilities and continues with similar coverage of tools to help you handle network problems. After that, you find out how to tackle troubles arising from an inactive or wacky Active Directory.

Part V covers the important bases when it comes to troubleshooting a Windows Server 2003 machine and the networks to which it is attached. Although we don't address every problem you might ever encounter, we do our best to steer you clear of the best-known (or at least the most-often-encountered) bumps in the road to networking success.

Troubleshooting is something everyone must do from time to time. Remember not to panic and to perform a systematic survey of the symptoms. You must try to identify what kinds of problems are manifesting themselves before you can figure out what might be amiss. Keep a record of problems and their solutions as you encounter and correct them. That way, you'll be able to not only solve most problems yourself, but also build a knowledge base that will help you out for the rest of your networking career!

Chapter 19

Using Windows 2003 Troubleshooting Utilities

• •

In This Chapter

▶ Using Event Viewer

▶ Dealing with crash dumps

▶ Checking out the System Information Tool

▶ Working with Windows 2003 Computer Management

▶ Plotting performance with Performance Monitor

▶ Investigating the Resource Kit utilities

• •

*A*lthough it's not necessarily the case that "where there's Windows 2003, there's trouble," trouble with a Windows Server 2003 system is certainly not unimaginable. As you survey the contents of this chapter, you have a chance to delve into some of the more well-known — and obscure — troubleshooting tools that Windows 2003 offers to savvy users.

And if that's not enough to satisfy your appetite, we mention some worthwhile Resource Kit troubleshooting utilities at the end of this chapter.

Event Viewer Reveals

Event Viewer is an essential troubleshooting tool for Windows Server 2003. One of the most valuable characteristics of this tool is that you can always count on Event Viewer to give you the messy details about what's going on when drivers or services fail to load during system startup. Event Viewer is also your entry point into analyzing what's going on with your system, whether you're auditing specific events by design or trying to figure out where problems and errors may be coming from.

To launch Event Viewer, follow this menu sequence: Start⇨Administrative Tools⇨Event Viewer. This produces the Event Viewer window shown in Figure 19-1.

Figure 19-1: The System Log in Event Viewer.

The small icons in the right column of the Event Viewer's various logs represent the following:

- **Red circle with an X:** Known as the error icon, it identifies an error report that may be worth investigating.

- **Blue quote bubble with a lowercase *i*:** Called the information icon, it indicates an event that describes the successful operation of a major server service.

- **Yellow triangle with an exclamation point:** Known as the warning icon, it indicates that an event occurred that wasn't necessarily serious but might indicate that potential problems lie ahead. This may be worth investigating, too.

To investigate any log entry, double-click the line where it appears. When we double-clicked one of the red circles in Figure 19-1, it produced the Event Detail report shown in Figure 19-2.

The System Log appears in Event Viewer by default. The utility also includes three other main log files (in addition to the System Log) and may include service- or application-specific logs, depending on what applications and services you have installed. Here's a rundown of what appears on our test system:

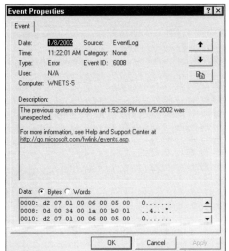

Figure 19-2:
An event
detail.

✔ **Application Log:** Records events logged by some applications or services. When developers build applications, they can instruct those applications to send event information to the Event Viewer as part of their installation. The icons that appear in the Application Log are the same as those for the System Log.

✔ **Directory Service:** Records events related to the Directory Service.

✔ **DNS Server:** Records events related to the Domain Name Service (DNS) server.

✔ **File Replication Service:** Records events related to the File Replication Service.

✔ **Security Log:** Records security-related events, such as changes to a machine's security policy and failed attempts to log on or access files or directories. This is where security audit information is recorded. The Security Log uses two special icons: A yellow key indicates an audited security event completed successfully, and a gray lock indicates that an audited security event failed.

✔ **System Log:** Records all events logged by Windows 2003 system components. By default, the System Log records all system-related hardware and operating system errors, warnings, and information messages.

Working with Event Viewer should become part of your regular system maintenance routine. Check the System and Application Logs at least once a week to see whether anything untoward has happened. If you audit security events, check the Security Log as often as makes sense.

Sick applications? Call Dr. Watson!

Throughout this book, you encounter loads of tools and utilities for troubleshooting Windows Server 2003 hardware, networks, and the operating system itself. But what do you do when the applications go awry?

The answer to this question is, Nothing!" Not because you can't *do* anything about application problems, but because such problems in the Windows 2003 environment automatically provoke error reports from the Dr. Watson utility. In fact, Dr. Watson's job is to report application difficulties whenever they occur.

Although you probably won't know what to make of Dr. Watson's content — unless you have

extensive Windows programming experience and are familiar with debuggers — rest assured that this is old hat for plenty of people out there. Your entire involvement with Dr. Watson will be to check where the crash dump resides, make a copy of that dump, and e-mail it to someone who can make heads or tails of this stuff! You can find the crash dump in the "Crash Dump" text box at the top of the Dr. Watson application window, which is displayed by entering **drwtsn32** in the text entry box of the Run command.

When applications get weird, Dr. Watson can be good for the tech support folks who will try to cure what ails your system.

Whenever you troubleshoot, the Event Viewer should be an early stop along your path. In addition to keeping you informed about most system problems, this tool can be counted on to keep you informed about any application or service problems that know how to use this facility to report warnings and errors. Unfortunately, this does not include all applications, but does include most server services and important applications, such as database managers and e-mail packages.

Dump Picking

Should you ever be unfortunate enough to uncover a bug in Windows 2003 itself — a painful process that begins with mysterious server failures and progresses to long, arduous calls to Microsoft's technical support staff — you'll probably have to create a crash dump for their use.

Reading crash dumps is well beyond the ken of ordinary system or network administrators. You just need to recognize the term and know how to create a crash dump for some expert to peruse at his or her leisure.

Therefore, we begin with a definition: A *crash dump* is a snapshot of everything in memory when a Windows 2003 system configured to capture a crash dump actually crashes. It includes information about the operating system, the hardware, applications, and all types of other information that Windows 2003 usually keeps hidden from view and uses to manage its own operations.

Experts can pick through a crash dump to pinpoint causes of a crash and use their knowledge to start formulating fixes or workarounds. This is one of the things that drives the creation of the patches and fixes that eventually show up in the service packs — in case you were wondering where that stuff comes from.

To enable a crash dump, your computer must first meet the following criteria:

✔ Your paging file must reside on the same partition where the Windows 2003 system files reside. This is called the *boot partition* in Windows 2003-speak. The paging file contributes to the bulk of the crash dump and must be accessible after the system quits working — that means it must be on the same drive where the crash dump utility resides.

✔ You must have sufficient free space on the boot partition to capture everything in RAM plus everything in the paging file. This means that the free space must equal the sum of those values (RAM and the paging file). To determine the amount of free space you need, open Task Manager, click the Performance tab, and look at the number reported in the Limit box in the Commit Charge pane. (To launch Task Manager, right-click any open area on the taskbar and choose Task Manager.) This represents the number of kilobytes of free space you'll need (to convert to MB, divide this number by 1024).

After you meet these criteria, you can enable crash dumps in the Startup and Recovery dialog box. To display this dialog box, choose Control Panel⇨ System, click the Advanced tab, and click the Settings button under Startup and Recovery. The Write Debugging Information section contains a pull-down list where you can select to write a small dump file, a kernel-only dump file, a complete dump file, or none at all. The default filename (`%systemroot%\ MEMORY.DMP`) is defined in the Dump File box. You don't need to change this default. The Startup and Recovery dialog box is shown in Figure 19-3.

After you select the dump file settings, the next time your system experiences a STOP error (a serious error that can result in data corruption if left unresolved), it writes the MEMORY.DMP file to your Windows 2003 system directory. By default, the value of the symbol `%systemroot%` is equal to C:\WINDOWS, assuming that you installed Windows Server 2003 on the C: drive with the default system root directory name.

Figure 19-3:
Selections
to capture a
crash dump.

A crash dump creates two interesting problems. First, because the sum of RAM and the paging file is probably 200MB or more, you must find a way to get a copy to technical support. (You'd better have a fast Internet link.) Second, you must remember to delete that file after you copy it; otherwise, your server is likely to run out of space on the boot partition.

Compressing crash dumps usually reduces them by 70 percent or more, so we recommend that you zip them (using a utility such as WinZip, which can be found at www.winzip.com) before you send them.

System Information Tool

You may recall the Windows NT Diagnostics tool from Windows NT 4.0. It has been transformed into the System Information tool. Windows 2000 included this tool in the Computer Management tool, but Windows 2003 has placed it exclusively in the System Tools subsection of the Start menu (Start⇨All Programs⇨Accessories⇨System Tools⇨System Information). By expanding the five subsections of System Summary (Hardware Resources, Components, Software Environment, Applications, and Internet Settings), you can obtain detailed information about the status, settings, configuration, and operations of the system. This is a great place to look before adding new hardware or when trying to find out why a device is failing.

Windows 2003 Computer Management

With the introduction of Plug and Play and Microsoft Management Console (MMC), several functions and applications found in Windows NT 4.0 and Windows 9x have been combined to create a versatile inspection tool for Windows 2003. The Computer Management tool (see Figure 19-4) gives you access to troubleshooting tools such as System Information and Device Manager. To open the Computer Management tool, choose Start⇨ Administrative Tools⇨Computer Management.

Figure 19-4:
The
Computer
Manage-
ment Tool.

Device Manager is a component borrowed from Windows 9x (and is the tool that Windows NT users have been begging for). This nifty tool maintains a complete list of installed devices. After expanding the device-type headings in the right pane to reveal the list of individual devices, you can double-click any device to reveal a Properties dialog box. From these Properties dialog boxes, you can

 ✔ Obtain device status

 ✔ Launch troubleshooting help

 ✔ Remove or replace drivers

 ✔ Change configuration settings

 ✔ Alter device-specific operational settings

From now on, you'll be able to reconfigure devices on the fly. And, in many cases, you don't even need to reboot for the changes to take effect.

Performance Monitor

Windows 2003's performance monitor utility (which is now called System Monitor) is an under-appreciated work of inspired genius. We say that not only because it's true, but also because we've come to rely on this outstanding tool to help us with all types of troubleshooting over the past few years.

When you first launch System Monitor (Start➪Administrative Tools➪ Performance), it presents readings from three default counters, as Figure 19-5 indicates. With a little work and planning, System Monitor can offer a broad range of useful information about the performance of your computer system and network.

Figure 19-5: The Performance Monitor.

You use the primary display of System Monitor to monitor either real-time or recorded measurements. Depending on which toolbar button you click, the display area can show measurements in graph form (such as an EKG), in histogram form (like a thermometer), or in report form (like a budget). See Chapter 20 for additional information on System Monitor.

Counting yer objects

Performance is measured on a counter and object basis. Chapter 16 goes into some detail about Windows 2003 objects. For this chapter, all you need to know is that everything in the Windows 2003 environment is an object, and each object has its own specific counters that measure certain aspects of the performance or activities of that object. The full context of performance is based on the following:

- ✔ **Computer:** The source system of the object
- ✔ **Object:** The subsystem of interest
- ✔ **Counter:** The aspect of performance of interest
- ✔ **Instance:** The specific object to be measured when multiple objects of the same type exist on a single system

Counters are added to the display area by clicking the big plus sign button on the System Monitor toolbar. This reveals the Add Counters dialog box, where you can select the context of the counters you want displayed. If you click the Explain button in this dialog box, details about the selected counter are revealed.

Here are some of the most important object and counter pairs to watch (in the following list, the object name appears to the left, followed by a backward slash, followed by the counter name):

- ✔ **Server\Bytes Total/sec:** Shows how much data your server is handling over time (for a basic measurement of how busy your system is). Other counters for the server object, such as Sessions Errored Out, Work Item Shortages, Errors System, and Blocking Requests Rejected, can all indicate potential system bottlenecks.

- ✔ **Memory\Pages/sec:** Shows how frequently the server is moving data from memory to disk, and vice versa. If this number gets large (more than 2500 pages per second on an average server), it can indicate a shortage of RAM on your server.

- ✔ **PhysicalDisk\Avg. Disk Queue Length:** Indicates how many disk requests are pending service. If this number stays over 2.0 for long, it can indicate a disk drive that's too slow to handle its load or one that's overwhelmed by current disk activity. Sometimes, this indicates a need for a faster drive or disk controller, or even a faster disk subsystem.

The objects used to monitor disk activity can cause performance problems even when System Monitor is not recording them. Therefore, by default, Windows 2003 enables only the PhysicalDisk counters and not the Logical Disk counters. Using the DISKPERF command-line tool, you can enable or disable both disk objects. For complete usage information, issue the `diskperf /?` command from a command prompt.

Some light summer reading

There are lots of books about performance monitoring and tuning for Windows NT 4.0 and Windows 2000, and we're sure that soon there will be many for Windows 2003 as well. Most of the tips for Windows NT 4.0 and Windows 2000 should apply to Windows 2003, but your mileage may vary.

Here are a few books we usually recommend for Windows NT 4.0 and Windows 2000 performance monitoring:

✔ *Windows 2000 Performance Guide* by Mark Friedman (published by O'Reilly & Associates)

✔ *Windows 2000: Performance Tuning & Optimization* by Kenton Gardinier (published by Osborne/McGraw-Hill)

✔ *Windows NT Server 4.0 Secrets* by Valda Hilley (published by Wiley Publishing, Inc.)

Keep an eye on these authors for Windows 2003 versions of similar titles.

Search for *Windows 2003 performance* at www.amazon.com and you may come across some books that weren't out when this book was written. Good luck and happy hunting.

Of logs and alerts

A major benefit of System Monitor is obtained through its logging capabilities. Through logs, you're able to capture performance data that you can review later. This not only allows you to collect data over extended periods of time without having to sit and watch, but also creates a historical paper trail for baselining, troubleshooting, and capacity planning.

Log files are created using the Counter Logs and Trace Logs selections of the Performance utility's main window. Counter Logs are used to record the measurements of specific counters (not just entire objects). Trace Logs are used to record memory and resource events.

Log files are created by highlighting either Counter Logs or Trace Logs in the left pane, right-clicking in the right pane, and then choosing New Log Settings. You need to name the log file and define the items it will record. For example, you may name the file server 1-2-2-02-cpu.log and record measurements from the CPU object. After you record a log file, you can view its content in the System Monitor display by clicking the View Log Data button (it looks like a cylinder) on the toolbar.

Another benefit (perhaps not so major) stems from the capability to define alerts. Alerts allow administrators to instruct System Monitor to watch certain counters and send a message when preset values are reached. Administrators use Alert view to issue warnings when disk space is running low or when network or CPU utilization becomes dangerously high. Think of Alert view as a type of system alarm capability. Generated whenever a counter's measurement crosses its defined threshold, an Alert event can do the following:

- ✔ Record an item in the Application log of Event Viewer
- ✔ Send a network message
- ✔ Execute a batch file
- ✔ Start logging performance data

You can define alerts in the Alerts area of the Performance utility's main window. Just select the Alert component in the left pane, right-click in the right pane, and choose New Alert Settings.

Windows 2003 Resource Kit Utilities

Many of the programmers and engineers who helped design Windows 2003 created tools and accessories that never made it into the official product release of Windows 2003. Many of these time-saving and headache-relieving tools are included in the Windows Server 2003 Resource Kit, along with lots of technical details and how-to's that the manuals and online help files simply don't contain.

The Windows Server 2003 Resource Kit was on the distribution CD with the main operating system in prerelease, but we don't know whether it will ship on the CD in the final form of the operating system. If it's not on the CD, you should be able to find it from an online bookstore or through TechNet (www.microsoft.com/technet/).

Whichever way you gain access to the Resource Kit, you'll find that it contains tons of troubleshooting utilities. Here, we provide a brief list of the categories and encourage you to explore this resource further for yourself:

- ✔ **Computer Management tools:** Includes a wide range of inspection, control, and profiling utilities.
- ✔ **Deployment tools:** Includes utilities for the Windows Server 2003 operating system and general software deployment, including specialty tools such as a Security Identifier (SID) monitoring tool and a system preparation tool.
- ✔ **Diagnostic tools:** Includes utilities for monitoring or inspecting applications, hardware, the network operating system, and the network.

✔ **Network Management tools:** Includes utilities for directory services, interoperability, network administration, performance, remote computing, security, and storage management.

✔ **Registry tools:** Includes a plethora of Registry tools that can be used to perform command-line actions, such as creating unique queries for values; adding, changing, or deleting values; copying subsections; and backup and restore operations.

✔ **Win32 Debugger tools:** Includes programmer-level utilities for troubleshooting and debugging custom code and software designed for the Windows 2003 platform.

To find out more about these utilities, search for the file named RKTOOLS.CHM on the Resource Kit Utilities CD or in the installed folder (\Program Files\ Resource Kit\). This file includes an explanation for each utility!

Chapter 20

Nixing Network Problems

. . . .

In This Chapter

▶ Knowing what happens when networks go bad

▶ Understanding the symptoms

▶ Nosing about with NetMon

▶ Double-checking network settings

▶ Finding a missing server

▶ Dealing with a slow network

▶ Accessing the network

▶ Fixing intermittent problems

. . . .

*E*ven with the best planning and equipment, the networks of even the best network administrators crash from time to time. Spotting trouble before it happens is best, but knowing how to quickly remedy trouble after it happens can be a lifesaver. Because of today's heterogeneous networking environments, many things can go wrong. In this chapter, we discuss some common network problems and tell you how to solve them.

When Good Networks Go Bad

Believe us when we say that you'll know when something goes wrong on your network! Your pager beeps (or vibrates), your phones ring, and people stand in your doorway tapping their feet. To help you lessen the chance of network problems, you should learn the warning signs associated with network problems and add preventative measures to your network.

Because networks consist of so many resources, when the network goes down, so too could the Internet connection as well as the e-mail, fax, and printing service. Whoops, that sounds like the business could come to a crashing halt! That's right, a broken network can cause lots of problems for an organization.

What's healthy? Creating a baseline

One way to monitor your network for trouble is to create a baseline report of what your network looks like on a day when it's healthy (that is, working properly). When you think the network is functioning poorly, you can compare snapshots of the network on a good day and a bad day. Some administrators like to take a baseline snapshot and then weekly snapshots.

You should monitor the network's memory, processor, logins, and utilization because these areas usually contain the warning signs that show up when something goes wrong. You can monitor these functions using the System Monitor tool that comes with Windows Server 2003. Choose Start⇨ Administrative Tools⇨Performance, and the Performance window appears. You'll notice that it has two functions: one is System Monitor and the other is Performance Logs and Alerts.

In System Monitor, you can view real-time information or load information from a previous capture of data that you made.

In Performance Logs and Alerts, you can look at the various logs in textual format to examine each individual alert. It's not really plain-old ASCII format; it's still a graphical user interface (GUI), but the alerts are listed as line items that you can view or filter.

To add counters and objects, right-click the Counters button at the bottom of the System Monitor and choose Add Counters. (You can also click the Add button, which is the plus sign in the right pane.) The Add Counters dialog box appears, as shown in Figure 20-1. Your computer is selected by default as the one to be monitored, but you can monitor any computer in your domain. Next, you need to select the performance object that you want to measure, such as Processor (which is selected by default), Print Queue, or Paging File. When you select the performance object, the performance counters for that object are displayed. After you select the counter, you may need to select an instance when you have more than one object on your system. For example, if you have more than one hard drive on your computer, you can choose which one you want to monitor.

You can check the server, processor, and memory for issues such as the total number of logons, how many logons your system is experiencing per second, how much memory is being used, and how much of the available sever bandwidth is being used. If you don't understand a particular object or counter, you can click Explain for more information.

While you have the Add Counters dialog box on your screen, you can add as many performance counters as you want. As you add each counter, it takes on a color that appears on the graph and in the legend at the bottom of the

Figure 20-1:
The Add Counters dialog box.

chart. Continue to click Add and choose the counters for the object until you're finished, and then click Close. Figure 20-2 shows System Monitor in action after we added several counters and began monitoring. Notice the real-time lines (one-second intervals) on the graph.

Figure 20-2:
A graph of System Monitor doing its thing.

You should establish a baseline when you first begin using Windows 2003. Then, set your alerts and counters to monitor performance during certain intervals of peak usage and other time frames. This allows you to analyze your network and server load after it's been used for a while. Make adjustments to your server and then look at the logs again to see whether the adjustments helped. For example, if you determined that more memory was needed in the server, add memory and then go back and view the logs again to make sure that this change improves performance. You may need to tweak some other setting besides the memory.

Because you want to monitor your server on a regular basis, save the configuration settings (File⇨Save As) and type a filename such as `Perfset.msc`. Then, each time you monitor the server, you can pull up your configured settings. If you save the settings to your desktop, Windows 2003 creates an icon for you that you can double-click the next time you want to monitor the server with these settings.

Documenting problems

We recommend that you grab a notebook and begin to document all network problems as they occur or immediately thereafter. You should record the symptoms, the items you changed to correct the problem, and the date and time. Documenting what you changed can give you a leg up if something else breaks that's related to a change you made. For example, you may need to give User A the permission to get to a spreadsheet application. Then, a week later, you notice that the master template file has been altered by that user and everyone on your network is complaining that their spreadsheet application has new defaults. You may have given that user too many rights.

You should include a drawing of your network (called a *network map*) in this documentation. Seeing your network at-a-glance helps with troubleshooting efforts because you can look at the various segments and their information. See Chapter 5 for more information on network maps.

If you have a computer room, you should lock the door and require visitors to sign a visitor log notebook — even the person who comes to change the light bulb in the ceiling should sign in, because the ladder could bump into some wires in your computer room and bring a segment of your network down.

What we've seen in organizations that have several network administrators is that while one administrator works on one problem, another lets the maintenance person into the computer room. When something on the network goes down, network administrators start looking for the problem, but don't know that there was someone in the computer room. If you keep access to all your equipment as restricted as possible, know exactly who goes near that equipment, and log all changes, you stand a better chance of troubleshooting problems quickly.

If you have more than one network administrator and a problem occurs, gather everyone and ask these questions:

- ✔ Has anyone made any changes to the network today that don't appear on the log?
- ✔ Has anyone outside our group been inside the computer room?

Then, check your network change log to see whether any changes to the network over the past week could be related to the current problem.

30,000-foot view

When your network breaks, try to step back and look at it from a distance. Ignore the panic that sets in because it won't help you keep your wits about you. Divide your network into segments so you can analyze which parts of the network are broken. Is it just one workstation, one segment, one server, one application, or one service? After you begin to isolate the problem, you can start to correct it.

If this network is connected to a wide area network (WAN), you have more work to do. Someone could have made changes on the WAN that affect your network. If you're connected to a WAN, be sure to use unique naming and addressing schemes. If everyone names their Windows 2003 servers and domains the same (for example, Server1, Server2, Server 3, and so on), things stop working well. For example, you can install a Windows Server 2003 in an isolated manner (not connected to any network) and then later connect it to a WAN. If no naming scheme is in place, other servers on the WAN may have the same names and addresses, which can really foul up the network.

In addition to using unique naming and addressing schemes, you need to build redundant paths or links in your WAN in case links go down. If you don't, you may find that remote offices are not available until the link is restored. Links can go down because of carrier problems or faulty equipment on your end. In some cases, you may want to disconnect your WAN connection to see whether the immediate problem goes away.

If you're using Active Directory Services and the directory isn't being administered properly, you may have some other LAN connected to yours via the WAN that's interfering with your network. Again, disconnect your WAN connection to see whether the problem goes away.

Flowcharts can help diagnose problems because they force you to think in a logical pattern (if the flowchart is logical). Draw a flowchart of your trouble-shooting technique and have it handy. Then, when trouble arises, you can look at your flowchart and make a quick determination.

Open Up and Say Ahhhhh!

Just as a runny nose can tell you that you're coming down with a cold, symptoms on a network can indicate when problems are about to occur. You should not only monitor your server and network for its general health, but also walk around the building and talk to your users. We find that a lot of users don't report problems as often as we would like. Sometimes you bump into users who casually tell you about a problem they have that forces them to reboot several times a day. The users just accept this instead of reporting it. We like to consider "walking the floors" as part of our general network-monitoring scheme.

The network's getting sleepy. . . very sleepy

Anytime the network begins to slow down, suspect trouble right away and start poking around at the disk space and memory on Windows Server 2003. Bad network interface cards (NICs) in workstations can cause a slowdown because the network tries to work around the malfunctioning board. You can use System Monitor and Network Monitor (NetMon) to poke around and gather information about what's messing up. If you have intelligent hubs on your network that are collecting Simple Network Management Protocol (SNMP)-type statistics to a centralized management console, look at those logs also. Often, they graphically depict a workstation NIC that's acting up.

Yeah man, it's NetMon

NetMon is a Windows Server 2003 utility that enables you to poke around the data on the network in a fashion similar to the way a protocol analyzer works. You can set up your Windows Server 2003 computer to capture frames from the network and analyze what's going on at an error level, protocol level, and more. NetMon is not that fancy because you can't view your entire network. You can view only the incoming frames to your Windows Server 2003 computer on which you install the agent and tools. If you want to view frames in an entire network segment, you have to use NetMon for Systems Management Server (SMS), simply because it's more robust and includes more features.

Network Monitor has two parts: the administrative tool (Network Monitor) and the network protocol (Network Monitor driver). You have to install both of these before you can begin to analyze the frames. Convenience then dictates that when you install Network Monitor, the driver is automatically installed along with it. That was nice of Microsoft.

The Windows Server 2003 installation doesn't install NetMon automatically. It's a service that you install separately and access through the Control Panel. Follow these steps to install NetMon on your server:

1. **Choose Start⇨Control Panel⇨Add or Remove Programs.**

   The Add or Remove Programs dialog box appears.

2. **Click Add/Remove Windows Components.**

   The Windows Components Wizard appears.

3. **Choose Management and Monitoring Tools, and then click Details.**

4. **In the Management and Monitoring Tools window, mark the Network Monitor Tools check box, and click OK.**

5. **Click Next.**

6. **If you are prompted for more files to complete the installation, do one of the following:**

   a. If you copied your Windows Server 2003 CD to the network, tell the wizard the path of the files.

   b. Otherwise, insert your Windows Server 2003 CD.

After you have everything installed, you can start NetMon through the Administrative Tools area (Start⇨Administrative Tools⇨Network Monitor). Your screen should look similar to Figure 20-3.

After you've launched NetMon, you can set up filters to capture only certain information. For example, you may not want to monitor NetBIOS multicast information, but you may want to hone in on Internet Protocol (IP) information. You set filters to separate what's captured and what's not.

You can set triggers on events so that "when this happens, take this action." For example, you may not want to capture all the data coming and going on the server. You may be looking for a certain pattern and when that pattern occurs, you want to begin the capture. These filtered captures help you further define what you're looking at in the capture trace.

Microsoft has a wealth of information about NetMon that you should become familiar with (Start⇨Help and Support⇨Administration and Scripting Tools⇨ Monitoring and Status Tools⇨Network Monitor). Always start with the Best Practices section to learn what Microsoft feels is the best way to set up a particular function on your network.

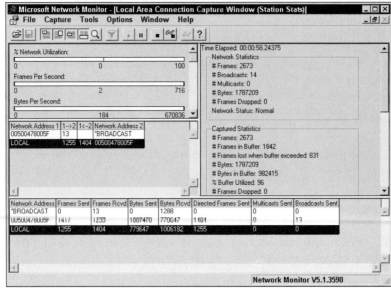

Figure 20-3:
The
Network
Monitor in
action.

Check Those Network Settings: Again!

A host of things can be configured improperly or changed that will affect network operation. The following list of questions can help you sleuth about and find things that may have changed:

- **Is proper addressing set (no duplicate addresses)?** Each node on the network (including servers) must have a unique address and computer name. If you can't PING (PING is an IP utility discussed in Chapter 14) or see the computer in the browser or Active Directory, make sure its identifiers are correct.

- **Are the proper IP ranges set?** If you're using an in-house IP numbering scheme and then connect to the Internet, your scheme may conflict with another registered set of numbers. Before connecting to the Internet, check with your Internet Service Provider to make sure that you don't set up your network using someone else's IP numbers.

- **Are the services on server running?** Sometimes the service you need stops running on the server. Choose Start⇨Administrative Tools⇨Services and check that the service is installed and running. Sometimes you need to start and stop a service.

✔ **Are any errors logged in Event Viewer?** Look in Event Viewer to see whether any errors have been logged (Start⇨Administrative Tools⇨ ✐Event Viewer).

✔ **Are there any conflicting devices?** Use the Windows 2003Conflicts/ Sharing Manager to see whether any devices are conflictingwith interrupt requests (IRQs) or memory. (Choose Start⇨All Programs⇨ Accessories⇨System Tools⇨System Information⇨Hardware Resources⇨ Conflicts/Sharing.) You can also look in Device Manager in that same area for more information.

✔ **Are the proper domains available?** Be sure that the proper domain controller for the server is up and running and that Active Directory is available.

✔ **Are access rights assigned correctly?** Be sure users have the proper rights to the groups and resources that they need to access.

✔ **Are the proper shares set?** Make sure that the resource in question is shared on the server and listed in Active Directory for all or some to see. Sometimes devices don't appear because they haven't been told to.

What Do You Mean the Server's Unavailable?

When users can't find the server from their workstations, they get antsy. Check to see whether only one user or several users have the problem. If just one user can't find the server, the problem is probably at his or her workstation. If several users can't find the server, you probably have a segment problem, such as a downed bridge or router. (For more information on bridges and routers, see Chapter 4.)

If one user has the problem, ask the following questions:

✔ **Is the user logged in?** Don't laugh, but sometimes users call you about not getting services on a network and they haven't logged in yet.

✔ **Has the user ever accessed the network before?** If this is a new user logging in for the first time, the account may not be set up. However, if the user recently transferred from another department, you may need to reassign the user to another group or alter his or her account policies.

✔ **Has the user tried to reboot the workstation?** Sometimes, if the user reboots his or her workstation, the one-time glitch disappears.

✔ **Does the user have the proper rights?** Check the user's account policies and permissions to make sure he or she has the proper access rights on the network or directory to access the needed resource.

✔ **Has anyone made changes to the workstation?** If any new devices were added to this workstation, the new device may have a conflicting IRQ or memory address problem. Look at the root directory on the workstation and sort the files by date and time to see when the latest changes were made. Then, check the Windows directory and search for *.ini files to see whether changes have been made to any of those files. If a new NIC was added, verify whether it was set to the proper speed of the network.

✔ **Can you PING the user's workstation?** If Transmission Control Protocol/Internet Protocol (TCP/IP) is installed on the workstation, try PINGing the workstation from your desktop, try PINGing the server from the user's workstation, and try to find the server in the browser or directory listing. For more information on how to PING, see Chapter 14. If you can PING the server but can't see the server in the browser, you can force a browser election on the network to reset the master browser. For information about browser elections, search TechNet (www.microsoft.com/technet/).

✔ **Does the user have a bad satin cable?** Satin cable is the silver-colored cable sometimes used for the network connection between the user's NIC and the wall plate. Sometimes housekeeping vacuums over the cables on a network and damages them. You can easily change out a cable to see whether it's bad. If the cable isn't the problem, try the NIC. (Of course, if this is a wireless workstation, the cable won't be the culprit!)

✔ **Does the user have a bad NIC?** NICs go bad sometimes. Replace the card with a card that you know works to see whether that solves the problem.

You may also want to check the following:

✔ **Logon time restrictions:** If the user can log on to the network at specific times only, check the user's configuration to make sure no restrictions apply.

✔ **Remote Access Service (RAS):** If the unavailable server is a RAS server, you must grant users a dial-in privilege in their accounts to connect to it.

✔ **Dynamic Host Configuration Protocol (DHCP):** If the unavailable server is a DHCP server, make sure that the DHCP service is installed and running. (Choose Start➪Administrative Tools➪Computer Management, and then expand Services and Applications.) If users who depend on DHCP services can't see the DHCP server, they can't obtain an IP address.

Slow Networking Services

When services on a network start to slow down, trouble is surely just around the corner. When this happens, it's possible that disk space on the server is running low, memory needs to be reconfigured, or a token ring board has gone bad and broken the ring. If the NICs in the server aren't capable of handling a lot of traffic, think about upgrading to higher performance NICs. Don't use old 8-bit NICs for your server; use 32-bit NICs at the very minimum.

Hark! I hear a board beaconing

Token ring is a funny creature because it forms a ring, and the data travels around the ring in a circular fashion. When a break in the ring occurs, data travels in a U shape instead. People located at the bottom of the U don't notice the slowdown as much, but those located at the tops see a tremendous slowdown. A token ring break typically happens when wiring gets out of whack or when one NIC starts beaconing. (This means the NIC is sending a signal that something is wrong with it.) If you use hubs that aren't intelligent, or Multistation Access Units (MAUs), you have to isolate the bad token ring board or port on the MAU by a process of elimination. We've had to take an entire ring and unplug one MAU at a time, and then unplug one port at a time. The older MAUs are actually relays, and you have to use a MAU tool to reset the relay. Other times, you need to replace the faulty NIC.

Oh where, oh where has the bandwidth gone?

You should check to see whether an application running on the network is consuming a lot of bandwidth. Applications consuming a lot of bandwidth occur frequently in 10-Mbps (10MB per second) Ethernet environments in which you have a lot of network activity and database applications. In some poorly designed database applications, when a user makes a database query, the entire contents of the database are downloaded to the user's workstation for processing. This creates a lot of extraneous traffic. To help alleviate this problem, you can upgrade to database software that has a database engine to do the record crunching; the user gets only the results. Another solution to this problem is to upgrade to a faster network-wiring scheme, such as 100-Mbps Ethernet.

High-volume printing can also cause this problem. If certain users or groups of users are printing volumes of data during the day, think about switching them to print at night (if possible) to alleviate network congestion. You can set up a print definition for those users that allows their information to be printed only during certain hours.

Some organizations elect to upgrade their existing network backbone to help relieve bandwidth congestion problems, but the associated cost is high. Organizations that have remote offices sometimes place an extra Windows 2003 Server in the remote office and install it as a domain controller. This allows user authentication to be performed locally at the remote office, which conserves WAN bandwidths. Other organizations elect to upgrade their current network backbone to 100 Mbps while leaving the users connected to the hubs at 10 Mbps. This involves upgrading the devices connected to the backbone to include 100-Mbps NICs and cables, plus adding a switch capable of changing between the workstation speed of 10 Mbps to the backbone speed of 100 Mbps. With this arrangement, even if users are going full throttle, the server still has 90-percent bandwidth available for other clients.

Congestion on the network

If you have an Ethernet network that's experiencing lots of collisions and errors, there could be a problem with the Carrier Sense Multiple Access/ Collision Detection (CSMA/CD) media access method. If you have intelligent hubs on the network, you can view information about the network either through a graphical interface or by looking at the LEDs on the hubs. A high collision rate is usually an indication of faulty wiring or bad boards. It can also mean that the bandwidth utilization is high. Ethernet has a lower utilization than token ring. Sometimes you need to segment off high-volume users.

Where did all the disk space go?

If your server's disk space is low, you're in for a fair amount of trouble because servers can contain print queues, as well as user's data and applications. When disk space begins to run low, all sorts of strange problems appear. You should buy a lot of RAM up front, because Windows 2003 uses much more than its predecessor, Windows NT. If you have the minimum RAM required by Microsoft, you'll run into problems trying to do more than one task, so add lots more on top of the minimum.

Windows 2003 uses disk space to swap recently used information back and forth from RAM. Therefore, if you have more RAM, you'll be able to access files faster. You can look at your memory information and how it's being used by choosing Start⇨All Programs⇨Accessories⇨System Tools⇨System Information⇨System Summary.

Low disk space causes Windows 2003 to encounter difficulties when trying to write to the Pagefile.sys file. To view and change the minimum and maximum size of this file, choose Start⇨Control Panel⇨System, click the Advanced tab, and then click the Settings button under the Performance heading. In the Performance Options dialog box that appears, click the Advanced tab, then click the Change button under the Virtual Memory heading. You see a screen similar to the one shown in Figure 20-4.

Figure 20-4:
The Virtual
Memory
dialog box.

Virtual Memory dialog box showing:

Drive [Volume Label]   Paging File Size (MB)
C: 384 - 768

Paging file size for selected drive
Drive: C:
Space available: 2063 MB
⊙ Custom size:
Initial size (MB):   384
Maximum size (MB):   768
○ System managed size
○ No paging file   Set

Total paging file size for all drives
Minimum allowed: 2 MB
Recommended: 382 MB
Currently allocated: 384 MB

OK   Cancel

You should have at least the same minimum and maximum numbers that Windows 2003 recommends.

Do it after hours

Is someone performing a network task that's transferring a large amount of data, such as restoring a lot of files? Or is someone performing a function such as remirroring drives? If a network has large storage drives that are mirrored and the mirroring breaks, you can remirror the drives, but doing it during working hours isn't a good idea. Check to see whether anyone is performing some sort of maintenance — either on the network or the server. If a large restoration of files is required across the network, try to do it during nonpeak hours.

If you check in System Monitor and see a heavy resource load, you can get a better handle on who's placing that load by choosing Start⇨Administrative Tools⇨Computer Management, expanding System Tools⇨Shared Folders, and checking the resource usage per share, per person.

Can't Get There from Here

When a segment of your network is down, getting "there" is impossible. Several factors can cause this, depending on how you configure your network. Try to PING different nodes of the network to pinpoint what's down. For example, if you can PING one interface of a router but not the other interface, the problem is probably inside the router. You can also perform a TRACERT (as discussed in Chapter 14) on TCP/IP to determine the time intervals between the current and final destinations. A slow response between two destinations could point you to the exact location of the problem. Try using PING and TRACERT from different locations on your network to further define what can be seen and from where.

Use more than one utility to determine where your network failure may be. For example, PING works with the TCP/IP protocol only: Try using another utility, such as NBTSTAT, which works with NetBIOS and TCP/IP.

Also, the following problems could prevent you from accessing portions of the network:

- ✔ **Router problem:** Routers connect different networks. If you've defined your router improperly, you can't see what's on the other side. Routers can also experience congestion and drop packets. In these cases, you may need more memory in the router. Older routers also require chip upgrades; for newer routers, upgrades can be written to the current chips. Check which software version your router is using and contact the manufacturer.

- ✔ **Bridge problem:** If your network contains bridges, sometimes you need to reboot the bridge. This may occur frequently, depending on the software and hardware used. Remember that bridges need high-end NICs because they pass a lot of packets between them. (See Chapter 4 for more information on bridges.)

✔ **WAN link problem:** If a T1 or 56 KB line goes down, you don't see anything on the other side of the line. Sometimes, you may have to call a telecom company to resolve this problem. You need to have circuit information and the customer support number handy.

✔ **Hub problem:** If you lose an entire segment of the network, check the hub that connects that segment. Hubs usually have power supplies and ports that can go bad. Sometimes, just plugging a node into a different port on the hub corrects a problem. Make sure you mark the port as bad so someone else doesn't plug a device into that port. Putting a circle around the port is often a good way to denote a bad port.

✔ **Wiring problem:** Wiring can degrade over time or can be moved around enough that the wires can go bad. Use a Time Domain Reflectometer (TDR) tool to check the cable for breaks. You may have to pull a new cable to the desktop or server. If you suspect that housekeeping has vacuumed over one of your satin cables and damaged it, replace that cable!

✔ **Server problem:** Check that the server in question is up and running. This seems obvious, but check it anyway.

✔ **Name resolution problem:** You may need to install Windows Internet Naming Service (WINS), DHCP, or a host file, depending on the protocols used on your network. (See Chapter 14 on TCP/IP for more information.)

Tracking Down Intermittent Problems

Intermittent problems are by far the most difficult to solve because they don't happen when you want them to and you can't always reproduce them. These types of problems occur after a sequence of events, usually in a particular order unbeknownst to you. Your work is to figure out the sequence of events. Impossible, you say. Not really!

If you started your system log, record the following items to help you eliminate possible causes of the problem:

✔ **Note the time and day of the problem:** For example, does the problem seem to occur only at 10 A.M. on Wednesdays? Perhaps a particular activity in one of the departments happens every week, such as right before a departmental meeting when everyone is trying to access or print reports. This extra activity could place a load on the server or the network. Look for trends in dates and time. Use System Monitor if you suspect this.

✔ **Note the equipment in use:** Does the problem occur only on a particular workstation or server? Does the problem occur only when a particular user logs on to the network? Check the user's account information, plus his or her desktop configuration files.

✔ **Note the application in use:** Does the problem occur only when a certain application is used? Reinstall the application. An application file can become corrupt, and the corruption can go unnoticed until a user performs a particular function of that application.

✔ **Note the environment in use:** Does the problem occur only on a certain floor, near a certain area such as an elevator? If so, you may have some wiring conflicts near heavy motors or fluorescent lighting.

✔ **Check the visitor's log:** Does the problem occur every time the maintenance person enters a wiring closet or the computer room? If so, follow this person in the next time and see what he or she is doing. (Don't forget the overcoat and sunglasses!)

✔ **Viruses:** Always an obvious possibility, viruses are often the last things checked. Viruses introduce random oddities onto networks. If you suspect one, immediately disconnect the server from the rest of the network and WAN, and scan it. Until recently, this would have been enough. However, it's important to instruct your users not to send any e-mail if you suspect a virus. You may have to disable the company post office to ensure that no e-mail is distributed at this time.

✔ **Known bugs:** Sometimes, you pound your head into the wall trying to solve a problem that is really a known bug. Check the Microsoft Web site regularly, and check for new service packs. Remember to check other organizations' Web sites as well. For example, if you use Microsoft Office, check Microsoft's site for service packs for that suite. If you use all 3Com Ethernet cards, check the 3Com Web site for driver updates that correct bugs. Staying on top of known problems can save you oodles of time.

Chapter 21

Reactivating Active Directory

. . . .

In This Chapter

▶ Cleaning house with Active Directory

▶ Getting help from the Help system troubleshooter

▶ Exploring common Active Directory problems

▶ Restoring a system from backup

. . . .

Active Directory is a vital part of Windows Server 2003. As described in Chapters 11 and 12, Active Directory contains and controls all the important objects in a network. Which important objects might those be? Well, they include user accounts, shared resources, computer membership, and group policy controls. In other words, Active Directory contains the items that enable and support a Windows 2003 domain.

When Microsoft designed Active Directory, it rightly perceived that any problems with this core service would cause network-wide problems. Therefore, it built powerful fault tolerance into the Active Directory service and provided several mechanisms that help Windows 2003 perform and maintain its regular functions. In this chapter, we look into these recovery and restoration features of Windows 2003 Active Directory.

A *fault-tolerant system* is one that can keep running during a software or hardware error. In addition, fault tolerance should prevent the loss of data.

Domain Controller, Heal Thyself

Active Directory is dynamically self-healing, or at least self-maintaining. It regularly checks itself for internal consistency, missing data, and expired entries. By default, a housecleaning operation is performed every 12 hours. This housecleaning consists of deleting logs, removing expired entries, and defragmenting the database file. The logs deleted by the housecleaning operation are change or transaction logs that temporarily store operations. After the system verifies that all actions listed in these logs have been performed successfully, the logs are deleted because they're no longer needed.

When you use a computer, the data on the hard disk naturally becomes fragmented (or split), which results in slower data access. The process of reorganizing this data back into the proper order to maximize performance is called *defragmentation*.

As Active Directory changes and adapts to the network environment, relationship and other object-related data becomes outdated or expires. This data, along with deleted items that still remain in the database, is removed. Defragmenting the database file compacts the data and reorganizes the file to maximize performance.

When defragmentation is performed by the system, it's called *online defragmentation*. Online defragmentation creates space within the existing database file for new Active Directory entries, but it does not release the space back to the file system for use by other files. Only offline defragmentation releases unused database space back to the file system. Microsoft recommends that offline defragmentation be performed only when absolutely necessary (such as when not enough drive space is available to perform normal system operations). To initiate an offline defragmentation, you must reboot and press the F8 key to access the boot menu. Then select Directory Services Restore Mode, which performs the offline defragmentation and boots the system into Safe mode. You'll have to reboot again to return to a fully operational network-supporting boot.

When All Is Not Quiet on the Western Front

Things go wrong. Sometimes, administrators' mistakes cause problems, a failed network connection prevents resource access, or a stray neutrino corrupts a data point in the database file. In any case, things need to be fixed to restore the normal productive activity of Active Directory.

The Help and Support Center system of Windows 2003 includes an Active Directory troubleshooter in the form of several problem-based scenarios with detailed causes and solutions. We've found this information to be immensely helpful in nearly every Active Directory-related problem we've encountered. To access the Active Directory troubleshooting information, follow these steps:

1. **Choose Start↪Help and Support.**

   The Windows 2003 Help and Support Center window appears.

2. **Click the Active Directory option in the list on the left, click the Troubleshooting subtopic, and then click Troubleshooting Active Directory.**

   In the right pane, you are presented with a list of possible Active Directory problems.

3. **In the right pane, click the topic that most closely resembles your current situation.**

   The list expands, displaying detailed causes and solutions. You'll probably find that your system is restored quickly with a simple fix.

Common Issues

The Help and Support Center troubleshooting section for Active Directory can lead you down the most direct path to the Promised Land of problem resolution. If you're an independent spirit, however, you may want to try to troubleshoot problems without any aid from the Help system. Luckily for you, the most common problems, which result from a failed or misbehaved Active Directory, are relatively easy to diagnose.

Communication interruption

The most common Active Directory problem is a communication interruption. Simply put, a communication interruption is anything that prevents clear and complete packet transactions between two hosts. These interruptions can result from something as simple as a broken network cable or an offline computer. More complex problems, such as a router with a corrupt routing table or a DNS server with wrongly defined entries, can also cause interruptions. When the problem is physical, you may need to replace the cables or reboot the system to restore functionality. When the problem is more complex, you need to investigate troubleshooting options specific to the ailing service.

If you suspect that a communication interruption is occurring, you can use common networking tools to help you obtain more specific information. For example, if your network uses the Transmission Control Protocol/Internet Protocol (TCP/IP), you can use tools designed for troubleshooting this protocol. The two most useful tools for this protocol are PING and TRACERT. (See

Chapter 14 for more information on PING and TRACERT.) PING informs you whether packets can traverse the network between your system and any other host. TRACERT informs you of each router jump between you and another host and whether transmission is not possible past a specific route point.

If the results of both PING and TRACERT show that packets may not even be leaving your computer, use IPCONFIG /ALL to verify that the TCP/IP protocol is properly installed and that its settings (IP address, subnet mask, default gateway, and so on) are correct. If any settings are incorrect, change them through the Local Area Connection interface (Start⇨Control Panel⇨ Network Connections⇨Local Area Connection) and reboot.

Group Policy problems

Another common problem arises from Group policies that either restrict access too much or contradict or overlap each other, which causes inconsistencies in the way the system functions. You'll need to examine the Group policies for each domain, user, group, and organizational unit to determine where the problem lies.

Domain controller communication

If Windows NT 4.0 backup domain controllers (BDCs) and Windows Server 2003 domain controllers are unable to communicate, you've probably enabled native mode for the domain. Active Directory in Windows Server 2003 can operate in four modes: Windows 2000 mixed, Windows 2000 native, Windows .NET, and Windows .NET interim.

Windows 2000 mixed mode is the default mode that allows both Windows Server 2003 domain controllers and Windows NT 4.0 Servers installed as BDCs to act as domain controllers interactively. *Windows 2000 native mode* prevents Windows NT 4.0 Servers from participating in domain controlling.

The *big* problem with the mode setting is that after it's set to native mode, it can't be reversed without a complete system reinstallation. Therefore, administrators should switch domains over to native mode only after they are *absolutely* sure that Windows NT 4 BDCs are no longer required.

The mode setting is made using the Active Directory Domains and Trusts tool (Start⇨Administrative Tools⇨Active Directory Domains and Trusts). Select the domain you want to switch over, right-click, and choose Raise Domain Functional Level. Then, in the Raise Domain Functional Level dialog box, choose a functional level (mode) from the Select an Available Domain Functional Level list.

If the combination of automated housecleaning, the instructions found in the Help and Support Center, and your own troubleshooting efforts fail to resolve your Active Directory problem, there's only one solution left — restoration from backup.

Backing Up and Restoring Directory Data

Restoring Active Directory from a backup requires one important item: a timely backup of the system. Without a recent backup of the system when it was functioning normally, you can't restore Active Directory — just as you can't build a brick wall if you don't have any bricks. The only way this solution can be employed is to prepare for it.

Preparing to restore Active Directory from a backup requires that you have a complete backup of your entire system. That means creating a backup using Backup Wizard and selecting Back Up Everything on My Computer (see Chapter 17).

When you have a backup, restoring the system is not difficult. Just follow these steps:

1. **Reinstall Windows Server 2003.**

   Be sure to install the system using the same partition and root directory names as before.

2. **Use the Backup tool to restore all data from the backup set back to its original locations.**

3. **After restoration is complete, reboot the system.**

   Windows 2003 automatically realizes that it's been restored from a backup and rebuilds the Active Directory database.

That's it. As you can see, your only real tool for repairing a severely damaged system is a recent and complete backup. As we stress in Chapter 17, you need to implement a regular, regimented backup procedure to protect your data (and your job).

If you would like more information on dealing with Active Directory problems, consult the Windows 2003 Help and Support Center (as described earlier in this chapter), the Windows Server 2003 Resource Kit, and TechNet (www.microsoft.com/technet/).

Part VI
The Part of Tens

The 5th Wave — By Rich Tennant

"Drive carefully, remember your lunch, and always make a backup of your directory tree before modifying your hard disk partition file."

In this part . . .

When Moses came down from the mountain, how many commandments did he carry? Ten. How many fingers do most people have? Ten. On a scale of one to ten, what's a perfect score? Ten. We're not entirely sure that all these things are necessarily connected, but that number shows up everywhere, even on the *Late Show with David Letterman.* Perhaps that's why The Part of Tens is a key ingredient in this and all other *For Dummies* books. Then again, it could just be a coincidence . . .

Each chapter in this part includes a list of tips, tricks, techniques, reminders, and resources for inspired information about your Windows Server 2003 system and its network. We'd like to claim the same source of inspiration that Moses had for his commandments, but our Part of Tens comes only from the "School of Hard Knocks" next door.

These chapters have been constructed to save you time, steer you around common networking potholes, and get you safely past common sources of chaos and confusion. The best part of tens, however, is one that doesn't appear directly in this part of the book — that's the part where you hold your breath and *count to ten* as you begin to lose your cool. If you try that part first, the other Part of Tens will do you a lot more good!

Chapter 22

Ten Tips for Installation and Configuration

*I*f you spend enough time working with Windows Server 2003, you undoubtedly will be required to install this software on multiple systems. This job can be more "interesting" than it has to be — not to mention that it can take more time than you may want it to.

This chapter provides some fact-filled sources of information, some tried-and-true guidelines, and some great repair tools and techniques to help you successfully survive the Windows Server 2003 installation process. Knowing these ten tips and not needing them is better than not knowing and needing them.

Exceed the Minimum Requirements

Table 22-1 offers a quick rundown of the minimum requirements to run Windows Server 2003 (and bonus realistic recommendations).

Table 22-1	Windows Server 2003 Minimum Requirements (Plus Realistic Recommendations)	
Item	*Minimum Requirement*	*Recommended*
CD-ROM	None	CD-ROM (12X or better) or DVD player
CPU	Pentium 133 MHz	Pentium 550 MHz or better
Disk space	1.5GB+ free	4GB free or more
Display	VGA	SVGA 800 x 600 or better
Floppy drive	3.5 inch (optional)	3.5 inch
NIC	At least one	PCI bus mastering NIC (at least 32 bit)
Pointing device	MS-Mouse or compatible (optional)	MS-Mouse or compatible
RAM	128MB or more	256MB or more (4GB max)

To configure a production server to simply meet the minimum requirements is a recipe for disaster. The performance (or lack thereof) you'd be able to squeeze out from such a machine would have a mob of users at your heels in no time at all.

When building a Windows Server 2003 computer, more of just about every-thing is better: This applies to more powerful (and more) CPUs, more RAM, and more powerful network interface cards (NICs). Servers do their things in quiet obscurity in most cases, so you don't have to install a 16MB graphics adapter, a fancy monitor, or a top-dollar mouse or touchpad. You can opt to skip the CD-ROM or DVD player on the Windows Server 2003 computer as long as you can access the server across the network from another machine where the contents of the CD-ROM have been copied to a hard drive.

If you install Windows Server 2003 on a machine that doesn't include a NIC, you won't be able to install or configure any of its network-related aspects. We're convinced that there's no point to installing a server that's not attached to a network, so don't install Windows Server 2003 on a machine unless it has a NIC (even better, a NIC connected to a real, live network).

Use Only Qualified Server Hardware

Before you even think about installing Windows Server 2003 on a machine, you'd best be sure that the hardware you're considering will make a good home for that software. Nevertheless, without a formal seal of approval or a guarantee from a vendor, how can you be sure that the software will work with your hardware?

Fortunately, you *can* be sure by checking the Windows 2003 Hardware Compatibility List (HCL). This is a comprehensive list of hardware that's been tested and certified to be compatible with Windows 2003. The HCL is available online at www.microsoft.com/hcl/.

You can also use the installation utility to automatically check your hardware for you. However, to use the latest HCL available, the system must also have Internet access. There are two ways to test your system for HCL compliance. The first is to insert the CD and let the auto-run mechanism start (or execute startup.exe from the root of the CD). Click Check System Compatibility and then click Check My System Automatically. The second method is to execute the following from the command prompt or Run dialog box:

```
i386\winnt32 /checkupgradeonly
```

Both methods attempt to first download the latest HCL and then test your system's hardware for compliance with the requirements of Window 2003. If any problems or incompatibilities are found, you see an on-screen report.

Many hardware vendors offer server machines with Windows Server 2003 preinstalled. When you're buying new servers, price one that includes the Windows Server 2003 operating system versus one that doesn't. You may be pleasantly surprised by the price breaks you can get when buying a preinstalled system.

Install from Your Network

The following may seem counterintuitive, but here goes: Copying files from a hard drive elsewhere on a network is faster than copying files from a local CD-ROM player (even a 36x or 40x player). Why? Because hard disks are still as much as 100 times faster than CD-ROM drives.

Savvy network administrators create a set of directories on a network drive and install Windows Server 2003 across the network when they can. This tactic is fast, easy, and requires only that you load a CD once, no matter how many times you install from it. In fact, network installation is what makes the next topic — namely, automated installations — feasible.

Let the Software Do the Work: Automating Installation

Normally, user input drives the Windows 2003 installation program: from character-based prompts during the initial load phase and by user navigation of menus and input items during the later phases. As an alternative, text files called answer files may drive Windows 2003 installation, making it possible to automate installation more or less completely. Script-driven installation can be especially handy when you must install more than two or three copies of Windows 2003 at any given time.

Windows 2003 supports more methods for automating installation than previous implementations (such as Windows NT 4.0), including the following:

- A new `[GuiRunOnce]` section in the answer file contains a list of commands to execute when a user logs on to the system the first time after the graphical user interface (GUI) mode portion of the installation completes.

- You can create a set of automated commands to complete the Setup process without requiring human intervention (at least, as long as no errors are encountered).

- You can even automate the first logon after Windows 2003's setup completes to install and configure selected applications, and then shut down the system thereafter — all from the magic answer files!

How do you get a piece of this magic? Well, you can search for and edit a predefined answer file called `unattend.txt` in the Windows Server 2003 Resource Kit. Or you can work with a utility called the Setup Manager, which you must install on your system after Windows Server 2003's base installation completes, to create an answer file for you from scratch. (To install Setup Manager, double-click `Support\Tools\deploy.cab` on the Windows Server 2003 installation CD.)

Windows 2003's Setup Manager is similar to the Windows 98 utility of the same name. This outstanding tool provides buttons that map to various sections of the installation process and guides you through interactive dialog boxes to specify a script for a single system installation or for multiple systems at the same time.

Windows 2003 also includes two utilities that are somewhat Ghost-like in their capabilities. (Ghost is a popular system imaging utility for Windows NT 4.0 that allows administrators to set up a single installation, take a snapshot, and then customize that same snapshot to install one, two, or many machines at the same time.) These two utilities follow:

✔ **Sysprep:** A utility designed to duplicate disk contents when installing multiple, identically configured machines at the same time. First you create a normal installation on a single machine, and then you install the applications you want to distribute. Next, you use Sysprep to distribute copies of this configuration to other identical systems elsewhere on the network. It doesn't get much easier than this!

✔ **Syspart:** A utility designed to clone installations across multiple machines where the hardware is dissimilar. It works as an extension of the unattended install facility with a default `unattend.txt` answer file.

Consult the *Windows Server 2003 Resource Kit* (published by Microsoft Press) or the TechNet CD to find out all you can about the various installation files before starting any big jobs. You'd also be well advised to try a couple of trial runs using these tools before attempting to automate the installation of one or more production servers.

Beating Installation Weirdness — Be Persistent

Despite your best efforts, and even if you've taken all the proper precautions, the occasional Windows 2003 installation will fail. We've seen causes of failure that range from defective media, to network congestion (trying to copy files to too many machines at once), to boot sector viruses. (We hate when that happens!)

When an installation fails, take a deep breath, count to ten, and try any or all of the following corrections:

✔ **Restart the installation:** If you get past the initial parts of the character mode portion of the installation, the software is often smart enough to pick up where it left off and carry on from there. If you're that lucky, count your blessings, and then go out and buy a lottery ticket!

✔ **If installation won't pick up where it left off, look for a directory named WIN_NT.~LS:** (If you're doing a floppyless install with the /B parameter, also look for WIN_NT.~BT.) Delete one (or both) of these directories and their contents. The Windows 2003 installation program looks for these directories and attempts to save time by picking up where it left off. This behavior works fine when copies are correct and pristine but can get in the way when problems surface. We include the DOS DELTREE command in our emergency install disk tool kit because it lets us dispatch these directories and their contents quickly and easily.

✔ **If all else fails, repartition and reformat the boot drive to remove all vestiges of your failed attempt:** You'll start over with a clean slate! Our emergency install disk tool kit also includes DOS Fdisk and a handy utility called Delpart.exe, which can remove even non-DOS partitions (such as NTFS) from a PC hard drive. Delpart.exe is available for free download from several Web sites. Search your favorite search engine for **Delpart.exe**.

If the final technique doesn't work, recheck the Windows 2003 HCL for potential sources of difficulty (see the "Use Only Qualified Server Hardware" section earlier in this chapter for the details on the HCL). Otherwise, look for guidance on your problems on Microsoft's TechNet CD or the Windows 2003-related newsgroups on the news:// msnews.microsoft.com news server.

Let [VGA Mode] Come to the Rescue!

You'll find out that Windows 2003 doesn't care a bit whether the display on your Windows Server 2003 machine is working. Windows 2003 continues to chug along quite happily — even if you can't see what the system is doing because the screen is totally confuzled or nothing is showing at all. The leading cause of display problems is loading a display driver that doesn't work with your graphics adapter, or your monitor, or both!

When this problem happens (and it's a common post-installation problem), don't panic. Simply reboot the machine (press the Reset button on the computer case if you can't read the screen at all). When the boot menu shows up, press F8 to access the Advanced Options, and then select Enable VGA Mode.

Doing so boots Windows 2003 with a plain-vanilla VGA driver. Then you can try a different driver (or troubleshoot the hardware). This time, use the test button to make sure the driver works before you change your display!

Use "Last Known Good" to Do Good!

After installation is complete, you must continue to configure your Windows Server 2003 to install additional software and add all types of information about system and user policies, account and group names, and so forth.

A generic boot floppy saves systems!

The problem with Startup disks is that it takes six of them to boot Windows 2003. Using these disks also takes you through a time-consuming set of steps to get a machine running. Fortunately, creative minds decided to develop a generic Windows 2003 boot floppy. It works on any system and kick-starts just about any balky Windows 2003 machine. Here's how to build one:

1. Format a floppy using the Windows Explorer (right-click the floppy drive icon in the left panel and select Format).

   You MUST format this floppy inside Windows 2003. A DOS-formatted floppy won't work as a generic Windows 2003 boot floppy!

2. Check your Windows Explorer settings to make sure you can see hidden files by choosing Tools⇨Folder Options, clicking the View tab, and then clicking the Show Hidden Files and Folders option in the Advanced Setting section.

3. Copy the following files from your server's root directory to the Windows 2003-formatted floppy disk:

   ✔ NTDLR

   ✔ NTDETECT.COM

   ✔ BOOT.INI

   ✔ NTBOOTDD.SYS (only if it appears)

This creates a boot floppy that can bring up a Windows 2003 system without using all six startup disks. Make this part of your standard Windows 2003 toolkit.

If this generic boot floppy won't boot the system, try the Startup floppies and attempt a full-fledged system repair!

Every time you make a change to Windows 2003, those changes are recorded in the Windows 2003 Registry. Sometimes, those changes can have unforeseen side effects — especially if you've been editing the Registry directly — and can make your machine falter or even fail to boot.

When your machine does falter or fails to boot, always try reverting to the last working version of the Registry. When the boot menu shows up, press F8 to access Advanced Options, and then select Last Known Good Configuration. You roll back to the version of the Registry that was in use the last time your machine booted successfully. The good news is that your machine will probably boot; the bad news is that you'll lose all the changes you've made since the last time you rebooted the machine. Bummer!

When you make lots of changes, either back up the Registry frequently or reboot frequently. This keeps the amount of work you can lose — from an ill-advised Registry change, a bad driver selection, and so on — to a minimum.

Use the Windows 2003 CD to boot

The Windows Server 2003 distribution CD is bootable. This means you can boot right off the CD. You no longer need to mess with half a dozen startup boot floppies. To get your system to boot from the CD, check out your CMOS for the boot device setting.

If your system doesn't support bootable CDs, it's really out of date. But if you can't afford anything newer, there's a workaround. Microsoft offers a startup boot floppy builder tool that you can download from its Web site. Just go to the Windows Server 2003 area of the Microsoft Web site at `www.microsoft.com/windowsserver2003/` and search for **setup disks for floppy boot install**.

When in Doubt, Back Up!

Windows 2003 is a reliable operating system, but accidents can happen. So, make sure you back up your Windows Server 2003 before you make *any* significant changes to that machine. Significant changes include adding beaucoups of new users or groups, making Active Directory changes, adding services or applications, or anything else that makes major changes to the Registry. This way, if the server goes down after the changes are applied, you can always restore the backup after booting from your startup disks and reactivating the backup software to get back to where you started. Don't leave home without it!

Prepare for the Real Work!

Although installing Windows Server 2003 by itself is no mean feat, the real work begins when that job is over. Formulate and then translate your plans for domain and directory structures, machine names, usernames, group names, and disk structures from concept to reality. This is the real work that makes Windows Server 2003 usable to your audience and capable of dealing with the demands they will put on your system. Remember to back up your system on a regular basis!

Chapter 23

Ten Steps to Networking Nirvana with Windows Server 2003

*W*indows Server 2003 without a network is like a bicycle without wheels or chips without salsa (our apologies in advance to the unicyclist and fat-free members of our audience).

Because Windows Server 2003 and networking go together like gangbusters, your gang (of users) may try to bust you when the network stops working. Try as you may to avoid it, it does happen from time to time. When the network goes on vacation, but you're still in the office, read over these tips and tricks to get things shipshape again.

Never Overlook the Obvious

The number one cause for failed networks is — you guessed it — loose connections. Always check a server's network interface cards (NICs) to make sure that the cables are still plugged in or otherwise attached. Also, be sure to check all hubs, the routers, the Integrated Services Digital Network (ISDN) box, the modem, and anywhere else the cables go (such as the client machines).

Networking experts often talk about a troubleshooting pyramid that follows the progression of network capabilities up from the hardware and cables, through the protocol stack, to the applications that request network services. In this analogy, the base of the pyramid is far bigger than the top. This pyramid illustrates that problems are most likely to occur at the physical level of networking. Why? Because that's where the cables and connections are. Go ahead — check them again.

Ensure Windows 2003 Routing

Windows 2003 happily enables you to insert two or more NICs or other devices that can carry network traffic — such as modems, ISDN boxes, or even Channel Service Unit/Data Service Units (CSU/DSUs) for high-speed digital networking. Doubling up on NICs (or the other network traffic devices listed) allows Windows 2003 to move traffic from one connection to another. This capability, known as *routing,* enables Windows 2003 to connect separate pieces of a network.

The most exposed and important part of many networks is the link that ties a local network to the Internet (or at least, to your local Internet Service Provider). If Windows 2003 fills that role on your network, be prepared to perform regular troubleshooting rituals to keep this all-important link to the outside world running.

If you can, you should isolate this function on a separate computer. This is a good idea for two reasons:

- ✓ Adding the burden of routing traffic and managing an Internet interface requires additional software and services that can tax a (possibly over-burdened) Windows Server 2003.

- ✓ You should limit the impact of system failure to as few services as possible. Chances are that your users will be less unhappy if they lose only Internet access or only access to shared files and applications, rather than losing both at the same time.

If you do use a Windows Server 2003 system as a router, especially if an Internet link is involved, think about installing firewall software, such as Microsoft's Proxy Server or Ositis Software's WinProxy, on that machine. A firewall protects your network from interlopers and allows you to monitor and filter incoming (and outgoing) content and information.

Open Your TCP/IP Toolkit

If you're going to attach to the Internet (and who isn't, these days?), you want to build a TCP/IP toolkit to help with the inevitable troubleshooting chores involved in keeping a TCP/IP network working properly.

Fortunately, Windows 2003 includes a fine collection of TCP/IP tools and utilities that you can use immediately. Table 23-1 includes some prime candidates for your IP troubleshooting toolbox. Given this arsenal of tools, you should be well prepared to shoot TCP/IP troubles before they shoot you!

Table 23-1	TCP/IP Diagnostic Utilities
Utility	*Description*
ARP	Displays the address translation tables used by the IP Address Resolution Protocol (ARP). Helps detect invalid entries and ensure proper resolution of numeric IP addresses to Media Access Control (MAC) addresses.
HOSTNAME	Displays your IP host name on-screen. Use this to check your machine's current name.
IPCONFIG	Displays all current network configuration values for all interfaces. Use this to check address assignments for your machine, the default gateway, and the subnet mask.
NBTSTAT	Shows protocol statistics and active connections using NetBIOS over TCP/IP. Use this to troubleshoot Microsoft naming issues.
NETSTAT	Shows active TCP and *User Datagram Protocol* (UDP) connections. Use this to check TCP/IP network connections and statistics.
NSLOOKUP	Displays information about known DNS servers.
PING	Verifies basic connectivity to network computers. Type PING loopback to check internal capabilities first, and then check local and remote machines to check overall connectivity.
ROUTE	Displays network routing tables and enables you to edit entries; useful primarily when static routing is in effect.
TRACERT	Determines the route from the sender to a destination by sending Internet Control Message Protocol (ICMP) echo packets that cause all stations between sender and receiver to announce themselves.

Install a Fast Server NIC

On a Windows 2003 Server, performance is the name of the game. In networking, because network traffic tends to congregate at the server, spending extra bucks on a fast, powerful NIC makes sense. At a bare minimum, you want a Peripheral Component Interconnect (PCI)-based NIC because it offers the best bus connection to the rest of the system. Other hardware enhancements worth purchasing for Windows Server 2003 NICs include the following:

- ✔ **Direct Memory Access (DMA):** Enables the NIC to transfer data directly from its on-board memory to the computer's memory without requiring the CPU to mediate.

- ✔ **Shared adapter memory:** Enables a NIC's on-board RAM to map into the computer's RAM. When the computer thinks it's writing to its own RAM, it's writing straight to the NIC; and when it thinks it's reading from its own RAM, it's reading straight from the NIC. Shared system memory works the same way, except the NIC reads from and writes to the computer's RAM instead of its own on-board RAM. Extra memory for NICs is almost as good as more RAM on Windows 2003 PCs!

- ✔ **Bus mastering:** Lets the NIC manage the computer's bus to coordinate data transfers to and from the computer's memory. Bus mastering enables the CPU to concentrate on other activities and can improve performance by 20 to 70 percent. This is the most worthwhile of all the enhancements mentioned here.

- ✔ **On-board coprocessor:** Puts an additional CPU on a NIC and allows the NIC to process data that the CPU would otherwise have to handle. Many NICs today use such processors to speed operations.

The idea is to put the processing power and speed where it does the most good: on the NIC that all the users must interact with to obtain data from (or move packets through) a server. In fact, if you have the money, you may want to investigate building backbones that use alternate or high-speed connections, such as FireWire (which is defined by IEEE 1394), Fibre Channel, Asynchronous Transfer Mode (ATM), or Gigabit Ethernet.

Know When to Divide and When to Conquer

When traffic reaches high levels on a network segment, traffic jams occur just like they do at rush hour on the highway. When this happens, you need to improve the existing roads (switch to a faster network technology) or add more roads (break up the existing network and put one subset of users on one new piece, another subset on another piece, and so on).

How can you figure out when traffic is starting to choke your network? Easy! Windows Server 2003 includes a service called Network Monitor (affectionately called NetMon) that you can install on your server to monitor the traffic moving into and out of your server (and on the cable segment or segments to which that server is attached).

NetMon doesn't install on Windows Server 2003 by default, but it's easy to add. Choose Start➪Control Panel➪Add or Remove Programs➪Add/Remove Windows Components ➪Management and Monitoring Tools. Then click the Details button, select the Network Monitor Tools check box, and click OK. After you follow the instructions from there, NetMon shows up in the Administrative Tools folder (Start➪Administrative Tools➪Network Monitor).

Get to know NetMon, and you get to know your network much better!

When in Doubt, Check Your Services

What do network servers do? They provide network services. When things get weird with Windows Server 2003 and you can't find anything wrong with the network, visit the Services tool, as shown in Figure 23-1.

Figure 23-1:
The Services tool indicates the status for all services installed on Windows Server 2003.

To view this display, follow this menu sequence: Start⇨Administrative Tools⇨Services. Then click the Services entry to view the list of services currently installed on Windows Server 2003.

Be sure to check the entries for key services such as Computer Browser, the Server service, and the Workstation service. Make sure that the Status field says Started and that the Startup field is properly set. (It should read Automatic for services that are supposed to launch upon startup.)

Many times, when the network shows no obvious problems, you may find that a key service has been paused or stopped or has simply quit for some reason. If the service has stopped, you should refer to Event Viewer to find out why because a stopped service usually indicates a serious problem that will recur.

Handle Names and Addresses Efficiently

The only way to find something on a network is to know its address. But alas, human beings are much better at remembering symbolic names than numeric addresses (or worse still, the arcane bit patterns that computers use to address one another).

This means many things when you operate a working network, but two primary concerns from a troubleshooting perspective exist:

- ✔ The services that provide name-to-address translation must be properly configured and working correctly for users to use a network effectively.
- ✔ Network addresses, subnet masks, and related information (such as default gateways, router addresses, and so on) must be unique, properly specified, and in substantial agreement for computers to use a network properly.

Symptoms of trouble in this area are many and varied. Duplicate addresses usually cause all holders of the same address to lose their capability to access the network. Invalid names or addresses simply can't be reached and may require serious troubleshooting to correct. Active Directory may be unavailable or not working for some reason or another. (In general, check the spelling of names carefully and the numeric values for addresses equally carefully.)

Fortunately, problems in this arena usually make themselves known during initial configuration or when settings change. If you can simply check your settings and assumptions against a known, working set of values, you can usually correct these troubles quickly and painlessly.

Ask What's New or Different

When troubleshooting a network, what's new or what's changed is often a source of trouble. Therefore, when you investigate network woes, be sure to ask yourself, "What's new?" and "What's different?" right away, and then answer in as much detail as possible. While digging up the details, you often uncover the source of the trouble and can determine its solution, all in one swift maneuver.

Savvy network administrators keep a log of changes and additions to the servers on their networks, so when those key questions are asked, answers are immediately forthcoming. You could do worse than to emulate these professionals!

If You Need Help, Ask

Occasionally, when troubleshooting a system, you run into problems that are so mysterious or baffling that you won't have a clue about how to correct them. When that happens, don't tear out your hair — ask for help instead.

If you're having a problem with Windows Server 2003, paying $245 for a Technical Support Incident with Microsoft may be worth it. (The cost of an online request is $99.) You can also check the TechNet CD (you can order it from www.microsoft.com/technet) or the Microsoft Developer Network (which you can join at www.msdn.microsoft.com/).

If the problem is with a piece of hardware, check the manufacturer's Web site or bulletin board for a driver update. If that doesn't lead to a happy dance, you may have to pay that vendor's tech support operation for some advice, too. If you can determine a problem's root cause, you can often get help from those who know that root the best. Even if it costs you, think of the valuable time (and aggravation) you'll save. Better to light a candle than curse the darkness!

Watch Network Trouble Spots

The best way to shoot network trouble and other types of system problems is to stop them before they ever happen. The only way to prevent problems and keep your network running is to study your network environment closely and carefully and figure out where its weak points are. Do this before your network demonstrates its weaknesses to the world at large by breaking.

If you keep an eye on potential trouble spots and perform regular maintenance and upkeep activities (such as scheduled backups, file system
cleanups, upgrades, service packs, and hotfixes), you can prevent problems.
And believe us, preventing problems isn't just less work, it's also the cause of
far less unwanted notoriety than fixing things after they break. Don't feel
compelled to learn this the hard way!

Index

• *X* •

•*Z* •

Notes

Notes

FOR DUMMIES®

The easy way to get more done and have more fun

PERSONAL FINANCE

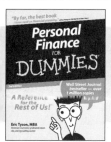

Personal Finance FOR DUMMIES
0-7645-5231-7

Investing FOR DUMMIES
0-7645-2431-3

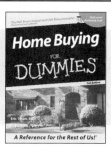

Home Buying FOR DUMMIES
0-7645-5331-3

Also available:

Estate Planning For Dummies
(0-7645-5501-4)

401(k)s For Dummies
(0-7645-5468-9)

Frugal Living For Dummies
(0-7645-5403-4)

Microsoft Money "X" For Dummies
(0-7645-1689-2)

Mutual Funds For Dummies
(0-7645-5329-1)

Personal Bankruptcy For Dummies
(0-7645-5498-0)

Quicken "X" For Dummies
(0-7645-1666-3)

Stock Investing For Dummies
(0-7645-5411-5)

Taxes For Dummies 2003
(0-7645-5475-1)

BUSINESS & CAREERS

Accounting FOR DUMMIES
0-7645-5314-3

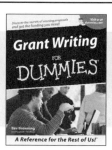

Grant Writing FOR DUMMIES
0-7645-5307-0

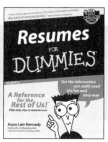

Resumes FOR DUMMIES
0-7645-5471-9

Also available:

Business Plans Kit For Dummies
(0-7645-5365-8)

Consulting For Dummies
(0-7645-5034-9)

Cool Careers For Dummies
(0-7645-5345-3)

Human Resources Kit For Dummies
(0-7645-5131-0)

Managing For Dummies
(1-5688-4858-7)

QuickBooks All-in-One Desk Reference For Dummies
(0-7645-1963-8)

Selling For Dummies
(0-7645-5363-1)

Small Business Kit For Dummies
(0-7645-5093-4)

Starting an eBay Business For Dummies
(0-7645-1547-0)

HEALTH, SPORTS & FITNESS

Fitness FOR DUMMIES
0-7645-5167-1

Golf FOR DUMMIES
0-7645-5146-9

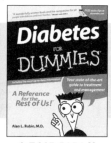

Diabetes FOR DUMMIES
0-7645-5154-X

Also available:

Controlling Cholesterol For Dummies
(0-7645-5440-9)

Dieting For Dummies
(0-7645-5126-4)

High Blood Pressure For Dummies
(0-7645-5424-7)

Martial Arts For Dummies
(0-7645-5358-5)

Menopause For Dummies
(0-7645-5458-1)

Nutrition For Dummies
(0-7645-5180-9)

Power Yoga For Dummies
(0-7645-5342-9)

Thyroid For Dummies
(0-7645-5385-2)

Weight Training For Dummies
(0-7645-5168-X)

Yoga For Dummies
(0-7645-5117-5)

WILEY

FOR DUMMIES®

A world of resources to help you grow

FOR DUMMIES®

Plain-English solutions for everyday challenges

COMPUTER BASICS

0-7645-0838-5

0-7645-1663-9

0-7645-1548-9

Also available:

PCs All-in-One Desk Reference For Dummies (0-7645-0791-5)

Pocket PC For Dummies (0-7645-1640-X)

Treo and Visor For Dummies (0-7645-1673-6)

Troubleshooting Your PC For Dummies (0-7645-1669-8)

Upgrading & Fixing PCs For Dummies (0-7645-1665-5)

Windows XP For Dummies (0-7645-0893-8)

Windows XP For Dummies Quick Reference (0-7645-0897-0)

BUSINESS SOFTWARE

0-7645-0822-9

0-7645-0839-3

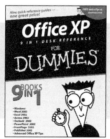
0-7645-0819-9

Also available:

Excel Data Analysis For Dummies (0-7645-1661-2)

Excel 2002 All-in-One Desk Reference For Dummies (0-7645-1794-5)

Excel 2002 For Dummies Quick Reference (0-7645-0829-6)

GoldMine "X" For Dummies (0-7645-0845-8)

Microsoft CRM For Dummies (0-7645-1698-1)

Microsoft Project 2002 For Dummies (0-7645-1628-0)

Office XP For Dummies (0-7645-0830-X)

Outlook 2002 For Dummies (0-7645-0828-8)

Get smart! Visit www.dummies.com

- **Find listings of even more *For Dummies* titles**

- **Browse online articles**

- **Sign up for Dummies eTips™**

- **Check out *For Dummies* fitness videos and other products**

- **Order from our online bookstore**

Available wherever books are sold. Go to www.dummies.com or call 1-877-762-2974 to order direct.

FOR DUMMIES®

Helping you expand your horizons and realize your potential

INTERNET

0-7645-0894-6

0-7645-1659-0

0-7645-1642-6

Also available:

America Online 7.0 For Dummies
(0-7645-1624-8)

Genealogy Online For Dummies
(0-7645-0807-5)

The Internet All-in-One Desk Reference For Dummies
(0-7645-1659-0)

Internet Explorer 6 For Dummies
(0-7645-1344-3)

The Internet For Dummies Quick Reference
(0-7645-1645-0)

Internet Privacy For Dummies
(0-7645-0846-6)

Researching Online For Dummies
(0-7645-0546-7)

Starting an Online Business For Dummies
(0-7645-1655-8)

DIGITAL MEDIA

0-7645-1664-7

0-7645-1675-2

0-7645-0806-7

Also available:

CD and DVD Recording For Dummies
(0-7645-1627-2)

Digital Photography All-in-One Desk Reference For Dummies
(0-7645-1800-3)

Digital Photography For Dummies Quick Reference
(0-7645-0750-8)

Home Recording for Musicians For Dummies
(0-7645-1634-5)

MP3 For Dummies
(0-7645-0858-X)

Paint Shop Pro "X" For Dummies
(0-7645-2440-2)

Photo Retouching & Restoration For Dummies
(0-7645-1662-0)

Scanners For Dummies
(0-7645-0783-4)

GRAPHICS

0-7645-0817-2

0-7645-1651-5

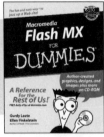
0-7645-0895-4

Also available:

Adobe Acrobat 5 PDF For Dummies
(0-7645-1652-3)

Fireworks 4 For Dummies
(0-7645-0804-0)

Illustrator 10 For Dummies
(0-7645-3636-2)

QuarkXPress 5 For Dummies
(0-7645-0643-9)

Visio 2000 For Dummies
(0-7645-0635-8)

FOR DUMMIES®

The advice and explanations you need to succeed

SELF-HELP, SPIRITUALITY & RELIGION

0-7645-5302-X

0-7645-5418-2

0-7645-5264-3

Also available:

The Bible For Dummies
(0-7645-5296-1)

Buddhism For Dummies
(0-7645-5359-3)

Christian Prayer For Dummies
(0-7645-5500-6)

Dating For Dummies
(0-7645-5072-1)

Judaism For Dummies
(0-7645-5299-6)

Potty Training For Dummies
(0-7645-5417-4)

Pregnancy For Dummies
(0-7645-5074-8)

Rekindling Romance For Dummies
(0-7645-5303-8)

Spirituality For Dummies
(0-7645-5298-8)

Weddings For Dummies
(0-7645-5055-1)

PETS

0-7645-5255-4

0-7645-5286-4

0-7645-5275-9

Also available:

Labrador Retrievers For Dummies
(0-7645-5281-3)

Aquariums For Dummies
(0-7645-5156-6)

Birds For Dummies
(0-7645-5139-6)

Dogs For Dummies
(0-7645-5274-0)

Ferrets For Dummies
(0-7645-5259-7)

German Shepherds For Dummies
(0-7645-5280-5)

Golden Retrievers For Dummies
(0-7645-5267-8)

Horses For Dummies
(0-7645-5138-8)

Jack Russell Terriers For Dummies
(0-7645-5268-6)

Puppies Raising & Training Diary For Dummies
(0-7645-0876-8)

EDUCATION & TEST PREPARATION

0-7645-5194-9

0-7645-5325-9

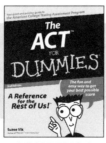
0-7645-5210-4

Also available:

Chemistry For Dummies
(0-7645-5430-1)

English Grammar For Dummies
(0-7645-5322-4)

French For Dummies
(0-7645-5193-0)

The GMAT For Dummies
(0-7645-5251-1)

Inglés Para Dummies
(0-7645-5427-1)

Italian For Dummies
(0-7645-5196-5)

Research Papers For Dummies
(0-7645-5426-3)

The SAT I For Dummies
(0-7645-5472-7)

U.S. History For Dummies
(0-7645-5249-X)

World History For Dummies
(0-7645-5242-2)